Disturbing Divine Behavior

Disturbing Divine Behavior

Troubling Old Testament Images of God

ERIC A. SEIBERT

Fortress Press
Minneapolis

DISTURBING DIVINE BEHAVIOR
Troubling Old Testament Images of God

Cover image: *The Flood*, The Art Archive / Museo del Prado Madrid / Alfredo Dagli Orti
Cover design: Laurie Ingram
Book design: PerfecType, Inc.

ISBN: 978-0-8006-6344-5

Library of Congress Cataloging-in-Publication Data

Seibert, Eric A., 1969-
    Disturbing divine behavior : troubling Old Testament images of God / Eric A. Seibert.
        p. cm.
    Includes bibliographical references and index.
    ISBN 978-0-8006-6344-5 (alk. paper)
    1. God—Biblical teaching. 2. Providence and government of God. 3. Bible. O.T.—Criticism, interpretation, etc. I. Title.
    BS1192.6.S45 2009
    231.7—dc22
                                            2009011354

Manufactured in the U.S.A.

13 12 11 10 09   2 3 4 5 6 7 8 9 10

Contents

Further resources including a sample syllabus and comments on using **Disturbing Divine Behavior** *in the classroom are available online at www.fortresspress.com/ seibert.*

For Nathan and Rebecca

two beautiful children
who are gifts from God,
and a spectacular source
of joy and blessing

Acknowledgments

I began writing the first draft of this book in the summer of 2003 and have appreciated the support and encouragement of many people along the way. Messiah College has been especially generous in providing both time and funding to assist my work on this project. This has come in the form of internal grants, an endowed chair, and a sabbatical leave. Beyond providing time and money, these awards strongly encouraged me to keep making progress on what turned out to be a considerable undertaking.

I want to express my gratitude to the many Messiah College students whom I have had the privilege of teaching over the years. Their questions and conversation have helped shape my discussion of some of the issues addressed in this book. At various places in the book, I include material from student assignments or from personal correspondence with friends. Thank you one and all for these contributions. I should also say a special word of thanks to the students who took my fall 2007 "Topics in Biblical Theology" class dealing with divine violence. Your level of engagement with the ideas presented was encouraging, and I appreciated your willingness to enter into dialogue even when you did not always agree with me.

I was especially fortunate to have several individuals read a draft of this manuscript along the way. To these individuals—Terry Brensinger, Andrea Dalton, Mike Huffnagle, and Elisa Seibert—I extend my sincere thanks. Thank you for your gift of time and your many helpful suggestions. While I take full responsibility for all remaining shortcomings and infelicities, I am confident they are far fewer due to your careful reading. I also wish to thank Randy Basinger, Pete Powers, and Dave Weaver-Zercher for taking the time to read the appendix on inspiration and the authority of Scripture and to offer feedback. It was helpful! I would also like to thank Sharon Baker and Richard Crane for using this book in draft form as a textbook in their college classes and for skillfully helping students think about important issues related to divine violence in the Bible. Thanks are also due to Joanna Barnhouse for undertaking the tedious job of compiling the indices, a task she completed with good cheer and care. At several points in the book, I quote from student assignments or email correspondence I received, and I wish to thank each of the individuals responsible for this material. To the others whose names I cannot remember, and to the many authors whose books and articles have assisted me along the way, I offer my thanks. I am also grateful to Fortress Press for accepting this book for publication and for working with me to complete it. Neil Elliott, in particular, deserves a special word of thanks for his many efforts on my behalf. Thank you for your time, patience, and assistance. I also benefitted from Andrew DeYoung's assistance in the latter stages of production, and wish to express my thanks for his help.

Finally, I wish to express my profound gratitude to Elisa, my wife and best friend. She has engaged in more conversations about disturbing divine behavior and related issues than any spouse should need to endure, and has done so with characteristic grace and goodwill. Her close reading of the manuscript resulted in a much better product and substantially improved this book in numerous ways. Thank you, Elisa, for your unfailing love, support, and good counsel. They mean the world to me.

To all who read this book, I sincerely hope you find it helpful as you endeavor to deal responsibly with disturbing divine behavior in the Old Testament, and as you seek to know and serve God.

The Story of the Man Who Gathered Sticks and Got Stoned

Tucked away in the book of Numbers, amid instructions about offerings and Israelite apparel, you will encounter a little-known story about a man who makes the ill-fated decision to gather some firewood on the Sabbath. The passage, in its entirety, is as follows:

> When the Israelites were in the wilderness, they found a man gathering sticks on the sabbath day. Those who found him gathering sticks brought him to Moses, Aaron, and to the whole congregation. They put him in custody, because it was not clear what should be done to him. Then the Lord said to Moses, "The man shall be put to death; all the congregation shall stone him outside the camp." The whole congregation brought him outside the camp and stoned him to death, just as the Lord had commanded Moses. (Num. 15:32-36)[1]

God's behavior in this passage is troubling to many readers. Why would God sentence a man to death for gathering firewood on the Sabbath? Doesn't that seem a bit extreme? It did to a former student of mine who made the following journal entry after stumbling across this passage:

> I was reading through Numbers, just skimming across the chapters, and I came across chapter 15 verses 32-36. This story seemed VERY harsh to me, especially from this "gracious" God I'm supposed to be serving! . . .
>   The story tells about a man who didn't honor the Sabbath, but instead "gather[ed] sticks." When you think about it, how harmless is gathering sticks? Apparently it is VERY harmful! The Israelites took the man, and brought him

before God. God told them to STONE THE MAN! This is horrible! It seems as if there are MANY reoccurring themes like this where God just seems ruthless in the OT. How could this God have people KILL a man for gathering sticks on the Sabbath? I really have no answer to this question.[2]

If you have ever felt like this student—disturbed by God's behavior in the Old Testament but unsure what to do about it—then read on. This book is for you.

Thinking Rightly about God and the Problem of the Old Testament

The overwhelming image of God in the Bible is that of a brutal, violent, and vengeful judge. In a world being torn apart by violence, there is no more urgent task than to counter the Bible's frequent and nauseating portraits of a ruthless and violent deity. The cruelty of God, however, is a problem that almost no one is willing to face squarely, including Christian interpreters.

—Jack Nelson-Pallmeyer[1]

Our understanding of God has enormous practical significance. . . . What we think of God and how we respond to Him are closely related. An inaccurate view of God can have disastrous effects on personal religious experience. We could never love a hostile, tyrannical being. . . . And we could not respect a mild, indulgent figure who never took us seriously. Our personal religious experience can be healthy only if we hold an adequate conception of God.

—Richard Rice[2]

In a course I teach titled "Issues of War, Peace, and Social Justice in Biblical Texts," we spend some time looking at the image of God as divine warrior in the Old Testament. The first couple of assignments require students to read passages like Exodus 1—15, Joshua 6—11, and 1 Samuel 15. These passages portray

God as involved in horrific acts of violence: sending devastating plagues on Egypt, commanding the total destruction of Canaanite cities, and commissioning Saul to utterly annihilate every last Amalekite. This is new terrain for some students, even for some who have grown up hearing Bible stories all their lives. One semester, after just the second day of class, a student wrote a journal entry revealing the significant impact reading these passages was having on her. She writes:

> I am very surprised at the nature of God and the character of God that is expressed in the Old Testament passages you have assigned to us. Perhaps it is because I have never really spent that much time reading the Old Testament before, and never before have I been asked to formally analyze or read the passages as in depth as I have been for this class. Of course, growing up in a church environment, I recognized almost every story I read about, especially Moses and the Egyptians, and Joshua and the city of Jericho.
>
> Somehow, after years of Sunday school and class, only the positive images of God were left to me, such as how He always helped Israel win and be victorious. But after the past two days of reading all these Old Testament scriptures and passages, I am very surprised at God's commands to slaughter every man, woman, and child in the cities. Somehow, these commands seem brutal, unfair, and unjust.
>
> So even after just two days of class, I find myself struggling with the image of God in the Old Testament and the image of God in the New Testament. The same God seems like two completely different people to me. On the one hand, God is this vengeful, merciless, unforgiving God but on the other hand, I have always understood Him to be a forgiving, compassionate, and merciful God. These war stories seem to utterly contradict the image of God in the New Testament.
>
> So I find myself trying to understand these passages and the motives of God in the Old Testament with the Israelites. Hopefully, as class continues, I will be able to understand the differences I am learning about in the character of God. Right now, I cannot understand the cruelty and violence of God and His commands to the Israelites to massacre everyone.[3]

 This student is not alone. Many readers of the Old Testament would be quick to echo her concerns and confusion. Some of the things God is reported to have said and done in the Old Testament are rather troubling, to say the least.

Throughout this book, I will generally refer to God's troubling conduct in the Old Testament as "disturbing divine behavior." This behavior, in turn, results in what I call "problematic portrayals" (or "troubling images") of God. Others refer to this disturbing divine behavior as the "dark side of God" and describe the passages containing it as "morally dubious" and "texts of terror."[4] Whatever words or phrases one uses, the point is the same: in the Old Testament, God sometimes acts in ways that leave readers perplexed and bothered.

In the chapters that follow, I will attempt to explain why some people—though certainly not all—find certain aspects of God's behavior in the Old Testament problematic. First, however, it may help to describe my own journey as it relates to the issues at hand. This will provide a context for understanding how my interest in this topic developed and for appreciating why it is so important to me.[5]

A Personal Journey

I consider myself very fortunate to have been born into a Christian home. My parents encouraged my regular participation in the life of the church, and we faithfully attended Morning Hour Chapel, one of three hundred Brethren in Christ churches in North America. As a denomination, the Brethren in Christ are theologically conservative with roots in the Anabaptist, Pietist, and Wesleyan traditions. True to its Anabaptist heritage, the denomination maintains a strong peace stance even though many members do not fully embrace the church's official position on militarism and war.

Both at home and at church, I learned the paramount importance of the Bible at an early age. The Bible was, after all, God's word. It was to be read, memorized, and, most importantly, obeyed. Though I have no recollection of anyone telling me this in so many words, I instinctively knew the Bible was not to be questioned or challenged. It was the supreme authority in matters of faith and practice.

Growing up, I had an unusual interest in the New Testament and devoted an inordinate amount of time to reading and studying that part of the Bible. But it would not be until my second semester at Messiah College in 1989 that I would discover my real passion. That semester, I took an Old Testament survey class with Terry Brensinger. Terry was one of those gifted professors who was able to bring the Bible to life. But he did more than that. Throughout the semester, he constantly demonstrated how the Old Testament applies to our lives. Realizing that these ancient texts could speak to me today was nothing short of amazing. In fact, it was life changing. I began to realize that the Old Testament was a virtual treasure trove I had barely begun to explore. Over the next three years, I took every Old Testament class I possibly could. But far from satisfying my hunger for Old Testament insights, all this simply whetted my appetite for more. So I continued my studies at Asbury Theological Seminary for the next four years.

During those eight years in college and seminary, the Old Testament came alive for me and profoundly shaped my understanding of God, the world, and humanity in more ways than I can recall. I came to appreciate how central trusting God is to Christian faith. I learned how dangerous it is for people to create their own solutions apart from God. I witnessed God's deep and abiding desire to be in relationship with people and observed how time and again God tenaciously stuck with the Israelites even *after* they repeatedly messed up. In short, I realized the Old Testament was teeming with theological insight and wisdom.

But as I was learning this, I also realized that the Old Testament raised certain problems for Christian readers like me. For example, how could the Old Testament's depiction of God as a warrior be reconciled with my belief that war is categorically wrong? As a member of a denomination with a strong peace position, this was an important question for me. During my final year at seminary, I wrestled with this issue in a master's thesis titled "Yahweh as Warrior: Old Testament Perspectives on God's Involvement in War." Although I devoted some 140 pages to the topic, trying my best to make sense of God's participation in war, I now judge my own conclusions to be completely unsatisfying.

After graduating from seminary in 1996, I returned to Messiah College, where I began teaching part-time before beginning doctoral studies in Old Testament the following year at Drew University. During the next five years, as I continued teaching at Messiah and working on my doctorate, I became troubled by an even greater array of disturbing depictions of God in the Old Testament. I discovered numerous texts in which God's behavior seemed highly problematic and seriously out of line with my beliefs about God's character. What was I to do with a story in which God reportedly drowned the entire human race except Noah and his family (Gen. 7:23)? What theological lesson was I to learn from God's genocidal decree that Saul utterly annihilate every last Amalekite, including "child and infant" (1 Sam. 15:2)? What sense was I to make of God's slaughter of seventy thousand people as punishment for a census that God had prompted David to take in the first place (2 Sam. 24:1, 15)? Nestled among the very same texts that had brought me such profound insights were passages which threatened to dismantle some of my most cherished beliefs. What was I to do?

I could have chosen simply to ignore these problematic passages. After all, that seems to be the way the church often "deals" with them. When was the last time you heard a sermon on God's attempt to kill Moses (Exod. 4:24-26)? Or, can you recall your Sunday school teacher ever getting out the flannelgraph board and placing hundreds of lifeless Egyptians along the shoreline, dead and bleeding, because God threw "horse and rider" into the sea (Exod. 14:30; 15:1)? Typically, these troubling images are not addressed in church. While some might be comfortable ignoring "problem passages" in this way, I was not. These portrayals were too pervasive, and their implications too problematic, to pretend they did not exist. Given the very real potential these problematic portrayals have of skewing one's view of God, I felt it was neither desirable nor prudent to act like the proverbial ostrich. Instead, I wanted to develop a responsible way of reading these texts that would value the Old Testament without encouraging false views of God. Therefore, I decided to address this problem directly.

My first concerted effort to do so came in the form of a Presidential Scholar's lecture at Messiah College titled "Reading the Old Testament without Losing Your Faith: Connecting Biblical Scholarship and Christian Belief." In that lecture, I emphasized the need to take the human origins of the Bible with full seriousness and to distinguish between the Bible's portrayals of God and God's true character. I also began discussing this topic in some of my classes and began giving related papers at professional conferences. Yet, given the complexities of this issue, I knew it was impossible to deal adequately with disturbing divine behavior in a single presentation or a few classroom conversations. Something more extensive was required.

My questions, concerns, and ideas on this topic have culminated in this present volume. They grow out of my own struggle with these troublesome texts and are guided by my respect for Scripture and my desire to use Scripture to think accurately about God. They are also motivated by a desire to help others who, like me, affirm the authority of Scripture yet sometimes struggle with certain Old Testament images of God. Writing this book has allowed me to examine more thoroughly disturbing divine behavior in Old Testament narratives and to propose a way of dealing with this in a theologically responsible manner.

The Importance of Thinking Rightly about God

A primary goal of this book is to help people know how to use Scripture to think as accurately as possible about God. The first chapter of A. W. Tozer's now classic book *The Knowledge of the Holy* bears the intriguing title "Why We Must Think Rightly about God." As Tozer sees it: "What comes into our minds when we think about God is the most important thing about us."[6] Therefore, he argues that it is crucial "that our idea of God correspond as nearly as possible to the true being of God."[7] This is important because the way we think about God strongly influences how we relate to God. As Old Testament scholar Terence Fretheim puts it: "The images used to speak about God not only decisively determine the way one thinks about God, they have a powerful impact on the shape of the life of the believer."[8] If we imagine God a demanding perfectionist or an absent father, these views undoubtedly will have an adverse effect on our relationship with God—if we choose to relate to God at all![9] On the other hand, if we believe God to be good and to have our best interests in mind, we are likely to maintain a life of faith regardless of what life throws our way.

Our view of God not only affects how we relate to God, it also influences our behavior. To illustrate this, consider how one's view of God influences one's perspective on a Christian's participation in war.[10] Those who view God as the kind of being who sometimes uses violence to protect innocent lives or to liberate oppressed people are likely to support a Christian's participation in war, at least in certain circumstances. Their view of God may lead them to conclude that God sometimes commissions

Christians to fight—and even kill—in war, as regrettable as that may be. Yet other Christians, who view God as nonviolent, as one who suffers rather than inflicts injury, regard war as an evil that should be avoided at all costs. Their conception of God as one who rejects violence naturally leads them to believe they should do likewise. From their perspective, joining the military or participating in war are never appropriate options for Christians to consider. As this simple example illustrates, our view of God can have an enormous impact on how we behave. What we think about God really matters! So then, how can we be sure that our thoughts about God are accurate? What resources do we have at our disposal to help us think rightly about God?

Most Christians would immediately reference the Bible as their primary source of information about God. They would say that God is revealed in the pages of Scripture and that by diligent study we can know a lot about what God is really like. While this is true, it is not without certain difficulties. For example, when people use the Old Testament to learn about God's character, they may discover that God is sometimes described behaving in ways that they find troubling or that do not correspond very well to some of their ideas about how God acts. As Old Testament scholar John Barton observes:

> Most Christians probably read the Old Testament to learn about God. They expect it to tell them what God is like, what he has done and what he requires of them. But those who approach the OT in this way are soon disappointed. They find that the God it shows them is, at best, something of a mixed bless-ing. Although at times he is loving, gentle and trustworthy, at others he seems capricious, harsh and unfeeling. . . . The information we get from the OT seems fairly ambiguous, and we would be hard put . . . to recognize in it the God in whom Jews or Christians now believe.[11]

This creates a real dilemma, causing considerable uncertainty about what to do with these images of God.

Who Should Read This Book?

As the prologue indicated, this book is for anyone who has encountered disturbing divine behavior in the Old Testament and wondered how to make sense of it. There-fore, I would expect this book to appeal to Christians from mainline denomina-tions, people from other faith traditions, and even "nonbelievers" who simply want to know what to do with these problematic portrayals of God. I particularly hope that this volume will be read by theologically conservative Christians who may ben-efit considerably from it even as they find parts of it challenging. This volume should especially interest college and seminary students who are preparing for ministry, since they will surely be asked questions about God's behavior in the Old Testa-ment. Similarly, religious professionals—clergy, professors, and the like—who feel ill-equipped to deal responsibly with disturbing divine behavior will find this book very useful. Finally, this volume should point the way forward to those courageous readers who attempt to use the Bible as a resource for peacemaking but feel that God's actions in the Old Testament are an obstacle in this regard.

Old Testament Narratives

In order to provide some focus for this study, I have chosen to deal almost exclusively with problematic portrayals of God appearing in Old Testament narratives. Old Testament narrative, the primary genre through which the stories of the Old Testament are told, is concentrated in such books as Genesis, Exodus, Joshua, Judges, Samuel, Kings, and Chronicles. There we read some of the most well known Bible stories, including Noah and the ark, Abraham and the near sacrifice of Isaac, Moses and the parting of the Red Sea, Joshua and the battle of Jericho, and many, many others. And it is there, in those familiar stories, that we encounter some of the most troubling portrayals of God.

Obviously, the portrayals of God many readers find disturbing are not limited to Old Testament narratives or to a select handful of books. Instead, they appear throughout various genres in the Old Testament (and the New).[12] For instance, troubling images of God occur with some frequency in prophetic literature.[13] In fact, one might argue that some of the most provocative Old Testament examples of disturbing divine behavior are found in the Prophets.[14] Still, I have chosen to limit this study to disturbing divine behavior found in Old Testament narratives for several reasons. First, many people are more familiar with Old Testament narrative than with prophetic literature. Since most readers of the Bible tend to know its stories better than its prophetic oracles, the images of God they find most disturbing will likely come from the narrative portions of the Old Testament. Second, dealing with disturbing divine behavior in prophetic literature requires a somewhat different discussion since a significant portion of it was first delivered orally and because it consists of poetry rather than prose. Third, focusing almost exclusively on the narrative portions of the Old Testament keeps this book within manageable proportions, and it seems better to concentrate on one genre rather than cover too much ground. Finally, many of the interpretive guidelines developed for dealing with disturbing divine behavior in narratives are easily transferrable to other portions of the Old Testament. For these reasons, it seemed prudent to restrict the parameters of this study to Old Testament narratives.[15]

Qualms about Questioning God

Finding an adequate way to handle disturbing divine behavior in the Old Testament will require us to ask a series of rather sensitive questions: Do Old Testament narratives record what actually happened? Must Israel's theological worldview be our own? Is the Bible's portrayal of God always trustworthy?[16] In what sense is it appropriate to speak of the Bible being divinely inspired? These are big questions, and how they are answered has important and far-reaching implications. The answers I suggest to these kinds of questions will not always be the ones many readers bring to this book. For that reason, I would ask that you journey graciously with me in the following pages, remaining open to entertaining new insights and ideas as they are presented.

Many Christians have never been encouraged to pursue the kind of questions raised in this book. In fact, they have been taught just the opposite. Somewhere along the way, they have learned that it is wrong to question God, the Bible, or time-honored Christian beliefs. They have not been invited to ask hard questions or to openly discuss controversial issues. Those few brave souls who dare to speak up are commonly met with suspicion and defensiveness rather than genuine openness. Jack Nelson-Pallmeyer relates an unfortunate episode from his youth that illustrates this point all too well.

> As a teen, I experienced church as a place of deep friendships and bewildering theology. During confirmation classes, I occasionally asked questions outside the box. I wondered why a loving God would drown nearly all of humanity, why God allowed earthquakes, and why a baby who died before being baptized went to hell. Musing like these met a stern response from a pastor who essentially told me to shut up and memorize truths found in the Bible and tradition.[17]

Why should questions like these be forbidden in the Church? What better place is there to discuss important matters of Christian belief and biblical interpretation than among a community of Christians committed to following the life and teachings of Jesus? Rather than stifling such inquisitiveness, the Church should encourage it. The community of faith is precisely the place where people should be able to actively engage and creatively explore challenging questions.[18] As Charles Kimball recognizes, demanding "blind obedience" to religious authorities is one of the warning signs that religion has become evil. Kimball writes: "Authentic religion encourages questions and reflection at all levels. When authority figures discourage or disallow honest questions, something clearly is wrong."[19]

Still, many church leaders feel quite uncomfortable dealing with questions like those asked by Nelson-Pallmeyer and like those we will explore in this book. When they are confronted by questions that cast doubt on their most basic assumptions about God and the Bible, they become combative rather than conversational. In doing so, they send a clear signal that these kinds of questions are unwelcome. The reason for this resistance varies from one church leader to another. Some, perceiving such questions as a challenge to their authority or to the Christian faith, quickly attempt to squelch them. Others are unsure how to respond to such questions since they themselves have never seriously wrestled with them. Even those with seminary degrees may find themselves struggling to handle questions about God's behavior in the Old Testament since this topic is not typically addressed in seminary classes. The Church's inability—and, at times, unwillingness—to constructively engage honest questions about these troubling images not only discourages people from asking such questions but sometimes gives the impression that doing so constitutes a lack of faith.

The Old Testament provides a better model, one that invites us to ask questions about God's behavior and to protest when we think God is acting inappropriately. In numerous Old Testament passages, we find people engaged in a feisty conversation with God about God's behavior. Abraham, for example, vigorously disapproves of God's plan to destroy the city of Sodom. He regards this divine plan as problematic because it threatens to wipe out the righteous along with the wicked (Gen. 18:23). Abraham objects to what he perceives as indiscriminate slaughter, asking God, "Shall not the Judge of all the earth do what is just?" (Gen. 18:25b). Apparently, Abraham had no qualms about confronting God or questioning God's intentions when he had serious misgivings about the morality of what God intended to do.

Moses also protested when he heard of God's plan to destroy Israel right after Aaron made a golden calf and the people engaged in their wayward worship. God says, "I have seen this people, how stiff-necked they are. Now let me alone, so that my wrath may burn hot against them and I may consume them; and of you I will make a great nation" (Exod. 32:9-10). But rather than meekly acquiescing to this divine declaration, Moses questions God's intentions.

> But Moses implored the Lord his God, and said, "O Lord, why does your wrath burn hot against your people, whom you brought out of the land of Egypt with great power and with a mighty hand? Why should the Egyptians say, 'It was with evil intent that he brought them out to kill them in the mountains, and to consume them from the face of the earth'? Turn from your fierce wrath; change your mind and do not bring disaster on your people." (Exod. 32:11-12)

And guess what? God listens to Moses. We are told that "the Lord changed his mind about the disaster that he planned to bring on his people" (Exod. 32:14).[20] Moses vigorously objects to God's behavior and convincingly persuades God that destroying Israel is a bad idea.

Questions about God's behavior are also raised by the psalmist. Consider, for example, the following accusations of divine inactivity:

> Why, O Lord, do you stand far off?
> Why do you hide yourself in times of trouble? (Ps. 10:1)

> How long, O Lord? Will you forget me forever?
> How long will you hide your face from me? (Ps. 13:1)

Apparently, the psalmist—and those who used these prayers—felt free to question God's behavior (or lack thereof) when it did not correspond to what they believed to be true about God.[21]

Passages like these encourage us to ask questions about God's behavior and to raise objections when that behavior appears morally or ethically problematic. While much more needs to be said about *how* to go about doing this, my point here is simply to reassure readers that there is nothing inherently wrong with raising questions about God's behavior in the Old Testament. On the contrary, the precedent for such questioning exists in the Old Testament itself.[22]

The Old Testament or the Hebrew Bible?

Some readers may be unaware that debate surrounds the appropriateness of labeling the first part of the Bible "the Old Testament." Quite apart from the problem of the adjective old, which has negative connotations for many readers, some object to this designation because it is a specifically Christian label. For example, it makes no sense for Jews to speak of an Old Testament since they do not regard the New Testament as authoritative. Instead, they refer to these writings as the Tanak, an acronym referring to the three major sections of the Hebrew Bible.[23] Many scholars—Christian and otherwise—simply use the designation "the Hebrew Bible" to refer to this collection of books. This religiously neutral designation, which reflects the primary language of these texts, is nonsectarian and avoids causing unnecessary offense.

That said, I have, nevertheless, opted to use the designation "Old Testament" throughout this study, since it is so commonly used to refer to this part of Scripture and since some readers would find references to "the Hebrew Bible" awkward, my choice in using this descriptor is pragmatic and intends no disrespect for those who label it otherwise. Whether "the Old Testament" is an appropriate designation for the first part of the Bible is another debate for another time, and I hope I may be forgiven for not entering it here.[24]

A Brief Overview

Part 1 of the book, "Examining the Problem of Disturbing Divine Behavior," consists of four chapters, each exploring the problem from a different angle. Chapter 1 analyzes numerous Old Testament passages that contain examples of disturbing divine behavior. These passages are categorized according to different kinds of divine behavior under such headings as "God as Instant Executioner," "God as Mass Murderer," "God as Divine Warrior," and so on. The chapter presents the scope and severity of the problem in some detail.

Chapter 2 identifies various types of individuals—religious pacifists, Christian educators, feminists, and so on—who have been bothered by these images and explores some of the images' negative impacts. Chapters 3 and 4 consider various ways people have responded to disturbing divine behavior in Old Testament narratives. Chapter 3 takes a historical look at some early expressions of discomfort with Old Testament images of God. Most notable is Marcion's rejection of the Old Testament and its God. This chapter also considers how the early church "saved" the Old Testament by appealing to such interpretive methods as typology and allegory. Since these methods are no longer regarded as appropriate for interpreting most of the Old Testament, chapter 4 discusses several contemporary "solutions" to the problem of disturbing divine behavior. Typically, these "solutions" try to explain and defend God's behavior. Ultimately, each approach discussed in this chapter is judged to be inadequate, prompting us to move in other directions in search of an appropriate response to problematic portrayals of God in the Old Testament.

The second part of the book, "Understanding the Nature of Old Testament Narratives," consists of four chapters that explore several interrelated issues crucial for dealing responsibly with disturbing divine behavior. Chapter 5 addresses the historicity of Old Testament narratives, challenging the popular assumption that everything the Bible reports actually happened. This opens the door for entertaining alternative possibilities for coming to terms with disturbing divine behavior in the Old Testament. Since this is such a sensitive issue for many Christians, chapter 6 responds to some of the objections raised by those who affirm the essential historicity of Old Testament narratives. This chapter also discusses some of the often overlooked dangers of demanding that everything (or most everything) in the Old Testament is historically accurate.

The conclusions reached in chapters 5 and 6 raise another question: If certain things did not happen as the Old Testament describes them, why have they been portrayed this way? Chapters 7 and 8 respond to that question. Chapter 7 considers what motivated Israelite historiographers (history writers) to write these stories in the first place. Among other things, it discusses how ancient writers routinely used the past to address a variety of issues in the present rather than for purely antiquarian interests. It considers some potential reasons for writing one of the most troubling texts in the Old Testament, the conquest narrative in Joshua 6–11. Chapter 8 introduces readers to several theological worldview assumptions commonly held by people in the ancient Near East. These assumptions—such as the belief that God/the gods fought for or against people in battle, and that God/the gods rewarded the righteous and punished the wicked in the here and now—influenced the way Israelites shaped their stories. Identifying these theological beliefs helps us understand *why* God was portrayed in certain ways in the Old Testament. Having a better knowledge of the nature of Old Testament narratives prepares the way for the interpretive guidelines offered in the final section.

The last part of the book, "Developing Responsible Readings of Troublesome Texts," builds on the previous discussion and provides readers with specific guidance for dealing responsibly with disturbing divine behavior in Old Testament narratives. Chapter 9 makes the case for the need to distinguish between the textual and actual God when reading the Old Testament. The importance of doing so is illustrated by an extended discussion of one of the most notoriously troubling passages in the entire Old Testament, the story of the Amalekite genocide in 1 Samuel 15.

Suggesting that we make distinctions between the textual and actual God inevitably raises the question of how we go about doing so. On what basis can these distinctions be made? The christocentric hermeneutic I develop in chapter 10 provides the basis for making these all-important distinctions between the textual and actual God. I argue that the God Jesus reveals should be the standard by which all other portrayals of God are evaluated. Old Testament portrayals that correspond to the God Jesus revealed can be trusted as reliable reflections of God's character, while those that fall short should be regarded as distortions of the same. Chapter 11 develops guidelines for using passages containing disturbing divine behavior in theologically constructive ways. People are encouraged to become discerning readers who employ a dual hermeneutic that allows them to reject certain Old Testament portrayals as unworthy of God without regarding the passages in which they reside as theologically useless. In this way, I attempt to demonstrate the enduring value of Old Testament narratives despite the problematic portrayals of God contained in many of them.

The final chapter of the book, chapter 12, is programmatic in nature. It offers general suggestions for how the church should deal with disturbing divine behavior in the Old Testament. A portion of this chapter is specifically designed to help religious professionals, including pastors and professors who preach and teach from these challenging texts and who regularly need to answer difficult questions students and parishioners ask about them.

The book concludes with a relatively brief afterword and two appendices. Appendix A responds to certain objections that might be raised to an assertion I make in chapter 10 about Jesus revealing a God who is nonviolent. The primary focus here is on how to deal with Jesus' comments about eschatological (end time) divine violence, which some believe contradict that assertion. Appendix B discusses the inspiration and authority of Scripture. Since this book inevitably raises questions about the nature and function of Scripture, it seemed necessary to address these matters. While some readers will undoubtedly need to rethink their view of Scripture in order to embrace the interpretive approach offered in this book, I maintain there is no inherent contradiction between utilizing this approach *and* affirming Scripture's inspiration and authority.

PART 1

Examining the Problem
of Disturbing Divine Behavior

CHAPTER 1

Problematic Portrayals of God

A cruel streak exists in the biblical depiction of God. The overwhelming evidence permits no other conclusion.

—James L. Crenshaw[1]

Many characters in the Bible—including God—sometimes act in ways that seem to transgress the moral code the Bible espouses. This conflict with the Bible . . . creates a dilemma. If God is good, how can he . . . seem bad sometimes?

—Ronald Hendel[2]

The well-known Trappist monk Thomas Merton once wrote: "It is of the very nature of the Bible to affront, perplex and astonish the human mind. Hence the reader who opens the Bible must be prepared for disorientation, confusion, incomprehension, perhaps outrage."[3] For many people, this "disorientation" is felt most keenly when entering the strange and unfamiliar world of the Old Testament, especially when confronted by its deeply disturbing stories of violence, deception, and sexual immorality.

Take, for example, the story of the Levite's concubine in Judges 19. An unnamed Levite, traveling toward his home, makes the fateful decision to lodge in the city of Gibeah for the night. While he is there, some of the men of Gibeah come to the house where he is staying and demand that he be sent out so they can have sex with him. The Levite's host refuses but offers an alternative. The men can have his virgin daughter and the Levite's concubine instead. Only the Levite's concubine is sent out, and she experiences extreme violence at the hands of the men of Gibeah who sexually abuse her throughout the night. The next morning, the Levite finds his dead (?) concubine on the doorstep. He puts her on his donkey and heads for home. When he arrives, he cuts her body into twelve pieces and sends various parts of her dismembered body "throughout all the territory of Israel" (v. 29). It is a gruesome tale, and readers are rightly repulsed by it.

To cite another example more briefly, consider what Amnon, David's oldest son, does to his half-sister Tamar (2 Sam 13). Amnon is smitten by his stunningly beautiful sister and desperately wants to go to bed with her. So, on the advice of his friend Jonadab, Amnon feigns illness as a pretext to be alone with Tamar. Then he rapes her. His behavior is outrageous and morally repugnant.

As troubling as these—and similar—Old Testament stories are, they do not raise insurmountable theological problems for one simple reason: they are stories about *human* wrongdoing.[4] They describe human beings behaving badly, as human beings regularly do. Therefore, the presence of such stories in the Old Testament is unremarkable.

What is surprising to many readers, however, is the inclusion of stories portraying God behaving in ways that appear ungodly and "ungodlike." For example, God is sometimes said to act unfairly, deceptively, and even abusively in the pages of the Old Testament. The Old Testament also describes God routinely participating in various acts of violence. As Raymund Schwager observes:

> The theme of God's bloody vengeance occurs in the Old Testament even more frequently than the problem of human violence. Approximately *one thousand passages* speak of Yahweh's blazing anger, of his punishments by death and destruction, and how like a consuming fire he passes judgment, takes revenge, and threatens annihilation. . . . No other topic is as often mentioned as God's bloody works.[5]

These descriptions of God bother many readers of Scripture and raise important questions. How can we explain God's behavior in these instances, and what do these portrayals suggest about God's character? But before tackling questions like these, we first need to discuss some of the passages in which these portrayals appear. This will help us better appreciate how prevalent and problematic these portrayals are. It will also enable us to be more specific about what makes God's behavior in these episodes particularly troubling to some people.

In what follows, I discuss several different categories of disturbing divine behavior.[6] While these categories draw general distinctions among various kinds of such behavior in the Old Testament, there is some overlap among them. Throughout this chapter, I raise various questions about God's behavior in the passages under consideration to demonstrate the kinds of questions that might occur to thoughtful readers of Scripture and to illustrate some of the potentially problematic dimensions of these portrayals of God. We will begin our exploration of disturbing divine behavior by briefly noting some examples in Old Testament law before turning our attention more extensively to numerous examples in Old Testament narratives.[7]

Disturbing Divine Behavior

God as Deadly Lawgiver

The books of Exodus, Leviticus, Numbers, and Deuteronomy contain 613 laws that God reportedly gave to the Israelites, most often through Moses.[8] These laws cover a broad range of issues, including agriculture, slavery, sexual behavior, war, and worship, to name but a few. Many of these laws simply state what people should or should not do without specifying what happens to lawbreakers. Certain laws, however, do indicate what should be done when infractions occur. While some of these consequences are quite reasonable—such as requiring a thief to make restitution for stolen goods—others seem disproportionate and morally questionable. Those laws stipulating that an offender is to die for his or her misdeeds are particularly disturbing. Consider the following sampling:

Whoever strikes father or mother shall be put to death. (Exod. 21:15)

Whoever kidnaps a person, whether that person has been sold or is still held in possession, shall be put to death. (Exod. 21:16)

Whoever curses father or mother shall be put to death. (Exod. 21:17)

Whoever does any work on the sabbath day shall be put to death. (Exod. 31:15b)

If a man commits adultery with the wife of his neighbor, both the adulterer and the adulteress shall be put to death. (Lev. 20:10)

If a man lies with a male as with a woman, both of them have committed an abomination; they shall be put to death. (Lev. 20:13a)

If a man has sexual relations with an animal, he shall be put to death; and you shall kill the animal. If a woman approaches any animal and has sexual relations with it, you shall kill the woman and the animal; they shall be put to death, their blood is upon them. (Lev. 20:15-16)

A man or a woman who is a medium or a wizard shall be put to death; they shall be stoned to death, their blood is upon them. (Lev. 20:27)

One who blasphemes the name of the Lord shall be put to death; the whole congregation shall stone the blasphemer. Aliens as well as citizens, when they blaspheme the Name, shall be put to death. (Lev. 24:16)

Anyone who kills a human being shall be put to death. (Lev. 24:17)

Regardless of one's position on the controversial question of the propriety of the death penalty, many of the offenses listed above certainly do not seem to warrant such extreme and irreversible measures. As unacceptable as kidnapping, adultery, and bestiality are to many of us today, who would seriously advocate executing those who engage in such behaviors? What legislator would rally behind legislation demanding death for children who strike or curse their parents? And what church body would advocate rounding up and routinely executing Sabbath breakers? Yet, as the Old Testament portrays it, for all of these offenses—and others—God stipulates demands that the wrongdoer be put to death! Such severe consequences seem rather harsh. The portrait of God as deadly lawgiver presented in these verses is difficult to reconcile with other portraits of God found elsewhere in the Bible, especially those in which God appears forgiving and kind.

God as Instant Executioner

In the prologue, we briefly discussed the tragic fate of a man who gathered sticks on the sabbath (Num. 15:32-36). In this incident, the unfortunate Sabbath breaker is executed by his fellow Israelites, who reportedly act on divine authority.[9] In several other Old Testament stories, the offender is killed directly by God without the use of human intermediaries. We will consider three such passages. In each instance, God's use of lethal force seems excessive—some might even say unwarranted— given the nature of the offense.

JUDAH'S SONS

In Genesis 38, we learn that Judah, Jacob's fourth son, has three sons of his own: Er, Onan, and Shelah (Gen. 38:1-6). In typical patriarchal fashion, Judah arranges the marriage of his firstborn son, Er, to a woman named Tamar. The next thing we are told is that Er "was wicked in the sight of the Lord, and the Lord put him to death" (Gen. 38:7). Since no explanation is given, we can only speculate about the nature of Er's wickedness. Judah then instructs Onan, his second-oldest son, to take the recently widowed Tamar to be his wife. Though such an arrangement seems odd to us, it was in keeping with an ancient custom known as Levirate marriage.[10] This law was intended to ensure the preservation of the deceased brother's name (in this case Er), since the first child of this union would be regarded as the deceased brother's son. Judah follows this custom and gives his second-oldest son, Onan, to Tamar. Since Onan knows the child produced by this marriage will not be regarded as his own, he refuses to impregnate her, practicing *coitus interruptus* instead (Gen. 38:9). Since Onan's actions were "displeasing in the sight of the Lord . . . he put him to death also" (Gen. 38:10). One can hardly blame Judah for being more than a little reluctant to give Shelah, his last remaining son, to Tamar. Marriage to Tamar seemed like a death sentence, and Judah "feared that he [Shelah] would die like his brothers" (Gen. 38:11).

The image of God in this passage is unsettling to say the least. Is God really in the business of summarily executing those who are "wicked" and "displeasing" in God's sight? If so, how does this fit with the ugly realities of the modern world? If God instantly executed individuals like these, then why were people like Adolf Hitler, Saddam Hussein, and Slobodan Milosevic allowed to live so long and do so much evil?

NADAB AND ABIHU'S UNHOLY FIRE

Another portrayal of God as instant executioner appears in a most unlikely place, the book of Leviticus. If you are familiar with the book of Leviticus, you know it is almost wholly devoid of stories. One notable exception is the story of two priests named Nadab and Abihu. Their very brief story of disobedience and death follows:

> Now Aaron's sons, Nadab and Abihu, each took his censer, put fire in it, and laid incense on it; and they offered unholy fire before the Lord, such as he had not commanded them. And fire came out from the presence of the Lord and consumed them, and they died before the Lord. (Lev. 10:1-2)

There is no indication of what motivated these newly ordained priests to offer "unholy fire." Whatever the reason, this act of ritual disobedience costs them their lives. God quite literally incinerates them. Why does God burn them alive for committing a single ritual offense? Why doesn't God extend grace and offer these men a chance to repent? It is not a pretty picture.

UZZAH AND THE ARK OF THE COVENANT

A third portrait of God as instant executioner appears in 2 Sam. 6:1-8 (see also 1 Chron. 13:1-11). In a politically savvy move, King David decides to bring the ark of the covenant, Israel's most sacred symbol of God's presence, to Jerusalem. This move is designed to centralize David's political and religious interests. As the ark is being transported on a cart, the oxen shake it, and an otherwise unknown man named Uzzah reaches out his hand to steady the ark (2 Sam. 6:6). For this act he is rewarded with death.

> The anger of the Lord was kindled against Uzzah; and God struck him there because he reached out his hand to the ark; and he died there beside the ark of God. (2 Sam. 6:7)

David is furious at this outbreak of divine anger, and many readers are similarly perplexed, if not perturbed, by God's behavior (v. 8). What has Uzzah done that is so terribly wrong that he deserved to die? The ark is about to tip over and he steadies it. It seems a most natural and reasonable response. You might even expect Uzzah to be praised for his quick thinking and decisive action, which presumably prevented the ark from sliding off the cart and crashing to the ground. Instead, he is struck dead by God.

Some have argued that Uzzah's actions were sinful because he overstepped his bounds and profaned something sacred when he touched the ark. We will consider that possibility later. But even granting that explanation, what makes this story so disturbing is the swiftness and severity of God's punishment. This is especially true when God's response here is compared to God's response in other stories. Sometimes, when people have committed what seem to be far more egregious sins, they get off the hook more easily. Just a few short chapters after the story of Uzzah and the ark, David commits adultery with Bathsheba, attempts an elaborate cover-up, and orchestrates the murder of Uriah in a foolhardy military operation that eliminates Uriah but also results in the death of eighteen Israelite soldiers (2 Sam. 11:24).[11] If anyone should have been killed instantly by the standards of the law, it was David! Yet the prophet Nathan comes to him and says, "The Lord has put away your sin; you shall not die" (2 Sam. 12:13). In fact, David lives well on into old age (see 1 Kgs. 1:1-4).[12] Why does God so quickly forgive David for a series of unambiguous, pre-meditated, and deadly sins but instantly execute Uzzah for what appears to be a split-second decision spontaneously made for the benefit of the ark? God's rather different response in those two episodes seems like an example of divine favoritism.

In each of these three accounts, the offenders are given no opportunity to repent and no second chances. Instead, they are instantly executed by God for their actions. Such rapid retribution seems to run counter to the Old Testament's claim that God is "slow to anger."[13] It creates the impression that God is Is God really like this?[14]

God as Mass Murderer

In addition to killing isolated individuals, the Old Testament also describes God as a mass murderer. This begins as early as Gen. 6:13 when God makes a startling announcement to Noah: "I have determined to make an end of all flesh, for the earth is filled with violence because of them; now I am going to destroy them along with the earth." Understandably, most modern depictions of the story focus primarily on the survivors: Noah's family and the fortunate animals in the ark. Yet, despite cute songs, child-friendly play sets, and colorful artistic renderings of the story, "Noah's Ark" is not a happy tale of giraffes and panda bears clambering aboard a floating zoo. It is a story of catastrophic death and destruction that, incidentally, results from a divine decree. Nearly the entire human population perishes because

God drowns them. It is a disaster of such epic proportions that even some of Hollywood's doomsday scenarios pale in comparison.

A similar story of mass murder is recorded in the book of Numbers. Once again, we witness divine destruction on a grand scale. In the short span of forty years, more than half a million people perish as punishment for their unwillingness to enter Canaan after hearing the unencouraging report that ten spies brought back to them (Num. 14:26-35). But unlike the flood narrative, this time the entire group does not perish in one great cataclysmic event. Instead, they die throughout the (approximately) forty-year period. During that time, there are several specific episodes in which God reportedly kills sizable numbers of Israelites.

> And the men whom Moses sent to spy out the land, who returned and made all the congregation complain against him by bringing a bad report about the land—the men who brought an unfavorable report about the land died by a plague before the Lord. (Num. 14:36-37)

> Moses said to Aaron, "Take your censer, put fire on it from the altar and lay incense on it, and carry it quickly to the congregation and make atonement for them. For wrath has gone out from the Lord; the plague has begun." . . . Those who died by the plague were fourteen thousand seven hundred, besides those who died in the affair of Korah. (Num. 16:46, 49)

> Then the Lord sent poisonous serpents among the people, and they bit the people, so that many Israelites died. (Num. 21:6)

Whether individually or in groups, at the end of forty years, hundreds of thousands of Israelites were killed "for the Lord had said of them, 'They shall die in the wilderness'" (Num. 26:65). This story and the flood narrative both portray God murdering on a massive scale.

These two stories are by no means the only ones that depict God behaving in this way. Many other Old Testament stories similarly portray God as a mass murderer. Consider the following sampling:

> Then the Lord rained on Sodom and Gomorrah sulfur and fire from the Lord out of heaven; and he overthrew those cities, and all the Plain, and all the inhabitants of the cities, and what grew on the ground. (Gen. 19:24-25)

> At midnight the Lord struck down all the firstborn in the land of Egypt, from the firstborn of Pharaoh who sat on his throne to the firstborn of the prisoner who was in the dungeon, and all the firstborn of the livestock. (Exod. 12:29)[15]

> The descendants of Jeconiah did not rejoice with the people of Beth-shemesh when they greeted the ark of the Lord; and he killed seventy men of them.

The people mourned because the Lord had made a great slaughter among the people. (1 Sam. 6:19)[16]

So the Lord sent a pestilence on Israel from that morning until the appointed time; and seventy thousand of the people died, from Dan to Beer-sheba. (2 Sam. 24:15)

That very night the angel of the Lord set out and struck down one hundred eighty-five thousand in the camp of the Assyrians; when morning dawned, they were all dead bodies. (2 Kgs. 19:35)

In these and many other stories, God is depicted as killing large numbers of people in one fell swoop. But does God really behave this way? Does God slay sizable groups of people in single acts of terror? If so, what does that suggest about the nature and character of God? These are not easy questions to answer.

God as Divine Warrior

One especially common way the Old Testament portrays God killing large groups of people is through his role as divine warrior.[17] This image of God is one of the most pervasive and unsettling in the Old Testament. One of the most striking examples of God's warring is recorded in the first half of the book of Exodus, as God decimates Egypt through a series of ten plagues before drowning the Egyptian army in the Red Sea. As the Israelites are trapped between the Egyptian army and the Red Sea, God fights on their behalf. The dramatic account is worth quoting at length:

> At the morning watch the Lord in the pillar of fire and cloud looked down upon the Egyptian army, and threw the Egyptian army into panic. He clogged their chariot wheels so that they turned with difficulty. The Egyptians said, "Let us flee from the Israelites, for the Lord is fighting for them against Egypt." Then the Lord said to Moses, "Stretch out your hand over the sea, so that the water may come back upon the Egyptians, upon their chariots and chariot drivers." So Moses stretched out his hand over the sea, and at dawn the sea returned to its normal depth. As the Egyptians fled before it, the Lord tossed the Egyptians into the sea. The waters returned and covered the chariots and the chariot drivers, the entire army of Pharaoh that had followed them into the sea; not one of them remained. But the Israelites walked on dry ground through the sea, the waters forming a wall for them on their right and on their left. Thus the Lord saved Israel that day from the Egyptians; and Israel saw the Egyptians dead on the seashore. Israel saw the great work that the Lord did against the Egyptians. So the people feared the Lord and believed in the Lord and in his servant Moses.

Then Moses and the Israelites sang this song to the Lord: "I will sing to the Lord, for he has triumphed gloriously; horse and rider he has thrown into the sea. The Lord is my strength and my might, and he has become my salvation; this is my God, and I will praise him, my father's God, and I will exalt him. *The Lord is a warrior;* the Lord is his name. Pharaoh's chariots and his army he cast into the sea; his picked officers were sunk in the Red Sea. The floods covered them; they went down into the depths like a stone." (Exod. 14:24—15:5, emphasis mine)

In various ways, this passage highlights God's very *active* involvement in warfare. God is not portrayed as sitting up in the heavens sending down divine directives while the Israelites slog it out on the field of battle. Rather, God is the one who reportedly "threw the Egyptian army into panic . . . clogged their chariot wheels . . . [and] tossed the Egyptians into the sea." According to this text, God is directly responsible for exterminating the Egyptians. It is God who obliterates the Egyptian army by drowning countless Egyptian soldiers. And as their lifeless bodies wash up on shore, Israel takes no credit for the victory but praises *God* for being "a warrior."

God's military prowess is also on display throughout the conquest narrative in the book of Joshua. As Israel enters Canaan and takes possession of the land, God is repeatedly described as fighting for Israel. In Joshua 10, for example, the Israelites are able to rout a coalition of kings whose armies are in retreat because "the Lord threw them into a panic" (Josh. 10:10). The following verse then provides a vivid description of the Lord's military tactics on this occasion:

As they fled before Israel, while they were going down the slope of Beth-horon, the Lord threw down huge stones from heaven on them as far as Azekah, and they died; there were more who died because of the hailstones than the Israelites killed with the sword. (Josh. 10:11)

Other Old Testament passages indicate God's involvement in war by referring to God "driving out" Israel's enemies and "fighting on behalf of" the people of Israel. For example, consider the words Joshua is said to have spoken to the Israelites just prior to his death:

For the Lord has driven out before you great and strong nations; and as for you, no one has been able to withstand you to this day. One of you puts to flight a thousand, since it is the Lord your God who fights for you, as he promised you. (Josh. 23:9-10)

Other texts indicate God's involvement in war by claiming that God "handed over" Israel's enemies.

And the Lord handed them [a coalition of northern kings] over to Israel, who attacked them and chased them as far as Great Sidon and Misrephoth-maim, and eastward as far as the valley of Mizpeh. They struck them down, until they had left no one remaining. (Josh. 11:8)

Each of these verses affirms God's role as divine warrior. While many more examples could be given, these should be sufficient to demonstrate that the Old Testament describes God as one who not only condones war in certain situations but actively participates in it.

Yet this is precisely what many readers find so troubling. As Walter Kaiser observes: "It is Yahweh's involvement with war in the Old Testament that poses the key problem for modern readers."[18] Similarly, Albert Winn believes "the main problem is not that the *people* of God were warriors, but that the Old Testament affirms that *God* is a warrior."[19] This portrayal of God as a divine warrior, as one who actively participates in so much bloodshed and killing, is problematic for many readers. It is little wonder it has been referred to as the "*skandalon* of the Old Testament."[20]

God as Genocidal General

On more than one occasion, the Old Testament portrays God ordering Israel to utterly annihilate a particular ethnic group, leaving no survivors. This represents what is arguably the most problematic way God operates as a divine warrior, namely, in the role of a genocidal general.[21] The most comprehensive command of this nature is related to the "conquest" of Canaan mentioned previously. As Israel prepares to occupy the land that God is said to have promised to Abraham, Isaac, and Jacob, Moses gives the people these stark instructions:

When the Lord your God brings you into the land that you are about to enter and occupy, and he clears away many nations before you—the Hittites, the Girgashites, the Amorites, the Canaanites, the Perizzites, the Hivites, and the Jebusites, seven nations mightier and more numerous than you—and when the Lord your God gives them over to you and you defeat them, then *you must utterly destroy them.* Make no covenant with them and *show them no mercy.* (Deut. 7:1-2, emphasis mine)

But as for the towns of these peoples that the Lord your God is giving you as an inheritance, *you must not let anything that breathes remain alive.* You shall annihilate them—the Hittites and the Amorites, the Canaanites and the Perizzites, the Hivites and the Jebusites—just as the Lord your God has commanded, so that they may not teach you to do all the abhorrent things that they do for their gods, and you thus sin against the Lord your God. (Deut. 20:16-18, emphasis mine)

In these passages, the Israelites are not just instructed to displace the Canaanites; they are commanded to destroy them. There is no room for compromise, and the Canaanites are to be slaughtered without mercy. Israel's total annihilation of the inhabitants of Canaan is regarded as the will of God.

> So Joshua defeated the whole land, the hill country and the Negeb and the lowland and the slopes, and all their kings; he left no one remaining, but utterly destroyed all that breathed, *as the Lord God of Israel commanded.* (Josh. 10:40, emphasis mine).

The ruthless program of violence and killing described here is explicitly said to be divinely sanctioned. In short, God is portrayed as a genocidal general who instructs Israel to act with utter disregard toward the countless Canaanite men, women, and children already living in the land.

This divine directive to utterly annihilate every last Canaanite makes God appear brutal and unmerciful. What kind of deity desires the absolute eradication of an entire group of people? Does the rationale for their destruction given in Deut. 20:18—"so that they may not teach you to do all the abhorrent things that they do for their gods"—justify such extreme measures, and could toddlers and infants ever pose such a threat? If not, what does this genocidal decree suggest about the character of God?

On another occasion, God is said to have commanded the extermination of all Amalekites. Consider the chilling command the prophet Samuel relays to King Saul:

> Thus says the Lord of hosts, "I will punish the Amalekites for what they did in opposing the Israelites when they came up out of Egypt. Now go and attack Amalek, and utterly destroy all that they have; do not spare them, but kill both man and woman, child and infant, ox and sheep, camel and donkey." (1 Sam. 15:2-3)

As the text portrays it, Saul is divinely commissioned to commit genocide by completely annihilating the Amalekites. Apparently, this is regarded as punishment for Amalek's attack on the Israelites hundreds of years prior, just after they had departed from Egypt (see Exod. 17:8-16).

Yet such a comprehensive command raises serious questions about the nature of God. If this text reflects "what really happened," as many Christians believe, what does it suggest about God's character? What kind of God commissions genocide? Such questions are particularly unsettling in light of the many atrocities committed in the twentieth century during the Holocaust and, more recently, in places like Rwanda, Kosovo, and Darfur. Moreover, narratives depicting God as genocidal become increasingly challenging to understand when viewed in light of other biblical stories in which God appears ready and eager to forgive those who repent of their wicked ways. Consider how the Ninevites escape destruction after responding favorably to the preaching of Jonah (Jonah 3). Why don't the Amalekites enjoy the same opportunity of divine grace? Such inequities further complicate this already problematic portrayal of a God who commissions indiscriminate killing by making God appear unfair and ungracious.

God as Dangerous Abuser

The portrayal of God acting abusively toward particular individuals reveals a somewhat different aspect of disturbing divine behavior from what we have already discussed.[22] To illustrate, we will look briefly at the stories of Hagar, Abraham and Isaac, and Saul.

HAGAR

When Abram's wife, Sarai, is unable to bear children, she encourages her husband to have sexual relations with Hagar, her Egyptian slave girl, as a means of having children by proxy, so to speak (Gen. 16:2). Abram complies, and Hagar conceives. But things quickly sour. Once Hagar has conceived, we are told she "looked with contempt" on Sarai (Gen. 16:4). Sarai responds by treating Hagar harshly and, understandably, Hagar runs away. While on the run, the angel of the Lord finds Hagar in the wilderness and asks where she has come from and where she is going.[23] After Hagar tells this divine messenger she is running from Sarai, her abusive master, she receives the following instructions: "Return to your mistress, and submit to her" (Gen. 16:9). That is like telling a battered wife to leave the women's shelter and return home to her abusive husband. Commenting on this troubling text, Phyllis Trible writes: "Without doubt, these two imperatives, return and submit to suffering, bring a divine word of terror to an abused, yet courageous woman. . . . God . . . here identifies with the oppressor and orders a servant to return not only to bondage but also to affliction."[24]

ABRAHAM AND ISAAC

A few chapters later, in Genesis 22, we encounter the story of the near sacrifice of Isaac. The narrative begins with these horrifying words:

> After these things God tested Abraham. He said to him, "Abraham!" And he said, "Here I am." He said, "Take your son, your only son Isaac, whom you love, and go to the land of Moriah, and offer him there as a burnt offering on one of the mountains that I shall show you." (Gen. 22:1-2)

Abraham unquestioningly follows the Lord's command and, after arriving at the designated spot, arranges the wood and binds his son, Isaac, to the altar. Then, with knife in hand, he is ready to make the required sacrifice when the angel of the Lord appears and stops him just in the nick of time (Gen. 22:11).

It is not uncommon for commentators to use this passage as an example of Abraham's amazing faithfulness and devotion to God, and at one level it certainly can be read that way. God had promised to make Abraham's name great by providing innumerable descendants through Isaac. God's promise would be worthless if Isaac were dead. By demonstrating a willingness to sacrifice Isaac, Abraham demonstrated his loyalty to God above all else, even that which had been promised to him.

While this reading of the text is constructive and compelling—and one that finds support in New Testament passages like Matt. 6:33 and Matt. 19:16-26—it does not diminish the troubling portrayal of God contained within this narrative. What kind of God asks a faithful follower to kill his own child? As Danna Nolan Fewell and David Gunn observe:

> We are not told what God wanted or expected to find in Abraham's performance. Most readings assume that what Abraham did met with God's approval. Abraham, on account of his radical obedience, becomes an exemplary character. Such a reading, on the other hand, leaves the character of God in a rather sticky situation. At the very best one might assert that God is simply unfathomable; at the worst, God is deranged and sadistic.[25]

James Crenshaw regards this as "a monstrous test" and believes "one labors in vain . . . to find the slightest hint of divine compassion in the dreadful story recorded in Gen 22:1-19."[26] Thus, while this text can be regarded as one that encourages total devotion to God, it has a shadow side. God is portrayed as acting in an emotionally abusive way toward both Abraham and Isaac—toward Abraham for having to contemplate and almost carry out this diabolical deed and toward Isaac for having to experience the trauma of being tied to an altar while his dad prepares to kill him.

SAUL

The story of Saul, Israel's first king, begins with his royal anointing in 1 Samuel 9 and ends with his ignominious death on Mt. Gilboa in 1 Samuel 31. Signs of Saul's unsuitable leadership first emerge in 1 Samuel 13, and just two chapters later the Lord rejects Saul "from being king" (1 Sam. 15:23, 26) and gives the kingdom to his "neighbor" David (1 Sam. 15:28). Samuel then anoints David as king, and we are told that "the spirit of the Lord came mightily upon David" (1 Sam. 16:13). What is especially troubling is what happens next. According to 1 Sam. 16:14, "the spirit of the Lord departed from Saul, and an evil spirit from the Lord tormented him." As the text describes it, this evil spirit from God came and went.

> And Saul's servants said to him, "See now, an evil spirit from God is tormenting you. Let our lord now command the servants who attend you to look for someone who is skillful in playing the lyre; and when the evil spirit from God

is upon you, he will play it, and you will feel better." . . . And whenever the evil spirit from God came upon Saul, David took the lyre and played it with his hand, and Saul would be relieved and feel better, and the evil spirit would depart from him. (1 Sam. 16:15-16, 23)[27]

This passage clearly claims that *God* was the one who sent an evil spirit to torment Saul. Is God in the business of sending evil spirits to afflict and torment people? If so, how can such behavior be reconciled with convictions about God's goodness? Portrayals of God acting abusively seriously complicate our efforts to think rightly about God.

God as Unfair Afflictor

There are several stories in the Old Testament in which God seems to punish the wrong person or persons. Our sense of justice is violated as we read these stories and observe God making decisions that seem unfair and that result in considerable suffering.

PHARAOH'S DIVINELY HARDENED HEART

In the book of Exodus, as God is doling out plagues designed to deliver Israel from Egyptian bondage and to display God's greatness, God repeatedly hardens Pharaoh's heart.[28] For example, after the sixth of ten plagues, we read, "But the Lord hardened the heart of Pharaoh, and he would not listen to them [Moses and Aaron], just as the Lord had spoken to Moses" (Exod. 9:12). This divine hardening of heart strengthens Pharaoh's resolve to keep the Israelites under his control as he refuses to let them go despite the increasing severity of the plagues on his land.

The image of God hardening Pharaoh's heart has troubled readers of the Bible for centuries. While many people would readily agree that God regularly *softens* hearts by making people receptive to divine initiatives, hardening hearts seems counterproductive and uncharacteristic of how God typically behaves. Why would God want to make someone more rather than less resistant to the divine will? Moreover, if God is at least partly responsible for Pharaoh's obstinacy, as the text clearly indicates, how can Pharaoh be held responsible for his refusal to let Israel go?[29] It just does not seem right. Pharaoh appears to have no other alternative. But why should God punish Pharaoh for resisting God's will when God was at least partly to blame for Pharaoh's ability to resist? These passages make God seem unjust and malicious.

DAVID'S "SINFUL" CENSUS

According to 2 Sam. 24:15, a verse previously cited in our discussion of God as mass murderer, seventy thousand Israelites die from a divinely initiated plague. Such an enormous death toll inevitably causes one to wonder what terrible evil these people had done to incur such monstrous divine wrath. Was it idolatry, sexual promiscuity, or social injustice? Not according to 2 Samuel 24. Instead, this lethal plague resulted from a census taken by David. But why? What is wrong with taking a census, especially given the fact that this particular census was authorized by God?

> Again the anger of the Lord was kindled against Israel, and he incited David against them, saying, "Go, count the people of Israel and Judah." (2 Sam. 24:1)

David does exactly what he is told but then is punished for it. This seems like entrapment, a deliberate setup designed to ensnare David and to provide a pretext for divine judgment.[30]

Upon completing this census, David is guilt stricken over what he has done, and he cries out to God (2 Sam. 24:10). God's reply to David comes through the prophet Gad, who instructs David to choose one of three options as his punishment. David can experience famine for three years, run from his enemies for three months, or experience a plague on the land for three days (2 Sam. 24:13). David chooses the latter, and by the end of "the appointed time," seventy thousand people are dead (2 Sam. 24:15).

This episode has many troubling dimensions. First, it portrays God as inciting, or prompting, David to sin. How can that be? Most people envision God as one who forgives sin—not one who causes it. Such behavior seems out of character for God (compare to Jam. 1:13).[31] Second, the *Israelites* are punished for something *David* does wrong. Is it fair for God to punish the Israelites for something their king does wrong? Third, by any standard of measure, the punishment seems totally disproportionate to the offense. Regardless of how "wrong" taking this census may have been, killing seventy thousand people seems grossly excessive. The whole ordeal seems terribly unjust and unnecessarily lethal. It makes God seem malicious and cruel.

SAMARIA'S DEADLY LIONS

One of the most unusual stories portraying God unfairly afflicting people is found in 2 Kings 17. This chapter describes the fall of Samaria, Israel's capital, to the Assyrians in 727 BCE.[32] When the Assyrians conquered people, they would take them from their homes and relocate them in various places around the Mediterranean world. Such a policy of deportation made it more difficult for a vanquished people to regroup since they were so widely dispersed. After the fall of Samaria, some Israelites were deported while foreigners were brought in to live on the land. According to 2 Kings 17, these new arrivals were in for quite a surprise.

> The king of Assyria brought people from Babylon, Cuthah, Avva, Hamath, and Sepharvaim, and placed them in the cities of Samaria in place of the people of Israel; they took possession of Samaria, and settled in its cities. When

they first settled there, they did not worship the Lord; therefore the Lord sent lions among them, which killed some of them. So the king of Assyria was told, "The nations that you have carried away and placed in the cities of Samaria do not know the law of the god of the land; therefore he has sent lions among them; they are killing them, because they do not know the law of the god of the land." Then the king of Assyria commanded, "Send there one of the priests whom you carried away from there; let him go and live there, and teach them the law of the god of the land." So one of the priests whom they had carried away from Samaria came and lived in Bethel; he taught them how they should worship the Lord. (2 Kgs. 17:24-28)

The text makes it unmistakably clear that the Lord is the one responsible for sending these deadly lions. Yet the deaths of these non-Israelite newcomers seem terribly unfair. These people came from distant places. Obviously, they were not going to know how to follow Yahweh. Still, they experience divine judgment for their ignorance all the same. Thankfully, the king of Assyria has the good sense to send a priest to teach these new arrivals "the law of the god of the land." Presumably, this stops the killing.

The portrayal of God in this passage is not attractive. God kills people for failing to follow "divine laws" that they had no way of knowing, a situation that God does nothing to remedy. It is up to a "pagan" king to solve this dilemma and to preserve the lives of these newcomers, people who have already suffered the humiliation of conquest, capture, and forced relocation. In this story, the king of Assyria appears more concerned than God is about these vulnerable people.

JOB

One of the most memorable portrayals of God afflicting an individual is found in the opening chapters of the book of Job. As the story begins, Job is described as being "blameless and upright, one who feared God and turned away from evil" (Job 1:1b). After a few verses detailing Job's enormous wealth—which, for ancient readers, would reinforce the impression that Job was a very righteous man—the scene shifts to the heavenly realm. There we see "heavenly beings" appearing before the Lord. One of these beings is referred to as *hasatan*, literally, the adversary.[33] After asking the adversary whether he has considered Job, the Lord proceeds to boast about Job's exemplary character. God's speech echoes the words of the narrator in verse 1: "There is no one like him on the earth, a blameless and upright man who fears God and turns away from evil" (v. 8).

The adversary is not impressed. He asserts that the only reason Job worships God is because of the way God has blessed him. The adversary believes Job's devotion to God is only skin deep and would quickly disappear if Job fell on hard times. The adversary then issues a frightening challenge: "But stretch out your hand now, and touch all that he has, and he will curse you to your face" (v. 11). Incredibly, God accepts the challenge and allows the adversary to wreak havoc on Job. In rapid succession, Job loses everything: his wealth, his property, his servants, and all of his children (Job 1:13-19). It is a tragedy of epic proportions.

Why would God do this to his blameless and upright servant? We find the answer in the following chapter. Once again, we are invited to peer into the heavenly realm as heavenly beings present themselves before God. And once again, God boasts about Job to the adversary, saying, "Have you considered my servant Job? There is no one like him on the earth, a blameless and upright man who fears God and turns away from evil." But this time God does not stop there. He continues by saying, "He [Job] still persists in his integrity, although you incited me against him, to destroy him for no reason" (Job 2:3). One could hardly imagine a more self-incriminating statement. What kind of God is willing to destroy someone—especially someone as devout as Job—"for no reason"?

But Job is not the only one who suffers at God's hands in this story; many others are affected as well. As the text portrays it, God permits—one might even say causes—the death of dozens of people "for no reason," or at the very best, to win a divine wager.[34] All of Job's children and nearly all of his servants are killed as a result of God's conversation with the adversary (Job 1:3, 15, 18-19). This kind of behavior casts a shadow over God's character, making God seem reckless and unjust. This again causes us to ask: Is God really like that? Does God treat people in ways that result in physical and emotional harm? If not, how should we interpret this image of God?

God as Divine Deceiver

The final problematic portrayal of God we will consider in this chapter is that of God as divine deceiver. As recorded in 1 Kings 22, King Ahab of Israel and King Jehoshaphat of Judah are seeking divine guidance to determine whether or not they should go to Ramoth-gilead and attempt to take it from the Arameans. Ahab rounds up four hundred prophets who advise the king to proceed as planned. They encourage him by saying, "Go up; for the Lord will give it into the hand of the king" (1 Kgs. 22:6). Jehoshaphat needs further assurance before he is ready to sign on and asks if there is another prophet of the Lord by whom they might inquire (v. 7). When Micaiah son of Imlah is brought forward, he initially mimics the words of these false prophets but eventually delivers his true message, saying:

> Therefore hear the word of the Lord: I saw the Lord sitting on his throne, with all the host of heaven standing beside him to the right and to the left of him. And the Lord said, "Who will entice Ahab, so that he may go up and fall at Ramoth-gilead?" Then one said one thing, and another said another, until a spirit came forward and stood before the Lord, saying, "I will entice him."

"How?" the Lord asked him. He replied, "I will go out and be a lying spirit in the mouth of all his prophets." Then the Lord said, "You are to entice him, and you shall succeed; go out and do it." So you see, the Lord has put a lying spirit in the mouth of all these your prophets; the Lord has decreed disaster for you. (1 Kgs. 22:19-23)

According to Micaiah's report, God uses deception to persuade King Ahab to go on a military expedition that would result in his death—and that is precisely what happens. Believing the deceptive words God put into the mouths of the false prophets, Ahab goes into battle, is wounded by an arrow, and dies (1 Kgs. 22:29-40). The image of God as a divine deceiver is not one we are accustomed to seeing in the pages of Scripture. Is this what God is really like? Does God sometimes use deception?[35] If so, how can we trust God? Once again, it seems we are left with a portrait of God that stands at odds with some of our most basic beliefs about the nature of God.

The Problematic Nature of These Passages

Before concluding, I want to summarize briefly some of the key difficulties we have identified with the portrayals of God discussed in this chapter. What is it that makes these images of God so troubling? First, these portrayals of God are problematic because God commonly appears to treat people inconsistently, especially when punishment is concerned. Uzzah is killed for trying to steady the ark (2 Samuel 6), while David is forgiven for committing adultery and murder, abusing the power of his office, and attempting to cover up his outrageous sin (2 Samuel 11). God's wildly different—and seemingly inequitable—responses to human behavior in this example and many others disturb our sense of divine fairness.[36]

Second, in numerous examples, God is portrayed behaving in ways that might be regarded as unethical or immoral. Perhaps the most egregious example of this is the portrayal of God as genocidal general. Images of God sanctioning—and, at times, actively participating in—genocide are deeply disturbing since this kind of behavior is exceedingly difficult to justify.[37]

Third, many of the passages we have considered are problematic because God is portrayed as one who kills indiscriminately. This is especially the case when God is portrayed as a mass murderer in such stories as the flood narrative, the destruction of Sodom and Gomorrah, and the Canaanite and Amalekite genocide. These stories speak of the wholesale slaughter of everyone: infants and toddlers, the aged and infirm, the mentally challenged. Today we routinely condemn such behavior in the strongest terms. For example, there is never a justifiable reason for killing an infant or a toddler. People who commit such atrocious acts are condemned and marginalized by society. Yet God is portrayed as sanctioning such behavior repeatedly in the pages of the Old Testament. This constitutes a serious problem for sensitive readers of Scripture.

Fourth, when engaging in acts of judgment and deliverance, God often appears to use excessive force. Take the Exodus narrative, for example. Was it really necessary to totally devastate the land of Egypt and kill every firstborn child in order to free the Hebrews? Wasn't there a less violent, less destructive way to liberate these people? Yet ironically, as the narrative describes it, God actually prolongs the devastation by strengthening Pharaoh's resolve to resist. One might reasonably expect the God of the universe to find more creative and less destructive ways to judge Egypt and deliver Israel.

Fifth, some of these portrayals are problematic because they depict God as one who provides no opportunity for offenders to repent. For example, when God is portrayed as an instant executioner, the affected individuals have no second chance. There is no opportunity to ask for forgiveness or to make amends. Their punishment is final and total. God's zero tolerance policy in these kinds of situations makes God appear harsh, exacting, and uncompassionate.

Sixth, God's behavior in Old Testament narratives is troublesome because God sometimes appears to act in self-contradictory ways. Many problematic portrayals of God are difficult to square with other images of God in the Old Testament. For example, though God is reportedly "merciful and gracious" (Exod. 33:6), such qualities seem utterly lacking when it comes to the divine directive to kill Canaanites and to "show them no mercy" (Deut. 7:2). Moreover, I suspect that those who were instantly annihilated by God—Er, Onan, Nadab and Abihu, and Uzzah—would beg to differ with the description of God as one who is "slow to anger, and abounding in steadfast love" (Exod. 33:6). These apparent discrepancies create difficulties for those wishing to use the Bible to speak coherently about the character of God.

Seventh, Christian readers of the Old Testament are often bothered by these portrayals of God because they seem so unlike the God Jesus reveals. Many of these Old Testament images of God appear to be totally out of sync with the God Jesus reveals in the New Testament: a God who calls us to love enemies and pray for persecutors (Matt. 5:44), a God whom Jesus describes as being "kind to the ungrateful and the wicked" (Luke 6:35), and a God who suffers violence rather than inflicts it on others. Trying to reconcile some of the Old Testament's most troubling images of God with the God revealed in Jesus is no easy task. Some would even say it is impossible.

———

This chapter has demonstrated both the broad range of problematic portrayals of God found in Old Testament narrative and the reasons why such portrayals can be so unsettling. The lengthy discussion of the portrayals was intended to familiarize readers with these images and to help them recognize some of the images' more troubling aspects. Even devout readers of the Bible do not always recognize the magnitude of the problem of disturbing divine behavior. Yet, regardless of whether one realizes it, the Old Testament contains a vast array of troubling images of God, which should concern all who regard these texts as normative for faith and practice. Regardless of how one tries to resolve the tension, it is hard to deny that the Old Testament presents God in ways that appear ethically questionable, if not down-right immoral. God is portrayed as one who sanctions violence, participates in war, executes individuals for seemingly minor offenses, and annihilates large groups of people in dramatic acts of divine destruction. If we are honest, many of us will admit that these images of God do not match up very well with some of our beliefs about God. Understandably, this creates a dilemma for those of us who affirm Scripture's authority yet remain at a loss for what to do with these problematic portrayals.

Obviously, not every Old Testament narrative portrays God behaving in disturbing ways. It would surely be an exaggeration to suggest that the Old Testament contains nothing but troublesome texts from Genesis to Malachi. Anyone who reads through the Old Testament will discover many wonderfully *un*problematic images of God to be savored and enjoyed. God's love, mercy, and grace are often displayed in grand fashion. Since this is not regularly recognized—and given many people's suspicion about the value of reading the Old Testament in the first place—perhaps I should have written a book about "inspiring" divine behavior rather than "disturbing" divine behavior. Yet, despite the obvious value of such a book, it would inevitably leave the problem of disturbing divine behavior unresolved and would provide no guidance for making sense of some of the most troubling images of God in the Old Testament. Thus, it is necessary to confront this issue head-on, with intentionality and care.

While this chapter has considered *how* various images of God are problematic, it has not considered *for whom* these images are problematic. The subtitle of this book—"Troubling Old Testament Images of God"—begs the question, Troubling for whom? Who specifically is bothered by the kinds of passages we have explored in this chapter, and why do they find these images of God so terribly troubling? The following chapter will address these questions by identifying various kinds of people who take issue with the way God is portrayed in certain Old Testament passages. By listening to what they have to say, we can better appreciate why these images are so disturbing for them. The seriousness of the problem we have raised in this chapter will come into even greater focus as we hear their stories.

CHAPTER 2

Problematic for Whom?

If reading the Bible does not raise profound problems for you as a modern reader, then check with your doctor and enquire about the symptoms of brain-death.

—ROBERT P. CARROLL[1]

Old Testament scholar William Holladay tells the following story in his book *Long Ago God Spoke*:

When I was pastor of a congregation many years ago, one of the church school teachers telephoned me one Sunday afternoon; she taught a class of fourth-grade boys, and she said the class had posed a problem she could not answer. They had been studying the events of the book of Joshua, particularly how Joshua led the Israelites to take possession of the land of Canaan. "But," the boys objected, "didn't the land belong to the Canaanites?" "Yes," she admitted. "But that isn't fair!" they all agreed. So here was her question: "What," she asked, "am I to tell the class?" It is indeed a problem, when the ethical sensitivity of a group of nine-year-old boys exceeds that of Joshua.[2]

These young boys were troubled by Israel's "conquest" of the land because it violated their sense of fairness. They clearly thought it was wrong that one group of people should take land belonging to another.

Many readers of the Bible have a similar reaction when encountering disturbing divine behavior in the Old Testament. They object to God's conduct on the grounds that it seems unfair and, at times, even unethical. But who are these readers, and what exactly do they find *so terribly* troubling about these portrayals of God? We will explore this question in the following pages by identifying several groups of people who seem particularly distressed by God's behavior in certain Old Testament passages and by considering why they feel that way. For the purpose of this chapter, I have construed these groups rather broadly, recognizing that an enormous amount of diversity exists among individuals in any one group. Not everyone who identifies with a particular group shares the same degree of discomfort or the same set of difficulties with problematic portrayals of God in the Old Testament. Instead, these groupings are meant to be illustrative, demonstrating common struggles certain kinds of people have had—and continue to have—with these texts.

Although most examples in this chapter come from people in the modern world who find disturbing divine behavior troubling, it would be wrong to conclude that this struggle is strictly a recent phenomenon. As we will see in chapter 3, discomfort with certain Old Testament portrayals of God dates back to the second century CE.[3] It is a problem that has been with us for a very long time.

Religious Pacifists

Many portrayals of God discussed in chapter 1 depicted God commanding or participating in acts of violence. Understandably, these images trouble religious pacifists since they seem to suggest that war has divine sanction in certain circumstances. By definition, a pacifist is someone who is opposed to participating in war personally; many pacifists also regard war itself as immoral.[4] This creates a real dilemma for religious pacifists who regard the Old Testament as Scripture since they read about a God who not only commands Israel to fight but sometimes even fights right alongside them. As two committed pacifists from my own religious tradition put it: "The wars of the Old Testament are a problem for Christians committed to biblical pacifism. How is it that the God who is most fully revealed in Jesus and His nonresistant way, commanded His people, Israel, to fight?"[5] They raise a good question. What are pacifists to do with sacred texts endorsing divinely sponsored violence? Doesn't this undermine the basis of their pacifistic convictions?[6] And don't such passages suggest that God sometimes approves of warfare, even today? Some Christians certainly think so.

In the fall of 2002, when talk of war with Iraq was gaining momentum, the Department of Biblical and Religious Studies at Messiah College produced a letter describing some of its concerns about the unprecedented preemptive strike on Iraq the United States was contemplating. The letter was published in the *Swinging Bridge*, the college's weekly student newspaper. As might be expected, not everyone agreed with the department's perspective, and the next edition of the *Swinging Bridge* carried a reply from an alum of the class of 1998. What I found disappointing—though not surprising—in his response was his attempt to use God's involvement in war in the Old Testament as justification for military action against Saddam Hussein. He writes: "Don't we have a God that is fierce? A God that has His providential hand in wartime? The Old Testament is filled with instances where God is present during war and leading His people into war. . . . Keep in mind that sometimes God uses war to stop evil that is against His kingdom. The Bible shows us this numerous times."[7] This is a familiar argument that is routinely advanced during times of war. For many Christians, God's involvement in warfare and killing in the pages of the Old Testament is incontrovertible evidence that such activities have God's blessing. In the words of one college student: "If killing was good enough for Joshua, then it's good enough for me!"[8] Attitudes like this are terribly troubling to religious pacifists and demonstrate the kind of problems these texts create for them.

In his recent book *Is Religion Killing Us?*, Professor Jack Nelson-Pallmeyer reflects on an experience from his student days that further emphasizes the unfortunate connection some people make between divine violence in the Bible and the appropriateness of war. He writes:

> As a college student involved in protesting the U.S. wars in Indochina, I wondered why my church, including most parishioners, gave uncritical support to the U.S. war effort. Friends and I who were former leaders of our youth group were shunned when we suggested that saturation bombing, defoliation, napalm, cluster bombs, maimed civilians, destroyed villages, and elevated body counts were hard to reconcile with Jesus, who blessed peacemakers and taught love of enemies. One angry parishioner told me that if I objected to war, I shouldn't be a Christian. To bolster his case, he challenged me to read the Bible. He said . . . that it was filled with stories in which a violent God approved of war.[9]

As Nelson-Pallmeyer sees it: "Acceptance of violence-of-God traditions within 'sacred' texts encourages human violence and sanctions abusive notions of power."[10] If so, then people who are committed to resolving conflict nonviolently are likely to find the Old Testament's violent images of God highly problematic. Such images seriously complicate their efforts to persuade people to engage in nonviolent peacemaking. How can they promote peace when God frequently seems to be at war? How can they claim it is inappropriate for Christians to participate in war when so much of the Bible seems to sanction it? God's involvement in war in the Old Testament creates real problems for religious pacifists, particularly for Christians committed to following the nonviolent way of Jesus.

Christian Educators

Disturbing divine behavior is also problematic for people I would classify rather generally as "Christian educators." Here I am thinking of religious practitioners—both clergy and academicians—who regularly use the Bible in their work as professionals. If asked, many of these individuals would acknowledge the difficulty of handling problematic portrayals of God from the pulpit or in the classroom. Because of that hindrance, these troubling texts are sometimes passed over for others deemed more suitable and spiritually edifying. As Elizabeth Achtemeier observes in the introduction to her book, *Preaching Hard Texts of the Old Testament*:

> God does and says things in the Old Testament accounts that we do not like, just as Jesus does and says similarly unsavory things in the New Testament. We preachers too, for all of our knowledge of the Scriptures, have stereotypes of God, and if his deeds and words do not match those preformed views, we reject or ignore them. We are very good at excising or omitting passages in the Old Testament that we cannot countenance.[11]

Achtemeier's comments highlight the very real problem these texts present for preaching. What should preachers do with these problematic passages? Is it advisable to ignore them? Not according to Barbara Brown Taylor, who advocates "Preaching the Terrors." She believes that "there comes a time in every preacher's life when the queasy-making parts of the Bible can no longer be ignored, when it is time to admit that the Bible is not a book about admirable people or even about a conventionally admirable God."[12] Still, the question remains: How can ministers use such passages responsibly as sermon texts?[13]

Many of the Old Testament images of God highlighted in the previous chapter also provide serious challenges to people who want to use the text as a source for Christian theology. In his book, tellingly titled *The Bible as a Problem for Christianity*, Robert Carroll demonstrates how problematic it is for Christians who try use the Bible this way. Carroll emphasizes the gap that exists between what the Bible says and what Christians actually believe. In his chapter "God the Hidden Problematic," Carroll gives several examples that illustrate some of the difficulties involved in using certain Old Testament portraits of God to do Christian theology. For instance, Carroll cites passages in which God is said to be the author of evil.

> I form light and create darkness, I make weal and create woe [evil]; I the Lord do all these things. (Isa. 45:7)

> Does disaster [evil] befall a city, unless the Lord has done it? (Amos 3:6)

On the basis of these and other texts, Carroll concludes: "A God who creates evil will not sit easily with a theological account of evil designed to exonerate God from responsibility for evil. Thus, if what the Hebrew Bible has to say is taken seriously, Hebrew statement and Christian theology will make poor bedfellows."[14] Ultimately, Carroll is not convinced that the Old Testament or its images of God have much value for the Christian theologian. If Carroll is right, this is a serious problem for Christian educators who want to use the Old Testament to help people understand what God is really like.

College and university professors who teach the Old Testament also face the challenge of knowing how to handle problematic portrayals of God in the classroom. They know from experience that it is nearly impossible to teach certain parts of the Old Testament without fielding questions from students bothered by God's behavior. Professor Katheryn Darr explores some of the most disturbing images of God in prophetic literature by examining Ezekiel 20, 23, and 26 in her article "Ezekiel's Justifications of God: Teaching Troubling Texts." Darr writes:

> Commentators express surprise when, for example, Ezekiel speaks of Yahweh giving "not-good laws", or when his descriptions of Jerusalem and Samaria's behavior become exceedingly lewd. But such responses are not limited to Hebrew Bible specialists. They are expressed also by students who encounter these texts, often for the first time, in introductions to the Hebrew Bible, or in courses on prophecy in ancient Israel. "How can I understand a God who gave murderous laws to this 'chosen' people?", they ask. And from one woman I heard: "Am I simply to accept the abusive husband's explanation of why his wife deserved to be murdered?" Such questions are rarely raised in disinterested ways. This is true for me, teaching in a School of Theology where most students have at least some faith commitment to the Bible. It was also the case, however, when I taught biblical studies courses to undergraduate college students. Even in graduate Departments of Religion, where one speaks of "religious beliefs," rather than "biblical theology," students oftentimes express confusion and dismay upon finding such passages within the Bible. "How do you deal with texts like these?", they ask.[15]

Christian educators of all sorts—pastors, theologians, and professors—need to find constructive ways to help their respective audiences "deal with texts like these." This is not an easy task, and it represents one way these texts are problematic for those who preach, teach, and theologize from them.

General Theists

Negative reactions to some Old Testament portrayals of God have also come from people I will refer to as "general theists." This category includes people who believe in a supreme being but who are not adherents of any particular religious tradition. Englishman Thomas Paine (1737–1809) is an especially colorful example of such a person from the eighteenth century. Paine could more precisely be described as a deist, a particular kind of general theist who believes God created the world but thereafter had nothing to do with the day-to-day affairs of its inhabitants. Paine was politically active in both the United States and France and wrote many influential articles and pamphlets. Through both writings and speeches, Paine exhibited a deep concern for the rights of poor and elderly people. He spoke out against the exploitation of workers and was one of the first to condemn the slave trade, urging that it be brought to an end nearly a century before the American Civil War began.

Paine was a highly controversial figure, and many of his writings elicited sharp criticism, though none provoked a more acrimonious response than his two-part work titled *The Age of Reason*.[16] Written in the 1790s, the second part of *The Age of Reason* is especially interesting for our purposes. Here, Paine's strong aversion to the Old Testament's depiction of God is unmistakably clear. Paine argued against accepting these views of God since he believed the Bible had no authority. His rationale for denying the authority of Scripture was based, in part, on his observation that many of the traditionally held beliefs about the authorship of certain biblical books was unwarranted.[17] Using only the Bible as evidence, Paine gave numerous reasons why neither Moses nor Joshua nor Samuel could have written the biblical books typically ascribed to them. By demonstrating why these books could not have been written by these particular individuals, and by arguing that it was impossible to know who actually wrote them, Paine concluded that the Pentateuch and many of the Historical Books were anonymous and, therefore, without authority. This allowed him to reject certain portrayals of God in the Old Testament. For example, by denying the Mosaic authorship of the Pentateuch, Paine could argue that "there is no authority for believing that the inhuman and horrid butcheries of men, women and children, told in those books [the Pentateuch], were done, as those books say they were, at the command of God."[18]

Paine's motivation for denying the authority of the Bible obviously grew out of his conviction that certain biblical portrayals misrepresented God's true character. Paine believed that the Bible promoted violence and cruelty, and he found it blasphemous to honor texts claiming that God sponsored much of this. He wanted to free people from the burden of laboring under an authoritative text he found morally problematic and from ideas about God he felt were unworthy of God.[19] That Paine regarded his work as a liberating corrective to the way many people of his day viewed the Bible is apparent in this especially revealing passage:

> The evidence I have produced, and shall produce in the course of this work, to prove that the Bible is without authority, will . . . relieve and tranquillize the minds of millions; *it will free them from all those hard thoughts of the Almighty which priestcraft and the Bible had infused into their minds*, and which

stood in everlasting opposition to all their ideas of His moral justice and benevolence.[20]

It seems that the "hard thoughts of the Almighty" Paine had in mind were those instances where the Bible portrayed God commanding mass murder and killing. He writes:

> To charge the commission of acts upon the Almighty, which, in their own nature and by every rule of moral justice, are crimes, as all assassination is, and more especially the assassination of infants, is a matter of serious concern. The Bible tells us, that those assassinations were done by the *express command of God*.[21]

Since Paine found such acts blasphemous and utterly incompatible with his view of God, he attempted to undermine the Bible's authority in order to exonerate God. Paine believed it was "a duty incumbent on every true Deist . . . [to] vindicate the moral justice of God against the calumnies of the Bible."[22] He asks: "For what can be greater blasphemy than to ascribe the wickedness of man to the orders of the Almighty?"[23]

In certain respects, I identify with Paine. He read the Bible and found certain portrayals of God to be highly problematic. So do I. He wrote hoping that his work would help people more accurately understand the character of God. So have I. But I differ sharply from Paine in the way he attempted to resolve the tension between his belief about God and the Bible's portrayal of God. For Paine, the solution was simple: disregard the Bible. From his perspective, this was totally unproblematic since he believed the Bible was "fabulous" and untrustworthy anyway. Moreover, as a deist, he felt people did not need this kind of "special revelation" to help them live rightly. Instead, he thought one's natural mind and reason were enough to guide one through this life and into the next. The approach taken in this book differs considerably since it presumes that the Bible is authoritative and indispensable in matters of faith and practice.

A more popular and well-known general theist who also had serious problems with the Bible's portrayal of God is Mark Twain. Despite his Presbyterian upbringing, Twain's rantings about God are unorthodox and unrelenting. Twain, who was influenced by Paine's writing, saw no connection "between the God of the Bible and the God of the present day" and had nothing good to say about the God of the Old Testament.[24] He speaks of the Old Testament God as "a fearful and repulsive character" and "an irascible, vindictive, fierce, and ever fickle and changeful master."[25] According to Twain, the God of the Old Testament has "evil impulses far beyond the human limit."[26] Of this God, Twain writes:

> In the Old Testament His acts expose His vindictive, unjust, ungenerous, pitiless and vengeful nature constantly. He is always punishing—punishing

trifling misdeeds with thousandfold severity; punishing innocent children for the misdeeds of their parents; punishing unoffending populations for the misdeeds of their rulers. . . . It is perhaps the most damnatory biography that exists in print anywhere.[27]

Words like these make Twain's absolute disdain for God's behavior in the Old Testament unmistakably clear.

Turning to a more recent example of a general theist who finds Old Testament portrayals of God problematic, we can briefly note the work of comedian, actor, and author Steve Allen, whose book *On the Bible, Religion, and Morality* has been compared to the writings of Thomas Paine.[28] Though he would not describe himself as a Christian, Allen is no stranger to Christianity. Raised Catholic, Allen was excommunicated in his early thirties because he chose to remarry. Afterward, he attended a Presbyterian Church in the Los Angeles area with his second wife for about twelve years. Although Allen believes in the existence of a supreme being, he does not believe this "Being" looks much like the God one encounters in the Bible.

Allen's book is a collection of essays, arranged from A to Z, on a variety of biblical texts and topics. The impetus for writing this book, which Allen originally intended to publish posthumously, grew out of his reading of Gideon Bibles he found in hotel rooms. In fact, by his own reckoning, about half of the book was written in hotels over a dozen years or so.

Allen's discomfort with portrayals of divine violence in the Old Testament is evident at various points throughout the book. In one place, he writes:

> Many children are taught Old Testament stories, as I was, but I somehow felt that the deity depicted in Exodus and elsewhere in the Old Testament was not the true God that I was supposed to pray to and worship. Yet at the same time I accepted as natural that the enemies of the Children of Israel were automatically the "enemies" of God. It never occurred to me to ask: If there is only one God, then he must have made the Egyptians, the Canaanites, the Philistines also, and if so why is he so violently angry with them? I was taught that Christians should not hate others—and indeed was greatly disappointed to learn that some of us were deeply prejudiced against Jews—and that we should try to love everyone, including even our enemies. Why, then, did God not do so in Old Testament times?[29]

God's behavior in the Old Testament ultimately leads Allen to reject the Old Testament as an untrustworthy source of information about God's character. Near the beginning of his essay on the book of Joshua, Allen writes:

> One of the most striking—indeed most typical—characteristics of Yahweh, from what one may learn about him in the Old Testament, is his savagery and bloodthirstiness. In the Old Testament he is often an utterly ruthless mass-

murderer, a military strategist and tactician as violent as any human tyrant known to history. Since I do not perceive God as bloodthirsty . . . it follows I cannot accept the accuracy of the Old Testament, except as a record of what the Hebrews believed at the time it was written.[30]

Allen finds portrayals of divine violence in the Old Testament particularly troubling because he believes these images are partly to blame for some of the violent behavior of the past century. He writes:

> That mankind is still capable of the murderous evils that have been committed in the 20th century may be due in part to the fact that Jews and Christians have totally incorporated, into their unconscious perhaps, extremely vengeful and "righteous" behavior as characteristic of the God they worship. If they have not, then why do not Jews and Christians reject publically the more sadistically violent portions of the Bible?[31]

Like Paine, Allen does not regard the Bible as a helpful resource for demonstrating God's goodness.[32] Unlike Paine, Allen does not want people to *stop* reading the Bible. On the contrary, he wants people to *start* reading the Bible—intelligently. He wants people to use their minds and their reason when coming to Scripture in order to distinguish between what is true and honorable and what is not. Since both Paine and Allen regard God as essentially good and merciful, they are deeply troubled by portrayals of God in the Old Testament that suggest otherwise.

Feminists

Since most biblical texts were presumably written by men, it comes as no great surprise to discover that the Bible overwhelmingly reflects a patriarchal perspective. Women are often portrayed unfavorably in biblical texts, and their voices are often marginalized—if not silenced altogether. This patriarchal bias can sometimes be detected in various portrayals of God. For example, in the legal sections of the Old Testament, numerous "God-given" laws privilege men over women. Professor Miguel De La Torre has identified these inequitable laws, and I have noted a few examples as follows:[33]

1. Male Hebrew slaves were to be freed after six years of service without needing to pay the owner anything for their freedom. No such provision existed for female Hebrew slaves (Exod. 21:2, 7).
2. If a man suspected his wife had been unfaithful, he could require her to drink a "water of bitterness" to determine whether she was guilty (Num. 5:11-31). A woman who suspected her husband of being unfaithful had recourse to no such option.

3. If a man believed the woman he married was not a virgin, he could ask for "evidence of her virginity" from the young woman's parents (Deut. 22:13-21). Again, no such option was available to women who suspected their husbands had sexual relations prior to marriage.

After examining these and other laws, De La Torre concludes: "One is left questioning if these laws were indeed the will of God or if these were the laws of men who attributed the regulations to God in order to protect their power and privilege within patriarchy. If these regulations came from God, then God stands accused of sexism."[34]

In addition to inequitable laws ostensibly given by God, there are various other divine actions that are particularly offensive to feminists. In the previous chapter, we cited God's alarming command to Hagar to return to an abusive situation and to submit to her abuser (Genesis 16).[35] Feminist Hebrew Bible scholar Phyllis Trible discusses various ways this portrayal of God is problematic for Hagar and, by extension, for all female readers.[36]

Another patriarchal portrayal of God is found in the way God responds to David for sins related to his adulterous relationship with Bathsheba, the wife of Uriah. As punishment for David's transgressions, the prophet Nathan declares:

> Thus says the Lord: I will raise up trouble against you from within your own house; and I will take your wives before your eyes, and give them to your neighbor, and he shall lie with your wives in the sight of this very sun. (2 Sam. 12:11)

According to this prophetic oracle, God takes an active role in carrying out this judgment involving the transfer of David's wives to someone else. This is problematic because it makes God complicit in acts of adultery and rape. By divine decree, numerous married women are required to have sex with someone other than their husband whether they want to or not. Such a portrayal of God is disturbing for obvious reasons. Of course, this portrayal of God made perfect sense in a patriarchal culture that regarded women as men's property. Viewed in that context, God's judgment can be understood as reflecting the patriarchal ethos of the time. Yet, even though such violent and violating behavior is understandable given the patriarchal context of ancient Israel, it is hardly appropriate to imagine God as one who initiates and sanctions such acts of violence against women. It is not difficult to understand why feminists—and others—find texts like these oppressive.

One place the patriarchal portrayal of God is felt most keenly and distressingly is in the prophetic literature. This is especially true in passages where God is portrayed as a faithful husband while Israel is portrayed as a faithless wife. Renita Weems has commented on the problematic dimensions of this marriage metaphor in Hosea, Jeremiah, and Ezekiel in her monograph *Battered Love: Marriage, Sex, and Violence in the Hebrew Prophets.* The portrait of God that emerges from these texts is not very attractive, to say the least. She writes: "God is described as an abusive husband who batters his wife, strips her naked, and leaves her to be raped by her lovers, only to take her back in the end, insisting that when all is said and done Israel the wife shall remain interminably the wife of an abusing husband."[37] What makes this image of God especially troubling is the power it has to legitimate spousal abuse in the real world. As Weems observes:

> As long as the metaphor's principal concern is to reinforce notions of hierarchy, power, and retribution, it is a problematic device for those of us committed to the work of mending the broken places in our generation and healing the damage done within our culture. If metaphors are what we live by, and if they help us imagine who God is, then we run the risk of making ourselves into the image of the deity who threatens, mutilates, and destroys.[38]

Although Weems believes there are ways to redeem the marriage metaphor, she rejects the image of God suggested by these texts. She regards it as unacceptable because it supports notions of domination, oppression, and violence that people in the ancient world may have accepted as the norm but which today are rejected as immoral.

Like Weems, Quaker writer Gracia Fay Ellwood also rejects violent patriarchal portrayals of God because of the tragic effects they have on women. She writes: "The image of the outraged divine patriarch is unacceptable because it encourages tendencies to violence and domination in human husbands/fathers."[39] When biblical portrayals of God have this undesirable effect—when they contribute to violent behavior against women—the problematic nature of these Old Testament images becomes painfully obvious. It is easy to understand why images like these present serious difficulties for self-identified feminists, for women generally, and for all who care about women's well-being.

Groups of Dispossessed People

Individuals who have been dispossessed, or who are part of a group that has been forcibly relocated at some point in time, find certain Old Testament images of God troubling. Take Robert Allen Warrior, a member of the Osage Nation of American Indians, for example. In an interesting article titled "Canaanites, Cowboys, and Indians," Warrior expresses concern over God's portrayal in the Exodus-conquest narrative and contends that "the story of the Exodus is an inappropriate way for Native Americans to think about liberation."[40] On the other hand, many individuals, particularly African Americans and those engaged in liberationist readings in Latin America, have found the story of God's deliverance of Israel from Egypt to be a powerfully positive narrative.[41] They celebrate the portrayal of God as one who frees people from slavery, oppression, and injustice.[42] This view of God clearly resonates with those who historically have been marginalized and disenfranchised.

So why would such a narrative, with its liberating God, not be especially meaningful to Native Americans who have been oppressed for more than half a millennium? The reason, according to Warrior, is that deliverance from bondage is only half the story. "The liberationist picture of Yahweh is not complete," he writes. "A delivered people is not a free people, nor is it a nation."[43] They need land. Although God promises to give them the land of Canaan, there is one "small" problem: it is already occupied. But not to worry. God promises to clear away the inhabitants of the land so that Israel can move on in. As Moses reportedly says to the Israelites just prior to their entry into the land:

> Hear, O Israel! You are about to cross the Jordan today, to go in and dispossess nations larger and mightier than you. . . . Know then today that the Lord your God is the one who crosses over before you as a devouring fire; he will defeat them and subdue them before you, so that you may dispossess and destroy them quickly, as the Lord has promised you. (Deut. 9:1a, 3)

As Warrior succinctly puts it: "Yahweh the deliverer became Yahweh the conqueror."[44]

Now that is all well and good as long as you are an Israelite. But what if you are a Canaanite? What happens if you identify with the indigenous people of the land, the people whom God defeats and subdues, rather than with the interlopers who move in? As Warrior observes: "The obvious characters in the story for Native Americans to identify with are the Canaanites, the people who already lived in the promised land."[45] Yet, according to this story, "the narrative tells us that Canaanites have status only as the people Yahweh removes from the land in order to bring the chosen people in. They are not to be trusted, nor are they to be allowed to enter into social relationships with the people of Israel. They are wicked, and their religion is to be avoided at all costs."[46] It is easy to see the kind of problems this raises for Native Americans who read this story. They rightly recognize that the God of the exodus is also the God of the conquest, a God who is ready and willing to forcibly remove indigenous people to make room for outsiders. Can Native Americans really identify with this kind of God? Warrior is uncertain and questions whether such a God can be trusted in the struggle for justice.[47]

As history sadly demonstrates, the Exodus-conquest narrative has not been very liberating for many Native Americans. In fact, one of the most shameful chapters in American history involves the mistreatment of Native Americans by Europeans who came to the "new land." Although most United States textbooks are very sympathetic toward the plight of these early European settlers, when the truth is told a different—and far more disturbing—picture emerges.[48] Time and again, we discover that they committed horrific atrocities against Native Americans. What makes this especially tragic is that they were "inspired" to do so by preachers who justified such barbaric acts by appealing to the biblical narratives of conquest and slaughter. The colonists were portrayed as the new Israel; the Native Americans, as Canaanites or Amalekites. As Susan Niditch describes it:

> On 1 September 1689 Cotton Mather preached his sermon "Souldiers Counselled and Comforted," a charge to members of the armed forces engaged in the ongoing battles with the native inhabitants of New England. . . . The mood is intense, electric with bloodstirring references to beloved friends killed by Indians (Mather: 9, 31, 32), to the need for courage, and to the faith owed a supporting but demanding God. . . . The Bible is alive to the people gathered at the Old North Meeting House, Boston, in the oral formulations of the Puritan preacher who combines traditional phrases and ancient images to describe perceptions of current realities. The cadences speak the listeners' myth. They are Israel in the wilderness, confronted by Amalek (Mather: 37), Israel who must approach the enemy with a priestly purity of body and soul (Mather: 17, 24, 25, 38). Amalek, deserving of vengeance and total destruction, is to be "beat(en) small as the Dust before the Wind," "Cast out as the Dirt in the Streets," (Mather: 28) eliminated, exterminated. The war against the Indians of New England is justified on grounds both explicit and implicit: they are accused of murdering Christians and therefore worthy of death . . . but also they are Ammon, Amalek, an indigenous population who will be displaced and disinherited by divine decision to make way for the new Israel.[49]

When texts are read in this way, when they are pressed into the service of murderous agendas, they are not liberating. Given this tradition, it is little wonder that some Native Americans have not found this narrative—or the God it portrays—particularly helpful.

Palestinians and some Jews also find the God of the conquest narrative problematic for similar reasons. They are deeply troubled by texts that portray God forcibly removing one group of people from their land in order to make room for another group. Jewish scholar Moshe Greenberg, for example, is particularly troubled by the way Jewish nationalists sometimes appropriate this view of God to legitimate acts of violence and to proclaim their absolute right to the land.[50] Greenberg does not find the biblical texts problematic in and of themselves, nor is he particularly uncomfortable with the conquest narrative as it now stands in the book of Joshua. His dispute is with the Jewish nationalists who have co-opted this view, and these texts, for their political agenda. Greenberg believes it is completely inappropriate to use Scripture to declare that Jews have a right to the land of Israel today. As he puts it: "Scripture knows of no general injunction of lasting validity to settle the land and expel its inhabitants."[51] For Greenberg, the notion "that present-day land seizures are scripturally grounded and that antipathy and rigor toward the inhabitants of those lands

... has scriptural warrant is ... far from self-evident."[52] And he cautions that we not "derive eternal lessons" from "conditional teachings or regulations."[53] His warning reminds us of the powerful influence these ancient texts can have in the world today and demonstrates the dangerous way they can be, and have been, interpreted.

After reading the conquest narrative, it is hard to imagine any dispossessed group of people cheering for the God of Joshua (unless they hold out the hope of dispossessing others!). This portrayal of God is problematic because it perpetuates the notion that dispossessing people is sometimes divinely sanctioned. A God who acts this way, who not only condones but actually commissions such terror and trauma, is not likely to inspire their worship.

Atheists and Agnostics

Some people who would consider themselves atheists or agnostics have also found the Old Testament troubling. For some, the problematic portrayals of God in the Old Testament present serious obstacles to believing in God or coming to faith in the first place.[54] Madalyn Murray O'Hair, arguably the most outspoken atheist of the twentieth century, is a case in point. According to her biographer Bryan R. Le Beau, O'Hair "returned repeatedly" to attacks on "the credibility of the Old and New Testaments" in her book *Why I Am an Atheist*.[55] It is obvious she had serious problems with portrayals of God in the Old Testament. She claimed that "the Jewish god is the most ruthless, sadistic monster ever invented."[56] While it would be overstating the case to claim that troubling depictions of God in the Old Testament kept O'Hair from believing in God, they certainly did not help. She recognized the problematic nature of the Bible and regarded it as an obstacle to faith. This is evident in a bold proposal she once made: "My suggestion to you is pick up the Bible and read it. More Atheists come from this exercise than any other single thing."[57] While the notion that reading the Bible can lead people to atheism may seem extreme, it should not be dismissed too casually. There is at least anecdotal evidence to support it, such as this story told by C. S. Cowles:

> A former student shared with me the sad story of his father, a dedicated lay leader of an evangelical church, who in mid-life set out to read the Bible through for the first time. He was first surprised, then shocked, and finally outraged by the frequency and ferocity of divinely initiated and sanctioned violence in the Old Testament. About halfway through the book of Job, he shut his Bible never to open it again and has not set foot inside a church since.[58]

I imagine there are many stories like this one, stories that demonstrate how God's behavior in certain Old Testament narratives has hindered rather than helped people come to faith.

During the writing of this book, I received e-mails from two individuals indicating that God's behavior in the Old Testament was an obstacle to belief for a family member. The relevant portions follow:

> I don't know how many or which ones that he read, but my father has claimed that God's actions in the OT (the war-like ones) keep him from believing.

> I remember distinctly a conversation I had with my older brother who had no need for God in his life. One of his intellectual difficulties was what to do with the disparity between the God of the New Testament and the "psychotic S.O.B." of the Old.

Sadly, I have no doubt many other people could share similar stories. Offensive portraits of God in the Old Testament sometimes do keep people from believing in God.

People of Faith

In contrast to atheists and agnostics, people of faith commonly have deeply held convictions about the trustworthiness of Scripture and the goodness of God. Many people of faith would claim that their beliefs about the Bible and their beliefs about God exist quite nicely together. But others would just as readily admit that serious tension exists between their core convictions about Scripture and the character of God.[59] They realize that some of the Bible's claims about God do not mesh very well with their beliefs about God, a situation that can be quite unsettling.

In his national bestseller *Rescuing the Bible from Fundamentalism*, Episcopal bishop John Shelby Spong shares how his careful reading of the Bible led him to some disagreeable discoveries about God. He writes:

> God appeared in some passages to be not only a nationalistic deity but also a sadistic one who delighted even in killing the firstborn in every Egyptian household (Exod. 11:4-6). . . . The picture of God that began to emerge from the Bible for me was neither a pleasant one nor one to which I was drawn in worship. It did not get better.

> The Bible confronted me with the picture of God rejoicing over the drowning of the Egyptians at the Red Sea (Exodus 15). Was this God not also the God of the Egyptians? I wondered. Later this God suggested that the children of the Edomites should have their heads dashed against the rocks for what the Edomites had done to the Jews (Ps. 137:7-9). In another instance, God was called "a man of war" (Exod. 15:3), a concept far removed from the one I had come to call the "Prince of Peace."[60]

Spong experienced a huge gap between the God he knew and the one portrayed in certain parts of the Bible. This created a terrible dilemma for him. Spong writes: "Time after time the things this God was thought to have commanded became repulsive to me. If all of these things were part of a Bible that had to be believed as the literal word of God, I found that increasingly I could not give myself in worship of such a deity."[61] Spong had a choice to make. He could either stop worshiping God or reject a literal reading of the Bible. He chose the latter. While not everyone bothered by these images resolves the tension as Spong did, his struggle illustrates the kinds of challenges facing people of faith who take the Bible seriously.

The conflict some people feel between their beliefs about God and the Bible's portrayal of God can be quite disconcerting. This was evident in an assignment I received from a student dealing with portions of 1 Samuel 16–18. Among other things, these chapters make repeated reference to Saul being terrorized by an evil spirit. In response, the student wrote:

> What really gets to me in these passages is the idea that the Lord sends evil spirits to torment people, causing them to act in crazy ways. Why would God do that? These troublesome portrayals of God tick me off. This is not the God that I think I know.[62]

People of faith find texts like these—along with many others discussed in the previous chapter—problematic, to say the least. Their high view of Scripture keeps them from dismissing these texts as theologically worthless, while their core convictions about the character of God make it difficult to accept what the Bible actually seems to be saying God is like. They are caught between a rock and a hard place.

Christians, in particular, are also troubled by the apparent disparities they find between the "God of the Old Testament" and the "God of the New Testament." As one of my students put it:

> A lot of times I wonder why God in the Old Testament is so dissimilar to God in the New Testament. It seems as if in the Old Testament he is very vengeful and angry with those who disobey him, but in the New Testament he forgives everyone who believes rather than punishing them. . . . It just seems crazy how radical God tends to be in the Old Testament. He had people killed and punished in horrible ways. Being raised thinking that the words God and Love and [sic] interchangeable seems strange to think about if one was only to read the Old Testament.[63]

This student articulates a tension felt by many Christians who find significant contrasts between portraits of God in the Old and New Testament. They expect to find a unified picture of God in the Bible and are troubled by conflicting portrayals of God, especially when some of those portrayals depict God behaving in ways that seem excessively violent and harsh.

In this chapter, I attempted to demonstrate why disturbing divine behavior is problematic for individuals from all walks of life, and have tried to illustrate both the scope and severity of the problem. For some, God's repeated use of violence in the Old Testament is troublesome because it seems to undermine peacemaking efforts. For others, God's behavior constitutes a real problem for preaching and teaching from these texts. Some are bothered by these portrayals because they have been used to justify their oppression, while others are troubled intellectually, unable to reconcile these images of God with their own personal beliefs. Whatever the particular nature of their concern, the kind of people we identified in this chapter would all agree on one thing: there are some troubling images of God in the Old Testament.

It was necessary to spend some time emphasizing the negative impact these texts have had on people since many readers of Scripture seem unaware of these deleterious effects. This would have aptly described me prior to entering college. I do not recall any of the texts discussed in the previous chapter troubling me when I was eighteen years old. (Then again, I do not think I had ever read many of these texts.) Nor was I aware that they bothered other people. As far as I was concerned, the Bible was the perfect word of God and its representation of God could be accepted unquestioningly. Even if I had felt some discomfort with certain images of God, my view of the Bible would have quickly neutralized any serious inquiry I might have undertaken.

This is precisely how many people initially deal with disturbing divine behavior. Holding tightly to clearly defined ideas about the nature and character of God, they immediately find ways to justify or resolve any theological tension they feel when reading potentially problematic passages. But doing so does not remove the difficulties. Instead, it makes them even more hazardous by masking them with pious justifications. You know the old adage: the cancer you don't know you have is more dangerous than the one you do know about.

Others do not find these passages problematic because of their comfortable familiarity with them. This familiarity effectively anesthetizes some readers of the Bible, preventing them from experiencing any significant discomfort with the unsettling images of God these stories contain. In short, they have grown so accustomed to these narratives that they are no longer troubled by them. In contrast to those who have little or no knowledge of the Old Testament, they have heard these stories so often that they sometimes fail to consider what the story is actually saying. The story of the worldwide flood in the book of Genesis, for example, becomes little more than a colorful tale about a floating zoo instead of a divine disaster of epic proportions. But even though some people are unaware of the problematic dimensions of passages like these, that does not eliminate the problem. These texts do create problems for many readers, and this chapter has demonstrated how deeply troubling God's behavior in the Old Testament can be for these individuals.

 The next two chapters consider several attempts, both ancient and modern, to address this perplexing problem. This will allow us to consider a wide range of "solutions" before charting a somewhat different way forward.

CHAPTER 3

Ancient Approaches
to Disturbing Divine Behavior

*Marcion threw out the Old Testament on account of the unworthiness of the
God it depicted. Origen retained the Old Testament and sought to interpret
it in such a way as to exclude from its depiction of God the qualities Marcion
condemned.*

—JOSEPH W. TRIGG[1]

In his book *Jesus against Christianity*, Jack Nelson-Pallmeyer shares this personal
story:

> Many years ago as a seminary student on retreat, I sat by a fireplace reading
> my Bible. I had my pen in hand, ready to highlight passages or paragraphs that
> struck me as particularly important or meaningful. On this occasion, another
> student saw me underlining in my Bible. He apparently knew of a passage
> that made writing in the Bible a punishable offense. "What are you doing?" he
> screeched, unable to conceal his rage. I looked up and said simply, "I'm cross-
> ing out the parts I don't like."
>
> At the time, this was a witty response to a hostile question. Today it is
> more. The biblical portraits of God as murderous, wrathful, hateful, and ven-
> omous are so widespread that they leave us no choice but to cross out parts of
> the Bible.[2]

While most contemporary readers of the Bible would be uncomfortable crossing out parts they find objectionable, some ancient readers employed even more extreme measures to eliminate problematic portrayals of God from the Old Testament. This chapter examines these—and other—ways people in the ancient world responded to disturbing divine behavior in the Old Testament.

Considering how people from the distant past dealt with problematic portrayals of God helps remind us that this problem has a long history. The discomfort many people today feel when they encounter these portrayals of God is nothing new; it has existed for a very long time. Our attempt to come to terms with these difficult images of God places us in a long line of people who have struggled with these texts in an effort to make sense of them. We are not alone.

The approaches we will consider in this chapter revolve around three general kinds of activity: changing the text, rejecting the text, and salvaging the text. As we will see, in each instance an effort is made to neutralize some of the more undesirable aspects of the Old Testament's portrayals of God. We begin by looking at a few examples of "textual tampering" in which ancient writers actually changed the text to alter portrayals of God they felt were inappropriate.

Changing the Old Testament

Replacing God with Satan

Some ancient writers apparently had very strong ideas about how God should—and should not—be portrayed. There is clear evidence in the Old Testament to this effect. Some writers found certain portrayals of God unacceptable and therefore decided to change them. To illustrate, we return to the account of David's "sinful" census discussed briefly in chapter 2. The narrative begins as follows:

> Again the anger of the Lord was kindled against Israel, and he incited David against them, saying, "Go, count the people of Israel and Judah." (2 Sam. 24:1)

According to this account, Yahweh is responsible for prompting David to count the people. But curiously, as the story unfolds, we discover that Yahweh punishes David for doing the very thing Yahweh had commanded him to do. Why would God prompt David to do something and then punish him for doing it? And why kill tens of thousands of Israelites in the process? This portrayal of God, which does not sit well with many modern readers, apparently bothered some ancient readers also. This discomfort is evident when comparing an alternate version of the story, written hundreds of years after 2 Samuel was produced. In this version, recorded in 1 Chronicles 21, the problematic portrayal of God is completely eradicated. This version begins with these words:

Satan stood up against Israel, and incited David to count the people of Israel.
(1 Chron. 21:1)

The Chronicler has made a slight—but not insignificant—change to the story, one that can be noticed immediately. In the Chronicler's account, Satan takes Yahweh's place. Satan, not Yahweh, is described as prompting David to take this sinful census.[3] The Chronicler presumably made this drastic alteration because of a disagreement with the notion that Yahweh would deliberately cause David to sin. By making Satan the culprit, the Chronicler conveniently eliminated all traces of God's problematic prompting, thereby exonerating Yahweh and relieving much theological tension.[4]

The decision to replace Yahweh with Satan illustrates a tendency that continued to develop for several hundred years. The people of Yehud—Jews living in the land of "Israel" after the exile—needed to find alternative explanations for the calamities that continually befell them. Previously, they were content to attribute everything that happened to them to the hand of God. But as time wore on and they continued to suffer at the hands of foreign oppressors, it became theologically unsustainable to maintain that God was responsible for all their misfortunes. Therefore, they began to posit secondary causes that provided a more acceptable rationale for some of the bad things that happened to them. Their view of God changed over time, and this alteration in the text accommodated that new understanding.

A similar phenomena took place in the pseudepigraphical book of Jubilees, a book dating to the second century BCE that retells portions of Genesis and Exodus 1–12. The writer of Jubilees clearly took issue with the way God was portrayed in certain passages and attempted to address this problem by correcting what was regarded as bad theology.[5] This was done by ascribing some of God's more questionable behavior to a Satan-like figure named Mastema.[6]

This substitution in Jubilees occurs in three episodes that portray God acting in morally questionable ways. These episodes are the binding of Isaac (Genesis 22), Moses's near-death experience (Exodus 4), and Pharaoh's pursuit of Israel into the Red Sea (Exodus 14). God commands child sacrifice in Genesis 22, attempts to kill Moses in Exodus 4, and hardens Pharaoh's heart in Exodus 14. In each story, God's behavior is both puzzling and troubling. The substitution of Mastema for Yahweh in Jubilees's retelling of these narratives eases the tension they otherwise generate. According to Wintermute's introduction to the book of Jubilees, the insertion of Mastema into these stories is part of a larger effort to come to grips with the source of evil in the world. He writes:

The author's interest in demonic powers provided a practical way of dealing with the problem of evil: How can one affirm both the omnipotence and goodness of God in the presence of manifest evil? In other words, where does evil come from? The author of Jubilees would teach us three things about evil: (1) It is superhuman; (2) but it is not caused by God; (3) therefore it comes from the angelic world, which has suffered a breach in God's good order. . . . The author of Jubilees is so certain of that point that he can recast the biblical traditions with confidence. *It was Mastema and not God* who tempted Abraham to kill Isaac (17:15-18:13; cf. Gen 22:1-19), who provoked the Egyptians to pursue Israel (48:12; cf. Ex 14:8f.), and who sought to kill Moses on the way to Egypt (48:2f.; cf. Ex 4:24).[7]

An interesting feature common to all of these passages is that in each one God is portrayed as bringing trouble against the people of God for no obvious reason. The idea that God would inexplicably bring evil against the people of God seems to have been particularly loathsome to the Chronicler and to the writer of Jubilees. They apparently regarded it as an inappropriate way to portray God and felt compelled to set the record straight.[8]

The Emendations of the Scribes

The *tiqqune sopherim*, or emendations of the scribes, represents another way some ancient writers responded to specific portrayals of God they felt were inappropriate. At specific places, it appears that scribes altered the Hebrew text of the Old Testament to modify views of God they found offensive.[9] These modifications are thought to have been made between 400 BCE and 100 CE.[10] Although it is unclear exactly how many changes of this nature were made, tradition puts the total at eighteen.[11] Two examples should suffice here.

Originally, Gen. 18:22 apparently read as follows: "So the men turned from there, and went toward Sodom, while the Lord remained standing before Abraham." The notion of the Lord standing before Abraham was regarded as problematic since the expression "standing before" implies subservience.[12] Understood in this way, the verse would imply that Abraham was superior to God! To avoid this inappropriate portrayal of God, a slight but very significant change was made: the positions of the two proper names were switched. This effectively eliminated the offense, resulting in the version we now find in our Bibles, which has Abraham standing before the Lord, not the other way around.

Another example of this type of scribal alteration is found in Num. 11:15. Moses complains to the Lord about the difficult task that has been laid on him, saying:

> I [Moses] am not able to carry all this people alone, for they are too heavy for me. If this is the way you [God] are going to treat me, put me to death at once—if I have found favor in your sight—and do not let me see *your* misery. (Num. 11:14-15, as it apparently originally read)

The word translated "misery" here could also be translated "evil" or "wicked-ness." It is easy to understand why some scribes would feel uncomfortable with this reference to God's misery or wickedness. Since this was thought to be an inaccu-rate and inappropriate way to speak about God, the final pronoun of the verse was changed from first to second person. This eliminated the offensive notion of God's misery by transferring it to Moses:

> If this is the way you are going to treat me, put me to death at once—if I have found favor in your sight—and do not let me see *my* misery. (Num. 11:15, emphasis mine)

Although changes like these "do not drastically alter the text," according to John Hayes, they demonstrate "that scribal activity could and did go so far as to produce alterations in the text" when scribes encountered descriptions they thought were unworthy of God.[13] They stand as indisputable witnesses that those who have gone before us also struggled with certain portrayals of God.

Obviously, making slight adjustments to the wording of just eighteen verses in the Old Testament hardly begins to address the magnitude of the problem. The presence of disturbing divine behavior is far too pervasive for that to be effective. Thus, it comes as no great surprise that some in the ancient world proposed a far more drastic and radical "solution."

Rejecting the Old Testament

Rather than changing the text a little bit here and there to neutralize specific prob-lematic portrayals of God, some Christians in the ancient world advocated a much bolder proposal: reject the entire Old Testament altogether. Given the seismic prob-lems they felt the Old Testament presented for Christian readers—not the least of which were problems related to its troubling images of God—they argued that the Old Testament had no authority for them and should be completely disassociated from truly Christian writings. The most prominent proponent of this perspective was a man named Marcion.

Marcion was born sometime around 85 CE. Although very little is known for certain about his early years, he is believed to have been a native of Sinope, a major Greek city situated on the southern shore of the Black Sea in the province of Pon-tus.[14] The son of a bishop, Marcion had the dubious distinction of being excom-municated by his own father for "his false teaching."[15] Although Marcion had some supporters in the region, he left for Asia Minor, hoping to find a more receptive audience for his ideas. He eventually arrived in Rome, possibly as early as 139 CE. He joined up with a group of Christians there and gave a sizeable monetary con-tribution to the church. For the next five years, Marcion was busily engaged in two writing projects. The first could be thought of as an edited New Testament. The second was a work entitled *Antitheses*.[16] Both were driven by Marcion's rather peculiar theological beliefs that most Christians today would regard as unorthodox.

As Marcion saw it, Christianity was a brand-new religion with absolutely no relation to the Jewish faith. In fact, he thought that the Creator God of the Old Testament was not the same as the God of the New Testament, the father of Jesus. Instead, Marcion believed the Creator God was an inferior deity who should not be associated with the true God whom Jesus reveals. According to Marcion, these two Gods had very different natures. The Creator God of the Old Testament appeared harsh, evil, and exceedingly violent, whereas the God of the New Testament was good and peaceful. As one early Christian writer put it, Marcion regarded the God of the Old Testament to be "a judge, fierce and warlike" while the God of the New Testament was "mild and peaceable, solely kind and supremely good."[17]

In contrast to some of his contemporaries who adopted an allegorical method of interpretation, Marcion pursued a very literal reading of the "Old Testament."[18] This led him to perceive a very sharp distinction between the portrayal of God in the Old Testament and the character of Jesus in the New Testament. To illustrate, consider a few of the "antitheses" he produced:[19]

- The Creator-God did not cause blind Isaac to see again,
    but our Lord, because he is good, opened the eyes of many blind persons

- The prophet of the Creator-God, when the people were locked in battle, climbed to the top of the mountain and stretched forth his hands to God, that he might kill as many as possible in the battle;
    our Lord, the Good, stretched forth his hands . . . not to kill men but to save them[20]

[handwritten left margin: forbade still can though]

- At the request of Elijah the creator of the world sent down fire;
    but Christ forbade his disciples to call down fire from heaven

    The prophet of the Creator-God commanded the bears to come out of the thicket and to eat the children; *[handwritten: not children]* *[handwritten: disrespect]*
    but the good Lord says, "Let the children come to me, and do not *[handwritten: vs.]* forbid them, for of such is the kingdom of heaven." *[handwritten: innocence]*

Disparities like these led Marcion to conclude that there were irreconcilable differences between the Creator God and Jesus. This led him to completely reject the Old Testament and its God. It also led him to produce an abbreviated "New Testament" that included only edited versions of Luke's gospel and ten of Paul's letters in which virtually all references and allusions to the Old Testament were excised.[21]

In July 144 CE., Marcion presented his writings to local church officials, who held an unprecedented hearing to evaluate them. The outcome was not favorable for Marcion. His teachings were rejected, and he was branded a heretic. That notwithstanding, many found his ideas quite attractive and Marcion's influence continued to grow and expand. This is evidenced by the emergence of Marcionite churches in such places as Rome and Carthage.[22] As Adolf von Harnack notes: "At the time of Clement [ca. 200 CE] there had already existed within Christianity for several decades an active and widespread movement which declared itself against the Old Testament and rejected the God of Israel because he was warlike and thereby contradicted the gospel."[23] Clearly, Marcion was not alone.

Marcion's widespread influence is also demonstrated by the fact that prominent second- and third-century writers felt the need to criticize him. Early church fathers like Irenaeus and Tertullian refuted his writings, judging them to be out of step with the church's beliefs about Scripture and God. Tertullian issued a particularly blistering critique of Marcion in a work aptly titled *Adversus Marcionem* (Against Marcion). This five-part refutation, written in 201 CE, indicates the significant impact Marcion and his ideas were having in the ancient world, one that Tertullian and others found both unwelcome and misguided. In contrast to Marcion, they believed that the God revealed in the Old Testament was the same God revealed in the New Testament since they regarded the Old Testament as an indispensable part of the Christian tradition that could not be dismissed so easily.[24]

Salvaging the Old Testament

In light of the challenges Marcion raised, particularly those relating to Old Testament portrayals of God, it is interesting to observe how the early church found a way to affirm the Old Testament as Scripture while simultaneously avoiding the excessively negative portrait of God that Marcion derived from it. Unlike Marcion, many in the early church felt there was a high degree of continuity between what God had done through Israel in the past and what God had done more recently through Jesus. They did not believe Jesus came to start a new religion but instead regarded Jesus as the fulfillment of all God had promised to Israel over the years. Given this perspective—that Jesus was the culmination of all that God was doing in and through Israel—it was natural to expect the Old Testament to say something about him. In fact, according to Luke's gospel, Jesus himself encourages this idea. In a postresurrection appearance, Jesus says to a group of his disciples in Jerusalem:

> "These are my words that I spoke to you while I was still with you—that everything written about me in the law of Moses, the prophets, and the psalms must be fulfilled." Then he opened their minds to understand the scriptures. (Luke 24:44-45)[25]

According to this passage, Jesus claims that there are things written about him in the Old Testament. The early church seized upon this idea. The notion that portions of the Old Testament referred to Jesus had far-reaching implications for how early church leaders read and interpreted certain Old Testament passages. Two common interpretive methods of the time—typology and allegory—greatly helped early Christian readers to "find Jesus" in the Old Testament. And, as we shall see, these interpretive methods also helped the church avoid some unpleasant conclusions about God's character they might otherwise have drawn from the Old Testament's portrayal of God.

Typology

The first of these two approaches—the typological approach—interprets people, objects, events, and ideas in the Old Testament as prefiguring, or symbolizing, some aspect of God's future activity, particularly as it relates to Jesus.[26] An example of this interpretive method is found in the Epistle of Barnabas, a noncanonical document thought to be written toward the end of the first century or beginning of the second century CE. In Ep. Barn. 12:1-7, two Old Testament passages involving Moses are interpreted typologically. In both passages, Moses's actions are regarded "as types of the cross of Christ."[27] The first allusion is to Exodus 17, a passage in which Moses's outstretched arms are instrumental in Israel's victory over the Amalekites. The second is to Numbers 21, a passage in which Moses is instructed to lift up a bronze serpent on a pole so that all those Israelites who had been bitten by poisonous snakes could look and live (Num. 21:8-9). In both episodes, something lifted up became the means of deliverance or salvation. Since Jesus himself had been lifted up on a cross (John 3:14), some early Christian interpreters believed these two Old Testament episodes prefigured this crucial event, teaching that salvation comes only to those who trust in Jesus.

Regardless of what one thinks about the accuracy of this interpretation, what makes this interpretive method especially interesting for our purposes is the way it evades problems related to the characterization of God in the Old Testament.[28] Both of the Old Testament passages typologized in Ep. Barn. 12:1-7 contain some disturbing divine behavior. In Exod. 17:8-13, God not only helps the Israelites slaughter Amalekites via Moses holding up the "the staff of God" but also issues a genocidal decree for the vanquished Amalekites by giving this chilling command to Moses: "Write this as a reminder in a book and recite it in the hearing of Joshua: I will utterly blot out the remembrance of Amalek from under heaven" (v. 14).[29]

The episode in Numbers 21 is similarly problematic. As punishment for speaking "against God and against Moses" (21:5), we are told that "the Lord sent poisonous serpents among the people, and they bit the people, so that many Israelites died" (21:6). While such swift and irrevocable punishment raises troubling questions about God's character, these questions are completely ignored by the typological approach, which passes over the grittier aspects of the text. Instead, this approach creatively uses Old Testament passages, even ones with problematic portrayals of God, to provide positive lessons about Christ and the church.

The ability to interpret the Old Testament typologically helped ensure its place among other important Christian writings, such as the Gospels and the Pauline epistles. In fact, one could argue that the usefulness of the Old Testament for the early church depended largely on its ability to see Jesus in these ancient texts. As Robert Grant and David Tracy put it: "Without the typological method it would have been almost impossible for the early church to retain its grasp on the Old Testament."[30]

Allegory

The allegorical method, which shares certain commonalities with the typological approach, was a well-respected and widely used interpretive method in the ancient world. It was especially popular in Alexandria, a major center of Christian teaching and instruction in North Africa. Examples of allegorical interpretation can be found in many early Christian writings, including the New Testament.[31] Reading allegorically involves looking for deeper, or hidden, messages in the details of a text. Secondary meanings are assigned to particular people, places, and events, allowing the details of the story to take on new significance as they function as symbols, or signposts, pointing to greater realities beyond themselves.

Origen (185–254 CE), a Christian leader in the first half of the third century CE, was the chief proponent of this method in the early church. Examples of Origen's allegorical approach can be observed in his numerous sermons, or homilies, on Old Testament texts. Many of Origen's allegorical interpretations are christocentric (Christ-centered) and in this way are similar to those that result from applying the typological method to Old Testament texts. In his first homily on the book of Joshua, Origen declares that "the book does not so much indicate to us the deeds of the son of Nun [referring to Joshua], as it represents for us the mysteries of Jesus my Lord."[32] This perspective is evident, for example, when Origen preaches about Rahab in Joshua 2. He believes Rahab represents the church and declares that the scarlet cord she hung out the window symbolizes the blood of Christ.[33] More generally, Origen used this method to draw out "spiritualized" or "moral" lessons from a text. For example, Origen associates the five kings who attacked Gibeon (Joshua 9) with the five senses in the body through which sin comes.[34]

By using the allegorical method, Origen was able to recognize various levels of meaning in the biblical text. There was, of course, the literal meaning, and Origen believed this was often historically accurate and edifying for Christians. Yet he also realized this was not always the case. Commenting on the incestuous story of Lot and his daughters in Gen. 19:30-38, Origen says, "If it teaches something useful in an elevated sense, God knows, as does that person who has received the gift of grace to expound these matters. As for the usefulness of the story itself, it would take quite a search to find it! Indeed, what profit can I find from the story of Lot and his daughters?"[35] Because Origen found no immediate value in the story's literal meaning, he focused on other levels of meaning made possible by an allegorical reading of the text. This enabled him to recognize what he considered to be a more significant dimension of the story at the spiritual level. Origen believed that Lot represented Old Testament law; Lot's wife, the Israelites who rebelled in the wilderness; and Lot's daughters, Jerusalem and Samaria.[36] Because Origen was convinced that the Bible was divinely inspired, he was confident that every single part was valuable. When he came across items that did not make sense or that reflected poorly on God, he did not despair. On the contrary, he thought such difficulties had been placed there intentionally by the Spirit and were meant to lead the mature reader to deeper insights.

To help us better appreciate Origen's use of allegory, it is useful to consider briefly one of the ways this interpretive method was used in relation to the *Iliad* and the *Odyssey*. These two Greek classics written by Homer were part of the educational curriculum for children in the Greco-Roman world. In addition to helping students learn to read and interpret literary texts, Homer's writings were used to teach students moral lessons. While some aspects of these texts functioned quite well in that regard, others did not. Some passages in the *Iliad* and the *Odyssey* did not reflect the kind of values people hoped to instill in their children. This was especially true in regard to the characterization and behavior of the gods. The god's actions often did not represent the kind of behavior parents wanted their children to imitate. As one scholar asks: "What was the schoolchild to make of gods who quarreled among themselves, had limited knowledge and power, played favorites, wreaked frightful vengeance on often trivial grounds, and frequently violated the most elementary principles of morality?"[37]

The theological and moral problems raised by these works elicited criticism from such individuals as Xenophanes in the sixth century BCE and Plato in the fourth. Plato actually considered these stories so problematic that he felt they should no longer be used to educate children.[38] But Plato's opinion did not win the day. Instead, these texts continued to be part of the educational program (and still are today!). Why? Two reasons can be given. First, many people held Homer's works in high regard. They had come to love and respect these works of literature and were not eager to dispense with them. Second, and more to the point here, these classic texts survived because people believed that interpreting them allegorically rendered their less attractive features harmless. As Joseph Trigg comments: "By Plato's time Homer's admirers had come up with what was to be a standard defense: Homer's poems were symbolic, and were perfectly acceptable when read allegorically."[39] The allegorical method defended these literary masterpieces against the critics by effectively neutralizing theologically and morally questionable passages.[40]

It seems the allegorical method functioned in much the same way for Origen in regard to the Old Testament. Because Origen was not limited to a literal reading of the text, he was able to find something of value even in the most theologically troubling biblical texts, such as those found in Joshua. As Joseph Lynch observes:

> Origen . . . showed the way to a defense of the Old Testament when he thoroughly allegorized its wars: for him, they were really battles against sin and the powers of darkness. In a homily on Joshua, a book full of war and violence, he wrote:
>
> > If the horrible wars related in the Old Testament were not to be interpreted in a spiritual sense, the apostles would never have transmitted the Jewish books for reading in the church to the disciples of Christ, who came to preach.
>
> Origen thus pointed the way to a learned solution for dealing with the difficulties of the Old Testament, including warfare and violence. For centuries exegetes and preachers allegorized the violence of the Old Testament narratives, making them refer to the moral struggles of the church against evil or of the individual soul against sin.[41]

For Origen and those who followed him, the allegorical method was the key to rendering otherwise objectionable passages acceptable. For a time, this proved very successful for dealing with disturbing divine behavior in the Old Testament. It provided a constructive approach for interpreting troublesome texts and offered a spiritually edifying way of using the entire Old Testament. This was particularly significant in light of Marcion's proposal to dispense with the Old Testament. Origen's use of the allegorical method allowed him to counter the charges of Marcion and "enabled Christians to use the whole Bible as the church's book."[42]

What is especially interesting and somewhat ironic about all this is that for all of Origen's protestations against Marcion,[43] he agreed with Marcion on one crucial point: some Old Testament portrayals of God are unworthy of God. Where Origen and Marcion differed was in how they responded to this problem. As Trigg puts it:

> Marcion threw out the Old Testament on account of the unworthiness of the God it depicted. Origen retained the Old Testament and sought to interpret it in such a way as to exclude from its depiction of God the qualities Marcion condemned. Marcion denied the validity of allegory. Origen spent his life employing allegory and seeking to justify the method.[44]

Since the allegorical method yielded interpretations of the Old Testament that were consistent with orthodox Christian beliefs, it ensured the Old Testament a permanent place in the Christian canon. Like typology, allegory served the church and saved the Old Testament by demonstrating ways of reading that were positive and constructive. Yet, despite its popularity, the allegorical method was only a temporary solution. The reason Origen could use the allegorical method so effectively was because people in the ancient world accepted it as a valid interpretive method. That assessment no longer holds true today. Most modern readers find Origen's allegorical readings quite fanciful. This is not surprising since the Achilles heel of the allegorical method is the lack of controls governing how correlations are made between details in the texts and the meanings assigned to them.

As typological and allegorical approaches fell out of favor, they were eventually replaced by other methods more concerned with the plain sense of the text. These interpretive shifts, which placed far greater emphasis on the importance of the literal meaning, once again raised uncomfortable questions about the problematic nature of the Old Testament and the disturbing divine behavior contained within its pages. The rise of the historical-critical method in the eighteenth century, for example, led some scholars—just like Marcion long before—to raise serious questions about the usefulness of the Old Testament for Christians. Some even suggested that the Old Testament, or at least certain parts of it, should no longer be included in the canon. To illustrate this, we will briefly consider two modern-day Marcionites (Friedrich Delitzsch and Adolf von Harnack) and one contemporary quasi-Marcionite (Hector Avalos).[45]

Modern-Day Marcionites

Friedrich Delitzsch

Friedrich Delitzsch (1850–1922), son of the beloved Old Testament scholar Franz Delitzsch, was a very prominent—and very controversial—German scholar. A famous Assyriologist, Friedrich gave the first of three lectures entitled "Babel und Bibel" (Babylon and the Bible) at the beginning of the twentieth century. Both the venue and the audience of his first lecture were impressive. The lecture was given in the royal German palace in the presence of Emperor Wilhelm II. In this lecture, Delitzsch drew many interesting parallels between the Bible and recent discoveries in Babylon. The prestigious setting and overwhelming response—both favorable and critical—guaranteed him a second lecture, the topic of which is particularly instructive for our purposes. In that lecture, Delitzsch denigrated ancient Hebrew culture and the value of the Old Testament. As the following statement reveals, one aspect of the Old Testament Delitzsch found particularly troubling was its portrayal of Yahweh.

> The more deeply I immerse myself in the spirit of the prophetic literature of the Old Testament, the greater becomes my mistrust of Yahweh, who butchers the

peoples with the sword of his insatiable anger; who has but one favorite child [Israel], while he consigns all other nations to darkness, shame, and ruin,[46] *no*

Many of the comments Delitzsch made in his second lecture seem to have been motivated by German nationalism and anti-Semitism. These ideological predispositions came to full expression in his 1920–21 publication titled *Die Grosse Täuschung* (The Great Deception). In this two-volume work, Delitzsch completely repudiated the Old Testament as having any value for Christians. Herbert Huffmon summarizes Delitzsch's work this way:

> The "Great Deception" was the Old Testament. He [Delitzsch] emphasized the many seemingly exaggerated claims and numbers in the biblical texts, the numerous minor variations in names and other specific data, the unfulfilled divine promises, the lowly cultural level of the Hebrews . . . the false attribution of writings to Moses, the false assertion that Yahweh, Israel's particular god, was God. All these points led him to the conclusion that the Old Testament was no book of Christian religion and should be excluded from Christian theology.[47]

Delitzsch, like Marcion of old, felt the Old Testament was fundamentally flawed and of no consequence for the Christian church. And while some of his reasons for thinking this way differed considerably from Marcion's, both regarded God's problematic behavior in the Old Testament as one reason to exclude this part of the Bible from the Christian canon.

Adolf von Harnack

Similar sentiments regarding the Old Testament were also expressed by Adolf von Harnack, a colleague of Delitzsch's. Harnack applauded Marcion's efforts to preserve God's good character. "It will always be to the glory of the Marcionite church," he writes, "that it would rather cast away the Old Testament than tarnish the image of the Father of Jesus Christ by mixing in traces of a warlike God."[48] Although Harnack regarded Marcion's dismissal of the Old Testament as ill-advised in the second century CE, he thought the time had come for the church to follow through with Marcion's suggestion. Harnack believed his contemporaries had outgrown their need for the Old Testament and should free themselves from it. Just prior to the publication of the first part of Delitzsch's *Die Grosse Täuschung*, Harnack wrote:

> The rejection of the Old Testament in the second century was a mistake which the great church rightly avoided; to maintain it in the sixteenth century was a fate from which the Reformation was not yet able to escape; but still to preserve it in Protestantism as a canonical document since the nineteenth century is the consequence of a religious and ecclesiastical crippling.[49]

If Harnack would have had his way, the Old Testament would no longer be part of the Bible. Admittedly, this would resolve the problem of disturbing divine behavior. As Old Testament scholar John Bright recognized: "The Old Testament is a problem because it is in the Bible, and because of what the church declares the Bible to be. If the Old Testament were not in the Bible . . . it would occasion the Christian no problem whatever."[50]

Hector Avalos

Hector Avalos's very recent quasi-Marcionite proposal to remove violent texts from the Bible is somewhat less extreme than what Marcion and his followers suggested, though equally problematic in my opinion. Avalos, a self-avowed secular humanist, argues for "the principled decanonization of violent texts" and the recanonization of Scripture based on the principle of nonviolence. In other words, he believes violent texts in both testaments should be removed from the Bible, resulting in a revised canonical collection. Rather than rejecting the entire Old Testament like Marcion, Avalos proposes selectively removing violent verses while leaving the rest intact. According to Avalos, nonviolence should "be the theological arbiter of whether a text is called sacred."[51] He urges Christian pacifists to take the lead and "to follow the logic of a pacifistic theological principle that any depiction of God as violent must be understood as false."[52] Thus, the only texts and portrayals of God allowed to appear in this recanonization of Scripture would be those deemed to be nonviolent.

Avalos's proposal to recanonize Scripture is motivated by his belief that violent texts encourage violent acts. Specifically, Avalos argues that the underlying causes of numerous wars "can be traced to the use of sacred texts to justify violence."[53] Since he finds this connection between Scripture and violence problematic, Avalos proposes severing this linkage by recanonizing the Bible. He regards this as a legitimate move because, he believes, "the current canon is the product of late and imperialistic decisions under Constantine" and "canonicity is ultimately a theological decision," the criteria for which has "been repeatedly revised in Christianity."[54] Therefore, his proposal to decanonize violent biblical texts—such as Genesis 6–7, Exodus 12:29, and 1 Samuel 15:1-3, to name a few—is entirely in keeping with the canonical process as he understands it.[55]

While I can appreciate the struggle such individuals as Avalos, Harnack, and Delitzsch had with the Old Testament and its troubling images of God, I cannot follow them when they advocate eliminating it—partially or fully—from the Christian canon. Physically removing problematic passages violates the integrity of the text and is not the way forward. Similarly, removing the entire Old Testament is unacceptable. Far too much is lost in the process. Despite various problems that arise from retaining the Old Testament as Scripture, the church rightly continues to regard it as foundational for Christian faith and practice. As Bill Arnold and David

Weisberg put it: "From the second century until the present, the church has continued to insist that any form of Christianity that can do without the Hebrew Scriptures is no genuine Christianity."[56] Any satisfactory solution to disturbing divine behavior must deal with the biblical text as it now stands.

Functional Marcionites?

Although few Christians would advocate the radical approach suggested by the likes of Marcion, Delitzsch, Harnack, Avalos, and others, the way many Christians actually use the Old Testament makes them appear quite sympathetic to it. Unwilling to remove the Old Testament from the canon, they simply ignore it, or at least large parts of it.[57] They behave like functional Marcionites since their attitudes toward various portions of the Old Testament echo those of Marcion and his ilk.[58] As Ellen Davis observes:

> Many Christians, both ordained and lay, view the Old Testament as a historical document that is impenetrably complex and morally problematic. Even in evangelical traditions, few pastors, teachers, or preachers feel confident in drawing on it for theological insight and guidance for their lives. In a word, the Old Testament is ceasing to function as Scripture in the European-American mainstream church.[59]

In light of this trend, perhaps we should not be too quick to judge Marcion and his followers. Instead, maybe we should first take a good look at ourselves and our own practices of reading the Bible. If we ignore the Old Testament, or even just those parts we find unsuitable in one way or another, how different are we from Marcion in certain respects? Doesn't such behavior render us functional Marcionites? It is a question worth pondering.

Over the centuries, the church has consistently labeled Marcion a heretic, dismissing his ideas as unorthodox.[60] Because of this, Marcion has become something of a "poster child" representing the perils of questioning disturbing depictions of God or of suggesting that there are glaring contradictions between the ways God is portrayed in the Old and New Testament. By condemning Marcion and labeling him a heretic, it becomes easy to write him off as a misguided individual whose ideas are not worth considering. But in doing so, we miss the very important contribution Marcion makes. For all his shortcomings, Marcion has done the church a service by raising a critical question that cannot easily be dismissed. Simply put, that question is, What are Christians to do with "the Old Testament God"? While the church may judge Marcion's response to that question as extreme, as throwing out the baby with the bathwater, it cannot ignore the very real problem Marcion identified. On the contrary, this question must be directly addressed if the church wishes both to affirm the Old Testament as Scripture *and* to use it to think rightly about God.

This chapter has demonstrated that misgivings about Old Testament depictions of God have a very long history. People who lived hundreds and even thousands of years ago—the Chronicler, the writer of Jubilees, Marcion, Origen, and many others—were all troubled by disturbing divine behavior in the Old Testament. They considered some biblical portrayals of God unworthy of God and attempted to solve this problem in various ways. Some opted to change certain troubling texts by rewriting them. Others took more drastic measures by rejecting not just specific problem passages but the entire Old Testament. Still others came to terms with these troubling images of God by interpreting them in nonliteral ways. Whatever the approach, all of these attempts to neutralize disturbing divine behavior in the Old Testament reveal how uncomfortable many people in the ancient world were with these problematic portrayals of God. In other words, this problem is not just a modern one, and this is a point worth emphasizing.

Sometimes, when concerns are raised about God's behavior in the Old Testament, some people assume that these concerns largely reflect *modern* sensibilities. They believe people today struggle with the more demanding portraits of God in the Old Testament because these portraits conflict with contemporary beliefs about God as tolerant, loving, and nonjudgmental. In this context, any critique of God's behavior in the Old Testament becomes suspect and is regarded as nothing more than an attempt to make God in one's own image. Yet, while that may be true in some cases, experiencing difficulties with certain Old Testament portrayals of God is not just a modern phenomenon. As we have seen, people have regarded these portrayals as problematic for centuries. In grappling with this issue, we continue a very important conversation that began many years ago.

This chapter highlighted the success of the early church in dealing with disturbing divine behavior by utilizing typology and allegory, especially the latter. These interpretive methods prevented the church from arriving at some unwanted conclusions and enabled the church to recognize the value and enduring significance of the Old Testament. Today, typology and allegory are no longer regarded as appropriate interpretive methods for reading most biblical texts. They are considered too subjective, and they fail to deal seriously with the plain meaning of the text.

Since the early church's best way of handling disturbing divine behavior is no longer viable today, other approaches are needed to deal with these troubling images. The next chapter considers several more recent approaches, each of which attempts to defend God's behavior in the Old Testament in one way or another.

CHAPTER 4

Defending God's Behavior
in the Old Testament

*Now, in each of these examples of God behaving very unpleasantly indeed,
I have simply spelled out what the Old Testament itself says. I have not read
into the stories what is not there. I have also hinted that in order to make
them acceptable to our modern ways of thinking about God, we have to do
quite a bit of doctoring.*

—J. C. L. Gibson[1]

In the first few chapters, we considered various dimensions of the problem of
disturbing divine behavior in the Old Testament. We discussed the biblical
evidence, explored reasons why people feel uncomfortable with these portrayals of
God, and noted some attempts to alleviate that discomfort. Most of the "solutions"
we examined in chapter 3 represented ancient responses to this dilemma, and we are
now ready to discuss several contemporary approaches to this perplexing problem.

But before we explore these more recent efforts to defend God's behavior, we
need to consider the possibility that the problem we have identified is one of our
own making, rooted in certain assumptions about God that are unfounded. One
of the primary reasons so many people find God's behavior in the Old Testament
unsettling is because it does not conform to their fundamental beliefs about God as
good, loving, and fair. But what if these beliefs about God are unwarranted or, at
least, overstated? What if the problem lies with our preconceived notions about God
rather than with the way the Old Testament portrays God? What if God actually

is both good *and* bad, just *and* unjust, loving *and* abusive? What if God really does have a "shadow side" that sometimes manifests itself in devious and diabolical ways? If so, then thinking rightly about God would require us to modify our beliefs in order to bring them in line with the Old Testament's description of God. Those who take this approach believe we should accept the difficulties of God's conflicted nature as portrayed in the Old Testament rather than struggling to find ways to justify it.

This approach is exemplified in the work of Jewish scholar David Blumenthal. In his book tellingly titled *Facing the Abusing God*, Blumenthal focuses on developing what he calls a "post-holocaust, abusive sensitive faith."[2] Utilizing the work of Gracia Fay Ellwood in her pamphlet *Batter My Heart*, Blumenthal cites several passages from the Pentateuch and the Prophets that depict God acting abusively.[3] He is critical of Ellwood's approach, which he regards as an attempt to "erase" the problem by suggesting that these texts do not accurately reflect what God is really like. From Blumenthal's perspective, that misses the point and denies God's true nature. He writes:

> *God is abusive, but not always.* God, as portrayed in our holy sources and as experienced by humans throughout the ages, acts, from time to time, in a manner that is so unjust that it can only be characterized by the term "abusive." In this mode, God allows the innocent to suffer greatly. In this mode, God "caused" the holocaust, or allowed it to happen.[4]

As this quote reveals, Blumenthal's understanding of God as abusive is rooted both in Scripture and in historical experiences like the Holocaust. Thus, while Blumenthal believes "God is loving and fair, even kind and merciful," he also believes that sometimes "God is an abusing God."[5]

If God sometimes is abusive, as Scripture suggests and historical experience seems to indicate, and if such behavior "is inexcusable, in all circumstances," as Blumenthal maintains, it is difficult to avoid the conclusion that God's abusiveness represents a pathological character flaw.[6] So what are we to do? How might this realization influence the way we understand and relate to God? Blumenthal proposes we recognize God's abusiveness and accept it. Accepting it does not, however, mean passively or silently submitting to it, according to Blumenthal. He argues that we can—and should—protest divine misconduct and believes we are free to charge God with gross injustice.[7] But regardless of our response, in the final analysis he believes we need to come to terms with this God who is sometimes abusive.[8]

Blumenthal's proposal represents a response to disturbing divine behavior that is about as far away from Marcion's as one can get. Blumenthal simply accepts the God of the Old Testament "as is" without trying to explain how God's behavior is good even though it seems bad at times, or how it is justified even though it seems immoral in certain situations. He believes all the portrayals found there—those that inspire and those that disturb—reflect God's character in all its complexity and moral ambiguity. Thus, Blumenthal's position exemplifies an all-inclusive approach to dealing with the diverse and conflicting portrayals of God in the Old Testament by arguing that God is both loving and abusive, both good and evil.

While some may find Blumenthal's approach refreshingly honest, few Christians would follow his lead or embrace his description of God. Fewer still would follow Marcion by excising virtually the entire Old Testament and rejecting the God it reveals. That leaves us with two extremes to be avoided and indicates that an acceptable solution to disturbing divine behavior must fall somewhere between Marcion's rejection of the Old Testament and its God and Blumenthal's acceptance of the same.

In recent years, Christians have developed a number of approaches that fall between these positions. Unlike Marcion, they refuse to dismiss the Old Testament and its portrayals of God. Yet neither do they accept Blumenthal's proposal that God sometimes is abusive and unjust. Instead, they have found various ways forward that attempt to preserve both the integrity of Scripture and the goodness of God.

The purpose of this chapter is to survey several of these approaches commonly used to defend God's behavior in the Old Testament. Generally speaking, these approaches are not mutually exclusive positions but a range of options people draw upon when grappling with some of the more difficult depictions of God in the Old Testament. In fact, it is not unusual to find people using multiple approaches as they attempt to make sense of God's behavior in the Old Testament.

Despite the popularity of these approaches none satisfactorily resolves the problem at hand. All are flawed in significant ways, and I will discuss some reasons I find these approaches inappropriate interpretive options for addressing the problem of disturbing divine behavior. My evaluative comments here are not intended to be a full-blown critique, but are designed to reveal certain weaknesses that render these approaches unsuitable for dealing responsibly with problematic portrayals of God in the Old Testament.[9] Beyond some of the specific concerns I raise about each of these approaches lies a more fundamental critique that applies to all of them; that critique will be discussed toward the end of the chapter. For the sake of convenience, I have taken the liberty of labeling each of these approaches.

The Divine Immunity Approach

The divine immunity approach defends God's behavior in the Old Testament by suggesting that everything God does is good and right because God can do no wrong. It is argued that, regardless of how God behaves, God cannot be charged with misconduct because all of God's acts are righteous by virtue of the fact that God is the one doing them. Because God is God, God is not subject to the kind of critique that would be leveled against human beings engaged in similar kinds of behavior. In this way, God is exempt from—or immune to—any and all charges of abuse, injustice, or immorality.

Divine immunity is granted on the basis of two fundamental theological convictions: God's absolute sovereignty and God's unquestionable goodness. Since God is thought to be in complete control of the world, God has the right to do whatever God wants. In the words of the psalmist: "Our God is in the heavens; he does whatever he pleases" (Ps. 115:3; see also Ps. 135:6). Moreover, since God is believed to be unquestionably good, whatever God does must be regarded as good. Those who appeal to this approach believe that God has the right to do anything and that anything God does is right—even when it seems terribly wrong! As Eugene Merrill observes: "If God is all the Bible says he is, all that he does must be good—and that includes his authorization of genocide."[10] This differs radically from Blumenthal's understanding of God. Whereas Blumenthal would regard God's genocidal decree as illustrative of God's abusiveness, Merrill believes it reflects God's goodness.

Proponents of this approach concede that it is difficult to understand how things that "seem" bad are actually good when God does them. But according to their way of thinking, that does not really matter. They believe that it is not always important to understand why God acts in certain ways or issues certain commands. In fact, they would argue we should not expect to be able to understand such mysteries fully given the limitations of our finite human minds. Instead, we must simply believe that whatever God does is good because God is good. As professor Daniel Gard writes:

> What appears to the human mind as "evil" acts of God (such as the genocide commands against the Canaanites) are in fact not "evil" acts at all since they come from the Lord himself. There simply comes a point in which human reason must bow to the divine and recognize that his ways are truly not ours and his thoughts are truly above our own (cf. Isa. 55:8-9).[11]

Similarly, Dutch Reformed theologian A. van de Beek believes that anything God does is good because it is God who does it. He writes: "What goodness is at a specific moment is determined by the action of God at that moment. And if today God acts differently than yesterday, goodness today is different from what it was yesterday. God is the criterion for good and evil. . . . There is no authority above him to which he could be subject."[12] To illustrate, van de Beek considers one of the most notoriously difficult passages in the entire Old Testament, God's command to annihilate the Amalekites. He writes: "When God commands Saul to destroy the Amalekites to the last man, woman, and child (1 Sam. 15:3), and the prophet with his own hands hews in pieces the survivor (1 Sam. 15:33), then at that moment that is good."[13]

Those who appeal to the divine immunity approach argue that, in the final analysis, it makes no difference whether we understand *why* God commanded the

Canaanite genocide or *why* God chose to instantly annihilate people like Er, Nadab and Abihu, and Uzzah. Nor does it matter if God's treatment of Pharaoh or Hagar *seems* unjust or abusive from our perspective. If God does it, it must be right—even if we cannot understand it. Our human limitations keep us from seeing the "big picture," they say, and we need to trust that God's actions are appropriate even if they seem problematic to us. Besides, who are we to judge God? And who is to say that God's standard of justice is the same as ours? Therefore, we should not question God's behavior no matter how heinous it might seem to us because there are things about God we cannot understand and simply must accept on faith.

The divine immunity approach has been with us for a very long time. It was used by Irenaeus (ca. 130–200 CE), a brilliant church father and contemporary of Marcion. Despite his impressive intellectual abilities, Irenaeus found himself unable to offer a reasoned defense against Marcion's criticisms of the Old Testament's portrayal of God. Instead, Irenaeus just said it was wrong for Marcion (and others) to make such criticisms. Much like those who take the "divine immunity approach," Irenaeus "extolled the virtues of simple faith" and contended "that there were many questions that simply should not be asked."[14]

In certain respects, I am sympathetic with some of the underlying concerns of the divine immunity approach. For example, I am quite willing to acknowledge that our understanding of God is limited. We are finite beings with significant limitations, particularly in terms of what can—and cannot—be known.[15] Our knowledge of God will always be partial and incomplete. It is both arrogant and naive to think we can "figure God all out" or put God in a box. It is not possible. There is much we just do not and cannot know, no matter how hard we try. To illustrate this in class, I have sometimes used the image of an iceberg. I point out that the tip of the iceberg, the part above the water, is analogous to what can be known about God. The much larger, unexposed portion of the iceberg beneath the water, I go on to say, is what we do not and cannot know about God. With those who advocate the divine immunity approach, I agree there is much about God that remains a mystery.

What bothers me about this approach, however, is the way it discourages certain kinds of questions and restricts honest inquiry about the character of God. It often stifles conversation and prematurely forecloses questions that deserve further exploration. By declaring that everything God does in the Bible is good and right, the divine immunity approach short-circuits critical thinking and leaves little room for vigorous engagement with questions of divine justice and fairness. And while I freely acknowledge we can never have all the answers to these kinds of questions, I believe we can know more about God than this approach implies.

While some believe the divine immunity approach exhibits great reverence for God by refusing to question God's actions in the Old Testament, I would suggest it does just the opposite. Rather than glorifying God, this approach actually dishonors God by suggesting God sometimes acts in ways that are incongruous with our most basic beliefs about what is right. In order to make this approach work, one must redefine evil behavior as good if God is the one portrayed doing it. But how can that be? Is genocide ever good? Can killing Canaanite men and women—not to mention defenseless children and infants—be "right" just because God orders it? Is abuse ever moral? Can injustice ever be just? Regarding bad behavior as good simply because God is the one described as doing it strikes me as a very simplistic and extremely dangerous way of handling problematic portrayals of God. As Gerd Lüdemann observes: "Cruelty remains cruelty even if the Bible attributes it to God."[16] Moreover, if God's standard of justice is so fundamentally different from ours that physical abuse and the slaughter of babies can be considered just, then it no longer seems possible to have a meaningful conversation about what constitutes justice. As professor C. S. Cowles puts it:

> If the indiscriminate slaughter of human beings for any reason can be called a "good" and "righteous" act . . . then all moral and ethical absolutes are destroyed, all distinctions between good and evil are rendered meaningless, and all claims about God's love and compassion become cruel depictions. It represents the ultimate corruption of human language and makes meaningful theological discourse virtually impossible.[17]

Therefore, despite the pious veneer of the divine immunity approach, it does not represent a theologically responsible way of handling disturbing divine behavior.

The Just Cause Approach

One of the most popular ways of defending God's behavior in the Old Testament is the just cause approach. In contrast to the divine immunity approach, this approach attempts to justify God's behavior. It does so by supplying a rationale for God's actions, explaining why it was both necessary and right for God to afflict this person or kill that one. In many cases, this rationale is supplied—or at least implied—by the biblical text itself. God's destructive behavior, for example, is regarded as justly deserved divine punishment. Consider God's decision to flood the earth:

> Now the earth was corrupt in God's sight, and the earth was filled with violence. And God saw that the earth was corrupt; for all flesh had corrupted its ways upon the earth. And God said to Noah, "I have determined to make an end of all flesh, for the earth is filled with violence because of them; now I am going to destroy them along with the earth." (Gen. 6:11-13)

According to this text, God's decision to destroy virtually the entire human race is portrayed as a response to widespread human wickedness.[18] Similarly, the fall of Jerusalem to the Babylonians is described as God's response to the sins of Manasseh and Judah.

The Lord said by his servants the prophets, "Because King Manasseh of Judah has committed these abominations, has done things more wicked than all that the Amorites did, who were before him, and has caused Judah also to sin with his idols; therefore thus says the Lord, the God of Israel, I am bringing upon Jerusalem and Judah such evil that the ears of everyone who hears of it will tingle. I will stretch over Jerusalem the measuring line for Samaria, and the plummet for the house of Ahab; I will wipe Jerusalem as one wipes a dish, wiping it and turning it upside down. I will cast off the remnant of my heritage, and give them into the hand of their enemies; they shall become a prey and a spoil to all their enemies, because they have done what is evil in my sight and have provoked me to anger, since the day their ancestors came out of Egypt, even to this day." (2 Kgs. 21:10-15)

Once again, the causal relationship between divine violence and human sinfulness is expressed with unmistakable clarity.[19] The operative assumption in these passages—and others like them—is that some sins are punishable by death. If so, then these passages clearly portray God acting appropriately. God has the right—some would even say the responsibility—to kill those who commit such sins since God is the judge of all creation and the only one with authority to take human life.

But there are problems with this defense of God's behavior. Some would challenge the appropriateness of the assumption that certain sins should be punished by death. But even granting that debatable assumption, there is another problem facing those who try to justify God's behavior in these passages—the problem of indiscriminate killing. Passages like Genesis 6 and 2 Kings 21 imply that divine judgment results in the death of people of all ages, *including infants and toddlers*. It is hard to imagine how anyone could persuasively argue that babies have committed sins worthy of death. If they have not, the just cause approach fails since it is unable to offer a satisfactory explanation for God's behavior in these instances.

In some passages, God's deadly response to a particular offense seems excessive. This is especially true when it is unclear why a particular act was so bad that the offender had to killed by God. In these instances, the just cause approach is often used to defend God's behavior by explaining why the individual(s) in question deserved to die. To illustrate, we can return to the incident of Uzzah and the ark (2 Sam. 6:1-11). Uzzah, you may recall from our discussion in chapter 1, makes one fatal mistake: he tries to keep the ark from falling off a cart. For this, he is instantly struck dead by God. Working on the assumption that God always acts justly, one would reasonably conclude that Uzzah committed a sin worthy of death. But after a careful reading of this passage, it is difficult to see why that is so. The text does not say why Uzzah's actions were wrong or why they elicited such a swift and deadly response from God. *Was it a punishment or a result?*

Old Testament scholar Walter Kaiser uses the just cause approach to fill in the gaps by explaining what motivated Uzzah and why God needed to instantly annihilate him. Despite the lack of textual evidence to this effect, Kaiser believes Uzzah did not intend to do anything wrong and asserts that Uzzah's *motives* were pure.[20] Still, Kaiser argues, Uzzah "disregarded the written Word of God," thereby forfeiting his life.[21] Here Kaiser is referring to rules relating to the transportation of the tabernacle that required specific parts of the tabernacle to be carried by certain groups of priests (Num. 4:15). One group, known as the Kohathites, was to carry "all the furnishings of the sanctuary" but was not to "touch the holy things," lest they die. The ark of the covenant was, of course, one of these untouchable "holy things." To carry the ark without touching it, poles were inserted through a series of outer rings on the ark, and these were used for transporting this most sacred object (Exod. 25:13-15). According to Kaiser, even though Uzzah did not intentionally set out to violate this legislation, that is precisely what his well-intentioned actions did.[22]

Even if one accepts Kaiser's explanation, it does not fully resolve the problematic portrayal of God that emerges. Instead, it leaves us with the image of an inflexible and uncompassionate deity, one more concerned with meticulous obedience to the law than with pure motives. It also raises questions about divine fairness. When God's behavior in this episode is set alongside God's behavior elsewhere in the Old Testament, it is difficult to explain. Why does God allow an apostate king like Ahab to do enormous damage to the spiritual well-being of Judah for twenty-two years (1 Kgs. 16:29-30) while smiting poor Uzzah, a man with no known history of wrongdoing, for a single, unpremeditated act? Or why is Manasseh allowed to transgress God's commands for years on end before there are any apparent divine repercussions?[23] In addition to encouraging the worship of other gods, we are told that Manasseh "shed much innocent blood, until he had filled Jerusalem from one end to another" (v. 16). In fact, his unparalleled—and reportedly unrestrained—wickedness is cited as the reason for Jerusalem's destruction, a point we noted earlier. Why would God let such an evil man live so long and die of natural causes, when Uzzah gets executed on the spot for a solitary "transgression." Such disparities—which could be multiplied many times over—violate all sense of divine fairness and raise serious questions about the justice of divine punishment.

In Old Testament passages where God's punitive actions seem unmerited or excessive, many Jewish interpreters alleviate the theological tension these passages create by "reading condemning circumstances into the situation."[24] In other words, these interpreters make the misdeed more explicit than the text suggests, thereby making it easier to justify God's behavior. Consider, for example, how Jewish interpreters explain the chilling divine command issued to King Saul in 1 Sam. 15:2-3:

> Thus says the Lord of hosts, "I will punish the Amalekites for what they did in opposing the Israelites when they came up out of Egypt. Now go and attack

Amalek, and utterly destroy all that they have; do not spare them, but kill both man and woman, child and infant, ox and sheep, camel and donkey."

In an interesting article titled "The Punishment of Amalek in Jewish Tradition: Coping with the Moral Problem," Avi Sagi detects two ways Jewish interpreters have clarified and emphasized Amalek's wickedness in an attempt to justify God's behavior.[25] Some, such as Yitzhak Abrabanel (1437–1508), have argued that Amalek got what it deserved because it violated "the norms of just war." Abrabanel believed Amalek's attack was unjustified since it was a war of aggression rather than one waged in self-defense. Others, such as Nahmanides (1194–1270), thought the reason for Amalek's destruction was their rebellion against God.[26] Following Nahmanides's line of reasoning, Abraham Sofer (1815–1871) wrote: "God did not command us to revenge and destroy Amalek, man and woman, infant and suckling, because they hurt us and afflicted us, but to uproot them from the world because they raised their hand against God, and God's enemies will be extinguished."[27] In both instances, these interpreters use a just cause approach to defend God's behavior, a move consistent with the predilection of many Jewish scholars. As Sagi notes: "Jewish tradition . . . prefers to stress the gravity of Amalek's deed in an attempt to justify the punishment" rather than just saying it is right because God commanded it.[28]

The difficulty with this interpretive approach, however, is that emphasizing "the gravity of Amalek's deed" results in explanations that outrun the biblical evidence. The text of 1 Samuel 15 does not claim the Amalekite attack was "a war of aggression," nor does it state that the Amalekites were in "rebellion against God."[29] This illustrates a fundamental weakness of the just cause approach.

The Greater Good Approach

The greater good approach is really a subcategory of the just cause approach. Specifically, this approach claims that God's behavior can be justified in certain instances because it serves a greater good. This approach asserts that God sometimes uses destruction and death for a higher purpose. In these cases, even though God's actions may seem unjust or morally questionable, they should not be regarded as such since they result in a greater good.

To illustrate this approach, we can look at two quotes from Gleason Archer. In the first one, Archer describes why the deadly flood described in the early chapters of Genesis was necessary. In the second, Archer justifies God's decree to exterminate the Canaanites. Regarding the flood, Archer writes:

> We must recognize that there are times when only radical surgery will save the life of a cancer-stricken body. The whole population of the antediluvian civilization had become so hopelessly infected with the cancer of moral depravity

(Gen. 6:5). Had any of them been permitted to live while still in rebellion against God, they might have infected Noah's family as well.

Regarding Canaanite genocide, Archer says:

> Much as we regret the terrible loss of life, we must remember that far greater mischief would have resulted if they had been permitted to live on in the midst of the Hebrew nation. These incorrigible degenerates of the Canaanite civilization were a sinister threat to the spiritual survival of Abraham's race.[30]

While you can detect the just cause approach at work in these statements, something else is evident here as well. According to Archer, God was not punishing these people just because of their wickedness. Rather, God eliminated these "wicked" people because they posed a threat to the "righteous" families of Noah and Abraham. As Archer sees it, the pre-flood civilization was utterly destroyed because their wickedness was highly contagious and would have "infected" Noah and his family. Similarly, the Canaanites were destroyed because they "were a sinister threat to the spiritual survival of Abraham's race."

To be sure, these ideas are not without biblical support, at least in the case of the Canaanites. In Exod. 23:31b-33, we read:

> I [Yahweh] will hand over to you [the Israelites] the inhabitants of the land, and you shall drive them out before you. You shall make no covenant with them and their gods. They shall not live in your land, or they will make you sin against me; for if you worship their gods, it will surely be a snare to you.

The Canaanites were to be driven out in order to preserve Israel's religious purity. This is stated even more forcefully in the instructions given to the Israelites in Deut. 20:16-18.

> But as for the towns of these peoples that the Lord your God is giving you as an inheritance, you must not let anything that breathes remain alive. You shall annihilate them—the Hittites and the Amorites, the Canaanites and the Perizzites, the Hivites and the Jebusites—just as the Lord your God has commanded, so that they may not teach you to do all the abhorrent things that they do for their gods, and you thus sin against the Lord your God.

This kind of rhetoric, which emphasizes the need to eliminate one group of people to preserve the "purity" of another, is extraordinarily dangerous. One need only recall Adolf Hitler's extremism as a case in point. His attempts to "purify" the human race, reflected in his manifesto *Mein Kampf* and actualized in concentration camps all across Europe, resulted in the extermination of millions. While Hitler's motivation for confronting "the Jewish problem" differs considerably from the biblical rationale for dealing with "the Canaanite problem," the final solution is frighteningly similar in both cases.

In biblical passages describing genocide and mass murder, the greater good approach does not seem particularly persuasive. First, it is difficult to believe that God would order the extermination of one group of people to preserve the religious purity of another, considering the fact that both groups were created in God's image. Second, it is unclear how eliminating the Canaanites would have ensured Israel's religious purity. Even if the Israelites had eradicated the Canaanites from their land, they would have still had constant contact with their "pagan" neighbors who worshiped other gods. Third, this approach posits a rather anemic view of the power and appeal of Yahwistic faith. As C. S. Cowles observes, "The 'sanitized land theory' presents an unflattering view of Israel's God. It was a virtual admission that in free and open competition with Canaanite religion, Yahweh worship would lose out."[31] Fourth, instructing people to commit genocide in order to preserve their moral purity is logically incoherent. As Cowles asks,: "What could be more morally bankrupting and spiritually corrupting than slaughtering men, women, and children?"[32] And finally, this approach falters because it suggests that God sometimes sanctions morally reprehensible behavior. You might think of it this way. While many of us would praise a parent who tries to protect his or her child from bad influences, few—if any—would applaud a parent who goes on a shooting spree, kills several neighborhood kids, and then claims the killings were justified because these kids were negatively influencing his or her child. Yet the greater good approach, in effect, does just that. This approach says it is fine for God to sanction otherwise reprehensible behavior as long as some greater good results.

An appeal to the greater good approach that is more sophisticated than Archer's is offered by Old Testament scholar Terence Fretheim, who has reflected on the problem of divine violence in several publications. In a recent journal article, he argues that God's use of violence is always purposeful, representing either God's judgment or salvation. According to Fretheim, divine violence advances God's redemptive purposes for the world. He believes it serves God's greater plan for creation and moves us one step closer to the day when violence will be no more. Fretheim illustrates this from the Old Testament by citing such examples as Israel's exodus from Egypt and subsequent return from Babylonian exile. He writes:

> Violence becomes the means by which God's people are delivered from violence. So, for example, violence *against* the Egyptians leads to Israel's salvation *from* Egypt's violence (e.g. Exod 15:1-3). Or, God uses the violence of the Persians under King Cyrus against the enslaving Babylonians as a means to bring salvation to the exiles (e.g., Isa 45:1-8).[33]

For Fretheim, this illustrates that "God's violence, whether in judgment or salvation, is never an end in itself, but is always exercised in the service of God's more comprehensive salvific purposes for creation."[34] Fretheim does not think that this is just an Old Testament phenomenon but is convinced that God still acts this way today. He believes that "in order to accomplish God's work in the world, God may respond in violent ways in and through various agents so that sin and evil do not go unchecked." Thus, according to Fretheim, "God chooses to become involved in violence so that evil will not have the last word. In everything, including violence, God seeks to accomplish loving purposes. *Thereby God may prevent an even greater evil.*"[35]

One could hardly imagine a clearer articulation of the greater good approach. Still, this approach rests on the very dubious assumption that it is right for God to use extreme acts of violence as long as the ends justify the means. But is it? Can mass murder and genocide ever be justified? Can it ever truly be regarded as moral? Even if we could demonstrate that the entire *adult* population of the antediluvian world and the Canaanite civilization was deserving of death, the same cannot be said for the children and infants living at the time.[36] The ends, however noble, do not justify such violent means, especially when this violence affects some of the most vulnerable members of society.

The "God Acted Differently in the Old Testament" Approach

A rather different way of dealing with disturbing divine behavior than what we have considered so far emphasizes discontinuity between God's past and present behavior. I have descriptively, albeit rather infelicitously, labeled this the "God acted differently in the Old Testament" approach. It comes in several variations, all of which understand much of God's involvement with Israel as a form of divine accommodation.[37] According to this approach, God met Israel where they were historically, developmentally, and spiritually, and interacted with them in ways they could understand even when that required God to behave in a manner that did not always represent God's fullest revelation. God's willingness to act in this way is thought to underscore God's commitment to relate to and communicate effectively with the people of Israel. This explanation attempts to reduce some of the difficulties associated with problematic portrayals of God by recognizing that God's behavior in these passages does not represent the final word about the nature and character of God. To consider how this approach works, we will consider two of the most common ways it is understood.

Progressive Revelation

People often explain differences between God's behavior in the Old and New Testaments by appealing to the notion of "progressive revelation." Simply put, progressive revelation is the idea that more and more of God's character and will was revealed over time. As one Christian ethicist describes it: "The Old Testament . . . contains a growing disclosure of God's moral designs for his people and all humanity. In the process of this self-disclosure, God, being deeply personal, often begins where people are in their understanding of his will and plan."[38] According to this perspective, each new divine revelation supplemented God's earlier self-disclosure without contradicting or superseding what had previously been revealed.[39] Practically speaking, this means that Israelites living in 500 BCE should have had a clearer understanding of God than those living in 700 BCE; those living in 700 BCE should have had a better understanding of God than those living in 900 BCE, and so on.

According to this view, God chose to self-disclose slowly and partially to ensure that the people of Israel could comprehend what was being revealed. Just as one cannot teach people calculus before they learn how to add and subtract, more advanced concepts about God's character and God's will were reserved until Israel had learned some basic theological lessons. They needed milk before they were ready for solid food—to borrow an expression from the New Testament.[40] This gradual unveiling was necessary because Israel started with a very limited understanding of God's ways and God's will.

If God wanted to be known in Israel, God had to communicate to people in ways they could understand, *even if* that meant getting involved in messy human affairs like warfare and killing. According to Tremper Longman, there is a "progressive pattern" that can be traced through "five distinct phases of divine warfare in the Bible."[41] For Longman, this demonstrates "God's progressive plan in motion,"[42] which illustrates "a pattern of ever-fuller revelation."[43] This explains why God's behavior in the Old Testament sometimes differs from God's behavior in the New Testament, and proponents of this approach believe it relieves some of the discomfort that problematic portrayals of God in the Old Testament create.

One problem associated with trying to use the notion of progressive revelation to deal with disturbing divine behavior in the Old Testament is that it is extremely difficult to demonstrate from the biblical texts themselves. As noted, progressive revelation works on the assumption that later texts display a more enlightened view of God, and God's will, than do earlier texts.[44] To illustrate progressive revelation at work, it is necessary to distinguish earlier texts from later ones and then to put them in chronological order based on the date of writing. This is no easy task. Scholars are often deeply divided over when certain texts were written, making any ordering of them from earliest to latest difficult to say the least. More to the point, even in those instances where the date of certain texts seems reasonably secure, it does not always appear that later texts reveal a higher understanding of God's will and ways. In fact, sometimes we find just the opposite. As Davies points out:

> The various views encountered in the Hebrew Bible concerning warfare, for example, do not suggest that attitudes in Israel necessarily became less brutal

and more humane with the passage of time. Thus we find Jeremiah in the sixth century BCE [relatively late in Israel's history] calling upon God to bring judgment against Babylon by "putting all her warriors to the sword" and leading them all "to the slaughter" (Jer. 50:27; cf. 51.3-4). . . . Hosea's disapproval of the bloody revolution that Jehu brought about at Elijah's request (Hos. 1.4) is *earlier* than the apparently approving tone of the Deuteronomic account preserved in 2 Kings 9. The evidence at our disposal simply does not support the view that Israel's ethics evolved in a gradually ascending scale of values.[45]

It seems that Israel's theological beliefs did not always progress from lower to higher, from ideas that were misguided to those that were more enlightened. The biblical evidence suggests that the development of their theological beliefs was a much more complicated affair than progressive revelation allows. This seriously compromises the usefulness of this approach for explaining the presence of disturbing divine behavior in the Old Testament.

A Theocratic State

Another variation of the "God acted differently in the Old Testament" approach emphasizes the unique way God related to Israel as a nation. As the Old Testament portrays it, Israel was a theocratic state, with God as its king and commander-in-chief. Because of this, God sometimes needed to participate in the unsavory acts of war and killing in order to maintain the integrity of the state. As Craigie puts it: "The state is a form of human organization through which God worked in the times of ancient Israel, and war was a form of human activity inseparably linked to the existence of the state."[46] In other words, if the state of Israel was to survive, God had to participate in war.[47]

Those who distinguish between the theocratic state of Israel and modern nations sometimes do so to explain why God condoned war in the past but not today. For example, although professor Daniel Gard believes Israel's political identity required God to use the people of Israel in human warfare, he no longer believes this is true of the church today since "no political, geography-bound nation on earth today can claim to be the people of God as ancient Israel once claimed." According to Gard: "The church has no territorial or political boundaries. She does not raise armies or fight battles with weapons, ancient or modern."[48] Similarly, Longman cautions readers against naively applying stories of conquest in Joshua to contemporary issues of war. He writes:

Clearly, we do need to exercise some caution as we think about contemporary applications of Old Testament stories. . . . We must take into account that *what happened in the past might have occurred under special circumstances* and no longer applies to us.

For instance, we may marvel at the story of Joshua fighting the Canaanites and then make the mistake of identifying our nation's armed forces with the Israelite army, concluding that whenever we go to war we're fighting a holy cause with God on our side. The "holy war" was a phenomenon of the Old Covenant when the people of God were one nation. Today the people of God are scattered throughout many nations and our holy war is now a spiritual conflict, not a physical one (see Ephesians 6:10-20).[49]

Explanations like these, predicated on Israel's uniqueness as a theocratic state, are thought to relieve some of the tension between the portrayal of God's behavior in the Old and New Testaments and to reduce the problematic nature of God's actions in many Old Testament texts.

One critique applicable to both variations of the "God acted differently in the Old Testament approach" relates to the necessity of God's involvement in violence. In the first instance, Israel's spiritual naïveté makes it necessary for God to participate in violence in order to self-disclose in a way that Israel can understand. In the second instance, Israel's unique relationship with God as sovereign of a theocratic state requires God to use war to preserve the state and work out the divine plan. Both claim that God had no other choice. But some feel this severely underestimates the creativity and resourcefulness of God. One might think the creator of the universe could have found a better way to achieve these ends than through the brutality of warfare and killing. Explanations that defend God's behavior by suggesting God had to use violence appear overly restrictive and seem to limit God's creative capacity.

Even if one believes that concepts like progressive revelation and theocracy explain *why* God behaved differently in ancient Israel, one is still left with troubling questions about what this behavior says about God's character. If God participated in acts of violence in the distant past for "noble" reasons, as this approach suggests, what does that teach us about the nature of God? Can we really call a being who commanded the wholesale slaughter of men, women, children, and infants "good"?[50] These are not easy questions to answer.[51]

The Permissive Will Approach

The final approach to be considered in this chapter is what I call the permissive will approach. This approach attempts to defend God by saying that even though God may have allowed certain "bad things" to happen, God is not ultimately responsible for them. This effectively removes the primary blame from God by assigning it to some secondary agent. This approach is one of several favored by Guy Hershberger in his book *War, Peace, and Nonresistance*. Hershberger is aware of the problems that God's behavior raises for many readers. He recognizes that some portions of the Old

Testament, such as God's command that Israel go to war, seem to contradict New Testament teachings, such as those found in the Sermon on the Mount. When comparing the two, one might conclude that God's standards have changed. But Hershberger disagrees, insisting that God's will is consistent and that God does not change.[52]

According to Hershberger, God sometimes commanded Israel to fight and kill—behaviors contrary to God's perfect will—because of human sinfulness. He writes:

> The various Old Testament commands of God requiring killing, such as the commands to slay the Amalekites, to hew Agag to pieces, and to kill the giant Goliath, were *permissive* commands given to a sinful, lean-souled people who had chosen to live on the lower, "sub-Christian" level. It was God's will that Israel should possess that land of Canaan and since they refused to live the nonresistant way of life in taking it, choosing rather the way which leads to war, He gave the *permissive* command to take this way. But the *permission* was given only because Israel chose to live on the sub-Christian level. It is not God's plan that men should sin, but if they choose to sin He can still use them to carry out His eternal purposes.[53]

According to Hershberger, if Israel had been fully obedient to God, they would not have needed to resort to military force or violence. Instead, God would have supernaturally removed all of Israel's enemies. Hershberger believes that God would have done this nonviolently by providing "the Canaanites with a motive to migrate as the new settlers approached."[54] But since Israel was disobedient, God permitted them to engage in physical combat against their flesh-and-blood enemies.

This approach is also used to explain certain texts in which God's behavior seems totally out of character with conventional notions about the nature of God. Take, for example, the affliction of King Saul in 1 Samuel 16. As the text portrays it, God sends an evil spirit to afflict Saul.

> Now the spirit of the Lord departed from Saul, and an evil spirit from the Lord tormented him. (1 Sam. 16:14)

This obviously bothers many readers and violates some of their most fundamental convictions about the character of God. Most Christians do not believe God is in the business of sending evil spirits to torment people! Yet that is precisely what this text claims. One way around this dilemma is to appeal to God's "permissive will" and to argue that there are some things God allows but does not directly cause. This is one way Walter Kaiser deals with this problematic passage. Regarding Saul's affliction, he writes: "We conclude that all this happened by the permission of God rather than as a result of his directive will, for God cannot be the author of anything evil."[55] Similar explanations could be offered for other problematic passages, such as the divine hardening of Pharaoh's heart. In each case, the interpreter attempts to ease the theological dissonance these passages elicit by appealing to secondary causes not explicitly mentioned in the text.

While this approach is attractive, it fails to do justice to what the text actually says. In the case of Saul, the text does not say that God "permits" an evil spirit to torment Saul. The text clearly claims that God is directly responsible. This is not surprising given ancient Israel's worldview, in which everything that happened, good or evil, was regarded as coming from the hand of God.[56] As Walter Brueggemann points out:

> It may trouble our positivistic minds that the disorder of Saul is attributed to an evil spirit, and it may trouble us more that the evil spirit is credited to God. We must remember that the world of biblical perspective is a world without secondary cause. All causes are finally traced back to God who causes all, who "kills and brings to life" (2:6). This narrative simply assumes that the world is ordered by the direct sovereign rule of God. All the spirits that beset human persons are dispatched from this single source (cf. 1 Kings 22:19-23).[57]

What Brueggemann does not say, however, is whether this "world of biblical perspective" should be our world as well. It is certainly not the world Kaiser inhabits. For Kaiser, "God cannot be the author of anything evil." I imagine many Christians would agree. But does this not render the permissive will approach invalid? If the text is actually claiming that God sent this evil spirit, then appealing to God's permissive will—an idea clearly not in the mind of the original writer—seems a forced attempt to make this passage fit into a predetermined theological box. The only way to use this approach credibly is to admit that the text inaccurately reports what "really happened" before applying the notion of God's permissive will to correct it. Since many inclined to use this approach are unlikely to concede the text is "flawed" in this way, appealing to God's permissive will seems a disingenuous way to defend God's behavior in these instances.

A Very Important Word about Control Beliefs

Each of the "solutions" to the problem of disturbing divine behavior considered in this chapter differ from one another in important ways. One appeals to God's inscrutability—God's ways are not our ways—while another emphasizes God's unimpeachable justice. One explains God's use of violence for the greater good, while another expounds on God's different *modus operandi* throughout history. Yet, for all their differences, each approach is guided by a fundamental assumption, or "control belief."[58] Before identifying this assumption, it is necessary to comment more generally on the nature of control beliefs.

Control beliefs can be defined as strongly held presuppositions that provide the framework within which we make sense of things. They "guide and control the way we investigate and interpret evidence" and "form the boundaries within which answers are possible."[59] These beliefs function as interpretive boundary markers, or gatekeepers, which limit the way data can be explained.

To illustrate how powerfully these beliefs shape the way we view the world, consider the undiscovered discovery of Christopher Columbus.[60] In 1492, Christopher Columbus set out on his maiden voyage across the Atlantic Ocean.[61] After leaving Spain and sailing a few thousand miles westward, he finally reached land. Apparently, he initially thought he was somewhere in the Indies.[62] His belief was based on two firmly held control beliefs: (1) Ptolemy's estimate that the circumference of the earth was eight thousand miles (it is about three times this), and (2) the belief that the world was six parts land and one part water. When Columbus landed, he was nowhere near Japan or China. Instead, he was in the Bahamas. He initially failed to realize what he had discovered because his control beliefs did not allow for the possibility of a much larger planet earth not to mention another continent in the Atlantic between Europe and Asia! Because his control beliefs were inaccurate, his interpretation was mistaken as well.

Columbus's undiscovered discovery teaches us a significant lesson. It reminds us of the importance of making sure our control beliefs are accurate. They must be carefully scrutinized to be sure they are reliable. Otherwise, our faulty premises may lead us to draw false conclusions.[63] As Sanders puts it: "All of us have and should have control beliefs. It would be impossible to live meaningfully without them. They give us stability as we encounter new ideas and experiences. But sometimes we need to examine and modify—or even reject—certain of our control beliefs."[64]

Returning to the topic at hand, we are now ready to identify the fundamental control belief operative in each of the interpretive approaches discussed in this chapter. Simply stated, that control belief is as follows: <u>God actually said and did what the Old Testament claims</u>. The influence this control belief exerts over many interpreters cannot be overemphasized. It defines the boundaries within which they believe "solutions" to disturbing divine behavior can be found. If these portrayals really do reflect what God actually said and did, it makes sense to offer a defense of God's behavior when it seems questionable or out of character. All the approaches we have considered in this chapter—with the exception of the divine immunity approach, which claims God's behavior cannot always be explained—function in precisely this way.

But what if this control belief is inaccurate? What if God did *not* actually say and do everything the Old Testament claims? What then? If this control belief is mistaken and we have determined that a solution to disturbing divine behavior can only be realized by working within its parameters, we run the risk of ending up like Columbus, insisting we have found Asia when our boat is docked in the Caribbean. More to the point, if this control belief is unreliable and we depend on it to guide our interpretation, we risk misconstruing the very nature of God. Given how much rests on the accuracy of this control belief, it behooves us to examine it carefully and thoroughly. Doing so will require us to ask some hard questions about the historical reliability of Old Testament narratives.

Generally speaking, those who use the approaches discussed in this chapter assume the basic historicity of the Old Testament.[65] That assumption—that the Old Testament is historically reliable—is the cornerstone for the control belief that God actually said and did what the Old Testament claims. But is this assumption warranted? Do these stories always report exactly what happened? If not, what does this suggest about God's reported involvement in them? For example, did the Israelites massacre all the inhabitants of Jericho except for Rahab and her family after the walls reportedly collapsed? Did Saul and his army annihilate every last Amalekite except King Agag in partial obedience to a divine directive issued through the prophet Samuel? Were 185,000 Assyrian soldiers instantly killed overnight by the angel of the Lord? If one concludes that some of the events found in Old Testament narratives did not happen as described, it opens the door to ask questions about the extent to which God was involved in them. And if it turns out that some of these events never happened at all, it stands to reason that God was not involved in them!

While reaching such a conclusion would obviously resolve some of the discomfort created by disturbing divine behavior in the Old Testament, it would open up a whole new set of questions. For instance, if the purpose of these texts was not to record "exactly what happened," then why were they written in the first place? If certain events did not actually happen—or at least not exactly in the way described—why are they described this way? Moreover, if God did not actually do many of the troubling things the Old Testament suggests, why did ancient writers portray God this way? These important questions will occupy our attention in the next section of the book as we reflect on the validity of the control belief that God said and did everything the Old Testament claims.

––––––––

This chapter has considered several modern attempts to defend God's behavior in the Old Testament. I have tried to give a fair, albeit brief, hearing to each of these. Despite the popularity of many of these approaches, none provides an adequate solution to the problematic portrayals of God we are studying. Each fails for a variety of reasons. While I discussed some of their inadequacies above, the objections raised in this chapter represent only a preliminary and partial critique. Other reasons could be added to demonstrate why these approaches are unsatisfactory. This will become apparent as we move throughout the book.[66]

I realize that the approaches discussed in this chapter are often held by sincere Christians, and I respect their attempt to grapple with some of the most challenging texts in the Old Testament. Still, while I am sympathetic with their efforts to defend God's behavior—I do not want to posit an unjust, uncaring, immoral God any more than they do—I fear these solutions may do more harm than good. By uncritically accepting problematic portrayals of God as reflective of God's true nature, these solutions further complicate efforts to see God as God really is. If we hope to think rightly about God, we need to find a more constructive way of dealing with disturbing divine behavior in the Old Testament that goes beyond just trying to defend it. The next section of the book moves us in this direction.

PART 2

Understanding the Nature of Old Testament Narratives

CHAPTER 5

Asking the Historical Question: Did It Really Happen?

The events of the Bible are as real as what happened to you today. So the first important principle of reading the historical books, or any book of the Bible that intends to teach history, is to learn how God treated His people in space and time in previous generations.

—Tremper Longman III[1]

The things that you're liable
To read in the Bible—
It ain't necessarily so.

—Ira Gershwin[2]

For some time now, serious questions have been raised about the historical veracity of the Old Testament. Were the patriarchs—Abraham, Isaac, Jacob, Joseph—real people? Did the exodus happen as described—or at all? Did the Israelites inherit the "promised land" by defeating fortified Canaanite cities through a series of stunning military victories? And so forth. Scholars are divided—sometimes sharply—over how best to answer these kind of questions. "Maximalists" adamantly defend the essential historical accuracy of the Old Testament,[3] while "minimalists," or "revisionists," believe it yields little historically reliable information about the people and events it describes.[4] In between these two positions, situated at opposite ends of the spectrum, are numerous other, less extreme options. It is obvious that many possibilities exist between denying that an event ever happened and believing that it happened exactly as described in the Bible. Without getting entangled in the details of this particular debate, the fundamental question it raises as it relates to this study must be explored: Do Old Testament narratives always describe what happened in the past?[5]

For many readers of the Bible, that question is answered with a resounding "Yes!" They believe that everything—or almost everything—in the Old Testament took place as described. They believe that there was a worldwide flood, that God sent ten plagues on Egypt, and that the walls of Jericho literally fell down after the Israelites circled the city seven times on the seventh day. In fact, virtually all of the well-known Old Testament stories—Jacob and Esau, David and Goliath, Daniel and the lion's den—are regarded as "true" stories about real people and historical events. While these readers might allow for the possibility of some embellishment, and may even regard a few stories as more parabolic than historical, by and large they believe the Old Testament contains an accurate rendering of Israel's past.

Many factors contribute to this view of the Old Testament. The notion that these stories are historical accounts of what happened in times past is often reinforced through sermons, Sunday school curriculum, and an assortment of books, videos, and DVDs that routinely give this impression. Our modern expectations about factuality and our assumptions about history writing also contribute to this view. Today, we put a premium on historical reliability and accuracy. We expect to be able to read a wide range of materials—history books, biographies, newspapers—that include "true" stories about real people, places, and events. And we expect these accounts to be reasonably accurate.[6] Many people expect no less of the Bible, assuming that similar standards for writing history existed then as do now. Also, belief in the Bible's divine inspiration naturally leads people to affirm its historical reliability. If God is the source of the Bible, its ultimate "author," it seems reasonable to assume that it contains a trustworthy record of the past. What need is there to question the historicity (historical reliability) of the Old Testament if God stands behind it all?[7]

Considering the cumulative effect of these factors, it is easy to understand why many people confidently believe the Old Testament is a reliable record of the past. But is it always? Is that a valid assumption? This is the fundamental question we will explore in this chapter. It is extremely important since it has a direct bearing on how we evaluate the Old Testament's claims about what God said and did. If the Old Testament's stories about Israel and the way God dealt with Israel (and others) are essentially accurate, then the best option for dealing with problematic portrayals of God would seem to be one of those discussed in chapter 4. On the other hand, if some Old Testament narratives are not historical accounts or do *not* accurately report what happened in the past, new options for handling disturbing divine behavior can be pursued.

As noted earlier, many biblical scholars have serious doubts about the historical veracity of certain portions of the Old Testament. Unfortunately, those who think this way do not always explain how or why they have arrived at their conclusions. This creates certain difficulties for individuals who have always assumed that the Old Testament contains an accurate record of the past. This became apparent to me while teaching a Bible course at Messiah College required for all students. One textbook I used was John Barton's short book *How the Bible Came to Be*. At one point in the book, as something of an aside, Barton writes: "The books of Ruth and Jonah, short stories about imaginary characters, have few signs of being compilations. They seem to be conscious works of fiction."[8] Inevitably, students would either ask me about this in class or write about it in their assigned journals. Barton's statement catches them off guard and challenges some of their most basic beliefs about the Bible. Regrettably, Barton never explains why he thinks as he does about these two Old Testament books. He simply declares them "fictional." But this casual proclamation is not very persuasive to people who have believed in the historical reliability of the Bible all their lives! Instead, unsupported declarations like these tend to do more harm than good, raising readers' defenses rather than inviting them to seriously consider alternate ways of viewing things.

In an attempt to avoid this undesirable state of affairs, I want to be explicit about the kind of evidence that leads some interpreters to question the historicity of certain parts of the Old Testament. To do this, I have chosen to examine two rather different Old Testament narratives—the story of Jonah and the conquest narrative in Joshua 6–11 both of which are regarded as historically unreliable by some interpreters. This discussion will put us in a better position to evaluate the accuracy of the assumption that the Old Testament records what took place in the past.

The Story of Jonah

The book of Jonah tells the story of an Israelite prophet who does everything in his power to escape God's call to preach to the people of Nineveh. Jonah attempts to get away from God by boarding a boat heading in the opposite direction from where he was supposed to go. His getaway plan is foiled, however, when a violent storm threatens to tear the ship apart. The sailors on board reluctantly throw Jonah overboard in an effort to calm the sea. As the prophet is near death in the Mediterranean Sea, he is rescued by a "great fish," which swallows him. After spending three days and three nights inside the belly of this beast, Jonah is vomited onto dry land. God then gives the wayward prophet a second chance, once again commanding him to preach to the Ninevites. This time, Jonah obeys. He travels to Nineveh and preaches a very brief sermon, which prompts the entire city to repent. In response, God relents and decides not to destroy the city. Curiously, this makes Jonah furious. Rather than rejoicing over this happy turn of events, the prophet climbs to the top of a hill and pouts. He would rather die than watch God show mercy to people he apparently hates. But instead of granting Jonah's death wish, God interacts with the prophet in a gracious attempt to readjust his attitude and broaden his perspective. It is uncertain whether God's efforts succeed, since the book ends with a question directed to Jonah that is left unanswered (Jon. 4:10-11). We are left hanging, wondering how Jonah will respond. So goes the book of Jonah.

For many people, this story is unquestionably historical simply because it is in the Bible. This assessment would seem to be validated by the fact that the story deals with historical locations like Joppa and Nineveh and features a real person named Jonah, an individual who prophesied during the reign of Jeroboam II, according to 2 Kgs. 14:25. Even Jesus referred to this story when the scribes and Pharisees requested a sign. He said:

> An evil and adulterous generation asks for a sign, but no sign will be given to it except the sign of the prophet Jonah. For just as Jonah was three days and three nights in the belly of the sea monster, so for three days and three nights the Son of Man will be in the heart of the earth. The people of Nineveh will rise up at the judgment with this generation and condemn it, because they repented at the proclamation of Jonah, and see, something greater than Jonah is here! (Matt. 12:39-41)

In the minds of many people, such evidence clinches the historicity of Jonah. But does it? Not necessarily. First, just because a story refers to real people and places does not necessarily mean it took place. Authors who write historical fiction routinely use real people and places to make their stories believable even though the particular stories they write never actually happened. Second, Jesus' reference to the story of Jonah is not sufficient to ensure its historicity. It is not unusual for people to refer to well-known stories without believing they actually happened. Consider, for example, J. R. R. Tolkien's masterful trilogy *The Lord of the Rings*. Suppose I wanted to emphasize my deep and enduring commitment to my spouse and said something like this: "Just as Samwise Gamgee was loyal to Frodo, so too will I be loyal to my wife, Elisa." Do my references to Samwise Gamgee and Frodo imply that I believe they were real people or that *The Lord of the Rings* actually happened? Of course not. I am just using characters from a well-known story, albeit a fictional one, to make a point.

When closely examined, several features seem to suggest that the book of Jonah represents something other than historical reporting. My purpose in discussing these features is not to make an unassailable case that the story of Jonah never actually happened. Rather, I hope to provide a better understanding of the kind of evidence that leads people to raise questions about the historical reliability of the book of Jonah and other Old Testament narratives. In the final analysis, you will need to decide what to do with the evidence. You will need to determine whether it is sufficiently persuasive to warrant rethinking your understanding of the historical nature of certain Old Testament texts.

Challenges to the Historicity of Jonah

A Physiologically Implausible Fish Tale

Jonah's famous fish ride is undoubtedly the best known part of the story. Yet his three day–three night underwater adventure is also extremely vulnerable to critique and has been challenged in various ways. For instance, it has been pointed out that the gullet of a "whale" is too narrow to swallow an adult.[9] Even if it were possible for a whale to swallow a person, the chances of that person surviving for three days and nights inside such a creature seem very slim indeed. The gastric juices—not to mention the lack of oxygen—would not tend to sustain human life. Also, it seems improbable that Jonah would have been in any state, physically or mentally, to compose the highly structured poem preserved in Jon. 2:2-9, which he supposedly wrote while inside the whale.

not a whale

Of course, there are counterarguments to these objections. For example, some have responded by claiming that what happened to Jonah was a miracle. Although humanly speaking such an event is impossible, God made it happen because God can do anything. Others have argued for the reliability of this part of the story by trying to "prove" it *could* have happened. This is done by appealing to modern stories about people who have been swallowed by a whale and have survived. The most popular story in this regard concerns a man named James Bartley. Bartley, who has been heralded as a "modern-day Jonah," is said to have survived in the belly of a whale for thirty-six hours. To be sure, it is a very interesting story and well worth reading.[10] Unfortunately, this story has no factual basis. In a fascinating article tracing the origin and evolution of this particular story, Professor Edward Davis convincingly demonstrates that it is fallacious.[11] No credible stories of individuals being swallowed by a whale and surviving exist.

The Enormous Size of Nineveh

Another problematic feature of the story, from a historical point of view, is the enormous size of Nineveh. According to the book of Jonah, traveling through Nineveh required "a three days' walk across" (Jon. 3:3). For a city to be a three days' walk across, it would have needed to be approximately fifty miles in diameter. Yet archaeological excavations at the ancient city of Nineveh have determined that the city was never that large. Instead, the city of Nineveh was no greater than seven and a half miles in circumference, and only about three miles in diameter at the oblong axis. Although this is still very large, by ancient standards, walking from one end of the city to the other could have easily been done in less than half a day.[12]

Defenders of the historicity of the book of Jonah respond by saying that what is meant in Jon. 3:3 is a three-day preaching mission. While this is an interesting suggestion, it is highly speculative. Nothing in the text would lead one to such a conclusion. In fact, it is doubtful that anyone would have suggested this unlikely interpretation were it not for the problems created by trying to reconcile this verse with the actual size of Nineveh. Others have argued that the three days' walk refers to "Greater Nineveh," a region that included both the city and the surrounding region. If this more extensive area is in view, it would explain why it took three days to walk across it.[13] But the plain meaning of the text seems to be that it took three days to walk from one end of the city to the other. This makes the Ninevites' repentance all the more remarkable. After Jonah has gone only partway across the city, just "a day's walk" (Jon. 3:4a), the whole place repents after hearing a very short sermon! Since none of these arguments seem to work very well, it seems we are left with our initial dilemma of needing to account for this reference to a huge city that stands at odds with the facts on the ground.

The Presence of Multiple Miraculous Events

The book of Jonah is part of the Latter Prophets, a group of prophetic books that includes Isaiah, Jeremiah, Ezekiel, and the twelve Minor Prophets. One striking contrast between the Former Prophets (Joshua, Judges, Samuel, and Kings) and the Latter Prophets is that miracles are virtually nonexistent in the Latter Prophets. Oddly, the opposite is true of the book of Jonah. As Leslie Allen writes:

> This little book is a series of surprises; it is crammed with an accumulation of hair-raising and eye-popping phenomena, one after the other. The violent sea-storm, the submarine-like fish in which Jonah survives as he composes a song, the mass conversion in Nineveh, the magic plant—these are not commonplace features of OT prophetic narratives. While one or two exciting events would raise no question, *the bombardment of the reader with surprise after surprise in a provocative manner suggests that the author's intention is other than simply to describe historical facts.*[14]

While I do not question that God performs miracles, the fact that this prophetic book contains so many miracles when other books in the same category contain none at all raises serious questions about what kind of story we are reading. The writer seems to be sending the reader important signals suggesting this book is not to be read as straightforward historical reporting.

The Exquisite Literary Artistry

Finally, a close reading of the book of Jonah reveals a highly sophisticated literary structure that makes it seem more like a carefully written piece of literature than a record of past events. For example, there are intriguing parallels between chapters 1 and 3. Both chapters describe an unnamed "pagan" acting decisively in a time of crisis—the captain in chapter 1 and the king in chapter 3—and both chapters begin with a nearly identical word from God to Jonah. Interesting parallels also occur between chapters 2 and 4. Jonah speaks to God in both chapters, though in the former Jonah thanks God for saving his life and in the latter he asks God to take it. The conversation that takes place between Jonah and God in chapter 4 is an especially striking piece of literary artistry. Both individuals speak the same number of (Hebrew) words in the following order: Jonah thirty-nine, God three, Jonah three, God five, Jonah five, God thirty-nine.[15] This level of linguistic coordination is difficult to explain if someone was simply recording what actually happened.

As we have seen, both external and internal evidence raises questions about how to evaluate the historicity of the book of Jonah.[16] For some readers, these features clearly indicate that this story was never meant to be taken historically. That is not to deny that Jonah was a real person, that cities like Joppa and Nineveh were actual places, or that some Israelites actually hated Assyrians. Rather, it is to say that these historical elements were used to create a story that is more like a parable and less like a report of what actually happened on a boat in the Mediterranean Sea—and in the streets of the Assyrian capital—more than 2,500 years ago. Others remain unconvinced and continue to insist that the story of Jonah happened as described. Regardless of your perspective on this particular Old Testament narrative, the purpose of this discussion has been to illustrate the kind of evidence that must be considered when seeking to ascertain the historicity of a biblical story and to demonstrate that there are good reasons for believing it did not actually happen.

I chose to begin with the book of Jonah because questioning its historicity is far less threatening than questioning the historicity of other portions of the Old Testament. Since the story of Jonah is not a major part of the basic Old Testament story line, those who conclude that it did not actually happen do not need to radically rethink their understanding of the history of Israel or the nature of the Old Testament. The same cannot be said about the conquest narrative in Joshua 6–11. The conquest narrative *is* a major part of Israel's story. Raising questions about its essential historicity necessarily generates broader and more serious concerns.

The Conquest Narrative (Joshua 6–11)

The conquest narrative describes how Israel entered the land and occupied it through a series of successful military operations. According to the biblical text, the bloodshed and killing required to take the land was commissioned by God and, on some occasions, God is described as actively participating in these battles. As noted earlier, these texts include some of the most disturbing depictions of God in the entire Old Testament. But what if the conquest of Canaan described in the book of Joshua did not actually happen, or at least not as it is portrayed? How would that influence our reading of this story and what might that suggest about how we should handle the view of God presented there?

The purpose of what follows is not a full-blown critique of the conquest model. Nor is it intended to conclusively prove or disprove the historicity of the conquest narrative any more than our earlier discussion was designed to do so in regard to the story of Jonah. This issue is too large and unwieldy to be explored satisfactorily in the few pages I am able to give to it. Many studies have been devoted to this topic, and I encourage the interested reader to explore these further.[17] My intentions here are much more modest. I again want to illustrate the kind of evidence that leads people to question the historicity of certain Old Testament narratives and to suggest that there are good reasons for not accepting the conquest narrative at face value.

A Description of the Conquest Narrative

According to the book of Joshua, Israel's incursion into Canaan unfolded in three stages corresponding to three different geographic regions, beginning in the center of Canaan (Joshua 6–8) before going south (Joshua 9–10) and finally north (Joshua 11). The battle of Jericho, the first military confrontation in the central campaign, is the most well-known story of the book of Joshua. After the walls of Jericho miraculously fall down, the Israelites slaughter all the inhabitants and burn the city to the ground (Josh. 7:20-21). Israel then moves westward to the city of Ai. After an initial defeat, Israel is victorious once again. The troops then return to "base camp" in Gilgal, where they are met by Gibeonites who claim to be travelers from a distant land (Josh. 9:6). The Israelites believe their story and enter into a covenant with them, something they were explicitly forbidden to do with the inhabitants of the land (Deut. 7:2). They soon realize their mistake but agree to let the Gibeonites live.

When the king of Jerusalem hears that the Gibeonites have made peace with the Israelites, he forms a coalition and lays siege to the city of Gibeon. The Gibeonites cry out for help, and Israel comes to their rescue. After defending the Gibeonites by defeating the five-king coalition in the South, the Israelites take three of their cities (Makkedah, Libnah, Lachish) along with others in the vicinity (Eglon, Hebron, Debir). The northern campaign is precipitated by news of what happened in the south. When King Jabin of Hazor hears what the Israelites have done, he amasses an enormous fighting force at the waters of Merom, a location in the far north. Although the army of this northern coalition is described as being more numerous than the sand on the seashore, Jabin and his allies are swiftly defeated when the

Israelites carry out a surprise attack (11:7). King Jabin is executed, and Hazor is destroyed. A similar fate befalls all the kings who sided with him (11:12). The conquest narrative comes to an end with the following summary statement:

> So Joshua took the whole land, according to all that the Lord had spoken to Moses; and Joshua gave it for an inheritance to Israel according to their tribal allotments. And the land had rest from war. (Josh. 11:23)

Based solely on a reading of Joshua 1–11, we can make several general statements about the conquest of Canaan: The Israelites (1) entered Canaan from the outside, (2) were a distinct ethnic group from the Canaanites, (3) conquered the land violently through numerous military confrontations, (4) occupied the land in a relatively short period of time,[18] (5) worked together as one united group, and (6) possessed all the land of Canaan at the end of the conquest. Despite this portrayal of events in the first half of the book of Joshua, many scholars fundamentally disagree with this explanation of how Israel came to possess the land. Why? What causes them to question the historicity of the conquest described in Joshua 6–11 and prompts them to present alternative explanations for Israel's emergence in the land?

Evaluating the Historicity of the Conquest Narrative

Various pieces of evidence seem to cast doubt on the historical veracity of Israel's conquest of Canaan as described in Joshua 6–11. My focus here is primarily on biblical and archaeological evidence, though I also briefly address other factors that raise questions about the historicity of the so-called conquest of Canaan.

BIBLICAL EVIDENCE

A careful reading of the *entire* book of Joshua challenges some of the statements listed above. For example, despite the claim at the end of the conquest narrative that "Joshua took the whole land" (Josh. 11:43), just two chapters later we read:

> Now Joshua was old and advanced in years; and the Lord said to him, "You are old and advanced in years, and very much of the land still remains to be possessed. This is the land that still remains: all the regions of the Philistines, and all those of the Geshurites (from the Shihor, which is east of Egypt, northward to the boundary of Ekron, it is reckoned as Canaanite; there are five rulers of the Philistines, those of Gaza, Ashdod, Ashkelon, Gath, and Ekron), and those of the Avvim, in the south, all the land of the Canaanites, and Mearah that belongs to the Sidonians, to Aphek, to the boundary of the Amorites, and the land of the Gebalites, and all Lebanon, toward the east, from Baal-gad below Mount Hermon to Lebo-hamath, all the inhabitants of the hill country from Lebanon to Misrephoth-maim, even all the Sidonians. (Josh. 13:1-6a)

According to this passage, the Israelites had not taken "the whole land" in just a few years. Instead, at the end of Joshua's long life, a considerable amount of territory was still out of their control. Since the Israelites could not have taken "the whole land" while "very much of the land still remains to be possessed," those interested in ascertaining what actually happened need to assess which of these perspectives is most accurate.

The claim that Israel possessed the whole land is further complicated by explicit references to Israel's failure to drive out all of its inhabitants. Although God promises to drive out various groups of people from the land, such as the Geshurites (Josh. 13:2, 6b), this clearly does not happen during Joshua's lifetime, if ever. "The Israelites did not drive out the Geshurites or the Maacathites; but Geshur and Maacath live within Israel to this day" (Josh. 13:13). Likewise, although Josh. 12:8 claims that Joshua gave the land of the Jebusites to the people of Israel, we are later informed that "the people of Judah could not drive out the Jebusites . . . so the Jebusites live with the people of Judah in Jerusalem to this day" (Josh. 15:63). The book of Joshua also reports Israel's inability to "drive out the Canaanites who lived in Gezer" (Josh. 16:10a) and those residing in the territory of Manasseh (Josh. 17:12). Instead, the Israelites made them slaves (Josh. 16:10b; 17:13). All of this suggests that Israel's control over the land did not come about as quickly or easily as Joshua 6–11 seems to suggest, nor was it as all encompassing.

Additional complications arise when turning to the book of Judges. Judges presents a picture of Israel's occupation of the land that differs radically from the one described in Joshua 6–11, suggesting that the process was far more protracted and complicated. In the book of Judges, there is no indication that the land was occupied as the result of a pan-Israelite endeavor with all tribes working together in one united effort. As the initial chapters of Judges describe it, various tribes commonly appear to have acted alone. Moreover, despite some victories, many of these tribes were not very successful in ridding the land of its inhabitants. The Benjaminites did not drive out the Jebusites (Judg. 1:21). Manasseh did not drive out the inhabitants of Beth-shean (Judg. 1:27). Ephraim did not drive out the Canaanites (Judg. 1:29). Zebulun did not drive out the inhabitants of Kitron (Judg. 1:30). Asher did not drive out the inhabitants of Acco (Judg. 1:31). Naphtali did not drive out the inhabitants of Beth-shemesh (Judg. 1:33). These references from Judges 1 are clearly at odds with the initial impression given by the conquest narrative in Joshua that Israel was unstoppable and had conquered all the land at the end of five years. They certainly contradict the sweeping claims made in the book of Joshua:

> Thus the Lord gave to Israel all the land that he swore to their ancestors that he would give them; and having taken possession of it, they settled there. And the Lord gave them rest on every side just as he had sworn to their ancestors; not one of all their enemies had withstood them, for the Lord had given all their

enemies into their hands. Not one of all the good promises that the Lord had made to the house of Israel had failed; all came to pass. (Josh. 21:43-45)

Various statements in the second half of the book of Joshua combined with the picture that emerges from the book of Judges suggest that Israel's hold on the land was only partial at best. There appear to have been many people in Canaan who successfully resisted the unwelcome Israelite advances. Thus, it seems that the final three statements discussed above—that the Israelites occupied the land in a short period of time, that they worked together as one united group, and that they were able to possess all the land of Canaan at the end of their military operations—need serious modification. These difficulties raise significant questions about the historical reliability of Joshua 6–11, difficulties that are compounded when archaeological evidence is brought to bear on the events described in this narrative.

ARCHAEOLOGICAL EVIDENCE

An earlier generation of archaeologists attempted to provide independent verification for the events recorded in the book of Joshua.[19] They tried to do this through extensive excavations at key sites the Bible claimed were destroyed by the Israelites shortly after entering the land. If the conquest actually happened as the book of Joshua said it did—and as these archaeologists believed it did—then they felt they should be able to find incontrovertible evidence of this in the archaeological record. Thus, with spade in hand, they went digging for evidence to corroborate the Bible's account of things. Initially, there actually did seem to be a correspondence between the facts on the ground and the biblical description. But, eventually, it became clear that much of the evidence did not match up with the biblical record. Ironically, rather than proving the historicity of the conquest narrative, their efforts had the opposite effect. To illustrate this, I have chosen to highlight a few key issues that demonstrate how difficult it can be to correlate the archaeological evidence with the biblical text.

Among scholars today, it is widely agreed that Israel appeared in Palestine at the end of the thirteenth century BCE.[20] Assuming that the basic story line of the book of Joshua is historically reliable, we would expect to find archaeological evidence that certain cities, such as Jericho and Ai, were destroyed by the Israelites around this time. According to the book of Joshua, after the walls of Jericho collapsed, the Israelites burned the city to the ground (Josh. 6:20, 24). The kind of conflagration envisioned here would inevitably have left behind a layer of ash and debris that archaeologists could identify. But no such destruction layer has been found for the city of Jericho during the time in question. The reason for this is simple: Jericho was unoccupied when the Israelites supposedly marched around it! As Israel Finkelstein and Neil Silberman report: "There was no trace of a settlement of any kind in the thirteenth century BCE, and the earlier Late Bronze settlement, dating to the fourteenth century BCE, was small and poor, almost insignificant, and unfortified. There was also no sign of destruction."[21] In other words, at the end of the thirteenth century, when Israel is believed to have entered Canaan, it appears there was nobody in Jericho to conquer. While not all scholars agree with this archaeological assessment, there is currently no compelling evidence to the contrary.[22]

A similar problem exists for the alleged destruction of the city of Ai. According to the conquest narrative, after defeating the inhabitants of the city, "Joshua burned Ai, and made it forever a heap of ruins" (Josh. 8:28). While it is true that Ai was "a heap of ruins" when Israel was in the land, it was not because the Israelites had made it that way. The city had been destroyed more than one thousand years earlier. According to Syro-Palestinian archaeologist William Dever, after this much earlier *pre-Israelite* destruction, "the site was totally abandoned until sometime in the twelfth or eleventh century BC, when a small Israelite village flourished on the centuries-old ruins." Dever continues: "Despite the vivid, detailed account of the battle and capture of 'Ai in Joshua 7–8, there was simply no trace of an Israelite destruction, and indeed no Canaanite city there to be destroyed in Joshua's time."[23] On this point, the biblical description of the conquest is at odds with the archaeological record, and efforts to correlate the two are not compelling.[24] Similar kinds of difficulties exist with regard to some of the other cities mentioned in the conquest narrative, highlighting the serious challenges that face those intent on asserting the historicity of the conquest narrative in the book of Joshua.[25]

Another archaeological indicator that casts doubt on certain aspects of the conquest narrative in Joshua is the similarity in material culture at Israelite and Canaanite sites. If the Israelites were outsiders, an ethnically distinct group of foreigners who came from another place, the archaeological record should reflect this. We would expect the Israelites to have a distinctive material culture—pottery, tools, weapons—that would set them apart from the indigenous people of Canaan. Yet, as archaeologist Amihai Mazar points out, "nothing in the archaeological findings from this period points to foreign traditions or objects brought by the Israelites from outside the country."[26] Instead, we find much continuity between the material culture of the Israelites and the Canaanites, particularly in regard to pottery.

Pottery is one of the clearest ways to distinguish one group of people in the ancient world from another. Yet the pottery discovered at the very earliest Israelite sites in the hill country looks strikingly similar to Canaanite pottery. As Dever observes:

> The common early Israelite pottery turns out to be nearly identical to that of the late 13th century BCE; it comes right out of the Late Bronze Age urban Canaanite repertoire. As someone who has spent 30 years studying this pottery, I can tell you that, based on the pottery evidence, we would not even suspect that the people living in these hill-country sites were newcomers at all.

One can't imagine nomads sweeping in from the desert, with no architectural or ceramic tradition behind them, suddenly becoming past masters of the potter's art in Palestine. This early Iron Age I (c. 1200 BCE) pottery goes back eight or ten centuries in a long Middle–Late Bronze Age tradition. Clearly the pottery alone suggests that these newcomers to the hill country were not newcomers to Palestine. They had been living alongside the Canaanite city-states for some time, perhaps for several generations, probably for several centuries.[27]

This evidence, along with a number of other factors, has led Dever (and others) to draw conclusions about Israel's origins in Canaan that are quite at odds with the biblical picture of the conquest in Joshua 6–11. Dever believes that the first Israelites were actually Canaanites who separated themselves out from the rest of their community and moved east, forging a new life for themselves in the hill country of Canaan. This certainly does not preclude the possibility that some of the people who settled at these "Israelite" sites came from other countries, possibly including a small group of escaped slaves from the Sinai Peninsula. Still, many scholars today believe that the majority of those who eventually come to be known as Israelites arose from *within* Canaan itself.

> Earliest Israel probably was a loose confederation of tribes and clans that "emerged" gradually from the pluralistic population of the land. Accordingly, Israel's ancestors would have been of diverse origins. Some may have been immigrants from Transjordan, possibly even from Egypt. But basically Israel seems to have emerged from the "melting pot" of peoples already in the land of Canaan at the beginning of the Iron Age.[28]

If true the whole OT is false [handwritten annotation]

If this is correct—if most Israelites did not enter Canaan from outside the land—then another major element of the conquest model appears to be historically unreliable.

MISCELLANEOUS EVIDENCE

In addition to the presence of contrasting biblical versions of Israel's "entry" into Canaan and the problems raised by the archaeological evidence, several other issues also raise doubts about the historicity of the conquest narrative in the book of Joshua. We only have time to mention these in passing. Some have wondered how plausible it is to believe that a group of recently freed slaves—who reportedly had lived in the wilderness for forty years with very little battle experience—could defeat the kind of fortified Canaanite city-states described in the book of Joshua.[29] Others point to the lack of external evidence indicating an incursion of foreign invaders destroying Canaanite cities at this time.[30] Such a dramatic shift in power in the region would surely have been reflected in some ancient documents, but it is not.[31] Still others have noted striking similarities between the conquest narrative in Joshua and other conquest narratives in the ancient Near East.[32]

These similarities raise questions about the nature and function of such narratives and the degree to which they were intended to reflect historical events. When all of these items are taken into consideration, they cause us to rethink how Israel actually came to possess the land of Canaan. Whatever conclusion one ultimately reaches, good reasons exist for questioning the description of events as narrated in the book of Joshua.

What Is an Old Testament Narrative?

So far, the reasons that have been given for why someone might question the historicity of the story of Jonah or the conquest narrative have related specifically to these particular Old Testament narratives. But there is also a more basic reason why some scholars raise questions about the historical veracity of these and other Old Testament narratives. This relates to the basic nature of Old Testament narratives as a distinct literary genre.

Defined simply, a genre is "a group of things with common characteristics."[33] In literature, these "common characteristics" are those elements that allow us to distinguish one kind of writing from another and which create certain expectations in us as readers. As we become familiar with certain literary genres, we learn what to expect of them. For example, suppose you heard someone reading from a book that began with the words "Once upon a time." Your familiarity with this genre would immediately allow you to classify it as a fairy tale and would govern your expectations of the story. You would not be surprised if the story included talking animals or the use of magic, and you might expect the main characters "to live happily ever after." On the other hand, you would not expect the characters in the story to be historical people nor would you expect the story to mention real places. That is just not how fairy tales work.

Consider how different your expectations would be if you were reading a biography of Abraham Lincoln. You would expect this book to provide many historical details about real people, places, and events that were important to Lincoln. You would anticipate hearing about Lincoln's early years, his education, the significant individuals who influenced him, his political failures and successes, and his presidency during the Civil War. You would not, however, expect the book to include a story about an animal that spoke to Abraham Lincoln and encouraged him to devise a magical potion that could help him defeat his political rivals! Talking animals and efficacious magic are not "common characteristics" of biographies. We know this because we are familiar with modern biographies and know what to expect of them. Knowing the characteristics of the genre we are reading establishes our expectations and helps us know how to read and evaluate the material at hand.

Becoming familiar with the genre we are reading is one of the most important steps we can take to understanding it properly. In fact, according to Old Testament scholar Hermann Gunkel, it should be the first step we take. As he so memorably puts it: "Anyone investigating an author without knowing the genre he uses is building a house beginning with the roof."[34] This is certainly true when it comes to reading and understanding the Bible. But here we immediately run into some difficulties. Unlike many books today, the Bible contains not one but many different literary genres—wisdom literature, parables, gospels, love poetry, law, and, of course, Old Testament narrative. This means we cannot read all parts of the Bible in the same way. Rather, the way we read depends on the genre we are reading. This is both exciting and challenging. It is exciting because it means the Bible offers a rich variety of texts for reflection and spiritual edification, and it is challenging because we run the risk of misunderstanding these texts if we do not recognize what genre we are reading.

Our ability to properly interpret these texts is further complicated by the fact that we are not naturally knowledgeable about the characteristics of many genres appearing in the Bible. This is understandable since many of these genres are "extinct." Nobody writes gospels, apocalyptic literature, or Old Testament narratives today. Unlike fairy tales or biographies, we do not instinctively know what to expect when reading these particular genres and we need to be extremely careful not to impose modern assumptions on these ancient texts. Old Testament narratives were written over two thousand years ago in a culture and language very different from our own. This fact alone should give us considerable pause when trying to make sense of what we are reading. It would be naive to assume that these ancient writers were guided by exactly the same presuppositions, assumptions, and standards used by writers today. They were not. The individuals who produced these stories were non-Western, pre-Enlightenment thinkers. Their worldview differs noticeably from ours in significant ways, and this is clearly reflected in the way they wrote. This must be taken into account when reading and interpreting these stories, lest we expect them to be something they were never intended to be.

Recognizing that Old Testament narratives are examples of ancient, not modern, historiography (history writing) leads many scholars to reject the popular assumption that these stories offer a trustworthy description of what took place in Israel's past.[35] While they would not deny that these stories often refer to real people, places, and events, and are at many points historically reliable, they realize that ancient historiographers were not principally interested in describing exactly what occurred. Assuming that Old Testament narratives were written to preserve a record of what actually happened is a modern—not an ancient—historiographic assumption. That is not to suggest that these ancient writers had no interest in history or historical matters. They certainly did. It is merely to emphasize that no simplistic equation can be made between modern history writing and Old Testament narratives. The way history is written today differs markedly from the way it was written in the ancient world. Old Testament narrative represents a distinct literary genre that needs to be understood on its own terms. Otherwise, we are likely to misunderstand and misinterpret it.

In what follows, I discuss several characteristics of Old Testament narratives that distinguish it from modern historiography. This will provide us with a better understanding of this particular genre. It will also reveal some additional difficulties with assuming that these narratives always report what actually happened and that God actually said and did everything these texts claim.

Old Testament Narratives Often Reveal More about the Author's Timeframe than the Story's

When you read an Old Testament narrative, it helps to remember that it has two separate time frames, which I refer to as the story's time frame and the author's time frame. The story's time frame refers to the setting of the story itself, the historical period in which it reportedly took place. The author's time frame refers to the time period in which the story was written down. For Old Testament narratives, these two time periods are commonly separated by decades, if not centuries. The same is also sometimes true of modern history writing. For example, if I decided to write a history of the Civil Rights Movement, the setting would be the 1950s and 1960s whereas the author's time frame would be the early twenty-first century.

One reason modern historians write about the past is to increase our understanding of the story's time frame, the time period about which they are writing. Whether describing a phenomenon like the Azuza Street Revival in the early twentieth century or Gandhi's nonviolent campaign leading to India's independence in the 1940s, modern historians discuss prominent people, events, and socioeconomic, political, and religious factors that help make sense of these historical moments. Therefore, when we read their work, we expect to learn a great deal about the historical period under investigation. Typically, we would not expect to learn very much, if anything, about significant people, places, and events from the author's time.[36]

In biblical literature, this situation is commonly reversed. For many ancient writers, it was more important to use the past to serve their interests in the present than it was to explore carefully what actually happened in times past. The past provided the raw material for crafting a narrative that could speak powerfully and persuasively to their own communities. Therefore, when they wrote, they used the past creatively to make a point in the present. Their goal was to communicate a message to their contemporaries rather than to provide a definitive rendering of the past. They were far less interested in fact checking or ascertaining the historical reliability of the sources they used than are modern historians.

Many readers of the Bible are unaware of how different Old Testament narratives are from modern history writing in this regard. Many people do not realize that these texts often yield more insight into the author's historical context than into the story's. Therefore, it comes as no great surprise to find them reading Old Testament narratives as though they were modern examples of history writing. When people read a narrative like Joshua 6–11 in this way, it is natural that they would expect it to yield reliable information about what actually happened when Israel "entered" the land of Canaan. But reading the conquest narrative this way fails to account for the striking differences between ancient and modern historiography. Equating the two invariably leads to confusion and misunderstanding.

Once we recognize that many Old Testament texts reveal more about the author's time frame than about the story's, we can shift our expectations for the kind of historical information that might be available to us. Take the book of Joshua, for example. Many scholars believe that at least one edition of the book of Joshua was produced sometime in the seventh century, approximately six hundred years after the proposed events took place.[37] The book is thought to be part of a larger literary work extending from Joshua through 2 Kings that was intended to support the religious reforms of King Josiah, who reigned over Judah from 640 to 609 BCE. Consequently, most scholars believe this text provides very little information about Israel's actual emergence in the land in the thirteenth century. The text seems to have been intentionally designed to address people in Josiah's day rather than to answer the historical question, How did Israel come to possess Canaan? In an article tellingly titled "Josiah in the Book of Joshua," Old Testament scholar Richard Nelson speaks of Joshua as a "prototypical Josiah" and "a forerunner of Josiah." In other words, Nelson believes the character of Joshua has been intentionally shaped to mirror King Josiah, during whose reign he believes a portion of the book of Joshua took shape. Nelson writes:

> Joshua is . . . presented as a royal figure, one that particularly resembles the great reformer, King Josiah (2 Kings 22-23). . . . Like King Josiah he practices undeviating obedience to the law (Josh 1:7; 2 Kgs 22:2) and consequently can demand the same standard of others (Josh 23:6). Like Josiah he celebrates a proper Passover (Josh 5:10-12; 2 Kgs 23:21-23) and restructures a covenant of loyalty with God (Josh 8:30-35; 2 Kgs 23:2-3). Joshua thus serves as a forerunner and model for royal leadership, especially for the reforming policies of Josiah.[38]

If Nelson is correct, a later writer portrayed Joshua—who reportedly lived hundreds of years earlier—in a way that would support to legitimate the actions of King Josiah in the seventh century BCE. The past has been shaped by, and pressed into the service of, the present.

This practice of using the past to address issues and concerns in the present can be illustrated by numerous Old Testament narratives. To cite one additional example, consider the patriarchal narratives in Genesis. Gary Rendsburg argues that the patriarchal narratives were shaped by the needs of the monarchy under David and Solomon. He writes: "On the face of it the narrative is about Abraham, Isaac, and Jacob, about their lives, about early Israelite history. But it reflects through and through the contemporary world of the author, the period in which he was living, the time of David and Solomon, and the characters who dominated the news in his day."[39] For example, Rendsburg notes how the stories in Genesis repeatedly emphasize the younger son being favored over the older—Isaac over Ishmael, Jacob over Esau, Judah and Joseph over their older brothers—even though this contradicts the ancient Near Eastern law of primogeniture, which privileges the older son. Why do these stories in Genesis emphasize the younger superseding the older? According to Rendsburg, it is partly because this is precisely what David (the youngest of Jesse's sons) and Solomon (one of David's younger sons) do when they assume the throne. They advance to power ahead of their older brothers. Establishing a precedent for this pattern in Israel's sacred history provides justification for the advancement of David and Solomon over their older brothers. For Rendsburg, however, this intentional shaping of the past does not mean that later writers simply created the patriarchs out of whole cloth. "The book of Genesis does not invent the material about the lives of these men," writes Rendsburg, "for I do believe in their basic historicity, but it casts the traditions in a new light."

While other examples could be given,[40] these should be sufficient to demonstrate the way Old Testament narratives use the past for the sake of the present. Interestingly, some of the same techniques used to accomplish this in antiquity are still being used today. Rendsburg cites several modern examples, the best of which he believes is Arthur Miller's play *The Crucible*.[41] Although the play is ostensibly about witch trials in Salem, Massachusetts, in the seventeenth century, the story is not really about the seventeenth century at all. Instead, it is really a play about the twentieth century, the author's historical context, since it critiques the McCarthianism of the 1950s. Another example is the motion picture and television series *M*A*S*H*. The movie and television show were set in Korea even though they were really about the war in Vietnam. "As with *The Crucible*, so with M*A*S*H: We are looking at the historical past, but we are seeing present day-events," writes Rendsburg.[42] Even though this technique can be used profitably in certain forms of literature and media today, it is not appropriate for modern historiography. This underscores one of the major differences between ancient and modern history writing.

Old Testament Narratives Were More Concerned with Literary Persuasion than with Historical Objectivity

Since ancient writers crafted their stories to address the concerns of their respective communities, they felt free to "massage" the facts in ways that suited their particular needs. After all, they were more concerned with persuasion than with precision. To this end, ancient historiographers sometimes engaged in practices that would be completely unacceptable to many of their modern counterparts today.

Consider the consistently negative portrayal of King Ahab in 1 Kings. The writer has nothing good to say about Ahab and claims he "did evil in the sight of the Lord more than all who were before him" (1 Kgs. 16:30). What is conspicuously absent from the story of Ahab in 1 Kings is any mention of his participation in the battle of Qarqar. From other sources, we know that a coalition of Syro-Palestinian forces successfully halted the advancing Assyrian army at Qarqar, a site in Syria on the West side of the Orontes River, in 853 BCE. Ahab's involvement in this coalition is recorded on what is known as the Monolith Inscription. According to this propagandistic Assyrian account of the battle—which naturally boasts a great Assyrian victory— *hmm* Ahab is said to have contributed two thousand chariots and ten thousand soldiers. Even though these totals are certainly exaggerated, they nevertheless suggest the significance of Ahab's participation in this conflict. So why does the writer of Kings fail to mention it? For one simple reason: it does not fit his historiographic agenda.

The writer of Kings believes that God blesses individuals who obey God, particularly those who worship only Yahweh and who do so in Jerusalem. Ahab fails on both counts, leaving the writer of Kings on the horns of a dilemma. Since Ahab's victory at Qarqar suggests divine blessing, it does not suit the writer's purposes. *not truely* Therefore, he conveniently omits any mention of Ahab's involvement in the battle. While it is true that historians need to be selective and must make difficult choices about what to include and what to leave out, mentioning Ahab without citing his involvement in the battle of Qarqar is a huge omission. It would be like writing a history of Abraham Lincoln and never mentioning the Civil War. Such an obvious omission clearly reveals the writer's bias against Ahab, and this raises legitimate questions about how accurate his presentation is at other points in the narrative.

Another example of a selective omission—this time used for more favorable ends—is the Chronicler's silence about David's adultery with Bathsheba and subsequent murder of Uriah. The Chronicler was certainly aware of these scandalous events. After all, one of the Chronicler's primary sources was the book of 2 Samuel, which is precisely where this ugly story unfolds (2 Sam. 11-12). Still, he consciously omits any mention of this sordid affair in 1 Chronicles 20, where we would expect to find it. The reason for this omission is simple. The Chronicler wants to portray David in the best possible light. Since this episode does not help his cause, he skips over it with nary a word. The result is an exceedingly sanitized portrayal of David. Literary practices like these suggest that scribes in ancient Israel were far more concerned with persuasion than with historical precision. While this certainly does not mean we cannot glean any historical insights about the events in question, it does require us to proceed with considerable caution given the obvious biases evident in some of these narratives.

Old Testament Narratives Put Words in People's Mouths

Another way Old Testament narratives differ significantly from modern historiography involves the creation and use of direct speech. Direct speech, or the words people say in Old Testament narratives, is a very important feature of these stories.[43] Naturally, many modern readers of the Bible assume that these words originated with the person who spoke them. Therefore, when they read Samuel's warning about the cost of having a king (1 Samuel 8), or Solomon's prayer at the dedication of the temple (1 Kings 8), they typically assume that these words more or less reflect what Samuel and Solomon actually said on those occasions. While this seems reasonable enough, it often appears not to have been the case.

In his groundbreaking work *The Deuteronomistic History*, German scholar Martin Noth examined some of the most significant "speeches" contained in the Old Testament and discovered that many of them sound alike because they share many of the same key words and phrases.[44] This is especially true of speeches made during transitional phases in Israel's story, when individuals were reflecting on the past or looking toward the future. Noth identified several speeches that shared these similarities, including Moses's speech to the Israelites prior to entering Canaan (Deuteronomy 1–4), Joshua's speeches before and after the conquest (Joshua 1, 23), Samuel's speech at the beginning of the monarchy (1 Samuel 12), and Solomon's prayer at the dedication of the temple (1 Kings 8).[45] Noth proposed that all these speeches were the creation of a single writer, whom he referred to as the Deuteronomistic Historian. This historian, who lived hundreds of years after these revered figures from Israel's past, apparently put his own words on their lips to promote certain theological ideas that were important to him.

While this practice would surely discredit a modern historian, creating speeches and putting them in the mouths of historical figures was common in the ancient world. Many writers put words into the mouths of the "greats" of the past. While this does not mean that everything spoken by this or that biblical character is suspect, it does force us to rethink some of our most fundamental convictions about the purpose and historical accuracy of these speeches. Once again, we are reminded of how different Old Testament narratives are from modern historiography.

Old Testament Narratives View the World Theologically

Finally, one of the most noticeable differences between ancient and modern history writing concerns the kinds of reasons given for why things happen. The writers of the Old Testament, and ancient historiographers generally, frequently provide theological explanations for events both large and small. In the Old Testament, God is routinely portrayed as active in human affairs. God speaks directly to individuals, opens and closes wombs, gives victory and defeat in battle, causes famines, and performs all sorts of miracles.

Obviously, this is quite different from modern history writing, which operates by a different set of principles. Modern historiographers look at a wide range of factors—social, political, economic, ethnic, and religious—to make sense of events but rarely assign the kind of overt theological explanations one encounters in the Bible. Very few historians, for example, would explain the Holocaust as God's punishment on the Jews or the terrorist attacks on September 11, 2001, as God's judgment on the United States of America. On this point, perhaps more than any other, it becomes apparent that ancient historiography and modern historiography represent two very different approaches to writing history. We will have much more to say about Israel's practice of writing "theologized history" in a later chapter since it is central to our effort to deal responsibly with disturbing divine behavior in Old Testament narratives.[46]

———

The first epigraph for this chapter was this quote from Tremper Longman: "The events of the Bible are as real as what happened to you today. So the first important principle of reading the historical books, or any book of the Bible that intends to teach history, is to *learn how God treated His people in space and time in previous generations.*"[47] A statement like this assumes that everything we encounter in the "historical books" is historically accurate. Although Longman does not say this in so many words, he clearly implies that we need not question the historicity of these texts. Nor should we ask if these events can be corroborated by other ancient Near Eastern texts or recent archaeological discoveries. According to Longman, such matters need not concern us.[48] We must simply assume the historical accuracy of these accounts, observe how God dealt with Israel, and accept this as revelatory of God's nature and character.

In this chapter, we observed how things like archaeological evidence and even differing accounts within the biblical text raise legitimate questions about the historicity of certain aspects of Old Testament narratives. More fundamentally, we explored some of the essential characteristics of Old Testament narratives and discovered that they differ markedly from those of modern history writing. This leads me to conclude, *contra* Longman and others, that we should not necessarily assume that things basically took place the way the Old Testament claims they did. I have no doubt that sometimes they did, but I am equally confident that at other times they did not. Those responsible for writing Old Testament narratives do not seem to have been primarily concerned with historical precision in order to create an account of what actually happened in this or that instance. Instead, as we will discuss later, they wrote for other kinds of reasons.[49]

By suggesting that Old Testament narratives were not written primarily to preserve a record of what took place in the past, I am *not* suggesting they are historically worthless. On the contrary, I believe these texts are of enormous historical value. But as we have observed, the historical value of these texts often has more to do with the author's historical context than the story's. When reading Old Testament narratives, we can learn a great deal about ancient customs, the nature of kingship, foreign relations, military practices, and so on. In some instances, we can also learn about specific historical events, such as the destruction of Jerusalem by the Babylonians in 587 BCE. This event, described in 2 Kings 25, is corroborated by other ancient Near Eastern texts and by the archaeological evidence. When dealing with the question of historicity, the challenge is to avoid extremes. To claim that everything recorded in the Bible actually happened is naive. But it is equally misguided to declare that nothing, or next to nothing, reported in the Bible actually happened. The truth lies somewhere in between those extremes and varies from text to text.[50] Answering the historical question must be done on a case-by-case basis.[51]

Acknowledging that there are some things in the Bible that did not happen, or did not happen as described, effectively exonerates God from certain kinds of morally questionable behavior. For example, if Jericho and Ai were not inhabited when the Israelites supposedly entered the land, this means the Israelites neither conquered these cities nor slaughtered their inhabitants. Therefore, it stands to reason that God never told Joshua, "See, I have handed Jericho over to you, along with its king and soldiers," (Josh 6:2), or "See, I have handed over to you the king of Ai with his people, his city, and his land. You shall do to Ai and its king as you did to Jericho and its king" (Josh 8:1b-2a). In these and many other instances, it is reasonable to conclude that God did not do or say everything the Old Testament claims. Such a conclusion has enormous implications for our study since it allow us to explore new options for addressing the problem of disturbing divine behavior. But accepting this conclusion also raises other challenging questions. If things did not happen the way the Old Testament claims, why did the Israelites portray them this way? And why would ancient writers depict God issuing such terribly troubling decrees if they knew full well God never said such things? These are important questions we will need to address.

Before we tackle these issues, however, more needs to be said about the conclusion I have drawn in this chapter—namely, that some of the things Old Testament narratives claim happened never did. I am keenly aware that some readers may find it very disheartening to learn that Jonah probably was not swallowed by a whale and that the walls of Jericho probably never came tumbling down, at least not in the miraculous way described in Joshua. Such revelations are often disappointing, especially for those who have always believed these stories referred to real people and actual historical events.

Others may feel more threatened, or even angry, than disappointed. Some may wonder: Doesn't raising questions about the historicity of the Bible cast doubt on its trustworthiness and reliability? Doesn't it corrode the very foundation of Christian faith? Who are we to stand in judgment on God's word? These are sensitive questions that need to be addressed before some people will be willing to entertain—let alone accept—the conclusion drawn in this chapter. Therefore, I have devoted the next chapter to this task. Chapter 6 responds to some of the objections people typically raise against denying the essential historicity of Old Testament narratives and also considers some of the dangers of demanding that every narrative be taken as a historically accurate rendering of the past.

CHAPTER 6

Concerns about Raising the Historical Question

Now I don't know if it happened this way or not,
but I know this story is true.

—NATIVE AMERICAN STORYTELLER[1]

In chapter 4, we spent a considerable amount of time discussing various ways people attempt to defend God's behavior in the Old Testament. Yet, despite these noble efforts, we concluded that none of these approaches provides a truly satisfactory solution to the problem of disturbing divine behavior. Instead, each was found wanting in certain respects. Toward the end of the chapter, we noted that all of the approaches discussed operated with the common control belief that God actually said and did everything the Bible claims. It was further noted that this control belief rests on the assumption that, by and large, the Old Testament accurately reflects what happened in the past.

Since one's acceptance or rejection of this assumption is critical in determining what kind of solutions can and cannot be proposed for addressing problematic portrayals of God in the Old Testament, it is essential to examine its validity. That was our primary task in chapter 5, where we explored evidence that challenged and problematized this assumption of historicity. It became clear that Old Testament narratives were not intended to be simple historical reports of past events. While these narratives certainly contain historical elements, we discovered that it is misguided to assume that all the events reported in the Old Testament took place, or took place just as described. Therefore, it is unnecessary to be constrained by this assumption when formulating a response to problematic portrayals of God in the Old Testament.

Despite the evidence cited in the previous chapter, some readers may still feel compelled to affirm the assumption that the Old Testament faithfully records what Israel—and God—actually said and did. For various reasons, they will resist the conclusion that the Old Testament sometimes describes things that did not occur. Since accepting this conclusion—that not everything in the Old Testament happened, or happened as described—is indispensable to the argument I am making in this book, it is important to explore some of the objections people typically raise to questioning the historicity of the Old Testament. In the pages that follow, I discuss several of these objections and offer some initial responses to them. I then go on to raise some concerns of my own, not about the propriety of questioning the historicity of Old Testament narratives but about the wisdom of assuming that Old Testament narratives are, in essence, historically reliable reports of exactly what occurred in the past. As I will argue, maintaining that position creates some serious difficulties for interpreters. But first, we turn our attention to some of the objections that have been raised to questioning the historicity of Old Testament narratives.

Objections to Doubting the Historicity of Old Testament Narratives

It Sounds Historical

Some people object to treating Old Testament narratives as anything other than historical accounts for the simple reason that this is what they seem to be. In their estimation, these stories appear to be straightforward historical accounts that provide numerous details about real people, places, and events. Since they see nothing in these narratives that would cause them to question their essential historicity, they naturally assume the text provides an accurate rendering of how things occurred.

At one level, this seems reasonable enough. At many, many points, the Old Testament does refer to real people, places, and events. Nevertheless, just because something "sounds historical" does not necessarily mean that it is. Writers can use real people, places, and events for fictional purposes. Novelists, such as James Michener, try to achieve verisimilitude when crafting their stories. They regularly use real settings, and they create believable characters in order to make their stories engaging and credible. Yet the stories they tell remain fictional. Just because a piece of writing contains certain "historical elements" does not automatically render it historical.

Moreover, I wonder whether the reason these stories *sound* historical to so many people has more to do with their preconceived notions about these stories than with the stories themselves. As noted previously, since many individuals have been conditioned to regard these stories as historical accounts, they can hardly hear them in any other way. I would argue that this "conditioning" is one of the main reasons people fail to see the indicators signaling that these stories are not purely objective reports of what happened in the past. But people who have never been sensitized to these "signals," and who have always been taught that everything in the Bible happened as described, are not very likely to notice them. Instead, their deeply held expectations that these stories took place override the evidence suggesting that something other than straightforward historical reporting is at hand. As discussed previously, it is crucial to recognize that Old Testament narrative is a unique literary genre that must be read and interpreted on its own terms.[2]

It Is Unnecessary and Irreverent to Question the Bible

Others object to questioning the historicity of Old Testament narratives because they feel such an interrogation is either unnecessary or irreverent. Their feelings about this are typically related to their view of the Bible and God's role in forming it. Since they believe that God was heavily involved in producing the Bible, they would argue that God prevented human authors from making any errors, or at least any really big mistakes. If God stands behind the process, why question the essential accuracy of these stories? Surely God would not allow these authors to write stories that never actually happened—especially when many of these stories speak of God's involvement in Israel's affairs.

These convictions about the Bible's divine origins and its relative "perfection" explain people's squeamishness about questioning its historical accuracy. To them it feels disrespectful to question the Bible. Most people do not like critiquing the work of a peer, let alone something believed to be the work of God. Who are we, as mere mortals, to question the accuracy of something God produced?

Obviously, this line of reasoning contains huge assumptions about the divine nature of the Bible. But if we come to a different understanding of the Bible's origins, one that allows much more room for human involvement in the process, this reticence to question its historicity is greatly diminished. Since this is a very important issue, and one that is dealt with at some length in appendix B, suffice it to say that various perspectives on the question of the divine inspiration of Scripture exist, not all of which suggest that God was concerned with ensuring that people only wrote about things that actually happened. Moreover, if people were *not* primarily writing these texts to preserve a record of what happened in the past, as previously argued, then it seems only natural to ask questions about the historical accuracy of what they wrote.

It Involves Doubting, and Doubt Is Bad

Another reason many hesitate to question the historical accuracy of the Bible is because they perceive questioning as doubting and they perceive doubting as being bad. Since doubt is often equated with a lack of faith, believers who have doubts are viewed as spiritual weaklings. Yet this seems a rather narrow and pejorative view of doubt. Doubt can be very positive and productive. It keeps us from being gullible. It compels us to ask questions and find answers. I would even go so far as to say that without doubt we cannot have genuine belief. Without doubt, we would take everything we hear at face value. We would "believe" everything and therefore believe nothing. Unless we really struggle with our beliefs and ask the hard questions, how can we know whether our faith is worth believing? Socrates once said: "The unexamined life is not worth living." In a similar vein, one might say that the unexamined faith is not worth believing. From this perspective, it would seem that questioning the Bible is actually a form of healthy inquiry that is necessary for a mature and robust faith.

Obviously, doubt can be taken to unhealthy extremes, and certain kinds of doubt can be symptomatic of deeper spiritual problem. For instance, if we confess a sin to God but doubt that God is either willing or able to forgive us, our relationship with God will certainly suffer. Similarly, if we have doubts about God's existence, it will probably be difficult to relate meaningfully to God; we are unlikely to worship and adore a being we are not even sure is real. Having persistent doubts like these that call into question God's willingness to forgive or God's very existence do not strike me as signs of spiritual health.

On the other hand, calling into question the historicity of the conquest narrative or the book of Jonah hardly seems to represent a "spiritual problem." The church has historically done a fine job of teaching people about the importance of belief, and belief is very important. The problem, however, is that the church sometimes encourages—even pressures—people to believe in the wrong things. It is vitally important to believe in the goodness of God, the forgiveness of sins, and the hope of life eternal, among other things. But is it really necessary to believe in the historicity of every Old Testament narrative, especially when the evidence clearly seems to point in other directions? Why is it regarded as a lack of faith to express genuine doubts about the historical reliability of the flood story, or about God's incineration of Nadab and Abihu, or about the divine mandate to wipe out the entire Canaanite population? Instead, I would argue that it honors God when we use all of our critical faculties to probe, question, and even challenge what we read in the Bible. God is pleased when we engage the text with our minds, not upset by such inquiry. Given the nature and function of Old Testament narratives, it is entirely appropriate—and sometimes even necessary—to raise questions about the historical reliability of these stories. This constitutes a faithful reading of this particular literary genre.

It Leads Down a Slippery Slope

One of the most common objections to questioning the historical accuracy of Old Testament narratives is the fear that such questions lead down a slippery slope. If we conclude that the story of Jonah did not really happen, what is to stop us from saying the same about all the rest? Are the stories about people like Abraham, Moses, David, and Solomon equally "untrue"? Where do we draw the line? It would be convenient to say, "Genesis 1–11 should be read nonhistorically, but once we get to the story of Abraham in Genesis 12 everything that follows is historical." Unfortunately, the situation is far more complicated. Old Testament texts resist such neat compartmentalization. There is no such "line" that can be drawn in the Bible between what did and did not happen.

Nevertheless, concluding that this or that Old Testament story did not take place does not mean the whole thing is nothing more than a bunch of campfire tales with little or no basis in history. Such a conclusion is reductionistic, unwarranted, and inaccurate. The Old Testament contains a great deal of extremely valuable historical information. It describes many real people and events, some of which are nicely corroborated by extrabiblical evidence.[3] We can learn a great deal about ancient Israel's leaders, international relations, beliefs, customs, hopes, and struggles from the pages of the Old Testament. But doing so requires skill and discernment. As we noted previously, ancient historiography differs considerably from its modern counterpart. One cannot simply open the Old Testament and expect it to immediately yield an objective report of exactly what happened in the past. Instead, when using the Bible to ask the historical question, one must weigh all the evidence—textual, archaeological, social-scientific—to determine what most likely did or did not occur in Israel.

It Undermines My Faith

Some Christians object to questioning the historicity of the Old Testament because they believe doing so undermines their faith. These believers see a close connection between their faith and the historical veracity of the Bible. Therefore, it is very important for them to be absolutely certain that the Bible—and the events it describes—are trustworthy and reliable. As Tremper Longman sees it: "Our faith is grounded in the veracity of the events recorded in God's Word."[4] If this is true, then questioning the accuracy of the Bible will be perceived as a challenge to their faith.

Of course, the critical question here is whether this linkage between the Bible and Christian faith is warranted. Is there a good reason to base one's faith on the historicity of the Old Testament? Does our faith rest on whether God actually sent a worldwide flood that killed everyone but eight survivors? Or would I need to abandon my Christian convictions if I concluded that God did not harden Pharaoh's heart, order the annihilation of Canaanites, or slaughter 185,000 Assyrian soldiers at the beginning of the eighth century BCE? I think not.

Let me be clear here. I am not suggesting that history is unimportant or that it makes no difference whether certain key events actually happened. On the contrary, I fully concur with the apostle Paul that if Christ was not raised from the dead, our faith is in vain (1 Cor. 15:14). But in relatively few cases, such as the one just mentioned, is it essential that the event in question actually took place as described. Most often, our faith does not hang in the balance based on how we answer the historical question. This is especially true when it comes to Old Testament narratives. Christian faith does not depend on whether the walls of Jericho came tumbling down, Jonah got swallowed by a really big fish, or David killed Goliath with nothing more than a slingshot and stone. While I am not suggesting that it makes no difference whether we believe these events actually took place, I am saying that our faith in God does not rest on the historical reliability of such events. Therefore, questioning the historicity of Old Testament narratives should not be regarded as an attack on Christian faith. Instead, raising these kinds of questions is a natural thing to do given the nature of Old Testament narratives and ancient historiographical practices.

It Diminishes Biblical Authority

Finally, many people feel that denying the historicity of the biblical narratives diminishes the authority of the Bible. How can something be true if it never happened? Doesn't the presence of "fictional" stories in the Bible undermine its credibility? These are important questions that require us to consider carefully the relationship between truth and history.

The importance of carefully distinguishing between "truth" and "history" cannot be overstated. Unfortunately, the common way the word *true* is used renders this task far more difficult. For example, suppose you and a friend have just finished watching a movie. As you are leaving the theater, your friend asks, "Do you think that movie was based on a true story?" By putting the question this way, your friend is asking whether you think the story really happened, whether it is rooted in historical events. Even granting considerable artistic license, your friend wants to know if you think the movie portrayed real people and real events. By asking if the movie was based on a true story, your friend essentially equates the words *true* and *historical*, using them as virtual synonyms.

This same semantic equalizing is reflected in the title of a relatively recent book authored by *U.S. News and World Report* religion writer Jeffrey Sheler. The book is titled *Is the Bible True?* A cursory look at the table of contents quickly reveals that Sheler is not debating whether the Bible's central theological claims are accurate. Instead, Sheler is interested in exploring whether certain parts of the Bible are historically verifiable, or at least historically plausible. As Sheler explains in his introduction: "It is a book mainly about history and about the evidence and arguments that scholars have raised in recent years that pertain to the Bible as history."[5] Given these concerns, it would have been far more appropriate—though I suspect far less marketable—to title the book *Is the Bible Historically Accurate?*

Although the practice of using "true" and "historical" as virtual synonyms is understandable, it is unfortunate because of how it conditions us to think about the Bible. Since we are taught to believe the Bible is true, we instinctively conclude that it must be historical given the way these two terms function in modern usage. No wonder so many Christians are adamant about defending the historicity of the Bible. Admitting that the Bible is not historical seems tantamount to admitting that it is not true. But this is not necessarily so. Determining whether something is historical and determining whether something is true are two fundamentally different kinds of questions. Something can be profoundly true even if it is not historical.

I routinely try to make this point in the basic Bible class I teach at Messiah College. Late in the semester, I show the class a Dr. Seuss video entitled *The Butter Battle Book*.[6] The video has a very simple plot. It describes a conflict between two groups of "people" (cartoon characters), the Yooks and the Zooks. As the story begins, we see a very small Yook and his grandfather walking toward a high stone wall. The grandson says:

> On the last day of summer, ten hours before fall, my grandfather took me out to the Wall. For a while we stood silent, and finally he said with a very sad shake of his very old head: "As you know, on this side of the Wall, we are Yooks. On the far other side of this Wall live the Zooks. And the things that you've heard about Zooks are all true, that terribly horrible thing that they do. And at every Zook house, and in every Zook town, every Zook eats his bread (shudder) with the butter side down!"

The Yooks hate the Zooks, and the Zooks return the favor, for one simple reason: they disagree over which side of the bread to butter. The Yooks butter their bread on top ("the true honest way"), while the Zooks butter their bread "down below." This causes great tension between these two groups, who seem to know virtually nothing else about each other. In order to keep an eye on the Zooks "in their land of bad butter," the elder Yook tells his grandson that he took a job on the Zook watching border patrol. Walking along the wall, he watched the Zooks closely. If they gave him any trouble, he just threatened them with a shake of his "tough-tufted prickly Snick-berry Switch." For a time, that was all that was needed to maintain order.

At this point, the story sours for the Yooks. "Then one terrible day," says grandfather Yook, "a very rude Zook by the name of VanItch, snuck up and slingshotted my Snick-berry Switch." An arms race ensues as each side builds bigger or comparable weapons. As the story draws to a close, the grandfather Yook and the Zook named Van Itch stand face-to-face on the wall, each armed with a "Big-Boy Boomeroo" (a nuclear weapon). Only then do we again hear from the grandson, who by this point has all but been forgotten. "Grandpa, be careful," he says. "Hey, easy. Oh, gee. Who's going to drop it? Will you or will he?" His grandfather replies, "Why, be patient. We'll see. We will see." A screen then appears with the words "The End," followed momentarily with the word "Maybe" underneath.

After watching this video, I ask the class three questions. First, I ask them whether what they just saw actually happened. Of course, the answer is "No." It did not actually happen because there are no such beings as "Yooks" and "Zooks." There are no such weapons as a "Stick-berry Switch" or a "Big-Boy Boomeroo." And besides, cartoons typically do not portray stories that actually happened. Next, I ask them if the story is true, to which they reply "Yes." Students easily recognize the story as symbolic of the Cold War. But beyond that there are many "truths" in the story. The story demonstrates how prejudice gets passed down from one generation to another by family members and through educational systems. Another "truth" in the story is that large conflicts often erupt over seemingly insignificant matters. After reflecting on the "truth" of the story, I then summarize what I am hearing: "It seems I hear you saying that even though this story didn't actually happen, it is still true in certain respects." Then I ask my final question: Might we apply this same line of thinking to the biblical text? In other words, is it possible that there might be things in the Bible that never actually happened but which are still profoundly true?

Some students are obviously uncomfortable with this move, but others recognize that at least some portions of the Bible contain stories that never occurred but are true all the same. The classic example is Jesus' parables. Consider one of Jesus' most well-known parables, the parable of the good Samaritan (Luke 10:30-37). Had you been in the crowd that day and asked Jesus the Samaritan's name or the town where he took the victim for lodging, the crowd would have had a good laugh at your expense! Jesus was telling a story to make a point, not to report a specific historical incident. To be sure, Jerusalem and Jericho were real cities, and there actually was a road between the two as the story claims. Moreover, we know that robbers and bandits frequently did assault people on this dangerous stretch of road in the first century. That notwithstanding, the story Jesus told about the good Samaritan did not actually take place. It was "only" a parable.

So is the parable true? Not according to the way we normally classify a story as being true. If a story must be historical to be true, then this parable is most certainly false. But this conclusion immediately exposes the inadequacy of our language and of our common notions of what constitutes a "true" story. To say this parable is not true is ridiculous. Of course it is true. It is true because it reveals God's will for how human beings are to relate to one another. Specifically, it teaches us who our neighbor is and how we should respond to someone in need, even when that someone is our enemy. The person whose question had prompted this bit of storytelling got the point. He realized that his neighbor was not just a fellow Jew, someone who looked like him or thought like him. His neighbor included even those whom he most despised, in this case a Samaritan.

In order to maintain that the Bible is true even though some parts of it might be nonhistorical, we need to move beyond narrow classifications that claim a story is true if it happened and false if it did not. Instead, we should realize that a story is true if it communicates truth. Its truthfulness does not depend on whether or not it took place. Truth can be delivered through many different genres. It can come through parables, historiographical writings, gospels—even fiction. Still, some people are uncomfortable with this because they believe a story is intrinsically more powerful if it happened in time and space. Consider this quote from Old Testament scholar Douglas Stuart in reference to the story of Jonah:

> If the events in the book actually happened, the audience's existential identification with the characters and circumstances is invariably heightened. People act more surely upon what they believe to be true in fact, than merely what they consider likely in theory. It is one thing to conclude that "Jonah is a story which illustrates the principle that we ought to allow God the right to show compassion to those whom we might think do not deserve it." It is quite another to conclude that "the ancient Israelite Jonah was a northern prophet who had to learn the hard way a lesson we ought to learn less stubbornly: our God has shown himself decisively to be a God of compassion and forgiveness—and not just toward us!" If it really happened, it is really serious. If this is the way God works in history, then a less narrow attitude toward our enemies is not just an "ought," it is a must; it is not simply a narrator's desire, it is God's enforceable revelation.[7]

According to Stuart, a story that actually took place is more powerful and authoritative than one that did not. While that certainly may be the case, it is not necessarily so. In fact, sometimes just the opposite is nearer the mark. Consider, for instance, J. R. R. Tolkien's fascinating fictional trilogy *The Lord of the Rings*. The trilogy emphasizes such values as being loyal, siding with good rather than evil, and doing the right thing even when it is extremely difficult. Tolkien's work has been enjoyed by millions of readers and contains many truths. It illustrates the value of companionship, the seductive and self-destructive nature of power, and the horror of warfare and killing. Still, in the final analysis, it is a story that never took place. Therefore, some would conclude that it cannot be as powerful as a story that actually did. To test this theory, consider this autobiographical account written while spending a summer in Warm Springs, Montana.

On Thursday, June 5, 2003, I drove to an establishment in town called "Suds and Pub" to do laundry. When I entered the shop and was contemplating which washers to use, a man informed me that the ones in front of me recently had gasoline poured down into them. Apparently, the owner's wife or ex-wife (I can't exactly recall) had a falling out. So I put my clothes in two other washers and went outside to do some reading. Later, I put my clothes in a dryer. When they were finished, I put them in the washbasket and got back in my car and drove home to Warm Springs.

This actually happened. But I doubt that anyone reading it will be particularly inspired by it. I have no confidence that it will cause anyone to change his or her thinking on topics such as loyalty, good versus evil, or the courage to act with moral conviction.

My point is simply this: a story that took place is not intrinsically more "true" or more powerful than one that did not. Stories that never actually happened can communicate profound truths and can be more powerful and persuasive than stories that happened in real time and space. In a brief article dealing the flood narrative in Genesis, Hebrew Bible scholar Ronald Hendel puts it this way: "The best stories, of course, are a vehicle for profound insights into our relationship to the world, each other, and God. . . . The biblical story of Noah's Flood is an exemplary and immortal narrative in this respect. Even if it didn't happen, it's a true story."[8] Similarly, John Goldingay makes these comments in reference to the book of Job: "That it is fiction in no way lessens its capacity to speak the truth about God and humanity. It may even do so more effectively by not being limited to the historical facts of one person's experience."[9] To claim that the Bible contains some of these types of stories—stories that did not happen or at least did not happen as described—does not necessarily diminish the "authority" of the Bible. It may, in fact, do just the opposite.

The Dangers of Demanding the Essential Historicity of Old Testament Narratives

Thus far, we have considered some typical objections raised by those who feel uncomfortable questioning the historicity of Old Testament narratives. I have attempted to demonstrate, albeit briefly, that these objections are not compelling and need not discourage us from inquiring about the historical veracity of Old Testament stories. In fact, rather than supporting Christian faith and beliefs, uncategorical assertions about the historical accuracy of these stories often have just the opposite effect. Those who insist that Old Testament narratives contain an accurate rendering of the past should be aware of the difficulties involved in maintaining this assumption and the dangers associated with demanding their essential historicity. We turn now to consider a few of these challenges.

It Misconstrues the Nature and Function of Old Testament Narratives

One of the problems with demanding the historical veracity of Old Testament narratives is that it misconstrues the nature and function of this ancient literary genre. As noted in the previous chapter, the primary purpose of Old Testament narratives was not to record exactly what took place. Though many of these stories do contain historically valuable information, assuming they were written to report what actually happened reflects a misunderstanding of their essential nature. Moreover, approaching Old Testament narratives in this way fails to acknowledge how significantly different ancient historiography is from its modern counterpart. Demanding the essential historicity of these stories imposes very modern assumptions on these very ancient texts, creating expectations in readers that these stories are unable to fulfill.

Ancient writers were not particularly interested in the "Did it actually happen?" question. They were not particularly concerned about the past in and of itself. That is not to suggest these writers had no concern with antiquarian interests. They clearly did. But *preserving* the past was not their primary concern. Instead, as noted previously, they were interested in *portraying* the past in a way that would inform the present. They used the past—and sometimes even invented the past—to address pressing questions and concerns in the present. They were not particularly concerned about making sure all the details in their stories "checked out" or were historically verifiable.[10] While that is not to suggest that these narratives have no connection to real people, places, or events, it is to say that their primary interest lies elsewhere. By demanding the essential historicity of these texts, we misconstrue the nature and function of Old Testament narratives and attempt to read this literary genre in a way it was never intended to be read. Divine inspiration

It Jeopardizes Christianity's Credibility

Demanding the essential historicity of Old Testament narratives has the unfortunate effect of jeopardizing Christianity's credibility. As noted earlier, some Christians make a strong connection between the foundations of their faith and the historical veracity of the Bible. But this is a dangerous move, one that puts them in an awkward situation. What will they do when archaeological discoveries and extrabiblical texts contradict certain aspects of the biblical story? How will they respond when biblical scholars conclude that a central biblical event—like the conquest—did not happen as told in the book of Joshua, if at all? They really have only one choice. Regardless of how persuasive the evidence may be, they must defend the historicity of the Bible at all costs. For them, their faith quite literally depends on it! People who do so, however sincere they may be, create unnecessary difficulties for themselves and others by reading the Bible in a way it was never intended to be read.

Some of the most embarrassing moments in the history of the church have been those in which Christians have publically attempted to "defend" the accuracy of the Bible. One need only recall the humiliating performance of William Jennings Bryan at the Scopes Monkey Trial as case in point.[11] The Scopes Monkey Trial was held in Dayton, Tennessee, in 1925 to determine whether a biology teacher named John Scopes was guilty of teaching evolution. Earlier that year, the state had made it illegal to teach evolution in public schools, but Scopes had blatantly disregarded the law. William Jennings Bryan, a well-known Christian lawyer, was called upon to be the lead prosecutor, while the ACLU brought in a team of lawyers to defend Scopes headed by an agnostic named Clarence Darrow.

The trial dragged on for many days in a sweltering Tennessee courtroom. It soon became clear that more was on trial than just a biology teacher named John Scopes. As George Marsden describes it:

> At the height of the proceedings he [Bryan] allowed himself to be cross-examined by the greatest trial lawyer of the day *on the subject of the precise accuracy of the Bible.* . . . The result was a debacle. Darrow forced Bryan into admitting that he could not answer the standard village-atheist type questions regarding the literal interpretation of Scripture. Bryan did not know how Eve could be created from Adam's rib, where Cain got his wife, or where the great fish came from that swallowed Jonah. He said that he had never contemplated what would happen if the earth stopped its rotation so that the sun would "stand still."[12]

Although Scopes was ultimately found guilty, making Bryan the winner, the case was a total failure for Christianity. Apart from appealing to God's miraculous power, there are no satisfying rational answers to such questions. Demanding that events like these took place as described jeopardizes the credibility of the Christian faith. It forces believers into an indefensible position from which they offer strained explanations that are neither convincing nor believable.

But it need not be this way. We are under no divine obligation to defend the historicity of Old Testament narratives. Instead, as we develop a more mature understanding of the nature and function of Old Testament narratives, we recognize that these stories were not written with the intention of reporting exactly what happened. We realize these stories do have historical value, but we also recognize how that value varies considerably from one narrative to another. This allows us to accept new discoveries that inform our understanding of the history of Israel, even when they present a different picture of the past than the one familiar to us from the pages of Scripture. Thus, we need not fear that archaeology or some other discipline will reveal a new piece of evidence that will undermine the essential truths of Christianity. Instead, we are free to incorporate the best science has to offer as we attempt to understand the Bible and evaluate its rendering of the past.

Unfortunately, the church sometimes gives the impression that taking the Bible seriously means reading all of it historically—unless, of course, the text explicitly suggests otherwise, as in the case of Jesus' parables. But in order to take the Bible seriously, must we really believe that Jonah got swallowed by a big fish, survived inside its belly for three days and nights, preached an astonishingly brief "sermon" resulting in the conversion of a city full of non-Israelites, and enjoyed the shade of a plant that grew overnight in *Jack and the Beanstalk* fashion and was destroyed the next day by a divinely appointed worm? Not according to William Placher. As he astutely observes: "If someone insists on the historical truth of Jonah—conversion of Ninevah [*sic*], big fish, and all—they are not taking the Bible more seriously than the rest of us. They are misunderstanding it."[13] If being a Christian is perceived as needing to believe such fantastic things actually happened, it is not difficult to understand why some people do not become Christians. While I have no doubt that God performs miracles, and think there are good reasons to believe that some miracles in the Bible happened as described, it is unnecessary and problematic to insist that *all* of them did.[14] Doing so jeopardizes the credibility of the Christian faith.

It Distorts the Character of God

One of the greatest dangers of demanding the essential historicity of Old Testament narratives is the damage it does to our understanding of who God is and how God acts in the world. When certain texts are believed to record what God actually said and did in the past, the picture of God that emerges is deeply disturbing. Take, for example, the divine command to exterminate the Amalekites:

> Thus says the Lord of hosts, "I will punish the Amalekites for what they did in opposing the Israelites when they came up out of Egypt. Now go and attack Amalek, and utterly destroy all that they have; do not spare them, but kill both man and woman, child and infant, ox and sheep, camel and donkey." (I Sam. 15:2-3)

For those who take this divine command as historical fact, it follows that the annihilation of the Amalekites was the will of God. Moreover, it reveals at least four highly troubling propositions about God: (1) God sometimes commissions and sanctions genocide, (2) God sometimes punishes people by commanding other people to kill them, (3) God sometimes punishes one group of people for the sins of another group, and (4) God sometimes demands the death of people who apparently have little or no opportunity to repent. These "truths" necessarily follow when reading the divine command as historical fact. But does this accurately represent the true nature and character of God? If so, it is certainly not the God many Christians today worship.

Reading a story like Jonah historically also raises significant theological problems. God's actions become terribly unsettling if we believe God specifically called Jonah to a task God knew the prophet despised. According to pastor Mark Buchanan:

> The story of Jonah confirms a dark suspicion we have about God. The suspicion is, God will always ask me to do the thing I least want to do, go to the very last place I desire to go. If I say I won't go to the prairies or India, God will send me there. If I tell him I hate Bosnians, or Tutsis, or French Canadians, that's exactly to whom he'll send me.[15]

wrong conclusion

Is this the God Christians worship? Does God search our hearts, discover what we least want to do, and then call us to go and do it? If you believe the story of Jonah is historically reliable and accept its view of God, you might think so. While many additional examples could be supplied to demonstrate how a historical reading of these texts can lead to distorted views of God, we need not linger here since extensive examples have already been considered.[16] Suffice it to say, demanding the essential historicity of all Old Testament narratives causes us to conceive of God in ways that are highly problematic.

———

For many Christians, questioning the historicity of the Bible is a very sensitive issue. This is especially true for those who link the historical accuracy of the Bible to their Christian faith. For them, separating these two is a very difficult and painful process. In this chapter and the previous one, I have tried to demonstrate why this linkage is both unnecessary and unwarranted. This chapter discussed many of the objections typically expressed by those wary of asking questions about the historical reliability of the Bible. This was done in an effort to explain why these are not particularly valid reasons for maintaining this presumption of historicity. We also noted some of the dangers of demanding that every Old Testament narrative is a historically reliable record of what happened in the past. These are substantial and cannot be easily dismissed.

If Old Testament narratives do not always reflect what actually happened, as I have argued, then new options for coming to terms with these difficult depictions of God are possible. Since there are no compelling reasons for assuming the essential historicity of all Old Testament narratives, in the final section of this book we will consider an alternate approach to dealing with disturbing divine behavior that is not constrained by this assumption.

To reiterate a point noted above, the fact that Old Testament narratives do not always record exactly what happened should not be seen as a threat to Christian faith. God is not limited to communicating truth only through historical accounts.

true

Rather, being infinitely creative and resourceful, God can speak to us through a broad range of literary genres. Moreover, since our faith is *not* inextricably linked to the historical veracity of Old Testament narratives, we need not be concerned that some of these stories do not reflect what actually took place. Rather, we should do our best to read and understand this unique literary genre on its own terms, fully confident that doing so does not threaten Christian faith or undermine the authority of Scripture. Christians who love God and live lives of faith and obedience can and do read Old Testament narratives in this way. It is a perfectly reasonable and responsible way to approach these texts.

But if the *primary* purpose of Old Testament narratives was not to preserve a record of past events, then why were they written in the first place? What motivated people to create these narratives, and what was their intended function? We have already answered these questions in a general way in the previous chapter. Now we are ready to inquire more specifically about some of the particular functions of these narratives. Doing so will significantly enhance our understanding of this literary genre. This, in turn, will put us in a better position to evaluate the role of God in these stories as we attempt to understand why God has been portrayed in various—and sometimes disturbing—ways.

CHAPTER 7

The Functions of
Old Testament Narrative

The past is a foreign country: they do things differently there.

—L. P. Hartley[1]

Since people write for many different reasons—to inform, to entertain, to persuade, to express deep emotion, to explore human nature, or just to earn a paycheck—it stands to reason that writing takes many different forms. Even a quick look on the shelves of your local bookstore will reveal a wide assortment of books written in a dizzying array of literary genres. The choices include technical writing, analytical writing, poetic writing, fictional writing, autobiographical writing, and creative writing, to name just a few.

One of the first things we notice about a book is the kind of book it is. This provides us with very important information and helps us know what to expect from it. Many modern authors state their purpose for writing in the preface or introduction of the book, which provides a general sense of what the book is about. Unfortunately, this is not the case with many ancient writings.

Typically, ancient writers did not explicitly state their purpose for writing.[2] This greatly complicates our reading of these texts, not the least of which those found in the Old Testament. The Old Testament comes with no preface or introduction, nor does it contain an overarching statement of purpose. Since the Old Testament contains a collection of books representing a wide range of literary genres written by many different authors over hundreds of years, it is somewhat artificial to ask generally about its purpose or function. Still, when the question is posed that way, a typical Christian response goes something like this: the Old Testament was written to record God's dealings with Israel so that future generations might know of God's loving faithfulness and might learn how to live in obedience to God. While it is true that the Old Testament does, at times, display God's love and faithfulness, and while it certainly can help people know how to live in obedience to God, this explanation does not account for why many of these texts were written in the first place.

This chapter explores some of the reasons why ancient writers produced the kind of narratives we now find in the Old Testament. After discussing several of these reasons for writing, we will use the conquest narrative in the book of Joshua as a case study to consider how this particular narrative may have functioned in Israel. By better understanding *why* these texts were written, we come one step closer to making sense of the problematic portrayals of God contained in them.

Reasons for Writing Old Testament Narratives

When discussing some of the general characteristics of Old Testament narratives in chapter 5, we emphasized that ancient writers often used the past for the sake of the present. We are now ready to look more specifically at how they did this and what they hoped to accomplish by using the past in this way. Although the reasons given below represent only some of many possibilities, they should be sufficient to illustrate the kind of factors that motivated people to write these narrative in the first place insofar as that can be determined.[3]

To Explain National Failures and Disasters

Some Old Testament narratives were written to provide explanations for Israel's national failures and disasters. They attempted to make sense of the past by answering nagging questions about what went wrong. In the opening chapters of the book of Judges, for example, the writer seems intent on answering a question that must have weighed heavily on the minds of many Israelites: If God gave us the land of Canaan, why don't we fully possess it? As the years passed, it is not difficult to imagine how Israel's partial possession of the land created real cognitive dissonance for some Israelites when set alongside the theological conviction that the whole land was theirs by divine right. This dilemma required some sort of explanation.

Scholars have observed that the book of Judges begins with two introductions set back to back: Judg. 1:1—2:5 and Judg. 2:6—3:6. In the first introduction, the reasons given for Israel's partial possession of the land are largely practical. We are told that the tribe of Judah, though partly successful, was ultimately unable to fully subdue "the inhabitants of the plain."

The Lord was with [the tribe of] Judah, and he took possession of the hill country, but could not drive out the inhabitants of the plain, because they had chariots of iron. (Judg. 1:19)

According to this verse, Judah's fighting force was technologically inferior to the inhabitants of the plain. Their adversaries had iron chariots, the stealth bombers of their day. Judah had no such military hardware and thus was no match for them. Although in this instance the people of Judah were *unable* to subdue their enemies, on numerous occasions the people of Israel appear *unwilling* to do so. Time and again, we find the Israelites reluctant to expel or exterminate the inhabitants of Canaan. Although the text does not explicitly say why, it provides a very good clue. Israel found it more advantageous to enslave people rather than to eliminate them (Judg. 1:28, 30, 33, 35)!

In addition to these pragmatic reasons, the first introduction also provides a theological explanation for Israel's less than total control of the land. Israel had failed to obey God in certain matters, which resulted in their failure to occupy the land fully. Specifically, Israel is charged with making forbidden covenants with the people of Canaan and refusing to tear down their altars (Judg. 2:2). Therefore, the angel of the Lord tersely informs them: "I will not drive them out before you" (Judg. 2:3).

The second introduction focuses exclusively on the theological reasons for Israel's failure and says nothing about Israel's inability or unwillingness to drive out the people of the land. According to Judg. 2:6—3:6, God has decided to stop driving out the inhabitants of the land because of Israel's flagrant disobedience.

So the anger of the Lord was kindled against Israel; and he said, "Because this people have transgressed my covenant that I commanded their ancestors, and have not obeyed my voice, I will no longer drive out before them any of the nations that Joshua left when he died." (Judg. 2:20-21)

In the second introduction, disobedience is not the only reason given for Israel's failure. We are also told that God intentionally allowed some of the indigenous nations to remain in the land in order to test Israel's obedience, to see if they would keep God's commandments. We read:

In order to test Israel, whether or not they would take care to walk in the way of the Lord as their ancestors did, the Lord had left those nations, not driving them out at once, and had not handed them over to Joshua. (Judg. 2:22-23)

They were for the testing of Israel, to know whether Israel would obey the commandments of the Lord, which he commanded their ancestors by Moses. (Judg. 3:4)

This is a test Israel promptly failed. "So the Israelites lived among the Canaanites, the Hittites, the Amorites, the Perizzites, the Hivites, and the Jebusites; and they took their daughters as wives for themselves, and their own daughters they gave to their sons; and they worshiped their gods." According to the divine mandate in Deut. 7:1-3, this is exactly what was *not* supposed to happen. (Judg. 3:5-6)

In addition to explaining the continuing presence of Canaanites in the land as a result of Israel's disobedience and as a test to determine whether Israel would obey God, the second introduction supplies yet another reason for their failure.[4] This is found in Judg. 3:1-3, a passage I recall troubling me as an undergraduate student taking a course on the book of Judges:

> Now these are the nations that the Lord left to test all those in Israel who had no experience of any war in Canaan (it was only that successive generations of Israelites might know war, to teach those who had no experience of it before): the five lords of the Philistines, and all the Canaanites, and the Sidonians, and the Hivites who lived on Mount Lebanon, from Mount Baal-hermon as far as Lebo-hamath. (Judg. 3:1-3)

According to this passage, God allowed some of the indigenous population to remain for military training.[5] Suppose all the Canaanites had been driven out right away. How would later generations of Israelites learn how to fight? This explanation, which suggests some Canaanites were left around for the express purpose of learning warfare, casts God in a rather dubious light.[6]

The presence of so many different—and at times competing—explanations about why Israel did not fully possess the land says something about how terribly distressing this situation was for some Israelites. These two introductions to the book of Judges reveal a community struggling to make sense of its undesirable situation.[7] They offer numerous reasons to explain why things are they way they are. We do much the same today.

Human beings seem to possess an insatiable need to make sense of the world. This is especially true in the wake of particularly devastating events. In the months after September 11, 2001, many articles, essays, and even books were written in an attempt to make sense of this horrific act of violence. People wanted to know what drove these men to commit such a heinous act. Others wanted to know where God was in all of this.[8] Many felt a deep need to make sense of this tragic event that shattered so many basic assumptions.

Arguably, the most traumatic event ancient Israel ever experienced was the fall of Jerusalem to the Babylonians in 587 BCE. In that moment, the unthinkable had happened. Jerusalem had been destroyed, the temple lay smoldering in ashes, and the people were taken from the "land of promise" to a foreign land hundreds of miles away. It has been argued that the impetus for writing and compiling large portions of the Bible, especially many of those referred to as the Historical Books, was an attempt to explain why this terrible tragedy happened.[9] While this may be too sweeping a claim, it is unmistakably clear that some narratives deal directly with the causes of Israel's fall from grace.[10] Ancient writers were clearly interested in offering explanations about why this or that tragedy happened, and this seems to be one of the motivating factors behind the creation of some Old Testament narratives.

To Support the Ruling Elite and to Promote Their Policies

Another reason for writing Old Testament narratives was to keep the ruling elite in power and to promote their policies. Writing for political purposes was a common practice in the ancient world, and many examples of such writing have survived. Sometimes, this kind of writing is rightly classified as political propaganda, especially when it asserts a ruler's divine right to rule or refutes accusations of impropriety or illegitimacy.[11] Before looking at some biblical examples, it might help to begin with an example from the ancient Near East in order to observe some of the prominent characteristics of political propaganda. For that purpose, we briefly turn our attention to the Tukulti-Ninurta epic.

The Assyrian king Tukulti-Ninurta ruled for over thirty-five years at the end of the thirteenth century BCE. One of Tukulti-Ninurta's most noteworthy achievements during his lengthy and illustrious reign was the sack of Babylon, which resulted in the acquisition of such treasures as the statute of Marduk and the literary archives of Babylon in addition to enormous amounts of gold, silver, and other items of significant value. But despite this victory and the wealth it brought to Assyria, not everyone approved of the king's military actions. Such dissension was dangerous to Tukulti-Ninurta since it cast doubt on his right to rule. In an attempt to "set the record straight" and to suppress malicious, or possibly even seditious, charges being leveled against the king, the Tukulti-Ninurta epic was born.[12]

Commissioned as a tool "to justify and explain his king's [Tukulti-Ninurta's] conquest," the epic begins by discussing various aspects of the political relationship between King Tukulti-Ninurta and his opponent, King Kashtiliash.[13] It culminates in a series of battles that result in the Babylonians' defeat and utter disgrace. Several features of this text suggest its intention was to defend Tukulti-Ninurta against those who were inclined to question the legality, sagacity, and propriety of his actions. This is typical of political propaganda. In what follows, we will focus our attention on two key characteristics of political propaganda that appear in this account.

If you were to read the epic, one of the easiest features to spot would be the unqualified praise given to King Tukulti-Ninurta coupled with the unrelenting criticism heaped upon his opponent, King Kashtiliash. This is one of the most common features of political propaganda. Within the world of the text, Tukulti-Ninurta can do no wrong, while Kashtiliash, the ill-fated Kassite king ruling in Babylon, can do no right. The first impressions we are given of Kashtiliash are unfavorable, to say the least. Early in the epic, he is decried as "the transgressor of an oath" (line 34; see also lines 54, 72, 75). Later, he is called "the wicked, the obstinate, the heedless" (line 109; see also line 136). In fact, the epic repeatedly "contrasts the treaty treachery of Kaštiliaš with the treaty loyalty of Tukulti-Ninurta. Indeed, Kaštiliaš can hardly be mentioned without being denounced for his treachery, nor Tukulti-Ninurta without being praised for his loyalty."[14]

A second propagandistic feature of this text is the care taken to illustrate how Kashtiliash lacks divine support while Tukulti-Ninurta is favored and assisted by the gods. Near the beginning of the epic, we discover that the gods are angry with the oath-breaking Kashtiliash and abandon their respective dwellings in Babylon. We read: "Marduk abandoned his sublime sanctuary, the city [Babylon]" and "Sin left Ur, [his] holy place" (lines 39, 41). Since abandonment by the gods is a sure sign of divine displeasure, Marduk and Sin's departures signal Kashtiliash's impending doom. Tukulti-Ninurta, on the other hand, is depicted as one who is exalted by the god Enlil (line 67) and who is precious in Enlil's family (line 68). In fact, when Tukulti-Ninurta wages the decisive battle against Kashtiliash, a plethora of gods (Assur, Enlil, Anu, Sin, Adad, Shamash, Ninurta, and Ishtar) rally to his side and fight on his behalf (lines 313–20). With the deck so heavily stacked in Tukulti-Ninurta's favor, his resounding victory over Kashtiliash comes as no surprise. Moreover, Tukulti-Ninurta's victory in battle further demonstrates the justness of his cause. It implies that the sun-god Shamash, who had been called to judge the dispute on the field of battle, has ruled in his favor (lines 150 and following). In short, the gods are for Tukulti-Ninurta and against Kashtiliash. The text does a superb job of justifying the sack of Babylon as divine punishment upon Kashtiliash for his unwarranted provocations on his northern neighbor and treaty partner, Tukulti-Ninurta.

The two key features of propagandistic literature we have identified in the Tukulti-Ninurta epic are also apparent in the narratives in 1 Samuel concerning David and Saul. Whereas Saul is accused of failing to keep "the commandment of the Lord" (1 Sam. 13:13), David is described as a man after God's own heart (1 Sam. 13:14). Although Saul chases David all over the countryside in a futile effort to kill him, David spares Saul's life not once but twice (1 Samuel 24, 26). Throughout the narrative, the writer seems intent on portraying David as blameless while depicting Saul in the worst way possible. This is just what we would expect of political propaganda. Additionally, it is clear that God's favor rests on David and not on Saul. This is especially evident in the following two passages:

> Then Samuel took the horn of oil, and anointed him in the presence of his brothers; and the spirit of the Lord came mightily upon David from that day

forward. Samuel then set out and went to Ramah. Now the spirit of the Lord departed from Saul, and an evil spirit from the Lord tormented him. (1 Sam. 16:13-14; see also 1 Sam. 18:12)

Then Samuel said to Saul, "Why have you disturbed me by bringing me up?" Saul answered, "I am in great distress, for the Philistines are warring against me, and *God has turned away from me* and answers me no more, either by prophets or by dreams; so I have summoned you to tell me what I should do." Samuel said, "Why then do you ask me, since *the Lord has turned from you* and become your enemy? The Lord has done to you just as he spoke by me; for the Lord has torn the kingdom out of your hand, and given it to your neighbor, David. Because you did not obey the voice of the Lord, and did not carry out his fierce wrath against Amalek, therefore the Lord has done this thing to you today. Moreover the Lord will give Israel along with you into the hands of the Philistines; and tomorrow you and your sons shall be with me; the Lord will also give the army of Israel into the hands of the Philistines." (1 Sam. 28:15-19, emphasis mine)

Both passages illustrate the theme of divine presence and abandonment. God has taken the kingdom from Saul and given it to David. God has departed from Saul—much like the gods departed from Kashtiliash—and come mightily upon David.

These texts clearly favor David and not Saul. They were written by someone sympathetic to the Davidic dynasty who went to great lengths to portray Saul as an inept and unfit ruler. Texts like these would have been very important for David and his heirs. They legitimated their right to rule, a right that was clearly disputed by the house of Saul.[15]

Another interesting example of political propaganda related to David is found in a narrative sometimes referred to as the History of David's Rise (1 Sam. 16:14—2 Sam. 5:10), a narrative that overlaps with some of the texts cited above. It seems that a primary function of this narrative was to defend David against accusations of wrongdoing that apparently were circulating during his reign. In his important study of this topic, Hebrew Bible scholar P. Kyle McCarter lists seven accusations he believes this text addresses. The accusations are as follows:

1. David sought to advance himself at court at Saul's expense.
2. David was a deserter.
3. David was an outlaw.
4. David was a Philistine mercenary.
5. David was implicated in Saul's death.
6. David was implicated in Abner's death.
7. David was implicated in Ishbaal's death.[16]

In each case, McCarter discusses how the text demonstrates David's innocence. Take, for example, the first accusation: that David was an opportunist who tried to advance his own interests in the court at Saul's expense. McCarter points to several passages that counter this claim. The text suggests that David enters the court at Saul's request (1 Sam. 16:19-22), was loyal to Saul, and rendered great service to him (1 Sam. 16:23; 19:4-5). Moreover, David's marriage to Saul's daughter, Michal, was not a self-promoting power grab to gain access to the throne. Instead, it was in response to Saul's request that David marry his daughter, a request David initially protested because of his unworthiness (1 Sam. 18:20-21a, 23). The cumulative effect of these passages neutralizes the accusation that David somehow weaseled his way into the court to gain power for himself at Saul's expense.

After examining a variety of texts in this narrative that counter each of the accusations set forth above, McCarter writes: "The history of David's rise . . . shows David's accession to the throne of all Israel, north as well as south, to have been entirely lawful and his kingship, therefore, free of guilt. All possible charges of wrongdoing are faced forthrightly, and each in its turn is gainsaid by the course of events as related by the narrator."[17] In this way, the text defends David, thereby increasing his power and control. The use of literature for political purposes, as we have noted in these examples, is quite common in the Bible and helps us understand why some of these stories were written as they were.

why don't the other kings use propaganda.

To Encourage Certain Behaviors and Beliefs

Old Testament narratives were also written to persuade people to behave in certain ways (or to stop behaving in certain ways, as the case might be!). These narratives represent powerful stories with the potential to change the way people thought and acted. For instance, while many Israelites were apparently quite comfortable worshiping Baal, others strongly disapproved of such behavior and regarded it as an act of unfaithfulness toward Yahweh. One of the function of the Elijah-Elisha cycle in 1 Kings 17—2 Kings 13 was to counter the popularity of Baal worship. Particularly striking in this regard is 1 Kings 18, a passage that clearly demonstrates Yahweh's superiority over Baal. Stories like this one were meant to persuade people to discontinue their worship of Baal, to switch allegiances, and to recognize the power of Yahweh.

To illustrate how some Old Testament narratives may have been created to persuade people to believe and behave differently, consider the following hypothetical scenario. Imagine you are part of a church that has become very self focused and self absorbed. The people in your congregation seem to have little concern for outsiders and are very intolerant of differences. You have observed this behavior for some time and find it alarming. From your perspective, this kind of exclusivism contradicts the mission of the church, a community called to reach out to others. How would you respond? What might you do to persuade members of your church to be more inclusive and tolerant? How would you encourage them to look beyond themselves to the needs of those outside the church community? If you are the pastor, or were given the opportunity to preach, you might be tempted to try what I misguidedly did as a college student. I preached a sermon entitled "The Forgotten God," which ended with a blistering critique of the congregation's apathy and lack of concern for *me* outsiders. But this kind of frontal assault is typically not very effective. A creative story can be much more subtle and persuasive.

The hypothetical situation I described above—about an ingrown community uninterested in seeing God's love and grace poured out on foreigners—is precisely the kind of situation some scholars believe gave rise to the book of Jonah. The story of Jonah is much more than a story about a wayward prophet who acts ridiculously, much more than a humorous tale told to entertain. Instead, it represents a profound critique of a community that has grossly misunderstood the nature of God's grace. But this critique comes in a form that makes it a little less painful to hear. As people are laughing at the ridiculous behavior of this wacky prophet, they slowly begin to realize that the story is not really about Jonah and the "whale." It is about them. It is about their own prejudice and hatred. It exposes the folly of their own reticence to see God's grace extended to outsiders, especially to their enemies. Numerous Old Testament texts bear eloquent testimony to Israel's desire to see her enemies "get what they deserve." Such texts reflect a longing for revenge and a desire to see divine punishment heaped on those who have harmed them. "O daughter Babylon, you devastator!," writes the psalmist. "Happy shall they be who pay you back what you have done to us! Happy shall they be who take your little ones and dash them against the rock!" (Ps. 137:8-9). The story of Jonah suggests that such wild enthusiasm for the destruction of one's enemies is misguided.

Old Testament scholar Douglas Stuart believes this story was intended to quell some of the enthusiastic eschatological yearning for the day of the Lord. The day of the Lord represented a time in which the people believed God would punish Israel's enemies. It was a day Israel anticipated with great delight.[18] But Stuart believes this story is saying, "Don't be like Jonah." Do not be ready to receive mercy while you remain unwilling to see your enemies receive it.[19] According to commentator Leslie Allen, this story is "challenging its audience to face up to the unwelcome truth of God's sovereign compassion for foreigners."[20] The God who had been so extensively merciful on Israel's behalf should not be denied the freedom to extend such mercy to others. In short, this story was intended to challenge and change people's behavior and beliefs about God's mercy and concern for those outside of Israel. Such a difficult message had much more chance of being successful by being packaged in an entertaining yet highly provocative narrative.

Obviously, we have only been able to scratch the surface here. The functions of Old Testament narratives are many and varied, and they go well beyond those discussed in this chapter.[21] For example, Old Testament narratives also helped Israelites develop a sense of national identity. This is especially true of the first half of the book of Exodus. Here we see a master narrative that describes how the

Hebrew people came into existence as a nation. Other parts of the Old Testament, at least at some stage, represent etiologies, stories intended to explain the "origin" of a particular people, place, or practice. Some Old Testament narratives appear to be political satire, stories intended to instill a sense of superiority by poking fun at other rulers and nations.[22] Still other narratives were inspirational, instrumental in helping the people of Israel find hope in difficult times.

A Case Study: The Book of Joshua

By this point, enough has likely been said to reinforce our earlier conclusion that Old Testament narratives were not written just to record what happened. As we have seen, the reasons for writing these texts are diverse. Part of the joy of reading Old Testament narratives comes from attempting to understand why they were written and how they might have functioned in the ancient world. Admittedly, this is not always an easy task.

Determining the function of an Old Testament narrative is a precarious endeavor because of many complicating factors. For starters, one must determine the boundaries of the narrative—where it starts and stops. In some cases, such as the book of Jonah, this is very straightforward. But in others, debate surrounds the specific parameters of the narrative. Second, many smaller narratives reside within larger narratives. For example, one can speak of the entire pentateuchal narrative (Genesis through Deuteronomy), the patriarchal narrative (Genesis 12–50), the Joseph narrative (Genesis 37–50), or the narrative about Judah and Tamar (Genesis 38). Different functions can be (and have been) assigned to each part.

A third difficulty is related to the recognition that some narratives existed independently before being incorporated into their present context. For example, scholars have argued that 2 Samuel 9–20 and 1 Kings 1–2 existed as a separate document before becoming part of 2 Samuel and 1 Kings. Scholars refer to this narrative as the Succession Narrative and believe it had a life of its own and a different function before getting incorporated into the Deuteronomistic History (Joshua–Kings). Fourth, it is quite likely that many narratives served multiple functions. Though some of these were likely to have been more primary than others, it is probably reductionistic to suggest that narratives were written for one reason alone. Fifth, as narratives grew and developed over time, their functions changed, further complicating our efforts to precisely describe the function of this or that particular narrative.

I point all this out to emphasize the complexity of this task and to keep us from glibly speaking as though we have identified the function of this or that narrative with absolute certainty. We need to exercise much humility as we attempt to determine how these texts functioned in their ancient settings. With these provisos in mind, we turn our attention to the conquest narrative to see what can be said about its function and purpose.

Based on the evidence discussed in chapter 5, it seems safe to say that the conquest narrative in Joshua 6–11 does not provide a historically reliable account of how Israel came to possess the land of Canaan. Then again, there is good reason to believe that was not the original purpose of this narrative. But if the purpose of the conquest narrative was not to provide historical information about Israel's "entry" into the land, why has it been presented this way? What was its purpose, and why was it written?

To answer these questions, it is important to realize that the "book" of Joshua, like many biblical books, grew over time. The first edition was originally much smaller than the final one. According to Richard Nelson, the book "grew" in three stages.[23] The accompanying chart illustrates Nelson's understanding of the book's development over time.[24]

Edition	Contents	Additions	Time Period
Edition 1	Joshua 2–11		Monarchical period
Edition 2	Joshua 1–12, 23	Chs. 1, 12, 23	DtrH
Edition 3	Joshua 1–24	Chs. 13–22, 24	Exilic/Postexilic

As this chart illustrates, the book of Joshua underwent several revisions. Each edition functioned somewhat differently in its own particular historical context, and Nelson explores these diverse functions. This demonstrates that narratives have multiple meanings, in part because they functioned in different ways at different times. To illustrate this, I want to examine some of the probable functions of the conquest narrative without trying to pin down precisely *when* it may have functioned in this or that particular way.

Possible Functions of the Conquest Narrative

To Justify Territorial Expansion

It is quite likely that the conquest narrative was sometimes used to justify Israel's territorial expansion. Expanding borders required subduing or displacing those already living on the land, and this, in turn, required the support and cooperation of key people in Israel. One way to gain this kind of support and to justify these acts of aggression was to claim that the land in question had been granted to Israel by God.

This claim of a divine right to the land is clearly evident in the book of Joshua.[25] Canaan is repeatedly described as the land Yahweh promised to Israel. Therefore, Israel had every right to claim this land as its own—or so it would seem. It is not difficult to envision how texts like these would have lent support to the expansionistic policies of an Israelite king like Josiah. By emphasizing that the land belonged to Israel by divine right, Josiah could justify his own territorial aspirations.[26] Rather than making Josiah look like a greedy land grabber, the book of Joshua makes him look like a righteous king, obediently finishing the job Joshua and the people had left undone hundreds of years prior. Understood this way, the conquest narrative—ostensibly a story about Israel's initial entry into Canaan—is really a story designed to legitimate the military aspirations of a king living hundreds of years after the events it seemingly reports.

To Build a Sense of National Identity

The conquest narrative may have also been designed to build a sense of national identity. Time and again, the early chapters of Joshua speak of "all Israel" participating in various aspects of the entry into—and conquest of—Canaan. The entire nation crosses the Jordan (3:17), listens as Joshua reads the law of Moses (8:33), and assaults Debir (10:38). The picture is of total group participation under the direction of one leader (Joshua) under God. By emphasizing that these formative experiences were common to "all Israel," the writer helps "to create and support" a sense of national identity.[27] Stories that focus on "us" (Israel) and "them" (Canaanites) would have encouraged group identity and helped inspire a sense of unity among the disparate tribes of Israel. This emphasis comes through with special clarity in the conquest narrative.

To Inspire Hope and Confidence in the Face of Powerful Threats

The conquest narrative, which tells of great victories over otherwise insurmountable foes, may have also inspired readers/hearers to have hope and confidence in the face of powerful threats. Nelson has argued that the book of Joshua was intended to encourage people who lived under the constant threat of attack from stronger and more powerful nations. He writes:

> The communities who formulated and read Joshua were groups always threatened by the loss of their land, or even landless exiles hoping for its restoration. It was most often Israel who was victimized as an indigenous people menaced by politically and technically superior outside forces. In Joshua, this superiority is illustrated by enemy kings with iron chariots and cities with impregnable walls. Israel perceived that its culture and religion were being endangered by hostile outsiders and alien groups with whom they shared the land. The book of Joshua was part of their reaction to this threat.[28]

By ancient Near Eastern standards, Israel was a relatively small country. Yet it was strategically located between major superpowers: the Egyptians to the south and the Assyrians and Babylonians to the east. This placed Israel in a precarious position. All travel between Egypt to the southwest, and Assyria or Babylon to the northeast, had to pass through Israel. The imperial powers on both sides desired, and sometimes demanded, Israel's loyalty and compliance. Whenever these countries engaged in armed conflicts, Israel was quite literally stuck in the middle of the road. It is not difficult to imagine how vulnerable Israel must have felt sandwiched between empires eager for more land and greater wealth. From this perspective, one can understand how encouraging the conquest narrative would have been to the people of Israel. It demonstrated that they could defeat foes who were militarily superior and far more powerful than they were if they were obedient to God, which leads us to the next point.

To Urge Obedience to the Laws of Moses and Unswerving Loyalty to Yahweh

Whatever else one says about the function of the conquest narrative, it must certainly have been intended to encourage faithfulness to God. It vividly demonstrates how unswerving devotion to Yahweh brings divine blessing and success. God tells Joshua that his success in possessing Canaan depends on strict obedience to the law of Moses (Josh. 1:7-8). Within the book of Joshua, Israel's dramatic victory at Jericho can only be understood as the result of Israel's absolute obedience to God (Joshua 6). On the contrary, the kind of disobedience Achan displays (Joshua 7) threatens the well-being of the entire community and jeopardizes Israel's right to remain in the land—a point Joshua drives home in his farewell address (Joshua 23). In this way, the conquest narrative—and the book of Joshua as a whole—illustrates the benefits of obedience and the dangers of disobedience. Presumably, it does so in order to persuade readers to obey God completely. Perhaps it is this function of the book that most resonates with many readers today.

As this brief survey demonstrates, there are many ways to understand the function of the conquest narrative that have nothing to do with describing events just as they happened. Instead, we have seen how these stories of conquest, ostensibly stories about "Israel's past," could be used to serve Israel's present needs and interests.

––––––––––

Throughout this chapter, we have explored some of the factors prompting people to write Old Testament narratives. Regardless of whether their reasons were political, theological, or inspirational, they wrote to address contemporary questions and concerns facing their respective communities, not just to record history for the sake of preserving the past. Since this is consistent with historiographic practices found across the ancient Near East, it comes as no great surprise. Still, it has been important to stress this point since many contemporary readers of Scripture are unaware of it and sometimes feel the only legitimate way to approach Old Testament narratives is as a record of what happened in the past. This chapter has presented many valid ways to read and understand these ancient texts that move beyond this limited understanding.

Many readers of the Bible believe that a primary function of Old Testament narratives is to teach us about God. By observing how God dealt with Israel, it would seem we should be able to learn a lot about who God is and how God operates in the world. This overtly theological function of Old Testament narratives has not figured prominently in our discussion thus far. This is partly due to the fact that it is based on the assumption that these narratives record what God actually said and did, an assumption we have called into question. But there is another reason. As John Barton puts it: "The Old Testament is not primarily a source of *information*, either about God or about other people's ideas of God."[29] This seems particularly true of many Old Testament narratives. According to Barton:

> They [narrative texts] were not written to provide information about these theological beliefs; they were written to tell a story or recount a history. In this sense the theology of the historical books is a secondary concern. Although God figures in the stories, and they do not make sense except on the basis of various beliefs about him, *they are not designed to tell the reader things about God*, but rather to narrate events from a particular point of view.[30]

While I think Barton is essentially right, his statement needs to be read carefully. It should not be taken to mean that Old Testament narratives provide no insight into the nature and character of God. They most certainly do! Nor is Barton suggesting that these stories tell us nothing about what Israelites thought about God. Instead, Barton is emphasizing that the *primary* purpose of these stories lies elsewhere. This is consistent with what we have discussed in this chapter. These writers had other motives and interests. What we learn about God from these narratives is often fortuitous and frequently secondary to other concerns.

That notwithstanding, God does feature prominently in many of these stories. Thus, it is reasonable to inquire about the creation of these literary portrayals of God. What guided the way God is portrayed in these narratives? What theological assumptions about God's nature and character shaped the way these stories could be told? What worldview assumptions governed how God could be depicted? And perhaps most important for this study, why was God portrayed in ways that seem morally objectionable and that sometimes seem to contradict other key Old Testament assertions about God as one who is good, just, and merciful? The next chapter—the final installment of part 2 of this book—explores these important questions.

CHAPTER 8

Israel's Theological Worldview

For centuries the Old Testament has been honoured as the sacred Scripture of Judaism, and as part of the sacred Scripture of Christianity. As such it presents standards of behaviour to be emulated, and images of God which provide models of his character and activity. In both religious traditions it possesses authoritative status. Here rests the problem. Not only is God seen as the caring shepherd, but also as the victorious warrior. Anthropomorphic representations of the deity are common and sometimes helpful in Scripture, but the sensitive reader must surely raise the question of the appropriateness of the image of God demonstrating the most violent and destructive side of human activity.

—T. R. Hobbs[1]

Why would an ancient storyteller present Yahweh in this way?

—K. L. Noll[2]

Portrayals of God as a Killer: Why?

Embedded in her well-known prayer in 1 Samuel 2, Hannah describes God in a most provocative way. She describes God as one who kills (1 Sam. 2:6a). At first blush, this may strike many readers as an unusual way to speak about God. Killing people is not the first thing most associate with divine activity. Nevertheless, as we have seen, killing is characteristic of God, or at least of the God described in the pages of the Old Testament.

Time and again, the Scriptures depict God using lethal force or authorizing others to do the same. Sometimes this divine violence is directed against particular individuals, such as priests like Nadab and Abihu in Leviticus 10, Abigail's foolish husband Nabal in 1 Samuel 25, or the unfortunate, ark-steadying Uzzah in 2 Samuel 6. Other times, God is described as killing people *en masse* by flooding the earth, throwing down hailstones from heaven, or annihilating a million-man army.[3] By any standard of measure, Old Testament narratives assign an enormous amount of killing to God.

The ubiquitous presence of this image of God—and many others that readers find equally distressing—raises a very important question. Why was God portrayed this way? Why did Israelites routinely depict God as one who kills and as one who sometimes engages in various other behaviors that seem unethical or immoral?

For some, the answer is obvious. They claim that God is portrayed as one who kills because it reflects what God actually did in time and space. They are convinced that the Bible's portrayal of God as one who kills—and as one who engages in other kinds of questionable activities—is fundamentally accurate. Others take a different approach. They believe ancient writers sometimes portrayed God in less than desirable ways because that was what was necessary to make a story work, not because God actually behaved in the way described. Those who take this approach believe the needs of good storytelling sometimes were allowed to override a writer's personal beliefs about God's character, resulting in literary portrayals of God that were at odds with the writer's own theological convictions. This way of understanding the Old Testament's portrayals of God is diametrically opposed to any approach that regards these portrayals as essentially accurate reflections of what God actually did.

To illustrate this approach, two examples should suffice. In an article dealing with the portrayal of God in the books of Samuel, Kurt Noll describes Samuel's God as follows:

> This is a deity who capriciously closes a woman's womb, and just as unexpectedly opens it, who delights in killing those he considers worthy of death, but who does not seem to concern himself with collateral deaths in the process, who chooses as king a man he has destined for failure, and who blames the victim for that failure.[4]

Given this unflattering portrayal of God in 1 and 2 Samuel, Noll raises the precise question we are considering: "Why would an ancient storyteller present Yahweh in this way?"[5] According to Noll, the answer is found in what he calls "narrative necessity."[6] Noll believes the problematic portrayal of Yahweh in the books of Samuel can be explained by the very practical needs of the writer, not by any personal religious convictions. Noll speaks of the story line of Samuel as "a Hebrew version of the timeless theme known as a 'simple twist of fate.'"[7] One person is charmed while another is cursed, and there is no good explanation for it. As Noll puts it:

this is not a fiction Book

> The storyteller requires a capricious deity to make the plot work. . . . The error we moderns often make is to assume that the characterization of Yahweh "mattered" to the ancient author and original audience—it almost certainly did not. That is to say, this tale was not designed to teach some religious truth about a god called Yahweh.[8]

According to Noll, the way God was portrayed in the books of Samuel was dictated by the needs of a writer wanting to tell a particular story a particular way, not by a desire to declare the "truth" about Yahweh. In fact, Noll believes that "in Iron Age Palestine, no sane reader would have worshiped the Yahweh of Samuel, though most if not all readers of Samuel worshiped *a* Yahweh."[9] He believes there is a gap—one might say a chasm—between the writer's portrayal of Yahweh and the writer's deepest beliefs about who this Yahweh really was.

This same general approach is briefly explored in a study by Michael Carasik dealing with divine omniscience in the Old Testament.[10] Carasik argues that the Hebrew Bible most often portrays God as one who is unable to access a person's interior thoughts and attitudes. In these examples, God does not seem to know what people are thinking, and thus would not be regarded as omniscient. Yet Carasik also recognizes that a handful of narrative passages do impute mind-reading abilities to God. While not denying that multiple authorship may account for these differing portrayals, Carasik believes God's omniscience, or lack thereof, has less to do with Israel's theological convictions and more to do with the mechanics of good storytelling. He writes:

> In stories, often one thing happens just so another (more important) thing can happen, or even just so that the reader can learn something important about a character. . . . The main reason God goes to Sodom and Gomorrah, for example, is not to check on things personally—that's simply a pretext. He goes there in order to give Abraham the opportunity to bargain with him. *The author limits God's omniscience to serve the needs of the narrative—that is, to tell a good story.*[11]

When it suits the story to have God know what is in the heart of a character like Abraham or Sarah, then God is omniscient; at other times, as in the story of the binding of Isaac, it makes a better story to keep the Almighty in the dark.[12]

For Carasik, like Noll, narrative necessity determines how God is portrayed.

If Carasik and Noll are right, it stands to reason that ancient writers some-times portrayed God in ways that did not necessarily correspond to their personal convictions. These writers could, and apparently did, render God in ways that vio-lated their most basic beliefs about God when such a portrayal was useful for the story they were writing. If this is true—if ancient writers sometimes portrayed God in ways that were at odds with their theological convictions for the sake of good storytelling—then this will certainly affect how we assess what they have to say about God. This may help us deal with some of the most disturbing divine behavior in the Old Testament, and we should keep this possibility in mind as we proceed.

I must confess, however, that I am not completely convinced by the argument that ancient writers were routinely willing to portray God in ways that differed radi-cally from their deepest convictions about God. While I do think some may have done this from time to time, I wonder how willing ancient scribes were to portray God in ways that fundamentally contradicted their core theological convictions. Moreover, even if we grant the possibility that some writers may have portrayed God in ways that were at odds with their personal beliefs, on what basis can we determine when a writer did so? What criteria would enable us to say that in a particular instance the writer is depicting God in a way congruent with personal beliefs but that in another instance the writer is not? It seems difficult to make such pronouncements with any degree of certainty.

From my perspective, neither of the extremes I have briefly sketched—that Old Testament portrayals of God accurately reflect what God actually did or that these portrayals are simply the product of narrative necessity—adequately explains what prompted these ancient writers to depict God in certain ways. Instead, I will attempt to demonstrate that Old Testament portrayals of God are generally consistent with what we might call Israel's basic theological worldview. Before pro-ceeding, however, it is necessary to say a few words about what constitutes a world-view and about some of the challenges of attempting to describe Israel's *theological* worldview.

Worldview Assumptions

In *The Universe Next Door*, James Sire defines a worldview as "a set of presuppositions (assumptions which may be true, partially true or entirely false) which we hold (con-sciously or subconsciously, consistently or inconsistently) about the basic makeup of our world."[13] These presuppositions include our beliefs about such things as the afterlife, the cause of weather patterns, the existence of spiritual beings, the source of sickness and disease, the nature of humanity, and the way God does—or does not—interact with the world. The presuppositions that constitute our worldview powerfully influence not only what we believe but also how we behave. Consider the following hypothetical scenario.

Suppose I am sitting in my office working at my desk when I begin to notice my back and neck starting to ache. At first, I do not think a lot about it. But as the hours go by, I begin to feel more and more uncomfortable. I start to feel sick to my stomach, and I realize that my forehead feels unusually warm. When I get home, I take my temperature and, sure enough, I have a fever. Before the day is through, I find myself staggering to the bathroom and there, hunched over the toilet bowl, I lose my lunch. What would I conclude? How would I interpret my experience? In spite of my limited medical knowledge, I would probably conclude that I had the flu, and chances are I would be correct. If so, I might decide to go to the doctor's office to get some medicine that could help my body deal with the illness.

What are my worldview assumptions in this hypothetical scenario? Obviously, I have assumed my illness resulted from *natural* causes. I believe microscopic organisms are responsible for my discomfort and pain. While I might never explicitly state this assumption as such, it is absolutely critical to my interpretation of the cause of my symptoms. Additionally, my belief that certain drugs will help my body fight this illness explains my decision to make a trip to the doctor in hopes of getting a prescription. In short, my assumptions about what causes and cures the flu dictate my behavior.

Let's suppose, however, that I was born and raised in a place where people have little or no knowledge that sickness is caused by microscopic organisms. And let's imagine that I have never seen a microscope and have no real understanding of infectious agents. How would I interpret my illness in that context? One possible explanation might be that my illness was caused by a curse someone had placed on me. Another might be that I had offended the gods. If I believed either of these to be the case, I might elicit the help of the local shaman. This individual could help me determine who had caused this and what could be done to counteract its effects, or could provide counsel about what I might do to appease the gods. In this situation, my interpretation of the event would be driven by a very different worldview assumption, one in which sickness and disease were believed to result from human or divine maleficence rather than from natural causes. As both of these scenarios indicate, worldview assumptions directly influence the way people make sense of their experiences and the way they respond to them. This is one reason it is so important to be certain that are worldview assumptions are as accurate as possible.

Difficulties of Determining Israel's Theological Worldview

Using the Old Testament to determine what the people of Israel actually believed about God, and trying to describe Israel's theological worldview, is complicated for many reasons. First, the possibility that some writers may have described God in ways that did not correspond to their core convictions, discussed above, complicates our task of discerning what they actually believed. Another challenge in determining what Israel actually believed is related to the fact that the Old Testament was written over hundreds of years. It is obvious that people's ideas about God change over time. Given this long period of production, it comes as no surprise that we find many differing—and sometimes even contradictory—views about God represented in the Old Testament.

no

Determining what Israel believed about God is also challenging because the Israelites never wrote anything akin to a systematic theology. The Old Testament texts that speak about God were not designed to provide an ordered account of Israel's beliefs about God. They make no attempt to systematize theological beliefs like modern theology books do. Instead, various ideas about God are expressed through a wide array of disparate texts, some of which were not written primarily for theological purposes. This suggests we must proceed with considerable caution when using them to determine what Israel believed about God.

Finally, there is the difficulty of the stories themselves as the medium through which their theology comes to us. The act of putting God into a story raises the very real possibility that God's character may be distorted in the process. As one scholar observes: "If you put God in a story, and you want it to be a good story, he is almost bound to end up as both the good fairy and the big bad wolf."[14] We must recognize the possibility that Old Testament narratives may only partially represent Israel's beliefs about God, given the nature of storytelling itself.

not .. lang

Despite these challenges, I still believe it is possible to identify some of Israel's core convictions about God and to speak generally about Israel's basic theological worldview. In what follows, I will highlight several key theological assumptions that reveal some of Israel's most fundamental beliefs about how God operated in the world. Doing so will help us better understand why God was portrayed in certain ways, especially those we may find troubling. It will also allow us to examine these theological assumptions more carefully in order to weigh their relative merit and to determine whether we should accept them as our own.

Obviously, in the space of just one chapter, the theological worldview assumptions discussed here are intended to be representative rather than exhaustive. Entire books have been devoted to exploring Old Testament theology.[15] What we can say here is necessarily selective. Also, it is important to keep in mind that not every Israelite would have shared all of these worldview assumptions. The Old Testament itself provides clear evidence that Israel was engaged in a lively conversation about some of these assumptions. Still, the worldview assumptions I have identified seem to have been shared by many in Israel over a long period of time. Moreover, as we will see, many of these worldview assumptions were not unique to Israel but were shared by Israel's neighbors. This further underscores just how prevalent some of these beliefs were in the ancient world.

Windows into Israel's Theological Worldview

God Controls the Natural World

One of Israel's most basic theological assumptions was that God controlled the natural world. Some of the most dramatic examples of God's control in this area are evident in the plague narrative (Exod. 7:14—12:36). In this story, God arrays the forces of the natural world against Pharaoh and all Egypt by turning the Nile's water to blood; multiplying frogs, gnats, and flies; causing animals and humans to suffer from pestilence and boils; producing hail to destroy flax and barley; sending locusts to eat wheat and spelt; and "turning off" the sun for three days! Regardless of how one assesses the historicity of this narrative, it reflects a worldview that assumes God's control of the natural world.

In other Old Testament narratives the emphasis is on God's control of the rain. Notice, for example, how the famine reported during the reign of David is described:

> Now there was a famine in the days of David for three years, year after year; and David inquired of the Lord. The Lord said, "There is bloodguilt on Saul and on his house, because he put the Gibeonites to death." (2 Sam. 21:1)

According to this account, the three-year famine was not merely a natural phenomenon, the result of a "dry spell." Instead, God is portrayed as causing this famine because of Saul's sins.[16] Only after this *spiritual* matter is addressed are we informed that "God heeded supplications for the land" (2 Sam. 21:14). In the ancient world, rain—or the lack thereof—had theological significance. When people experienced a drought that led to a famine, it was interpreted as an "act of God" in the most literal sense. Things we today call acts of nature had metaphysical meaning in the ancient world and were often regarded as indicators of God's favor or displeasure.

Another striking example of God's control of nature is evident in Elijah's confrontation with Ahab and the prophets of Baal in 1 Kings 17–18. Baal was a popular deity in the ancient world who was believed to have the power to produce rain. As the story begins, the prophet Elijah tells King Ahab that "there shall be neither dew nor rain these years, except by my word" (1 Kgs. 17:1b). For an extended period of time, the land is without rain. Then, "in the third year of the drought," God tells Elijah to appear before Ahab to inform him that rain is coming (1 Kgs. 18:1). Before the rain comes, Elijah and the prophets of Baal engage in a dramatic demonstration designed to reveal who is truly God: Yahweh or Baal. Yahweh, the God of Israel, is the clear winner. Despite their herculean efforts, the prophets of Baal cannot even get their god to respond to them (1 Kgs. 18:20-28)! Yahweh, on the other hand, not only responds to Elijah in a spectacular display of power but also sends rain (1 Kgs. 18:36-45). This narrative clearly works on the assumption that rain was no mere natural phenomenon.[17] The writers of the Old Testament, and their neighbors, believed that rain and all "forces of nature" were under divine control. This belief—that God/the gods controlled the natural world—was a pervasive worldview assumption throughout the ancient world.

God Causes Personal Fortunes and Misfortunes

Many Old Testament narratives also operate with the assumption that God bears ultimate responsibility for personal fortunes and misfortunes. This assumption is articulated with special clarity by Hannah, the mother of Samuel. After leaving her precious son under the care of Eli the priest, she prays:

> The Lord kills and brings to life;
> > he brings down to Sheol and raises up.
>
> The Lord makes poor and makes rich;
> > he brings low, he also exalts.
>
> He raises up the poor from the dust;
> > he lifts the needy from the ash heap,
> to make them sit with princes
> > and inherit a seat of honor. (1 Sam. 2:6-8a)

Hannah's words reflect the belief that death and life, as well as riches and poverty, come from God. They were regarded as divine blessings or judgments, not the results of human efforts or chance.

One specific way Israelites thought God brought personal fortune or misfortune was through a woman's ability to conceive. Several Old Testament passages depict God regulating conception, enabling some women to conceive while preventing others.[18] The portrayal of God in the book of Genesis is particularly striking in this regard. Here God seems especially (pre)occupied with procreation; several passages portray God closing or opening wombs.[19]

> For the Lord had closed fast all the wombs of the house of Abimelech because of Sarah, Abraham's wife. (Gen. 20:18)

> Isaac prayed to the Lord for his wife, because she was barren; and the Lord granted his prayer, and his wife Rebekah conceived. (Gen. 25:21)

> When the Lord saw that Leah was unloved, he opened her womb; but Rachel was barren. (Gen. 29:31)

> Jacob became very angry with Rachel and said, "Am I in the place of God, who has withheld from you the fruit of the womb?" (Gen. 30:2)

Then God remembered Rachel, and God heeded her and opened her womb. (Gen. 30:22)

According to these verses, the ability to conceive rests with God.

But this God who has the power to give life is also portrayed as having the power to take it away. In the book of Ruth, we learn that Naomi, a resident of Bethlehem, travels with her husband and two sons to the neighboring country of Moab in search of food on account of a famine. Her husband dies during their sojourn there. Though the situation is tragic, initially all is not lost. Naomi still has two sons to provide for her. As the story goes, both sons take Moabite wives and live for some time in the land. Then, about ten years later, tragedy strikes again when both of Naomi's sons die. This is devastating for Naomi, a widow in a foreign land without any male protector. In the ancient Near East, a more vulnerable person could hardly be imagined. When Naomi learns that the famine back home has ended, she decides to return. Her arrival causes quite a stir among the townswomen, who ask, "Is this Naomi?" Note her very revealing reply:

Call me no longer Naomi, call me Mara, for the Almighty has dealt bitterly with me. I went away full, but the Lord has brought me back empty; why call me Naomi when the Lord has dealt harshly with me, and the Almighty has brought calamity upon me? (Ruth 1:20-21)

Naomi's speech clearly reflects the belief that God stands behind her misfortunes. The deaths of her husband and two sons are not regarded as "natural" occurrences. They are the direct result of divine activity. Since no reason is given for why this devastating divine activity occurred, the reader is left wondering. There is certainly no intimation that Naomi had sinned and was being punished. Nor is there any indication that her husband and two sons had done anything "worthy" of death. Apparently, the writer was not concerned with such matters. What we do have is a clear statement of divine causality. Naomi was suffering, and she held God responsible. Presumably, this kind of thinking was quite common in Israel. Those who faced personal tragedy believed their calamity came from the hand of God.

God Rewards the Obedient and Punishes the Disobedient

In many Old Testament passages, it is clear that the writers wanted to explain why people experienced blessing or suffered disaster. These explanations tend to follow a rather fixed formula that is sometimes referred to as the doctrine of retribution. The formula goes something like this: Those who obey God can expect good health, wealth, and a very long life. Those who do not obey God can expect sickness, poverty, and a premature death.[20] These ideas are expressed in classic form in the book

of Deuteronomy, and Deuteronomy 28 draws this stark contrast between the blessings of obedience and the dangers of disobedience.

> If you will only obey the Lord your God, by diligently observing all his com-
> mandments that I am commanding you today, the Lord your God will set you
> high above all the nations of the earth; all these blessings shall come upon
> you and overtake you, if you obey the Lord your God: Blessed shall you be
> in the city, and blessed shall you be in the field. Blessed shall be the fruit of
> your womb, the fruit of your ground, and the fruit of your livestock, both the
> increase of your cattle and the issue of your flock. Blessed shall be your basket
> and your kneading bowl. Blessed shall you be when you come in, and blessed
> shall you be when you go out. (Deut. 28:1-6)

> But if you will not obey the Lord your God by diligently observing all his
> commandments and decrees, which I am commanding you today, then all
> these curses shall come upon you and overtake you: Cursed shall you be in
> the city, and cursed shall you be in the field. Cursed shall be your basket and
> your kneading bowl. Cursed shall be the fruit of your womb, the fruit of your
> ground, the increase of your cattle and the issue of your flock. Cursed shall
> you be when you come in, and cursed shall you be when you go out. (Deut.
> 28:15-19)

This formula provided many writers with a convenient theological framework
for explaining *why* things happened. This way of thinking is especially evident in
Joshua through Kings, a block of material often referred to as the Deuteronomistic
History. It seems the writers who put this material together were guided by many of
the ideas found in what is now the book of Deuteronomy, not the least of which is the
doctrine of retribution. Every success or failure, blessing or loss, could be understood
as coming from the hand of God. Since this way of explaining things is so prevalent
in many Old Testament narratives, just a few examples should suffice. I begin with a
positive example that describes how Caleb was rewarded for his obedience.

> Then the people of Judah came to Joshua at Gilgal; and Caleb son of Jephunneh
> the Kenizzite said to him, "You know what the Lord said to Moses the man
> of God in Kadesh-barnea concerning you and me. I was forty years old when
> Moses the servant of the Lord sent me from Kadesh-barnea to spy out the land;
> and I brought him an honest report. But my companions who went up with me
> made the heart of the people melt; yet *I wholeheartedly followed the Lord my God.*
> And Moses swore on that day, saying, 'Surely the land on which your foot has
> trodden shall be an inheritance for you and your children forever, *because you
> have wholeheartedly followed the Lord my God.'* And now, as you see, the Lord
> has kept me alive, as he said, these forty-five years since the time that the Lord
> spoke this word to Moses, while Israel was journeying through the wilderness;

and here I am today, eighty-five years old. I am still as strong today as I was on the day that Moses sent me; my strength now is as my strength was then, for war, and for going and coming. So now give me this hill country of which the Lord spoke on that day; for you heard on that day how the Anakim were there, with great fortified cities; it may be that the Lord will be with me, and I shall drive them out, as the Lord said." Then Joshua blessed him, and gave Hebron to Caleb son of Jephunneh for an inheritance. So Hebron became the inheritance of Caleb son of Jephunneh the Kenizzite to this day, *because he wholeheartedly followed the Lord, the God of Israel.* (Josh. 14:6-14, emphasis mine)

Three times in this passage the writer emphasizes Caleb's "wholehearted" obedience to the Lord. It is precisely because of his obedience that Caleb is rewarded with the city of Hebron. The clear message here is that God blesses the faithful.

Far more common, however, are examples in which individuals or nations are punished for their wickedness.

Then the Israelites did what was evil in the sight of the Lord and worshiped the Baals; and they abandoned the Lord, the God of their ancestors, who had brought them out of the land of Egypt; they followed other gods, from among the gods of the peoples who were all around them, and bowed down to them; and they provoked the Lord to anger. They abandoned the Lord, and worshiped Baal and the Astartes. So the anger of the Lord was kindled against Israel, and he gave them over to plunderers who plundered them, and he sold them into the power of their enemies all around, so that they could no longer withstand their enemies. Whenever they marched out, the hand of the Lord was against them to bring misfortune, as the Lord had warned them and sworn to them; and they were in great distress. (Judg. 2:11-15)

According to this passage, Israel's wayward worship precipitates divine judgment. Israel's apostasy prompts God to use foreign nations to oppress and to rule over the Israelites.

The idea that a person's, or nation's, sinfulness resulted in divine judgment was common in the ancient Near East. For example, in an ancient Mesopotamian text, we discover that King Assurnasirpal I, who reigned during the eleventh century, is suffering from an illness. He believes the goddess Ishtar has caused this sickness because she is angry with him for some unspecified reason, and he asks Ishtar to heal him.

For how long, Mistress [Ishtar], have you afflicted me with this interminable illness? I am Assurnasirpal, in despair, who reveres you, who grasps your divine hem, who beseeches your ladyship. Look upon me, let me pray to your divine ladyship(?), you who were angry take pity on me. May your feelings be eased! May your even benevolent heart grow pained on my account. Drive out my illness, remove my debility![21]

Later in this study, we will evaluate the relative merits of this theological assumption.[22] Does this idea—that God punishes the wicked with sickness, poverty, and death and rewards the righteous with health, riches, and life—accurately reflect the way God works in the world? If so, what explanation can be given to righteous persons who suffer, and how can we explain the great wealth and comparative ease of many wicked people? On the other hand, if we conclude that this does not represent how God operates, then what are we to do with the many texts that portray God behaving this way?

God Sanctions Warfare and Brings Victory and Defeat in Battle

To extend the previous point, we can explore one particular way the doctrine of retribution got worked out on a national level—namely, through victory and defeat on the battlefield. People in the ancient Near East commonly believed that God/ the gods divinely sanctioned their battles and even fought on their behalf.[23] As discussed in chapter 1, the Old Testament routinely portrayed the God of Israel as a divine warrior. This widespread "divine warrior" motif is attested to in numerous texts, monumental inscriptions, and artifacts from antiquity.

In the ancient world, people believed their land was a gift from God, often acquired through divinely assisted military exploits. This is evident in the story of the bitter conflict between the Israelites and the Ammonites in Judges 11. Their dispute is over competing claims to a tract of land in Transjordan. The Ammonites hope to reclaim land they contend Israel wrongly took from them many years prior. But Jephthah, an Israelite "judge," maintains that this land rightfully belongs to Israel. He bases his claim on the conviction that God gave Israel this land hundreds of years earlier through a series of military victories (Judg. 11:14-22). In a diplomatic effort to avoid going to war against the Ammonites, Jephthah appeals to this commonly held assumption that people possess the land given them by their God. He says:

> So now the Lord, the God of Israel, has conquered the Amorites for the benefit of his people Israel. . . . Should you not possess what your god Chemosh gives you to possess? And should we not be the ones to possess everything that the Lord our God has conquered for our benefit? (Judg. 11:23-24; see also Deut. 32:8-9)

People in the ancient world commonly believed the land they inhabited was theirs by divine right, regardless of the actual historical circumstances that caused them to occupy it. Obviously, as the narrative in Judges 11 demonstrates, this becomes highly problematic when more than one group lays claim to the same piece of land.

Another common feature of the divine warrior motif is how God/the gods used the forces of nature to fight against opponents. For example, when the Amorite coalition gathered against the Gibeonites at Gilgal, we read:

And the Lord threw them into a panic before Israel, who inflicted a great slaughter on them at Gibeon, chased them by the way of the ascent of Beth-horon, and struck them down as far as Azekah and Makkedah. As they fled before Israel, while they were going down the slope of Beth-horon, the Lord threw down huge stones from heaven on them as far as Azekah, and they died; there were more who died because of the hailstones than the Israelites killed with the sword. (Josh. 10:10-11)

Another example of God's use of the forces of nature in battle is seen in Israel's fight with King Jabin and Sisera, the commander of his army. This battle, led by the Israelite prophetess Deborah and a reluctant "judge" named Barak, is recorded in both narrative (Judges 4) and poetic (Judges 5) form. The battle is waged in the Wadi Kishon, and this is crucial to the story (Judg. 4:7). A wadi is a dry riverbed that can quickly become a raging river when it rains. As the narrative describes it:

The Lord threw Sisera and all his chariots and all his army into a panic before Barak; Sisera got down from his chariot and fled away on foot. (Judg. 4:15a)

Obviously, God does something that makes it difficult for the chariots to operate properly. But what? The answer emerges from the poetic version of the battle as Deborah and Barak sing:

Lord, when you went out from Seir, when you marched from the region of Edom, the earth trembled, and the heavens poured, the clouds indeed poured water. . . . The torrent Kishon swept them away, the onrushing torrent, the torrent Kishon. (Judg. 5:4, 21a)

This song celebrates a divine rainstorm that flooded the Wadi Kishon, effectively defeating Sisera's army. Chariots do not work well in mud! An interesting nonbiblical example of how divine rainmaking made military victory possible is found in King Mursilis's first-person description of his battle against a rival named Sunupassaer. The Hittite king Mursilis says:

The proud Weather-god, my lord, stood beside me. It rained all night so that the enemy could not see the campfire of the troops. But as soon as the weather became clear in the early evening, the proud Weather-god suddenly raised the storm and brought it and it went before my troops, making them invisible to the enemy. So I arrived at the land of Malazzia and burnt and destroyed it utterly.[24]

This Hittite king attributes his victory in battle to a weather-god who fought on his behalf.

Many additional similarities exist between the divine warrior motif in the Old Testament and other ancient Near Eastern texts and inscriptions. The Moabite

Stone—or Mesha Inscription, as it is sometimes called—is particularly interesting. Found in 1868 in Dhiban (ancient Dibon), a city located about twelve miles east of the Dead Sea, the inscription dates to the ninth century BCE. It celebrates the Moabite King Mesha's victory over Israel and chronicles the many places he occupied and built.[25] It appears that Mesha's predecessor had been subdued by an Israelite king named Omri, who had required him to pay tribute to Israel. Mesha inherited this unhappy arrangement upon his accession sometime during the reign of King Ahab, Omri's son.[26] Rather than continuing this practice, Mesha led several effective military campaigns, primarily in northern Israel. He successfully captured Israelite territory and ultimately freed himself from Israel's grasp.

Of special interest to us is the theological interpretation given to these military operations. According to the inscription, Moab's initial defeat at the hands of Omri was caused by Chemosh, Moab's national deity.[27]

> As for Omri, king of Israel, he humbled Moab many years (lit., days), for Chemosh was angry at his land.[28]

Although the motivation for Chemosh's anger is left unspecified, a reference to divine anger preceding military defeat is echoed throughout many Old Testament narratives.[29] We shall return to this idea momentarily.

Sometime later—presumably when Chemosh's anger subsided—King Mesha was divinely ordered to retake the land. Chemosh told him, "Go, take Nebo from Israel!" and "Go down, fight against Hauronen." Similar divine instructions are found in several Old Testament war narratives.

> Then the Lord said to Joshua, "Do not fear or be dismayed; take all the fighting men with you, and go up now to Ai. See, I have handed over to you the king of Ai with his people, his city, and his land." (Josh. 8:1)

> David inquired of the Lord, "Shall I go up against the Philistines? Will you give them into my hand?" The Lord said to David, "Go up; for I will certainly give the Philistines into your hand." (2 Sam. 5:19)

When King Mesha fights against Israel, Chemosh is actively involved in the battle. As the Mesha Inscription reports:

> And the king of Israel had built Jahaz, and he dwelt there while he was fighting against me, but Chemosh drove him out before me.

King Mesha's victories are not portrayed as the result of his superior military strategy or more powerful fighting force. Instead, this inscription claims he was able to throw off the burdensome yoke of the Israelites because Chemosh "drove out" the enemy. Similar language is used to describe Yahweh's warfare in the Old Testament. In his farewell address, Joshua reminds Israel that "the Lord drove out before us all the peoples" (Josh. 24:18a; see also 1 Kgs. 21:26). On another occasion, a prophet tells the Israelites: "I [the Lord] delivered you from the hand of the Egyptians, and from the hand of all who oppressed you, and drove them out before you, and gave you their land (Judg. 6:9). The idea that victory in battle was the result of the will of God/the gods was widespread in the ancient world. So too was the idea that defeat in battle was a sign of divine displeasure and abandonment.

As noted above, biblical texts sometimes make a clear connection between God's anger and Israel's defeat in battle. This is seen with special clarity in one intriguing story in the book of Joshua. After Israel's seemingly effortless victory at the battle of Jericho, the people travel West to the city of Ai. A reconnaissance mission prior to engagement results in a very encouraging report. The city of Ai should be easily taken since the population is rather small. Because there are so few in the city, the spies recommend taking only some of the troops—two thousand to three thousand—since the limited number of inhabitants does not require an all-out military offensive. This tactical advice is heeded, but instead of an easy victory Israel is soundly defeated, returning back to camp with <u>thirty-six</u> fewer soldiers. This causes *[handwritten: ?]* great fear and considerable distress among the people. Joshua's cry to God clearly *[handwritten: if untrue]* reveals his belief that this defeat came directly from God's hand. He asks: *[handwritten: why the exact number]*

> Ah, Lord GOD! Why have you brought this people across the Jordan at all, to hand us over to the Amorites so as to destroy us? (Josh. 7:7a)

God immediately responds and informs Joshua that the reason for this defeat does not represent evil divine intentions, as Joshua's question seems to insinuate. Instead, God reveals the real reason for Israel's defeat: disobedience. Prior to the battle of Jericho, Joshua had issued an order forbidding the people from taking any spoil.

> As for you, keep away from the things devoted to destruction, so as not to covet and take any of the devoted things and make the camp of Israel an object for destruction, bringing trouble upon it. But all silver and gold, and vessels of bronze and iron, are sacred to the Lord; they shall go into the treasury of the Lord. (Josh. 6:18-19)

Yet this order is disregarded by an Israelite named Achan.

> But the Israelites broke faith in regard to the devoted things: Achan son of Carmi son of Zabdi son of Zerah, of the tribe of Judah, took some of the devoted things; and the anger of the Lord burned against the Israelites. (Josh. 7:1)

Although we the readers know this, Joshua does not. So the Lord informs him.

> Israel has sinned; they have transgressed my covenant that I imposed on them. They have taken some of the devoted things; they have stolen, they have acted deceitfully, and they have put them among their own belongings. Therefore

the Israelites are unable to stand before their enemies; they turn their backs to their enemies, because they have become a thing devoted for destruction themselves. I will be with you no more, unless you destroy the devoted things from among you. (Josh. 7:11-12)

When Achan is identified as the culprit, he confesses. He has hidden some of the forbidden spoil in the ground underneath his tent: a mantle from Shinar, two hundred shekels of silver, and a bag of gold weighing fifty shekels (Josh. 7:21). This transgression is cited as the reason for Israel's surprising defeat. In accordance with the Lord's command (7:14-15), Achan and his family are stoned to death. They are then burned along with Achan's possessions and the forbidden spoil. Only then are we informed that "the Lord turned from his burning anger" (7:26). As this text so clearly reveals, military losses were understood theologically in the ancient world.

The divine warrior motif was extremely widespread throughout the ancient Near East and is clearly reflected in the way Israel and her neighbors made sense of their military engagements. They believed that God/the gods commissioned wars and fought in them, and they understood victory or defeat in battle theologically, as a result of divine favor or displeasure. If it was generally assumed that victory or defeat in battle corresponded to divine favor or displeasure, it stands to reason that Israel would also think this way. Does this mean Israel simply adopted the worldview of her neighbors? If so, then in what sense is Israel's interpretation of God's involvement in those battles accurate, much less "authoritative"? This is an important question to which we will return later. For now, the point to keep in mind is this: a crucial component of Israel's theological worldview was the belief that warfare was divinely ordained and that Yahweh often fought for—and sometimes even against—Israel.

God Is the Sole Divine Causal Agent

Whenever the writers of the Old Testament wanted to provide an explanation for an event they could not explain—or perhaps did not want to explain—in exclusively human terms, they portrayed God (Yahweh) as the sole divine operative. In these situations, the writers did not suggest that other supernatural beings (gods, demons, angels, and so forth) may have played a role in this or that event.[30] Instead, they portrayed God as the sole divine causal agent. This idea is reflected in Isa. 45:7, in which God reportedly says, "I form light and create darkness, I make weal (shalom) and create woe; I the Lord do all these things." By portraying God as fully in control, these writers functionally deny the efficacy—if not the existence—of other powers. Obviously, this does not imply that Israelites did not believe in other gods or spiritual powers. They certainly did; as a quick glance through the Old Testament makes abundantly clear. Still, the "official" perspective preserved in the pages of the Old Testament is that things happened because Yahweh either willed them or caused them to happen. Yahweh is routinely portrayed as the prime—and the only—mover and shaker in the divine realm.[31]

The obvious theological advantage of this assumption is that it marvelously preserves God's sovereignty. The disadvantage is that it seems to compromise God's morality since it attributes evil to God. As Robert Carroll puts it: "There is no other source for evil in the Hebrew Bible than God. All the disasters and terrible experiences which befall humans come from the one divine origin."[32] Yet it does not seem that the writers of the Old Testament were terribly troubled by this. According to Carroll: "Most biblical writers had no difficulty in presenting Yahweh/Elohim as the author and source of evil."[33] Be that as it may, it does create serious discomfort for many readers today.

To illustrate how problematic this emphasis on Yahweh as the sole divine causal agent can be, we return to the plague narrative in Exodus. Throughout the narrative, God's power and control are absolute. God is portrayed as being superior to Pharaoh, the Egyptian gods, and the imperial army. As noted earlier, this narrative depicts God as one who can change water into blood, smite the land with pestilence, afflict humans and animals with terrible boils, and even hide the sun for a few days. But there is also this troubling business of God hardening Pharaoh's heart—repeatedly. For many, this behavior offends their most basic notions of God's goodness. Be that as it may, it is understandable given Israel's beliefs about God's control of the world. As Thomas Mann keenly observes: "Theologically, the authors appear more willing to throw into question the morality of God than to risk undercutting the sovereignty of God. The hardening motif illustrates the Hebrew Bible's adamant refusal to assign evil to some force outside Yahweh's power and control."[34] J. C. L. Gibson views this notion of regarding God as the sole divine causal agent as a way of understanding what he calls "three particularly repulsive passages in the Old Testament," one of which includes the hardening of Pharaoh's heart.[35] He writes:

> There is a theological reason for, or at least explanation of, this way of speaking about God. . . . By and large the Old Testament accepts that God causes evil as well as good, that . . . he has built into the fabric of the universe a dualism of light and darkness, good and evil, and is therefore himself as much responsible for the one as for the other. God is always in control and at the end of the day evil is admitted to derive from him.[36]

While this might help us understand why God is portrayed in certain ways in these stories, this part of Israel's theological worldview will not sit well with many modern readers. It raises serious questions about how we move from Israel's theological worldview to our own.

To What Extent Should We Adopt Israel's Theological Worldview as Our Own?

Our discussion of several of Israel's theological worldview assumptions has revealed a great deal about how the people of Israel believed God acted in their world. Since they believed God was directly and intimately involved in their experiences, and saw the hand of God in both natural disasters and historical events, they attempted to explain what God was doing and why. Their theological worldview allowed them to make sense of their experiences and provided them with a way to explain the unexplainable.

Recalling Sire's definition of a worldview, it is "a set of presuppositions (assumptions which may be true, partially true or entirely false) which we hold (consciously or subconsciously, consistently or inconsistently) about the basic makeup of our world." As this definition indicates, our presuppositions are "assumptions which may be true, partially true or entirely false." So then what can be said about ancient Israel's theological presuppositions? Are they true? Partially true? Entirely false? The way we answer this question has a direct bearing on how we address the problem of disturbing divine behavior in the Old Testament. But before we consider the validity of Israel's theological presuppositions, it is helpful to pave the way by briefly considering the validity of two of Israel's *nontheological* presuppositions. Admittedly, making a distinction between theological and nontheological presuppositions is somewhat artificial since Israelites would not have compartmentalized things this way. Still, for the purpose of this discussion, it is reasonable to differentiate between Israel's beliefs about how God interacted with human beings, on the one hand, and Israel's beliefs about things like the basic structure of the world and certain social arrangements, on the other, even if these things do have certain theological dimensions to them.

Two of Israel's Nontheological Assumptions

COSMOLOGY: UNDERGROUND PILLARS AND A FLAT EARTH

Cosmology refers to the way people understand the physical structure of the world. Here I'm interested in Israel's perception of the physical structure of the world—not God's role in creating and sustaining it—and for that reason I discuss it here as a "nontheological" assumption. Israelites, like everyone else in the ancient world, believed the earth was the center of the universe.[37] From their perspective, the earth remained stationary while the sun revolved around it (see Josh. 10:12-13). The Israelites also had certain ideas about what supported the earth and kept it from drifting about in the waters believed to surround it on every side. Pillars were thought to be underneath the earth supporting it. This belief is reflected in Hannah's prayer: "The pillars of the earth are the Lord's, and on them he has set the world."[38]

Understandably, the Israelites also believed the earth was flat and square. This can be deduced from a passage that refers to the regathering of Israel in which the prophet Isaiah declares: "He [God] will raise a signal for the nations, and will assemble the outcasts of Israel, and gather the dispersed of Judah from the four corners of the earth" (Isa. 11:12). Such a statement implies that the earth is flat and presumably square. Today, of course, it would be ridiculous to argue that the earth is flat, stands motionless, or is supported by pillars. The knowledge we have gained over the past several hundred years has allowed us to advance beyond this prescientific worldview.

POLYGAMY: MANY WIVES FOR ONE MAN

A second nontheological presupposition in ancient Israel has to do with the nature of marriage. Polygamy was acceptable in that culture, and there are numerous accounts in the Bible of a man having more than one wife. Polygamists in the Old Testament include such individuals as Lamach (Genesis 4), Jacob (Genesis 29), David (1 Sam. 25:42-44; 2 Sam. 5:13), and Solomon (1 Kgs. 11), to name just a few. The Old Testament never explicitly condemns this practice or regards it as being morally problematic. Presumably, Israelites found no fault with this social arrangement, at least in principle. Yet today, we no longer believe this practice is appropriate. In fact, in the United States it is illegal to have more than one wife. Our thinking about the number of spouses one may have at any given time differs considerably from our ancient forebears.

The Question

Based on this very brief look at a couple of Israel's nontheological worldview assumptions, it is clear that each differs considerably from our own. The same would have been true had we explored other common practices in Israel, such as casting lots or sacrificing animals. We look at the world very differently from the way Israelites did. Stating this is meant not as a judgment on that culture but simply as an acknowledgment that, despite points of continuity, we do not share all of Israel's nontheological worldview assumptions.

One aspect I especially appreciate about Sire's broad description of presuppositions as "assumptions which may be true, partially true or entirely false" is that it reminds us that our presuppositions need to be tested and evaluated. They should not be just taken for granted. Instead, they should be examined carefully to determine whether they accurately represent reality. Otherwise, we run the risk of clinging to false beliefs that may lead us to make bad choices based on faulty premises.

All this brings us back to the question at hand: How accurate and reliable are Israel's *theological* worldview assumptions, particularly in terms of how God interacts with the world? If Israel's *nontheological* worldview assumptions were culturally conditioned and sometimes in need of revision, might the same be true of Israel's *theological* worldview assumptions? If so, it would seem we should proceed with caution, being careful not to *uncritically* adopt Israel's theological assumptions as our own.

For example, most Christians I know do not believe people go to a place called *Sheol* when they die, though this is clearly what some Israelites believed.[39] Likewise, most Christians today would be hesitant to say that God uses the forces of nature to punish people. They would not claim, for example, that the devastating tsunami of 2004 in South Asia, which killed more than 225,000 people, was an act of divine punishment. Thus, despite Old Testament portrayals of God as one who floods the world (Genesis 6) or casts horse and rider into the sea (Exodus 14–15), Christians today do not believe God is in the business of drowning tens of thousands of people in cataclysmic acts of divine wrath.

Similarly, while most Christians affirm God's sovereignty, few would accept the notion that God is the sole causal agent in the world. As Gibson observes: "Ancient Israel had only one God, and she was not afraid to draw the corollary that he sent evil as well as good. The New Testament and later Judaism tend to remove evil from God's direct responsibility and assign it to the Devil or some other power."[40] In other words, we think differently about these matters today. When Christians try to make sense of evil in the world, they tend not to attribute it directly to God. Instead, they appeal to such things as human freedom, the consequences of sin, and the activity of evil spiritual beings, such as demons.

Whether we do so consciously or not, we all reject some of Israel's theological worldview assumptions as inadequate. We do this, in part, because we have more data to work with. We have the benefit of thousands of years of human exploration and discovery to inform our understanding. Our understanding of God has grown and expanded over the years. Christians know more about the plans and purposes of God than people in ancient Israel did because Christians have the distinct advantage of knowing Jesus, God incarnate. The life, death, and resurrection of Jesus have radically transformed how we understand the work of God in the world and has given us a clearer vision of God than our forbears could have ever hoped for. Therefore, while it is natural to expect points of continuity between ancient Israel's theological worldview and ours, it would be foolhardy to completely adopt Israel's theological worldview as our own. Israel's theological worldview need not—and in some cases should not—reflect our beliefs about God. The real challenge when reading the Bible is to figure out where the lines of continuity and discontinuity should be drawn. That will be part of our task in the pages that follow.

This chapter brings the second part of the book to a close. Throughout part 2, we have explored the nature and function of Old Testament narratives. The understanding we have gained puts us in a better position to evaluate the presence of problematic portrayals of God in these narratives. This will inform the approach taken in part 3.

In addition to enhancing our understanding of this particular literary genre, our discussion of Old Testament narratives has raised serious questions about the validity of the control belief that asserts that God said and did everything the Old Testament claims. It has been important to reflect carefully on this control belief since it significantly limits the possibilities for dealing with problematic portrayals of God in the Old Testament. If this control belief is justified, then the best solutions to disturbing divine behavior are those discussed (and dismissed) in chapter 4.

But, I have attempted to demonstrate that this control belief is unwarranted. This is due, in part, to the fact that Old Testament narratives were not primarily written to record exactly what happened. We discovered that some events found in Old Testament narratives did not happen as described, while others did not happen at all. In these instances, one should proceed cautiously, realizing that some of the Bible's portrayals of God are not historically grounded. This opens the way for new approaches to problematic portrayals of God in the Old Testament. For example, if there really never was a worldwide flood as Genesis 6–8 implies, it stands to reason that God never said to Noah, "I have determined to make an end of all flesh, for the earth is filled with violence because of them; now I am going to destroy them along with the earth" (Gen. 6:13). If God never said this, and if God never actually flooded the earth as described, then we are free to raise questions about the accuracy of this particular portrayal of God. *blasphemy/*

Yet, even when reading about events that certainly did take place, questions remain about the legitimacy of some of Israel's depictions of God. For example, the Bible's claim that Jerusalem was destroyed by the Babylonians in 587 BCE is an indisputable historical fact corroborated by other kinds of extrabiblical evidence. But Israel's *theological interpretation* of that event remains open to question. What was God's role in this national disaster? Was Jerusalem destroyed because God was punishing Judah for the sins of Manasseh and those he caused the people to commit, as 2 Kgs. 21:10-15 claims? Or is this interpretation of the event a product of a theological worldview that understood military defeat as a sign of divine punishment? In other words, is it possible that Israel mistakenly understood God's involvement in this national tragedy? More generally, is it fair to say that the people of Israel sometimes made claims about God's involvement in their affairs that are perfectly understandable given their theological worldview but that are, nevertheless, inaccurate? If so, what does that suggest about the trustworthiness of these portrayals of God?

For those who accept the basic argument of this chapter—that our theological worldview need not be identical to ancient Israel's—new possibilities for dealing with disturbing divine behavior emerge. If we recognize that some of Israel's portrayals of God reflect culturally conditioned interpretations of God's involvement and may or may not reflect what God actually did or what God is actually like, new ways of thinking about this material become available to us. We are now free to question, and even critique, portrayals of God in Old Testament narratives. In the next, and final, part of this book, I will develop a particular way of approaching problematic portrayals of God that does just that. It is an approach that takes into account what we have learned about Old Testament narratives. It is also an approach that attempts to deal honestly with these difficult portrayals of God and to deal constructively with the texts in which they reside.

PART 3

Developing Responsible Readings of Troublesome Texts

CHAPTER 9

Distinguishing between the Textual God and the Actual God

The Amalekites, Genocide, and God

Rather than simply being human thoughts and opinions about God, the Old Testament is God's presentation of himself, *that is, his self-revelation.*

—JOHN WALTON AND ANDREW HILL[1]

The notion that the figure God in the biblical text is actually God who is worshiped by Jewish and Christian believers seems to us to be, ironically, a form of idolatry such as biblical voices constantly warn against.

—DANNA FEWELL AND DAVID GUNN[2]

I t is possible you turned to this part of the book after a brief glance at the table of contents rather than after reading the preceding chapters. That is understandable since this chapter marks the beginning of the section of the book that deals more directly with "solutions" to the problem of disturbing divine behavior. Still, if that is how you have arrived here, I would urge you to return to the beginning and read the first two parts of the book before proceeding. In what follows, my attempt to offer a constructive method for dealing with problematic portrayals of God in Old Testament narrative depends largely on arguments made earlier in the book.

The Textual God and the Actual God

The epigraphs for this chapter make it clear that scholars differ considerably over the extent to which biblical portrayals of God actually reflect God's true nature. Some believe that these portrayals faithfully reflect God's character, while others conclude that they bear little, if any, resemblance to the God many people worship today. Individuals such as John Walton and Andrew Hill, who think "the Old Testament is God's presentation of himself," are convinced the Bible accurately portrays God as God really is.[3] Therefore, whatever the Bible claims God said and did must necessarily reveal something about the character of God. If this is true—if all the portrayals of God in the Old Testament constitute God's self-revelation—then it is extremely difficult to offer a coherent description of the character of God since God seems terribly conflicted. The God portrayed in the pages of Scripture is not only gracious and compassionate but sometimes also violent and vindictive, a God both slow to anger and at times quick to kill, one who is willing to liberate one group while obliterating another. That notwithstanding, if the Old Testament portrays God as God really is, then these and many other discordant images must somehow be reconciled since they all reveal God's nature.

On the other hand, if the Old Testament's diverse descriptions of God are understood differently, not as divine self-portraits but as human portrayals of God, it is not necessary to assume that every Old Testament image of God reflects what God is really like. While some certainly do, others apparently do not. Appreciating the human origins of these portrayals allows us to recognize that literary representations of God in the Old Testament both reveal and distort God's character.[4] Therefore, any effort to use the Old Testament to know God as God really is requires us to distinguish between the *characterization* of God in Scripture and the *character* of God in reality. Doing so, in my estimation, represents the first step toward addressing some of the difficulties raised by problematic portrayals of God in the Old Testament.

To deal responsibly with disturbing divine behavior in the Old Testament, we must differentiate between the "textual God" and the "actual God," to borrow language from Terence Fretheim. According to Fretheim, the textual God is the God located within the pages of the Bible while the actual God is the God who transcends those pages.[5] One is a literary representation; the other, a living reality. As Fretheim observes: "The God portrayed in the text does not fully correspond to the God who transcends the text, who is a living, dynamic reality that cannot be captured in words on a page."[6] I find Fretheim's distinction between the textual God and the actual God very useful, and I will argue that it is imperative to distinguish between the textual God and the actual God if we wish to use the Old Testament to think rightly about God.[7]

At this juncture, I am aware that some may be uneasy with this notion of differentiating between the textual God and the actual God. If all Scripture is inspired by God, why should we need to differentiate between the textual God and the actual God?[8] Moreover, who are we to say which portrayals reveal God's character and which distort it? And what will keep people from simply picking and choosing portrayals they like while rejecting those they do not? These are significant concerns, all of which will be addressed to some extent in the remaining chapters. In this chapter, I want to make the case for *why* we must—and often unconsciously do—make distinctions between the textual God and the actual God all the time. Chapter 10 will then consider *how* we can make these distinctions in a hermeneutically responsible manner.

The Need to Distinguish between the Textual God and the Actual God

There are numerous reasons why an informed reading of the Old Testament compels us to make distinctions between the textual God and the actual God, and several of these have already been raised in the preceding section of the book. In chapter 5, I argued that not everything reported in the Old Testament happened as described. This implies that, in certain cases, God did not actually say or do what the biblical text claims. As noted at the end of chapter 8, if the worldwide flood described in Genesis 6–8 is not rooted in historical reality, as many scholars conclude, we are free to ask questions about the accuracy of the portrayal of God in those chapters. While this portrayal may reflect God's character, then again it may not. Similarly, if the Israelites did not massacre the inhabitants of Jericho and Ai as the book of Joshua suggests, then the text's description of God's involvement in these battles represents a literary construct, not a historical fact.

Therefore, since some Old Testament portrayals of God do not appear to correspond to God's actions in the real world, we should ask questions about the appropriateness of these portrayals. Once we recognize that God did not say and do everything the Bible claims, it becomes obvious that we must make distinctions between the textual God and the actual God if we hope to think rightly about God. Otherwise, we run the risk of describing God in ways that are not only inaccurate but possibly even antithetical to God's true nature.

Second, the need to distinguish between the textual God and the actual God arises from the fact that biblical texts are products of a particular historical and cultural context. When people wrote about God, they did so through the lens of their own time and place. Therefore, their descriptions of God are, to a greater or lesser degree, culturally conditioned. We explored this notion at some length in chapter 8. There we noted that Israel's view of Yahweh as a divine warrior, for example, was generally consistent with the way people in the ancient world understood divine involvement in war. They typically envisioned their patron deity as a divine warrior who routinely took part in their armed conflicts. Victory or defeat was explained theologically. You won because God was on your side, fighting for you. You lost because God was punishing you for some offense.

Given the ubiquity of the divine warrior motif in the ancient world, Israel's description of Yahweh as a warrior is neither surprising or remarkable. Israel often spoke about God's involvement in war in ways that were quite similar to how other people in the ancient Near East did. Therefore, care must be taken when doing theology with passages depicting Yahweh as a divine warrior. While this image may provide insight into the character of God, it may just as likely reflect commonly held ideas about divine involvement in war in antiquity.

To make this same point from a slightly different angle, recall that people in the ancient world believed that natural disasters (earthquakes, famines, and the like) were acts of God. They regularly supplied theological explanations for such events, explanations that many people today would find unwarranted and inappropriate. For example, when the Bible claims God sent an earthquake to swallow some disobedient Israelites (Numbers 16), or a famine to punish the house of Saul (2 Samuel 21), it is sensible to ask whether these theological interpretations are accurate. When natural disasters occur today, we typically regard them as just that—*natural* disasters. We do not claim God intentionally caused this tsunami or that hurricane to punish a certain group of people. Instead, we realize that such events occur from time to time when certain conditions present themselves. They are explainable—and sometimes even predictable—acts of nature. They are not acts of divine judgment. Arguably, the same was true in the ancient world despite the theological interpretations assigned to various natural catastrophes. If so, then these theological explanations seem to represent misguided attempts to make sense of natural disasters. While these explanations are understandable given the historical and cultural context in which they arose, they may lead us astray as we endeavor to think rightly about God. A responsible reading of Scripture requires us to recognize this possibility, and to allow for significant disjunctures between what the Old Testament claims about God in this regard and what God is really like.

Finally, the need to differentiate between the textual God and the actual God is necessary given the conflicting portraits of God in the Old Testament. The issue here is not just the presence of diverse images of God. Anyone who spends even a little time with the Old Testament will quickly realize that God is portrayed in many different ways. Often, these diverse portrayals do not stand in tension with one another but contribute to a multifaceted portrait of God. Yet there are times when one image stands in such contrast to another that the two seem mutually exclusive. For example, while one passage speaks of God as the kind of being whose mind cannot change, another clearly states that "God changed his mind" (1 Sam. 15:29; Jon. 3:10). One passage claims that God punishes "children for the iniquity of their parents" while another portrays God emphatically stating that a child will not suffer for the iniquity of a parent (Exod. 20:5; Ezek. 18:20). On numerous occasions God is described as being "slow to anger," while other passages seem to belie that affirmation (Exod. 34:6; Num. 11:1). Similarly, despite declarations that God is gracious and merciful, God is sometimes portrayed as hardening people's hearts for the express purpose of allowing them to be slaughtered mercilessly (Exod. 34:6; Josh. 11:20). In each of these instances, we see competing and contrasting views of certain attributes of God. Contradictory portrayals like these could be multiplied many times over if images of God in the Old Testament were compared with those in the New Testament. But I have chosen only Old Testament passages to demonstrate that conflicting views of God reside within the pages of the Old Testament itself.

Conflicting images require us to make choices if we wish to speak about God in a meaningful, coherent fashion. God either does or does not punish children for their parent's sins. God either is or is not merciful. To claim that all these statements reveal something about the character of God is to claim that God's character is inconsistent, unpredictable, and ultimately unintelligible. Therefore, distinctions must be made between competing portrayals of God, which is another way of saying we must differentiate between the textual God and the actual God.

Actually, if we are honest with ourselves, most of us will admit that we make distinctions between the textual God and the actual God all the time. Even though we may not do so systematically or self-consciously, we validate certain portrayals of God while ignoring or tacitly rejecting others. Few Christians I know conceive of God as one who commands genocide, instantly annihilates sinners, or sends plagues to afflict oppressors. Yet all of these images are soundly "biblical." Still, these and other images are conveniently set aside in favor of those judged more suitable. We do this because we instinctively realize that all biblical portrayals of God are not compatible. Choices must be made between competing and contrasting images in order to speak consistently and coherently about the character of God. If we hope to use the Bible to think rightly about God, we need to differentiate between literary representations and the living reality, between the characterization of God in the Bible and God's true character. While there are certainly points of connection between the two, there are also points of significant difference.

The Amalekites, Genocide, and God

To illustrate why it is so important to make this critical distinction between the textual God and the actual God, I want to revisit 1 Sam. 15:1-3. God's genocidal decree in this passage is clearly one of the most troubling divine pronouncements in the entire Old Testament.

> Samuel said to Saul, "The Lord sent me to anoint you king over his people Israel; now therefore listen to the words of the Lord. Thus says the Lord of

hosts, 'I will punish the Amalekites for what they did in opposing the Israel-ites when they came up out of Egypt. Now go and attack Amalek, and utterly destroy all that they have; do not spare them, but kill both man and woman, child and infant, ox and sheep, camel and donkey.'" (1 Sam. 15:1-3)

This brief, but chilling, divine directive is disturbing to say the least, and many read-ers are rightly bothered by the merciless, indiscriminate slaughter God ostensibly commands.[9]

The story of the Amalekite genocide stands at the critical juncture just prior to David's election and Saul's ultimate rejection. The instructions given to Saul in 1 Samuel 15 seem straightforward enough. He is to "utterly destroy" everyone—and everything—Amalekite. This divinely sanctioned slaughter is described as punishment on Amalek for attacking the Israelites shortly after they left Egypt. Apparently, this "attack" refers to the battle between Israel and Amalek recorded in Exod. 17:8-16. Yet, given the severity of the prescribed punishment, it is curious that neither Exodus 17 nor 1 Samuel 15 says anything about the specific nature of Amalek's transgression. Neither passage describes the nature of the attack or the motivation behind it. Exodus 17:8 simply reports that "Amalek came and fought with Israel at Rephidim," while 1 Sam. 15:2 cryptically describes the Amalekites' punishment as the result of "what they did in opposing the Israelites when they came up out of Egypt."[10] This vague and general description makes it all the more difficult to understand why Amalek received this particularly harsh divine sentence. A somewhat fuller picture emerges when reading Moses's retelling of the story in Deut. 25:17-19:

> Remember what Amalek did to you on your journey out of Egypt, how he attacked you on the way, when you were faint and weary, and struck down all who lagged behind you; he did not fear God. Therefore when the Lord your God has given you rest from all your enemies on every hand, in the land that the Lord your God is giving you as an inheritance to possess, you shall blot out the remembrance of Amalek from under heaven; do not forget.

According to this passage, the Amalekites are accused of attacking Israel at a very vulnerable moment, when the people were "faint and weary." Worse still, the Ama-lekites unmercifully "struck down" those Israelites "who lagged behind." In other words, they are portrayed as going for the easy kill, murdering those who were unable to keep up with the rest of the group. Still, even with these extra details, the motivation behind their apparent act of aggression remains unclear.

Assuming there is some historical memory preserved here, one wonders how the Amalekites would have told this story. How would they have described this confrontation in the Sinai Peninsula? What reasons would they have given for this armed conflict? And who would have been the aggressor in their version of the story? Unfortunately, there is not enough historical data available to answer these questions. As the biblical text describes it, Amalek was the aggressor and the Israelites were never to forgive or forget their act of violence. After the battle, the Lord commanded Moses: "Write this as a reminder in a book and recite it in the hearing of Joshua: I will utterly blot out the remembrance of Amalek from under heaven" (Exod. 17:14b).[11] This is precisely what God intends to happen under the command of King Saul, a king who has been given a comprehensive and unequivocal command to seek and destroy the entire Amalekite population.

This portrayal of God—as one who commissions genocide—is among the most disturbing in all of Scripture. But is it trustworthy? Does this characterization of God reliably reflect the character of God? And does the literary portrayal of God in 1 Samuel 15 represent what God actually said and desired thousands of years ago regarding the Amalekites? There are significant reasons to think not.

As noted earlier, numerous studies have quite convincingly suggested that various portions of 1 and 2 Samuel originally functioned as political propaganda supporting David and the Davidic dynasty.[12] Clearly, not everyone in Israel was happy about the dynastic change from the house of Saul to the house of David. Some were fiercely loyal to Saul and regarded David as an illegitimate usurper. One way the pro-Davidic contingent attempted to counter such charges was through the production of literary propaganda. Thus, it comes as no surprise that many features in 1 Samuel 15 seem intent on persuading the readers/hearers of this text that Saul was an unfit king who needed to be removed.[13]

One way this was accomplished was by casting doubt on Saul's faithfulness to God.[14] As we can see from 1 Sam. 15:2-3, the divine directive is unmistakably clear. Saul and the Israelites are not allowed to take prisoners or livestock but are to kill everyone and slaughter all the animals.[15] But Saul fails to carry through with God's stated plans. Instead, he spares King Agag and the best animals (v. 8). This casts Saul in a very bad light, raising questions about his fitness to serve as king. According to the text, Saul's disobedience causes God to "regret" having made him king (v. 11). The prophet Samuel then informs the disobedient king that God has rejected him (vv. 23, 26) and taken the kingdom from him (v. 28). As discussed previously, expressions of divine displeasure like these are standard fare for political propaganda and were routinely used to discredit a particular leader.

Viewed from this perspective, the text appears to have less to do with the character of God and more to do with the character of Saul. The focus here is really not on a genocidal God but on a disobedient king. Thus, the disturbing divine directive in 1 Sam. 15:2-3 is primarily intended to serve a *political* rather than a *theological* function. It is, in short, a pretext for sullying Saul.[16] Given this historiographic agenda, it is quite possible—even probable—that the divine directive in 1 Sam. 15:2-3 was created "to serve the needs of the narrative," which in this case happen to be political and propagandistic.[17] On this basis, it is reasonable to conclude that

God never issued this genocidal decree.[18] Instead, 1 Sam. 15:2-3 is best understood as a literary creation designed to serve as a canvas to display Saul's "sin" in bold relief. If so, then it is inappropriate to assume without question that this portrayal accurately reflects God's character.[19] If God did not actually command genocide, as this passage suggests, then one need not necessarily conclude that this portrayal of God reliably reflects God's character.[20] Hence, the importance of distinguishing between the textual God and the actual God.

The Danger of Equating the Textual God with the Actual God

If God did not issue the disturbing decree in 1 Sam 15, it is unnecessary to defend God's behavior in this story since God did not actually behave as the text claims. Yet interpreters who are unwilling to make distinctions between the textual God and the actual God are forced to do just that. They must defend divine actions like these since they essentially equate the textual God and the actual God, believing that Old Testament portrayals of God faithfully preserve God's actual words and deeds. But this effort, as well intentioned as it may be, results in hermeneutical gymnastics and strained interpretations.

To illustrate this, consider Walter Kaiser's attempt to deal with this difficult passage in his popular book *Hard Sayings of the Old Testament*.[21] Kaiser attempts to exonerate God of any wrongdoing by emphasizing the Amalekites' utter depravity and God's amazing forbearance, thereby demonstrating that God's directive to eliminate the Amalekites was both just and gracious. To do so, Kaiser assumes the Amalekites were unusually evil and fully deserving of the divine punishment pronounced against them.[22] He supports this by appealing to Deut. 25:17-19, the passage that situates Amalek's attack at a moment of great vulnerability for Israel. Kaiser also mentions the view "that the Amalekites . . . were attacking God's chosen people *to discredit the living God*" and suggests that Haman's genocidal desires reported in the book of Esther reflect "this nation's deep hatred for God."[23] In doing so, Kaiser insinuates that the Amalekites not only behaved wickedly toward the Israelites but also actively and aggressively opposed God.

A major problem with this approach is that the text demonstrates no special interest in emphasizing the Amalekites' awful wickedness, a point noted earlier. Even though the passage in Deuteronomy claims the Amalekites "did not fear God" (25:18b), taking that to mean the Amalekites were trying "to discredit the living God" seems a real stretch. Kaiser's concerted efforts to portray the Amalekites as irredeemably evil seem more conditioned by his theological desire to legitimate God's behavior than by the texture of the text. Moreover, even if one grants Kaiser's assumption that the text portrays the Amalekites as exceedingly sinful, we are left with no independent witnesses to adjudicate whether such an assessment is even remotely accurate. In fact, realizing that propagandistic texts routinely demonize the enemy in order to justify acts of violence should warn us against uncritically accepting this unflattering portrayal.

The other major feature of Kaiser's "solution" involves an effort to portray God as slow to anger and abounding in mercy vis-à-vis the Amalekites. He writes: "God never acted precipitously against them; his grace and mercy waited to see if they would repent and turn from their headlong plummet into self-destruction."[24] Kaiser attempts to demonstrate this by appealing to the "prediction" God made to Abram in Gen. 15:13-16.[25] According to these words, God ostensibly tells Abram that his descendants "shall be oppressed for four hundred years" in a land not their own (Gen. 15:13) and only afterward return to Canaan since "the iniquity of the Amorites is not yet complete" (Gen. 15:16b). For Kaiser, this illustrates God's patient mercy. Even granting the very dubious claim that God made this prediction,[26] it is inaccurate to equate the Amorites with the Amalekites. They are different groups of people.[27] The "prediction" from Genesis 15, which Kaiser employs in an effort to demonstrate God's patience and long-suffering, is totally unrelated to 1 Samuel 15. There is nothing in this passage to indicate that God's "grace and mercy waited to see if they would repent and turn from their headlong plummet into self-destruction."

Similarly unconvincing is Kaiser's attempt to soften God's extermination order by offering a peculiar interpretation of the practice of the ban. He contends that "God dedicated . . . things or persons to destruction because they violently and steadfastly impeded or opposed his work *over a long period of time*."[28] If this were true, it would nicely illustrate God's great patience in waiting so long to punish the Amalekites for their long-standing aggression against Israel. Yet there is no indication in 1 Samuel 15 that the Amalekites were being punished for their long and violent history with Israel over an extended period of time. On the contrary, 1 Sam. 15:2 unequivocally states that the sole reason for this divine directive is a single conflict with Israel some four hundred years prior.[29]

Thus, while I am sympathetic with Kaiser's efforts to exonerate God his imaginative explanation is hardly convincing. Because of his unwillingness to draw distinctions between the textual God and the actual God, Kaiser is forced to justify God's disturbing divine directive to utterly annihilate the Amalekites. This is a difficult task given the nature and comprehensive scope of this divine decree. Is genocide ever justifiable? Can the slaughter of babies and infants ever be regarded as good or right? Kaiser has no choice but to answer these questions affirmatively. His certainty that biblical portrayals of God reflect what God actually said and did— that the textual God equals the actual God—severely limits his interpretive options and impedes his ability to consider alternative explanations. It causes him to resort to ill-founded explanations in an unpersuasive attempt to make a genocidal God look good. In doing so, Kaiser asserts things about God that are, in my estimation, both untrue and unworthy of God. That is precisely why refusing to differentiate between the textual God and the actual God is so dangerous.

The folly of defending divine behavior that never actually happened can be illustrated by the following analogy. Suppose I have a good friend named Dan who is a bachelor with no children. One day, Dan is visited by a couple of social workers who severely criticize him for his poor parenting skills and accuse him of neglecting his two children. Since I care deeply about Dan, I decide to come to his defense. I attempt to argue passionately and persuasively that Dan is not a bad parent. I admit that Dan does not spend very much time with his children but explain that is due to his need to work long hours to make ends meet. I also acknowledge that Dan sometimes feeds his children nothing more than macaroni and cheese for weeks at a time, though I assure the social workers that he always makes certain they have enough money to buy a good lunch at school. I concede that Dan disciplines his children harshly and sometimes too severely, but I point out that he does so with love in his heart in hopes of teaching his children how to behave properly. In every way, I try to make Dan's accusers see that despite Dan's shortcomings, he is trying to be the best parent he can be given the circumstances. Are the social workers convinced? Do they see Dan in a new light? Perhaps. But wouldn't it have been better to tell the social workers that their accusations about Dan's poor parenting are baseless because Dan is not a parent! He has no children. With that simple acknowledgment, accusations that Dan has neglected and abused his children are easily dismissed.

My attempt to defend Dan's *alleged* behavior in this hypothetical scenario, as well intentioned as it might be, is unnecessary. No defense is needed since Dan never behaved in the ways described. Yet this is exactly what many Christians try to do for God. They attempt to defend God's behavior in the Bible when, in reality, God may not have done what the text claims. If God did not actually engage in certain worrisome behaviors, it makes little sense to rush to God's defense on account of them. In such cases, it is better to acknowledge that God never did what the text claims rather than to defend divine behavior that appears unethical or immoral.

Only a First Step

Acknowledging that a distinction exists between the textual God and the actual God is an essential step in dealing responsibly with problematic portrayals of God. It is, however, only a first step, and one that takes us only so far in our attempt to address the problem of disturbing divine behavior in Old Testament narratives. While denying the historical reality of the divine directive in 1 Sam. 15:2-3 solves the nasty problem of needing to accept a genocidal God, it creates others, especially for those who want to use this text in theologically constructive ways. Even if we believe that God did not command Saul to slay all the Amalekites and conclude that this particular portrayal of God is a literary creation, how can we be sure it does not reflect something essential about God's character? Despite our historical conclusions in this instance, how do we know God is not genocidal? To ask the question more generally, is it possible that nonhistorical depictions of God sometimes faithfully depict what God is really like?

When movie producers make films that are "based on a true story," they sometimes create situations that did not actually happen but that powerfully illustrate a defining characteristic of a person's life. These vignettes, though contrived, nevertheless provide the viewer with an accurate depiction of a person's personality or character. Similarly, telling a story about a person that never actually happened may accurately reveal that person's character. Take the well-known story of George Washington cutting down a cherry tree. As the story goes, when Washington is confronted by his father, he confesses what he has done, saying, "I cannot tell a lie." Historians do not believe this particular incident actually happened. Nevertheless, it presumably reveals something true about Washington's character, namely, his honesty. Nonhistorical vignettes can provide reliable information about a person's character. On the other hand, they may also distort a person's character. To illustrate, consider the following nonhistorical story about me:

> One day, Eric received a phone a call from Aunt Gertrude, who shared some bad news. She had recently been diagnosed with a terminal illness, was now bedridden, and had only months to live. After getting off the phone, Eric quickly hopped in his car and drove to her home in Arizona. Once there, he snuck in the back door and went from room to room stealing cash and jewelry. Once he had collected all he could carry, he quietly left through the back door, got into his car, and drove home.

Thankfully, this story does not describe an actual event in my past. For starters, I do not have an Aunt Gertrude and, to my knowledge, none of my relatives live in Arizona. If the story actually happened, it would be difficult to deny that I am greedy and opportunistic (or at least have been for some period of my life). But since this incident did not happen, it is quite possible that I am a very different kind of person from the one in this story. Realizing that there is a difference between the "textual Eric" and the "actual Eric" is crucial for assessing my true character. Let's hope I am not as greedy and opportunistic as this story suggests! While this story may reflect my true character, it is equally possible that it may not.

What all this suggests is that distinguishing between the textual God and the actual God is only a first step in the process of dealing responsibly with disturbing divine behavior. Merely recognizing that there is a difference between the textual God and the actual God does not automatically enable us to determine whether a particular portrayal of God reveals or distorts God's character. Other interpretive guidelines are needed to help us make these kinds of decisions. Still, making this distinction is extremely helpful in one critical way: it frees us from the need to defend all of "God's actions" in the Old Testament. Once we acknowledge that some stories do *not* reveal what God actually said or did, we are free to ask questions about whether these stories accurately reveal the character of God. This, it seems to me, is the first step toward reading these texts responsibly.

Degrees of Correspondence

Recognizing the need to differentiate between the textual God and the actual God inevitably raises questions about how the two are related. In this regard, it seems there are two ditches to avoid. First, as we have already discussed, simplistically equating the textual God and the actual God is inappropriate. To think we can just open the Bible, read what it says about God, and then uncritically accept it as revealing God's nature is naive. As David Clines expresses it:

> If we were to imagine that the God of whom it [the Pentateuch] speaks so extensively is identical with the "true God"—the God who is worshiped and theologized about—we might have some serious theological problems on our hands, and at the very least we should be tempted to modulate what we read in the text . . . in order to harmonize it with what we already believe we know of the "true God."[30]

There is not a perfect degree of correspondence between the textual God and the actual God. In fact, given the portrayals we have been considering in this study, there sometimes seems to be very little, if any, correspondence at all!

The flip side of simplistically equating the textual God and the actual God is denying that there is any connection whatsoever. Once we realize that some portrayals of God in the Old Testament do not accurately reflect God's character, it may be tempting to regard all of them as theologically spurious. In fact, some interpreters are convinced that the Old Testament's portrayals of God are virtually useless for doing Christian theology. They do not believe that any of its descriptions of God can be regarded as reliable reflections of what God is actually like. This sentiment is boldly expressed by Robert Carroll who declares: "It is not possible to make any equation between the Yahweh of the biblical narratives and the God of the creeds and confessions of the churches, even though clever theologians may be able to adjust the gap between the two so that it is narrower under certain conditions."[31]

I am not nearly so pessimistic. While I obviously agree that one cannot simplistically draw a straight line between the textual God and the actual God, it seems that many Old Testament portrayals of God—even those that exemplify disturbing divine behavior—have more to offer Christians than Carroll is willing to allow. To be sure, some Old Testament portrayals capture a great deal more of God's true essence than others, and some positively distort what God is really like. But I believe that most—if not all—provide us with opportunities to gain *some* insight into the character of God. In my estimation, the way forward lies somewhere between the extremes of total acceptance and total rejection sketched above. In saying this, I suppose Carroll might accuse me of being one of those "clever theologians" trying to "adjust the gap" between the textual God and the actual God. Perhaps I am. But I prefer to think of what I am doing less in terms of "adjusting" a gap and more in terms of discerning just how wide or narrow that gap really is in the first place.[32]

I have argued that making distinctions between the textual God and the actual God represents an important first step in dealing responsibly with disturbing divine behavior in the Old Testament. It keeps us from blindly accepting everything the Old Testament claims about God and raises our awareness of potential differences that exist between the characterization of God in these stories and the character of God in real life. In order to think rightly about God, we need to determine the degree to which the textual God and the actual God correspond—if at all. That is the crucial issue. Of course, this begs the question, How does one do that? What criteria can be used to determine the extent to which this or that portrayal of God accurately reflects what God is really like?

Unfortunately, there are no simple answers here. There is no precise formula that can be rigidly applied to ascertain the exact degree of correspondence between the textual God and the actual God. Still, I believe there is an interpretive approach that can help us make these determinations with a fair degree of reliability. This interpretive approach, which privileges Jesus and the God Jesus reveals, will be developed in the next chapter. Utilizing this approach should keep us from simply picking and choosing those portrayals we like while rejecting those we do not. This is important if we are serious about thinking rightly about God. It does little good to create a God in our own image if our goal is to know God as God really is. Instead, we need to adopt a principled approach that encourages us to embrace all characteristics of the textual God that are judged to accurately reflect God's character, regardless of whether they suit our own personal preferences. Then again, we must also be ready and willing to reject those aspects of the textual God that do not correspond to the actual God. This can be difficult for those who have always equated the textual God and the actual God and have assumed that all portrayals of God in the Bible are trustworthy. Still, this is absolutely essential if we want to use the Bible to speak responsibly about God.

CHAPTER 10

Evaluating Disturbing Divine Behavior by the God Jesus Reveals

Toward a Christocentric Hermeneutic

If a biblical concept corresponds to what we know of God in Christ, it is acceptable, if not, it is invalid. Had this principle guided the Crusaders and the Conquistadors the world would have been a better place for millions of people.

—GARETH LLOYD JONES[1]

In chapter 9, I argued that using the Bible to think rightly about God requires making distinctions between the textual God and the actual God and, more specifically, between literary portrayals that help us see God clearly and those that do not. But how can we determine which Old Testament portrayals distort God's character and which reveal it? That is a crucial question for our study. In what follows, I will describe an interpretive method that will help us make such determinations responsibly rather than arbitrarily.

Is the New Testament the Answer?

Ideally, it would be nice if we could just turn to the New Testament, look at the view of God presented there, and rest assured that this provides us with a clear and accurate picture of God's character. This would then give us a standard for determining which Old Testament portrayals reveal, and which distort, God's character, and to what extent they do so. But unfortunately, that is not the case. The New Testament contains numerous portrayals of God that are not all compatible with one another. If fact, some seem mutually exclusive. This again requires us to make choices among various images of God to determine which most accurately reveal God's character. Moreover, not all New Testament portrayals of God are unproblematic. Disturbing divine behavior is present in the New Testament as well. In the book of Acts, for example, King Herod's hubris is said to be the cause of his gruesome death, ostensibly by the hand of God.

> On an appointed day Herod put on his royal robes, took his seat on the platform, and delivered a public address to them. The people kept shouting, "The voice of a god, and not of a mortal!" And immediately, because he had not given the glory to God, an angel of the Lord struck him down, and he was eaten by worms and died. (Acts 12:21-23)

In this passage, God is portrayed as an "instant executioner," a role God also assumes in several Old Testament passages.[2]

Other potentially problematic portrayals of God are found in the book of Revelation. This is especially true when certain passages are interpreted literalistically and futuristically. Consider the way Jerry Jenkins and Tim LaHaye, coauthors of the best-selling fictional *Left Behind* series, handle a passage like Rev. 20:11-15:

> Then I saw a great white throne and the one who sat on it; the earth and the heaven fled from his presence, and no place was found for them. And I saw the dead, great and small, standing before the throne, and books were opened. Also another book was opened, the book of life. And the dead were judged according to their works, as recorded in the books. And the sea gave up the dead that were in it, Death and Hades gave up the dead that were in them, and all were judged according to what they had done. Then Death and Hades were thrown into the lake of fire. This is the second death, the lake of fire; and anyone whose name was not found written in the book of life was thrown into the lake of fire.

According to Jenkins and LaHaye, this passage actually "describes the final judgment of unredeemed mankind."[3] If so, then it portrays God using massive violence on an unprecedented scale. In fact, according to Tremper Longman, "no more fearful picture of a vengeful, violent God may be found than that described in Revelation 20:11-15."[4] As Longman sees it: "Those who have moral difficulties with the genocide in the conquest of Canaan should have even more serious difficulties with the final judgment."[5]

Since the New Testament, like the Old, contains various problematic portrayals of God, we cannot simply turn to the New Testament, breathe a sigh of relief, and naively assume that every portrayal accurately represents God's character. If we want to use the New Testament to develop a clear picture of what God is really like, we will need to narrow our focus. To that end, I propose looking at the Gospels and, particularly, at the God Jesus reveals. This holds the key to helping us construct an accurate view of God's character.

A Christocentric Hermeneutic

In what follows, I will develop a christocentric hermeneutic—or Christ-centered method of interpretation—to address the problem of disturbing divine behavior in the Old Testament.[6] Although a christocentric hermeneutic can function in various ways, I am particularly interested in demonstrating how it can be used to evaluate problematic portrayals of God in the Old Testament.[7] To that end, I will argue that the God Jesus reveals should be the standard, or measuring rod, by which all Old Testament portrayals of God are evaluated. Old Testament portrayals that correspond to the God Jesus reveals should be regarded as trustworthy and reliable reflections of God's character, while those that do not measure up should be regarded as distortions. Using a christocentric hermeneutic in this way employs a principled approach to determining the degree of correspondence between the textual God and the actual God that keeps us from simply making choices based on our own preferences.

The interpretive approach I am proposing rests on two major assumptions, and these need to be identified and discussed before proceeding. First, this approach assumes that God's moral character is most clearly and completely revealed through the person of Jesus. Obviously, some divine attributes, such as God's eternality and omnipresence, are not most clearly revealed through Jesus, since Jesus set these aside to take on human flesh.[8] But the assumption here is not concerned with these kinds of attributes. Rather, it is solely concerned with God's *moral* character. God's moral character refers to such things as God's goodness, mercy, love, and justice, to name but a few. It is the character of God that is revealed in God's interactions with humanity.

This assertion—that God's moral character is most clearly and completely revealed through the person of Jesus—is supported by the New Testament witness in various ways. For example, in the first chapter of John's gospel, we are told that God took on human flesh in the person of Jesus and "dwelt among us" (John 1:14). The incarnation, as Christian theologians refer to this event, yields a unique and unparalleled look into the heart of God. Since Jesus actually *was* God—"in the beginning was the Word, and the Word was with God, and the Word was God" (John 1:1)—the incarnation allows us to see God in action. Therefore, the life and teachings of Jesus, God incarnate, provide a definitive revelation of the character of God. As the writer of Colossians puts it, Jesus is "the image of the invisible God" and the one in whom "all the fullness of God was pleased to dwell" (Col. 1:15, 19).[9] Jesus is elsewhere described as "the reflection of God's glory and the exact imprint of God's very being" (Heb. 1:3a). If Jesus truly is "the image of the invisible God" and "the exact imprint of God's very being," then it stands to reason that the most reliable picture of God available to us is the one Jesus provides. As C. S. Cowles observes: "In the New Testament, Jesus is not defined by God; rather, God is defined by Jesus. Jesus is the lens through whom a full, balanced, and undistorted view of God's loving heart and gracious purposes may be seen."[10] Accordingly, Jesus becomes "our final authority . . . in determining the true nature and character of God."[11]

New Testament scholar Oscar Cullmann refers to Jesus as "God in his self-revelation."[12] According to John's gospel, this was Jesus' perspective as well. On one occasion, after Philip expresses his desire that Jesus show the Father to the disciples, Jesus replies:

> Have I been with you all this time, Philip, and you still do not know me? Whoever has seen me has seen the Father. How can you say, "Show us the Father"? Do you not believe that I am in the Father and the Father is in me? The words that I say to you I do not speak on my own; but the Father who dwells in me does his works. (John 14:9b-10)

To see Jesus is to see God. A christocentric hermeneutic privileges Jesus not simply because Jesus is the cornerstone of Christian faith but because Jesus provides unparalleled access to the character of God. Practically, this means that the God Jesus reveals will be the standard by which to measure all other portrayals of God. As Anabaptist scholar David Janzen describes it: "The stories that reflect the God revealed in Jesus Christ . . . function as the lens through which we interpret the rest of the biblical material and will be our guide to a truer understanding of the character of God."[13]

Second, this interpretive approach assumes the consistency of God's character. If God's character changed over time, the revelation of Jesus would be partial and incomplete. It would reflect God's character only at a particular point in time. On the other hand, if God's character is consistent and unchanging, then we can be confident that the character of God revealed by Jesus reflects God's true nature. While this does not preclude the possibility that God used different *means* to accomplish things throughout history, it does preclude the possibility that God's essential attributes changed over time. God is not malicious at one time and merciful at another. Rather, there is a fundamental consistency to God's character.

The notion of the consistency of God's character is a key component of Janzen's christocentric hermeneutic, which is based on two concepts: a hermeneutic of obedience to Jesus and trinitarian doctrine. Regarding the latter, he writes: "A specific implication of the trinitarian doctrine is the consistency of God, or the belief that how God acts at one time is consistent with God's action elsewhere."[14] Therefore, he rightly recognizes "that the character of God as God cannot differ fundamentally from God as revealed in Jesus Christ."[15]

If we accept these two assumptions—that Jesus reveals God's character most fully and clearly and that God's character is consistent over time—it stands to reason that the God whom Jesus reveals should be the standard by which all portrayals of God are measured and evaluated. Every image of God, biblical or otherwise, can be judged by Jesus' revelation of God. Portrayals that correspond to the God Jesus reveals should be accepted as accurate reflections of God's nature. Those that stand in tension with Jesus' revelation of God should be regarded as distortions of the same. In the words of Gareth Jones noted earlier: "If a biblical concept corresponds to what we know of God in Christ, it is acceptable, if not, it is invalid."[16] This will be our guiding principle as we address the problem of disturbing divine behavior in Old Testament narratives.

The Quest for the Historical Jesus

Determining the kind of God Jesus reveals requires us to look closely at Jesus' life and teachings as reported in the Gospels. But doing so immediately raises a potential problem. How can we be sure the literary portrayals of Jesus in the Gospels accurately reflect what Jesus actually said and did? Biblical scholars have invested an enormous amount of time and energy discussing this very question. Some believe it is necessary to differentiate between the historical Jesus (the actual Jesus) and the Christ of faith (the textual Jesus). This has resulted in a series of "quests" to determine which portions of the Gospels reflect what Jesus, the Jew from Nazareth, actually said and did.[17] In their attempt to identify the historical Jesus, scholars have developed various criteria to evaluate Jesus' words and deeds in an effort to distinguish which are authentic and which represent secondary accretions by the Church. The fruit of these efforts is disputed, and some scholars even question the probability (not to mention the usefulness) of trying to discover the historical Jesus.

For the purposes of this study, it is not necessary to enter heavily into this debate, though I do need to provide some context for what follows. First, I agree with the basic premise that some portrayals of Jesus in the Gospels do *not* reflect what Jesus actually said or did. It is unnecessary to assume that everything the Gospels say about Jesus accurately reflects the words and deeds of the historical Jesus. They clearly do not, a point that is quite evident when comparing a parallel account in two or more Gospels. Second, while it is true that the Gospel writers attribute things to Jesus he never said or did, the degree of distortion between the textual Jesus and the actual Jesus is typically far less severe than that which sometimes exists between the textual God and the actual God in the Old Testament.

I think there is a very simple reason for this. The Gospel writers had the benefit of eyewitness accounts of Jesus' miraculous power and authoritative teaching.[18] When writing the Gospels, they could utilize the traditions that had been handed down to them by those who had firsthand experience with Jesus, God in human flesh. The writers of the Old Testament, on the other hand, did not have access to an incarnate deity who lived among them. Instead, they tried to discern the hand of God in historical and natural events and regularly used worldview assumptions typical of their day to do so. Obviously, theirs was a much more difficult task, one open to far more speculation and potential misrepresentation of God's character than what we generally find in the Gospels. Third, despite the presence of inauthentic Jesus sayings in the Gospels, I believe the general portrait of Jesus that emerges is reliable enough to serve as a standard by which to evaluate portrayals of God in the Old Testament and elsewhere. Therefore, for the purposes of this study, it is generally not necessary to make fine distinctions between the textual Jesus and the actual Jesus. Where there are difficulties relevant to our study, they can be handled on a case-by-case basis (and will be given limited attention in appendix A).

Reintroducing God

My proposal to use the God Jesus reveals as the standard to evaluate literary portrayals of God raises an obvious question: What kind of God does Jesus reveal? I will attempt to answer this question in two ways, first by making some general comments about the God Jesus reveals vis-à-vis the Old Testament, and then by identifying several key characteristics central to Jesus' understanding of God.

To begin, it is important to be absolutely clear about one thing: Christians believe the God Jesus revealed is the same God the Bible describes as the God of Abraham, Isaac, and Jacob. This God was Israel's God, the one Jews and their ancestors worshiped for hundreds of years. Contrary to Marcion's beliefs, the Bible does *not* describe two different supreme beings who share little in common. Marcion was clearly wrong on this point.

What got people's attention—and what got Jesus in a lot of trouble—was that Jesus spoke about their God, the God of Israel, in ways that did not conform to their expectations. He described God in unconventional ways that irritated those who had fixed ideas about who God was and how God behaved. Through both word and deed, Jesus challenged some of their most deeply held theological convictions. He demonstrated how their view of God was fundamentally flawed in certain respects; it was much too exclusive and far too violent. Jesus tried to correct these and other misperceptions by reintroducing God to them.

One way Jesus attempted to help people see God more clearly was by utilizing "Old Testament" stories that revealed positive characteristics of God that were otherwise often overlooked.[19] For instance, consider Jesus' inaugural address in Luke 4.

After quoting a passage from Isaiah and engaging in a brief interchange with his audience, Jesus cites two Old Testament stories—and is nearly killed for doing so! Jesus says:

> But the truth is, there were many widows in Israel in the time of Elijah, when the heaven was shut up three years and six months, and there was a severe famine over all the land; yet Elijah was sent to none of them except to a widow at Zarephath in Sidon. There were also many lepers in Israel in the time of the prophet Elisha, and none of them was cleansed except Naaman the Syrian. (Luke 4:25-27)

The two stories Jesus refers to—one from 1 Kgs. 17:8-24 and the other from 2 Kgs. 5:1-19—are stories about God's grace toward outsiders during the prophetic ministry of Elijah and Elisha, respectively. They are stories Jesus uses to emphasize God's involvement with—and care for—non-Israelites.

The first story describes God's use of a foreign woman from Sidon to provide for Elijah's physical needs. Her faithfulness in doing so was rewarded by Elijah's presence and her survival. When Elijah first arrived at her doorstep, she had been preparing her last meal, which she planned to eat with her son before they died of starvation. Yet, as long as Elijah remained with her, the food she had to eat and the water she had to drink miraculously multiplied and never ran out. What makes this story so scandalous, especially to first-century Jews, is its emphasis on God's positive involvement with non-Israelites. While God certainly could have used one of the "many widows in Israel in the time of Elijah," God uses a foreigner to sustain the prophet. The second story repeats this same theme. Here the focus is on a man named Naaman, a Syrian army commander, who has leprosy. Once again, despite the presence of many lepers in Israel, it is only this foreigner whom the God of Israel heals.

The God Jesus reveals through these stories is one who is embracing and inclusive rather than parochial or nationalistic. As New Testament scholar Joel Green puts it: "In Jesus' address, the role of Elijah and Elisha as agents of healing to (and thus the exercise of God's grace among) outsiders is paramount."[20] These stories portray God as one whose concern for others crosses traditional boundaries, while emphasizing that the same would be characteristic of Jesus' ministry also. Suffice it to say, Jesus' audience did not receive this message very well.

> When they heard this, all in the synagogue were filled with rage. They got up, drove him out of the town, and led him to the brow of the hill on which their town was built, so that they might hurl him off the cliff. (Luke 4:28-29)

Jesus' vision of God was clearly at odds with theirs. Despite the fact that Jesus appealed to Scripture to make his case, his audience did not appreciate what he was claiming about God. In fact, they found his view of God so threatening that they tried to kill him. Murder seemed an entirely appropriate response to such "blasphemy."

Jesus certainly would have been familiar with a wide range of portrayals of God, including the problematic ones we have been considering in this study. Nevertheless, the more troubling Old Testament images did not govern his view of God. Instead, Jesus embraced other portrayals of God in the Old Testament, such as those found in the stories from 1 and 2 Kings noted above. These alternate portrayals of God—portrayals that offer a counterpoint to the most disturbing depictions of God in the Old Testament—are the ones that seem to have most influenced his thinking about the nature of God.

The God Jesus reveals is not a new deity unconnected to Israel's past but the one already found in the pages of the Old Testament. Jesus attempts to reintroduce this God to the people by correcting certain misperceptions and by emphasizing certain key characteristics that seem to have been overlooked. Jesus does this by selectively using some images of God from the Old Testament while avoiding others altogether. For example, Jesus never speaks of God as one who commands genocide. Nor does he describes God as one who abuses, deceives, or acts unjustly. These unsavory characteristics, which are evident in certain Old Testament portrayals of God, do not factor into Jesus' description of God. On the contrary, we will see that the God Jesus reveals is one who loves enemies and is kind to the wicked.

On occasion, Jesus does refer to certain Old Testament narratives that contain disturbing divine behavior. For example, in Luke 17:26-30, Jesus mentions the worldwide flood and the destruction of Sodom and Gomorrah recorded in the book of Genesis. It is interesting to note, however, that Jesus does not explicitly identify God as the cause of either of these disasters. Although his audience presumably would have assumed this to be the case, the way Jesus tells these stories keeps the problem of divine violence in the background. More significantly, it is clear that Jesus' purpose in using these stories was *not* to suggest that God's behavior in these narratives was representative of how God operates *in* history. Instead, Jesus used both stories as analogies that could help people understand what will happen at *the end* of history, when "the Son of Man is revealed" (v. 30).[21] My point here is simply to emphasize that Old Testament narratives containing problematic portrayals of God rarely occur in Jesus' discourse and, when they do, are not used to make theological claims about how God behaves in history.

The God Jesus Reveals

We are now ready to consider the kind of God Jesus reveals. This can be done by identifying some key characteristics of God that Jesus emphasized through his life and teaching. As noted above, Jesus' understanding of God's character was clearly influenced by certain Old Testament portrayals of God. Although Jesus typically does not cite particular narratives, much of what he says is compatible with certain Old Testament images of God, and some of these points of continuity will be discussed below. This serves the important function of reminding us that there are many positive and constructive images of God in the Old Testament. Despite the focus of this book, divine behavior in the Old Testament is not always disturbing! On the other hand, it will quickly become obvious that some of the claims Jesus makes about God stand in serious tension with certain Old Testament portrayals of God. While these differences can be disconcerting to many readers, I would argue that it is precisely these points of discontinuity that make a Christocentric hermeneutic so necessary and helpful for dealing responsibly with problematic portrayals of God.

While a fully satisfactory discussion of the kind of God Jesus reveals would require a book all its own, we can develop a rudimentary portrait of Jesus' God by looking at selected gospel passages. This portrait will then become the standard by which all other depictions of God in Scripture, especially the problematic ones, can be evaluated.

Jesus Reveals a God Who Is Kind to the Wicked

One of the first things we notice when looking at the life and teachings of Jesus is that Jesus reveals a God who is kind to the wicked. Hints of divine kindness toward the wicked are not absent from the Old Testament either. Recall the story of Jonah discussed earlier. God calls the prophet Jonah to "go at once to Nineveh, that great city, and cry out against it; for their wickedness has come up before me" (Jon. 1:2). After a failed attempt to flee from God's presence, Jonah does go as commanded, preaches a very brief sermon, and is dismayed to see the whole city turn to God. On the other hand, "when God saw what they did, how they turned from their evil ways, God changed his mind about the calamity that he had said he would bring upon them; and he did not do it" (Jon. 3:10). As this story portrays it, God spares a city full of Assyrians—people the Israelites would have considered some of the most wicked in the world—when they repent. Even in the Old Testament, God is sometimes portrayed as one who is kind to the wicked.

Admittedly, this image of God in the Old Testament is often overshadowed by the preponderance of portrayals of God meting out divine devastation on the wicked. Yet, despite the overwhelming presence of these problematic portrayals in the Old Testament, Jesus does not envision God as one who uses lethal force to destroy wicked people. Rather, the God Jesus reveals has more in common with the picture of God that emerges from the book of Jonah. This can be demonstrated in various ways. Embedded in the Sermon on the Mount, we find one of Jesus' most familiar sayings:

> You have heard that it was said, "You shall love your neighbor and hate your enemy." But I say to you, Love your enemies and pray for those who persecute you, so that you may be children of your Father in heaven; for he makes his sun rise on the evil and on the good, and sends rain on the righteous and on the unrighteous. (Matt. 5:43-45)

The importance of this verse for understanding Jesus' view of God can hardly be overestimated. Jesus doesn't command his followers to love their enemies just because he thinks it is a good idea. Jesus commands them to love their enemies because that's what God does. Their behavior is to mirror God's behavior. Followers of Jesus are to love enemies and pray for persecutors in order to "be children of your Father in heaven."

It is not uncommon for people who know my dad to look at me and easily recognize me as Laverne's son. For better or worse, we look alike. Similarly, people will know that we are related to God when we behave like God does. And this, fundamentally, involves loving our enemies. We are called to love our enemies because that is exactly what God does. As the apostle Paul reminds us: "God proves his love for us in that while we still were sinners Christ died for us" (Rom. 5:8). When people see Christians loving their enemies and see a family resemblance and get a glimpse into the very heart of God.

Jesus further describes God as one who "makes his sun rise on the evil and on the good, and sends rain on the righteous and on the unrighteous." By saying this, Jesus reveals his view of God as one whose blessings extend to everyone. Sunshine and rain, "good gifts" from God, are not reserved for the upright alone; they are extended even to those who are wicked.[22] In a parallel passage in the Gospel of Luke, Jesus says:

> But love your enemies, do good, and lend, expecting nothing in return. Your reward will be great, and you will be children of the Most High; *for he is kind to the ungrateful and the wicked*. (Luke 6:35, emphasis mine)

The God Jesus reveals, one who is "kind to the ungrateful and the wicked," is clearly at odds with Old Testament pronouncements declaring God to be "far from the wicked" (Prov. 15:29) and one who "make[s] the wicked stumble" (Zeph. 1:3). Jesus' view of God as one who "makes his sun rise on the evil and on the good, and sends rain on the righteous and on the unrighteous" similarly undermines the psalmist's claim that God hates all evildoers (Ps. 5:5) and that God's face "is against" them (Ps. 34:16).[23]

By what he said and did, Jesus revealed a God who abounds in mercy. This is not surprising since this was part of Israel's core confession about the character of God. Israel celebrated God as one who is "merciful and gracious" (Exod. 34:6). Jesus affirmed this view of God and allowed it to inform his ministry. As Gerd

Lüdemann observes: "At the heart of Jesus' *picture of God* is not the figure of a vengeful, zealous God but one of a God who turns to men and women in mercy."[24] A clear example of this is found in Jesus' treatment of the woman caught in the act of adultery recorded in John 8.[25]

> Early in the morning he came again to the temple. All the people came to him and he sat down and began to teach them. The scribes and the Pharisees brought a woman who had been caught in adultery; and making her stand before all of them, they said to him, "Teacher, this woman was caught in the very act of committing adultery. Now in the law Moses commanded us to stone such women. Now what do you say?" They said this to test him, so that they might have some charge to bring against him. Jesus bent down and wrote with his finger on the ground. When they kept on questioning him, he straightened up and said to them, "Let anyone among you who is without sin be the first to throw a stone at her." And once again he bent down and wrote on the ground. When they heard it, they went away, one by one, beginning with the elders; and Jesus was left alone with the woman standing before him. Jesus straightened up and said to her, "Woman, where are they? Has no one condemned you?" She said, "No one, sir." And Jesus said, "Neither do I condemn you. Go your way, and from now on do not sin again." (John 8:2-11)[26]

Jesus undoubtedly knew what the law required in this situation. This woman and her partner were to be executed. As Lev. 20:10 plainly states: "If a man commits adultery with the wife of his neighbor, both the adulterer and the adulteress shall be put to death." According to the book of Leviticus, this lethal legislation was a mandate straight from God (see Lev. 20:1). Yet Jesus felt the freedom to ignore it. Why? Apparently, Jesus did not envision God as a "deadly lawgiver." Instead, Jesus recognized God as one who is merciful, gracious, and compassionate. Jesus knew that God desires mercy (Matt. 9:13; 12:7), and this knowledge gave Jesus the freedom to reject the requirements of the law, even one ostensibly given by God. As this incident testifies, the God Jesus reveals is one who deals mercifully, not murderously, with sinners, while still calling them to leave their sinful ways behind.

In fact, when reading through the Gospels, you get the distinct impression that the God Jesus reveals was more interested in eating with sinners than executing them.

> And as he [Jesus] sat at dinner in Levi's house, many tax collectors and sinners were also sitting with Jesus and his disciples—for there were many who followed him. When the scribes of the Pharisees saw that he was eating with sinners and tax collectors, they said to his disciples, "Why does he eat with tax collectors and sinners?" When Jesus heard this, he said to them, "Those who

are well have no need of a physician, but those who are sick; I have come to call not the righteous but sinners." (Mark 2:15-17)

Jesus was regularly "banqueting with the bad," to borrow an expression from New Testament scholar Ben Witherington.[27] According to Jewish standards of the day, Jesus regularly hung out with the wrong crowd. He ate with sinners, touched lepers, welcomed tax collectors, and even talked to prostitutes! Yet these were the very people whom respected religious figures, familiar with the Old Testament and its problematic portrayals of God, knew to avoid. As Witherington puts is: "That the scribes object to Jesus' behavior . . . is quite understandable in view of some of the things the Old Testament says about the wicked (cf. Ps. 10:15; 141:5; and esp. Prov. 2:22; 10:30; 14:9: 'God scorns the wicked, but the upright enjoys his favor')."[28] Yet Jesus is not bound by these unattractive images of God. Instead, he affirms an alternate vision of God found in the Old Testament—namely, that God is gracious, merciful, and kind to the wicked.

We are so familiar with Jesus' friendship with the "wicked" that we fail to appreciate the scandal his behavior caused. By meeting and eating with such people, by forgiving their sins and welcoming them to participate in the reign of God, Jesus radically challenged some of the most problematic portrayals of God in the Old Testament. The God Jesus reveals is one characterized by a gracious hospitality that will stop at nothing to seek and save those who are not yet participating in the kingdom of God. While it is true that Jesus reveals a God who relentlessly pursues sinners, it is for the purpose of bringing them into the kingdom, not casting them out (see Luke 15). It is a pursuit of love, not punishment. In fact, when God sees even the slightest hint of repentance, the divine arms are wide open. The God Jesus reveals is a friend to sinners, not an enemy. Such a vision of God forces us to reassess those Old Testament portrayals of God that are at odds with these striking images of divine kindness and compassion.

Jesus Reveals a God Who Is Nonviolent

A number of years ago, I stumbled across a book with the intriguing title *Our God Is Nonviolent*. The book, written by a Jesuit priest named John Dear, highlights various practitioners of nonviolence, such as Martin Luther King Jr., Dorothy Day, Thomas Merton, Daniel Berrigan, and, of course, Jesus. The book's stated thesis is as follows: "Our God is a God of love and is nonviolent; God calls us to be nonviolent toward one another in order to transform our world of violence and war."[29]

While I imagine most Christians would have no problem speaking of God as a God of love, I wonder how many agree with Dear's declaration that God is nonviolent. Tremper Longman and Daniel Reid certainly do not. After quoting a passage from Isa. 13:6-14, these two biblical scholars begin their article "When

God Declares War" with these words: "Isaiah won't let us escape the fact that our God is violent. In fact, Scripture often describes him as a warrior, a warring king who obliterates his enemies."[30] My guess is that many Christians resonate more with Longman and Reid's bold declaration than with Dear's. But is theirs an accurate assessment of the character of God? Is the God whom Jesus reveals violent?[31] I think not.

Time and time again, the life and teachings of Jesus reveal a God who is non-violent. Recall Jesus' command to love enemies. As stressed earlier, the rationale for this command is rooted in the very nature of God. We are to love enemies because that is what God does. By calling us to love our enemies in imitation of God, Jesus effectively subverts some very popular first-century ideas about the fundamental nature of God's character—ideas, I might add, that had strong "biblical" support. Many Jews living in first-century Palestine looked forward to a day when God would fight on their behalf. They expected God to liberate them from foreign occupation by violently slaughtering their Roman oppressors. But when Jesus called people to love their enemies because God does, Jesus directly challenged their notions of a vengeful deity bent on the destruction of the wicked—in this case, the Romans. In doing so, Jesus invited his hearers to consider an alternative vision of God, one that did not include violence.

Implicitly at least, this is a feature of Jesus' inaugural address in Luke 4. Reading from the scroll of Isaiah, Jesus stops just prior to "getting to the prophetic punch line," as Cowles puts it.[32] The part that Jesus leaves out refers to the much anticipated "day of vengeance" when God would settle accounts with Israel's enemies (Isa. 61:2). According to Cowles, Jesus' "editing of this Scripture passage was not accidental but intentional and . . . represented an entirely new way of thinking about God." Cowles argues that Jesus was engaging in "an entirely new rewrite of Jewish theology" that "would introduce the shocking, unprecedented, and utterly incomprehensible news that God is nonviolent and that he wills the well-being of all humans, beginning with the poor, the oppressed, and the disenfranchised."[33]

As you read through the Gospels, you discover that Jesus never endorses or promotes a view of God as a divine warrior who fights physical battles on behalf of a "chosen people." As New Testament scholar Ben Witherington observes: "The call to throw off the yoke of Roman rule and retake the land is missing in Jesus' message. He did not use (as far as we can tell) the ancient Near Eastern myth of the divine warrior to articulate his vision of the coming dominion of God."[34] Thus, while certain passages in Isaiah might lead one to believe that God is violent, as Longman and Reid contend, it is clearly not the way Jesus understood God.

Jesus himself lived nonviolently throughout his life and ministry. Various stories in the Gospels illustrate Jesus' explicit rejection of violence. Since Jesus was God incarnate, God in human flesh, these stories are instructive and illustrative of the character of God. Jesus' commitment to nonviolence reflects the nonviolence of

God since the character of God is revealed in and through the words and deeds of Jesus. Luke records a very telling story in which Jesus rejects a violent response to an indignity he and his disciples suffer:

> When the days drew near for him [Jesus] to be taken up, he set his face to go to Jerusalem. And he sent messengers ahead of him. On their way they entered a village of the Samaritans to make ready for him; but they did not receive him, because his face was set toward Jerusalem. When his disciples James and John saw it, they said, "Lord, do you want us to command fire to come down from heaven and consume them?" But he turned and rebuked them. Then they went on to another village. (Luke 9:51-56)

There was no love lost between Jews and Samaritans during the first century. Jews regarded Samaritans as half-breeds, the descendants of those Israelites who had intermarried with foreigners in the land after the northern kingdom of Israel fell to the Assyrians in 722 BCE. As this story clearly illustrates, feelings of animosity ran deep between these two groups. On this occasion, Jesus is heading toward Jerusalem, the Jew's most holy place of worship. The Samaritans, on the other hand, believed Mount Gerizim, rather than Mount Zion (Jerusalem), was the proper place to worship God. Thus, when Jesus and his entourage enter this Samaritan village en route to Jerusalem, these Samaritans refuse to offer them the most basic hospitality of food and lodging. In response to this affront, James and John suggest that the Samaritans be punished for their actions (or lack thereof). Inspired by a violent Old Testament narrative, the disciples ask if they should command fire to come down from heaven to consume these inhospitable "half-breeds."[35] Jesus not only rejects their violent response but also rebukes his disciples in the process. According to some ancient manuscripts, Jesus says, "You do not know what spirit you are of, for the Son of Man has not come to destroy the lives of human beings but to save them."[36] As Cowles observes:

> They [the disciples] were ready to consign all of Samaria to destruction because of the inhospitality of a few. Apparently, it never crossed their minds that not only would the recalcitrant males perish but women, children, and the infirm, the very people Jesus had come to redeem. They would have thereby annihilated the woman at the well, who became the gospel's first evangelist, as well as the very people who would be the first beyond Judea to receive and welcome the good news of Christ's resurrection and the first to experience an outpouring of the Holy Spirit after Pentecost.[37]

Jesus rejects this violent option because it is inconsistent with the nature of God and the purpose of the kingdom. The God whom Jesus reveals is not one who goes around slaying sinners.

Jesus' rejection of violence is also strikingly illustrated on the night he is betrayed. As Jesus stands with his disciples in the Garden of Gethsemane, Judas approaches Jesus and betrays him with a kiss. What happens next once again exemplifies the nonviolence of God revealed through Jesus.

> Suddenly, one of those with Jesus put his hand on his sword, drew it, and struck the slave of the high priest, cutting off his ear. Then Jesus said to him, "Put your sword back into its place; for all who take the sword will perish by the sword." (Matt. 26:51-52)

Jesus forbade his disciples from using violence to protect him because he understood the mimetic nature of violence.[38] Jesus knew that violence would only lead to more violence. Violence is contrary not only to the will of God but to the very nature of God. As God incarnate, Jesus' nonviolent words and deeds enable us to see clearly the true nature of God.

The nonviolence of God is most plainly visible in Christ crucified on the cross.[39] Unfortunately, many people have turned this supreme act of nonviolent love into an act of divine violence by suggesting that God (the Father) willed—and thus was ultimately responsible for—the death of Jesus. Throughout the history of the church, various theories of the atonement have been put forward to explain the meaning of Jesus' death on the cross. Today, penal substitutionary atonement is one of the most popular theories held by many Christians. According to this view, the primary reason God sent Jesus to earth was to die on the cross. This theory of the atonement claims that on the cross, Jesus took upon himself the punishment each of us deserved. Jesus' death is what makes the forgiveness of our sins and a relationship with God possible. This theory of the atonement—like many others—maintains that the death of Jesus on the cross was divinely willed violence necessary for our salvation.

While this is not the place to engage in a thorough assessment of this (or any other) theory of the atonement, a few brief comments are in order.[40] One fundamental problem with penal substitutionary atonement is the way it drives a wedge between God the Father and God the Son, essentially maintaining that the Father required the death of the Son to save humanity. In its most troubling rendition, this view sometimes suggests that God the Father poured out all the divine wrath for the sins of humanity upon Jesus. Biblically speaking, such a view is utterly without merit. Penal substitutionary atonement has also been criticized for conceiving of the cross in largely forensic, rather than relational, terms. It regards Jesus' death on the cross as something necessary to settle a matter of cosmic justice without which it would have been impossible for God to forgive sins and be reconciled with humanity.

But this raises some sticky theological questions related to forgiveness and the justice of God. For example, does divine forgiveness require punishment? Moreover, if Jesus actually paid the debt, in what sense can we speak of this as "forgiveness," especially if forgiveness is understood as being released from a debt that cannot be paid? And in what sense is it just for someone who is innocent to suffer on behalf of someone who is guilty? Despite its popularity, penal substitutionary atonement is problematic at a variety of levels. I do not consider it an appropriate way to understand the significance of Jesus' death.

When attempting to understand the meaning of the cross, it helps to keep in mind that the church has never taken an official position on this issue. While the church has developed established creeds about such things as Jesus' nature—born of a virgin, fully God, fully human, of the same essence as the Father—the church has never done so with regard to the atonement. No ecumenical council has ever declared penal substitutionary atonement—or any other theory for that matter—to be the "orthodox" one.

Today, a growing number of scholars reject theories of the atonement that are predicated upon notions of divine violence. Instead, they understand the significance of Jesus' death in ways that are compatible with a nonviolent view of God.[41] As professor J. Denny Weaver writes:

> Jesus did suffer and die a violent death, but *the violence was neither God's nor God directed. Suffering and dying were not the purpose or goal of Jesus' mission.* Death resulted when Jesus faithfully carried out his life-bringing and life-affirming mission to make the rule of God present and visible. Since saving his life would have meant abandoning his mission, his death was necessary in the sense that faithfulness required that he go through death.[42]

Weaver and others emphasize the significance of Jesus' life. They argue that Jesus came to live, not to die. Death was the tragic—though predictable—result of Jesus' life, a life committed to inaugurating the kingdom of God, God's reign of peace and justice, on earth.

Jesus' willingness to die on the cross for the sake of the truth rather than to use force to preserve his own life speaks volumes about the nonviolent love of God. As Jesus hung on the cross, he spoke words of forgiveness rather than condemnation for those who tortured and crucified him. There is no call to arms or thought of revenge, only words of pardon and release (Luke 23:34). In that moment, we see straight into the heart of God. On the cross, the nonviolent character of God is displayed most dramatically and definitively. It is there we see God as a suffering servant, not a dominating warrior. God liberates by enduring pain, not by inflicting it. As John Dear puts it:

> In the revelation of Jesus, we find that our God is completely nonviolent. . . . Jesus reveals our God to be a suffering God, constantly loving, sacrificing God's self, dying for love of us, suffering the pain and violence we show to God, yet

constantly responding to that violence with nonviolent love. This is what Jesus taught and revealed with his life and death and resurrection.[43]

Both Jesus' life and death testify to the nonviolence of God. The fact that Jesus, God among us, never condoned violence, resorted to violence, or encouraged his followers to use violence reveals something profoundly true about the nonviolent nature of God.

Some have disputed the assertion that Jesus was nonviolent.[44] They regard such things as Jesus' dramatic actions in the temple when he overturned tables and drove out moneychangers (Matt 21:12), and his instructions that his followers lacking a sword sell their cloak and purchase one (Luke 22:36), as evidence that Jesus sometimes used and sanctioned violence. Since helpful responses to these and similar objections are readily available, I have chosen not to address them here.[45] In my estimation, when passages like these are properly understood, they are fully consistent with the claim that Jesus was nonviolent.

A potentially more serious objection we have not yet discussed, and that might seem to cast some doubt on the characterization of God as nonviolent, concerns Jesus' teachings about eschatological (end-time) judgment. How does Jesus' teaching about God's judgment of humanity, particularly the fate of those judged unfaithful, relate to this assertion that Jesus reveals a God who is nonviolent? To put it bluntly, how can a God who consigns people to "eternal punishment" be considered nonviolent?[46] This is an important question that needs to considered in some detail. For that reason, I have devoted a significant portion of appendix A to this issue. Anticipating my conclusions, I argue that Jesus' teachings about eschatological judgment are actually less problematic than they initially appear and do not undermine the characterization of God as fundamentally nonviolent.

While it is impossible to know exactly how Jesus' views about the nonviolence of God developed, he would have had some basis for viewing God this way from the opening chapters of the book of Genesis. Here, in the first two chapters, God is portrayed as a nonviolent creator. These texts affirm that when God created the world, whenever and however God actually did that, God created it without using violence. According to Genesis 1, God speaks the world into existence. God says, "Let there be light," and there is light (Gen. 1:3). God says, "Let the dry land appear," and it does (Gen. 1:9). God speaks, and creation happens. Likewise, in Genesis 2, God's creative acts do not require violence of any sort. God forms Adam from the dust. God plants a garden. God makes trees grow. At every point in the creative process, God operates nonviolently.[47]

This image of God as a nonviolent creator is particularly striking and noteworthy when set alongside other ancient Near Eastern creation accounts that routinely include divine violence as an integral part of the story. To cite one celebrated example, consider the Mesopotamian creation story known as the *Enuma Elish*. In this story, a fearsome goddess named Tiamat plans to kill certain gods because of their complicity in the death of her husband. The god Marduk agrees to fight Tiamat and is victorious. He kills Tiamat and then tears her body into two pieces. Half becomes the earth; the other half, the sky. Order is established, and the world as we know it is formed as a result of this violent act. But the story doesn't end there. Marduk kills Kingu—the ringleader of a group of devilish beings who had aided Tiamat—and Ea, the god of wisdom, uses the blood of this slain demon-god to create human beings. Once again, creation by divine violence is central to this story.

When you consider Genesis 1–2 alongside a story like the *Enuma Elish*, the contrast is striking, especially as it concerns the portrayal of God/the gods in each. Whereas the *Enuma Elish* envisions both the earth and humanity resulting from divine violence, Genesis 1–2 eschews any intimation of the use of violence in the creative process, choosing instead to portray God as a nonviolent creator.

The presence of this nonviolent image of God at the very beginning of the Bible is especially important. As professor J. Richard Middleton contends:

> By its alternative depiction of God's non-violent creative power at the start of the biblical canon, Gen 1 signals the Creator's original intent for shalom and blessing at the outset of human history. . . . As the opening canonical disclosure of God for readers of Scripture, Gen 1 constitutes a normative framework by which we may judge all the violence that pervades the rest of the Bible.[48]

Obviously, the extent to which this particular passage, Genesis 1–2, may have shaped Jesus' views about the nonviolence of God can never be known. But the point I wish to emphasize once again is that the God Jesus reveals stands in continuity with certain Old Testament images of God. While Jesus clearly distances himself from some renderings of God in the Old Testament, others are fully compatible with the way Jesus understands and reveals the character of God.

Jesus Reveals a God Who Does Not Judge People by Causing Historical (or Natural) Disasters or Serious Physical Infirmities

As discussed in chapter 8, Israelites—and people in the ancient world generally— interpreted historical disasters (such as defeat in battle) and natural disasters (such as famine) as signs of divine judgment. Similarly, they believed that people who contracted certain diseases, such as "leprosy," were being punished by God for their misdeeds.[49] Tragedies like these were most commonly understood as signs of divine judgment. This popular notion of divine retribution is challenged by Jesus on more than one occasion. Jesus suggests that neither historical disasters nor physical infirmities should necessarily be interpreted as signs of God's judgment.

One striking example of Jesus' alternative perspective on God's activity in the world in this regard is found in the Gospel of Luke:

At that very time there were some present who told him [Jesus] about the Galileans whose blood Pilate had mingled with their sacrifices. He asked them, "Do you think that because these Galileans suffered in this way they were worse sinners than all other Galileans? No, I tell you; but unless you repent, you will all perish as they did. Or those eighteen who were killed when the tower of Siloam fell on them—do you think that they were worse offenders than all the others living in Jerusalem? No, I tell you; but unless you repent, you will all perish just as they did." (Luke 13:1-5)

In this passage, Jesus reflects on two recent tragedies people typically would have regarded as signs of justly merited divine punishment. Yet Jesus directly challenges that kind of thinking. He does not believe that those killed were worse sinners than any of those in his immediate audience, nor does he suggest they had been intentionally targeted by a violent God exacting lethal punishment for their offenses. In both examples—the sacrificial massacre and the collapse of the tower of Siloam—Jesus emphasizes that those who experience such calamity are not "worse sinners" than those who do not. Instead, Jesus asserts that all people stand in need of God's mercy and grace and will experience the consequences of divine judgment ("will perish") unless they repent. As Charles Talbert puts it:

Just because people pass through life unscathed by suffering they should not assume that therefore they please God. Tragedy is no sure sign of sinfulness, just as absence of tragedy is no sure sign of righteousness. All alike—those whose lives are tragic and those whose lives are tranquil—are sinners and all alike must repent (change directions in life) before God's judgment comes upon them.[50]

Thus, while Jesus certainly does not exclude the reality of divine judgment, he does reject the notion that all personal tragedies are the direct result of divine judgment. Importantly, the divine judgment to which Jesus alludes in verses 3 and 5 is best understood as referring "to the last judgment," not to some kind of earthly calamity such as those referred to in Luke 13.[51]

On another occasion, Jesus and his disciples came across a man who had been born blind. Seeing this man, the disciples ask a revealing question: "Rabbi, who sinned, this man or his parents, that he was born blind?" (John 9:2). Jesus' disciples automatically assume that this man's physical infirmity was the result of divine punishment. Their interpretation of this man's condition is not surprising since it was commonly assumed that physical suffering resulted from sinful behavior. What is surprising is Jesus' response. His answer to their question—who sinned, this man or his parents?—is "Neither" (John 9:3). Jesus did not interpret this man's blindness as the result of divine punishment for human sin. According to Jesus, that is not the way God operates. Jesus rejected the doctrine of retribution because it was at odds with his understanding of how God works in the world.

The very nature of Jesus' ministry further challenges the notion that God is the kind of being who punishes sinners by inflicting them with serious physical infirmities. As Cowles observes: "It is surely a fact of inexhaustible significance that Jesus never used his supernatural miracle-working power to hurt, maim, coerce, conquer, or destroy."[52] Jesus' ministry was characterized by healing people, extending compassion, blessing children, and, yes, even forgiving sinners. Jesus made the lame walk, the blind see, the deaf hear, and the dead live. The God whom Jesus revealed was one who helped and healed people, not one who relentlessly pursued sinners to harm and kill them.

While this view of God stands in stark contrast with many Old Testament portrayals of God, there are some points of continuity between this Old Testament image and Jesus' understanding of God. Foremost among these is the simple fact that it is God's prerogative to judge sinners. Both Old Testament portrayals and the teachings of Jesus affirm that view of God. Thus, *that* God will judge sinners is not at issue. Rather, what is at issue is *when and how* that judgment will come.[53] In contrast to the Old Testament's insistence that God doles out punishments here and now, Jesus claims that divine judgment occurs at the end of the age. Therefore, Jesus tries to disabuse his hearers of the notion that God's judgment befalls sinners in predictable ways here and now. That unrepentant people will perish and that judgment will come are not in question. What Jesus is saying, however, is that this judgment will not come through direct acts of divine violence in history, the way it is so often portrayed in the Old Testament. Instead, divine reckoning is reserved for a future time, when God, "the judge of all the earth," will "do what is just."[54] In this instance, Jesus challenges a traditional way of understanding God's activity in the world and, in so doing, helps people see the character of God in a different light.

Jesus Reveals a God of Love

Finally, the God whom Jesus reveals is fundamentally characterized by love. This is the most primary characteristic of Jesus' God and the one that undergirds all the others. It is God's love that explains God's nonviolence and kindness to the wicked. It is God's love that restrains God from using lethal force to punish people through natural and historical disasters or serious physical infirmities. While the love of God is certainly evident in numerous Old Testament passages, it is most clearly visible in the person of Jesus. The incarnation, life, death, and resurrection of Jesus assure us beyond a doubt that God's primary disposition toward us is loving. This love is not some squishy, sentimental feeling. Rather, it represents a profound and costly choice to be with us and for us. As we read in John 3:16, one of the most well known verses in all the Bible: "For God so loved the world that he gave his only Son, so that everyone who believes in him may not perish but may have eternal life."

God wants to be in relationship with us and has gone to great lengths to make that possible.

God's love for us and desire to be in relationship with us is perhaps most poignantly expressed in the well-known parable of the prodigal son (Luke 15:11-32). In this parable, the God Jesus reveals is one whose love for all people, even those who have sinned grievously, is deep and real. The father in this parable, who symbolically represents God, exemplifies God's love in his response to his youngest son. When this wayward son returns home after going "to a distant country" where "he squandered his property in dissolute living," the father breaks with all Middle Eastern decorum and comes running out of the house to greet him.

> But while he [the wayward son] was still far off, his father saw him and was filled with compassion; he ran and put his arms around him and kissed him. Then the son said to him, "Father, I have sinned against heaven and before you; I am no longer worthy to be called your son." But the father said to his slaves, "Quickly, bring out a robe—the best one—and put it on him; put a ring on his finger and sandals on his feet. And get the fatted calf and kill it, and let us eat and celebrate; for this son of mine was dead and is alive again; he was lost and is found!" And they began to celebrate. (Luke 15:20b-24)

In this parable, along with two others recorded in Luke 15, Jesus emphasizes God's amazing love for the lost and God's deep desire that they be found.

Numerous other New Testament passages affirm that love is an essential characteristic of God. The writer of Ephesians claims that "God, who is rich in mercy, out of the great love with which he loved us even when we were dead through our trespasses, made us alive together with Christ" (Eph. 2:4-5a). And 1 John 4:8b simply states: "God is love." In fact, our love toward others is grounded in the realization that God "first loved us" (1 John 4:19). It is this God, a God of love, whom Jesus reveals with clarity and power.

The love of God is often on display in the Old Testament, especially—though not exclusively—when it concerns the people of Israel. Israel celebrated and basked in God's committed love toward them. Witness, for example, the antiphonal refrain of Psalm 136, "for his [the Lord's] steadfast love endures forever." We also find specific passages that emphasize the deep love God felt toward the people of Israel. God's tenderness toward Israel is expressed with special poignancy in Hosea 11:

> When Israel was a child, I loved him, and out of Egypt I called my son. . . . It was I who taught Ephraim to walk, I took them up in my arms. . . . I led them with cords of human kindness, with bands of love. I was to them like those who lift infants to their cheeks. I bent down to them and fed them. (Hos. 11:1, 3-4)

As with the other characteristics of God Jesus reveals, the notion of God as fundamentally loving has its antecedents in the Old Testament.

Applying the Standard of Jesus

Although more characteristics could be discussed, enough has been said to develop a reasonably clear picture of the God Jesus reveals. Jesus understands God to be kind to the wicked, nonviolent, disinclined to punish people here and now through disasters and physical infirmities, and fundamentally loving. The Christocentric hermeneutic I am advocating suggests that this view of God should function as the standard by which to evaluate all other portrayals of God in Scripture. Since portrayals of God in the Bible can sometimes hinder our efforts to think rightly about God, a Christocentric hermeneutic is essential to help us determine which depictions distort rather than display God's character. Portrayals that correspond to the God Jesus reveals should be considered trustworthy, while those that stand at odds with this view of God should be regarded as unsatisfactory.

Using the God Jesus reveals as a measuring rod to evaluate other depictions of God will inevitably lead to the conclusion that certain Old Testament portrayals only partially reveal God's character while others badly distort it. This means we will sometimes need to reject certain portrayals of God in the Bible as being fundamentally incompatible with God's true nature. For example, when we encounter passages in the Old Testament that portray God commanding or engaging in acts of violence, we should conclude that such portrayals do not accurately reflect how God actually behaves. As Cowles observes: "If ours is a Christlike God, then we can categorically affirm that God is not a destroyer. . . . God does not engage in punitive, redemptive, or sacred violence. . . . God does not proactively use death as an instrument of judgment."[55] God is not a deadly lawgiver, an instant executioner, a mass murderer, a divine warrior, or a genocidal general, despite what many Old Testament texts suggest. These problematic portrayals of God, discussed in chapter 1, do not describe the character of God. Instead, they can largely be viewed as culturally conditioned understandings of God that need to be evaluated—and critiqued—in light of the God Jesus reveals.

If God is fundamentally loving and nonviolent, it stands to reason that God never has—and never will—commission, sanction, or participate in acts of genocide. God never orders one group of people to massacre another. Applying a christocentric hermeneutic to our reading of the Old Testament requires us to say that, regardless of the text's claims, God never commanded the Israelites to commit genocide by slaughtering Canaanites or annihilating Amalekites. Such horrific violence stands against everything God stands for. This is why it is so crucial to distinguish carefully between the textual God and the actual God lest we confuse the two and make God the author of unspeakable evil.

Old Testament portrayals of God commissioning one nation to attack another as divine punishment for their sins must also be understood as culturally conditioned explanations that do not accurately reflect the way God works in the world. As professor Katheryn Darr writes:

When students ask me what I think about Ezekiel's . . . assertion that Israel's experience of exile, destruction and death at the hands of Nebuchadrezzar's troops was the punishment of a just God, proportionate and thoroughly merited . . . I must suggest that in a world where holocausts happen, we dare not follow Ezekiel when he insists that suffering, alienation and exile are God's just punishments for sin. I do not believe Nebuchadrezzar's destruction of a troublesome vassal [Judah] was God's way of punishing people for sinfulness, whether their own or the sin of the second wilderness generation. In a world where holocausts happen, I must tell Ezekiel, "No, in this, I cannot follow you."[56]

Darr realizes that this portrayal of God is inadequate. It is not a trustworthy reflection of the way God works in the world. God is not in the business of using one nation to punish another. Nor does God take sides in military confrontations. Divine judgment is not worked out on the field of battle.

Using the God Jesus reveals as the standard to judge other portrayals of God allows us to take a major step forward in our efforts to deal responsibly with disturbing divine behavior in the Old Testament. It removes the need to justify God's behavior and helps us recognize that certain portrayals do not reflect what God is actually like. As we begin to see God through the lens of Jesus, we realize there are times when we simply must say, "This is not God!" God is not in the business of acting unjustly, abusing people, or perpetuating acts of violence. Whenever we encounter portrayals of God engaging in such behaviors, we must unambiguously declare that God never did (or willed) such terrible things. Literary descriptions of God like these do not faithfully reveal who God really is. Therefore, instead of rushing to God's defense, attempting to explain why God was justified to act in such ethically and morally problematic ways, we should acknowledge that these portrayals do not display God's true nature.

Domesticating God?

Some might question whether my proposal to apply a christocentric hermeneutic to problematic portrayals of God is motivated by a desire to remake God in my own image, by rejecting some of the nastier depictions of God in the Old Testament. It might seem like this interpretive approach is really intended to tame, or domesticate, God by reducing God to a harmless deity who is soft on sin But is that the case?

To be sure, understanding God to be nonviolent does result in a gentler, less lethal God than many textual portrayals suggest. Likewise, privileging the life and teachings of Jesus, which speak of God as one who is kind to the wicked and who loves enemies, certainly results in a "nicer" God than one who commands genocide and instantly annihilates people. But does that mean I have domesticated

God, that I have whittled away all the challenging aspects of God's character in order to end up with an easygoing, undemanding deity? Does it imply that I have removed all the difficulties associated with knowing and serving God, so that the God emerging from this reading of the Bible is one with whom I am fully comfortable? Hardly! There is nothing comfortable about a God who calls me to deny myself and take up my cross. There is nothing cozy about a God who tells me to love my enemies. There is nothing undemanding about a God who challenges my middle-class attitudes toward wealth and personal property by calling me to sell what I have and give to the poor. And there is nothing permissive about a God who calls me to repent or perish.

Just because a christocentric hermeneutic leads me to conclude that God is not the kind of being who commands genocide, instantly annihilates people, or judges nations by subjecting them to the horrors of war does not mean that I believe God is a spineless deity who could not care less about how people behave. What we do really matters to God. God abhors sin and is constantly encouraging people to make life-giving choices and to avoid doing evil. Furthermore, just because I do not believe God uses lethal force to punish people, as numerous Old Testament portrayals suggest, does not mean I believe God refuses to discipline people here and now. Like any good parent, God disciplines us so that we might mature and grow. I can attest to this divine chastening in my own life. When people go astray, God is present and active, ready to convict and correct as necessary. God always does so, however, *in ways that are congruent with God's character.* Thus, using a christocentric hermeneutic to reject violent, culturally conditioned portrayals of God neither diminishes nor domesticates God. Rather, it helps us move beyond barriers that keep us from seeing the true character of God more clearly.

———

What I have proposed in this chapter is obviously not a foolproof way of determining the degree of correspondence between the textual God and the actual God. It is not possible to be absolutely certain that in every instance we have used the biblical text to think rightly about God. Such is the challenge of reading and interpreting Old Testament narratives. Still, applying a christocentric hermeneutic can help us put problematic portrayals of God in perspective as we attempt to discern the degree to which these portrayals distort or reveal God's character. Moreover, it reminds us that the reason for rejecting certain portrayals of God is not because they do not suit our particular theological preferences. Instead, it is because they fail to measure up to the God Jesus reveals.

Throughout the Gospels, Jesus demonstrates familiarity with, and respect for, the Old Testament without perpetuating some of its most problematic views of God. For example, Jesus does not portray God as one who slaughters Egyptian children or hurls down hailstones upon Canaanites. Jesus never even mentions God's role as divine warrior in the Exodus-conquest narrative despite the prominence of this motif in the Old Testament. In fact, Jesus rarely speaks about *any* of the problematic portrayals of God we highlighted in chapter 1. On the contrary, Jesus presents an alternative view of God, one that differs considerably from what we find in the troubling texts considered in this study. Since Jesus is the clearest and fullest revelation of God—a point developed at the beginning of this chapter—the view of God that Jesus reveals trumps all other views of God. The God Jesus reveals is the closest we get to seeing God as God really is. Therefore, this vision of God should function as the standard by which all other portrayals of God in the Bible are evaluated.

As we use the God Jesus revealed as the standard to evaluate other portrayals of God, we will inevitably discover numerous passages in which the "actual God" content is fairly low. We will find various portrayals of God that significantly distort rather than display the character of God, the living God. What are we to do in these instances? Should these portrayals and the passages containing them quickly be bypassed in search of greener pastures? Or are there valuable lessons to be learned from such texts despite their limitations? Questions like these are important for people who desire to use the Bible responsibly *and* constructively.

In the next chapter, I will demonstrate how problematic passages, even those containing portrayals of God we partially or totally reject, have something positive to offer the theologically resourceful reader. The challenge is to develop a way of reading these passages that allows us to be honest about the problems they raise without dismissing the valuable insights they provide.

CHAPTER 11

Using Problematic Passages Responsibly

Becoming Discerning Readers

As long as there are women and men who still read the Bible for its theo-ethical value . . . then there remains—for those of us who care to do so—the responsibility to help contemporary readers to read the Bible with a suspicious hope, careful of the Bible's distortions and mindful of its possibilities.

—Renita J. Weems[1]

Anyone who spends even a little time in the Old Testament will soon discover it exhibits a clear and pervasive patriarchal ethos. Unfortunately, this ethos has both directly and indirectly led to the oppression of women. In his book *The Dissenting Reader*, Eryl Davies surveys a variety of approaches that feminist biblical scholars have used to wrestle with the problem of patriarchy in the Bible.[2] According-ing to Davies, feminist biblical scholars who use an interpretive approach known as reader response criticism are best able to counter these deleterious effects.[3] In this approach, "the task of the reader . . . is to engage in a vigorous dialogue and debate with the Hebrew Bible, resisting statements that appear to be morally objectionable, and taking a critical stance against what he or she may regard as the excesses of the biblical text."[4] Davies realizes that this approach to the Bible is unfamiliar to many readers. He writes:

> Such resistance clearly involves a radical departure from the way in which the Bible is customarily read, for traditionally readers have been conditioned

to remain slavishly respectful to the text's claims and to respond to its demands with uncritical obeisance. They have regarded themselves as passive recipients of the text, and have felt obliged to submit to its authority and to acquiesce in its value judgments. They have read—and frequently studied—the Hebrew Bible with an untroubled admiration instead of with a restless questioning.[5]

Yet Davies believes that a responsible reading of the text requires individuals to engage in such "restless questioning" if they are to resist those elements that are oppressive to women.[6]

Davies suggests that the usefulness of this approach extends well beyond the problem of patriarchy and "can be applied to all passages which appear offensive or unacceptable to the modern reader," including problematic portrayals of God.[7] He illustrates this in an article dealing with what he calls "morally dubious passages of the Hebrew Bible."[8] Here again, Davies encourages people to be dissenting readers, ready to critique and reject certain aspects of biblical texts that are judged unacceptable. This is precisely what he does with the conquest narrative in the book of Joshua. He writes:

> The biblical passages describing the annihilation of the Canaanites in Josh. 6-11 must surely feature prominently in the list of biblical texts that modern readers of Scripture would wish to question or reject, for the depiction of God encountered in these chapters is seriously defective and the actions attributed to his people are clearly morally offensive. . . . As we contemplate such passages of Scripture we must learn to become "dissenting readers" . . . just as we might readily concede that parts of the Hebrew Bible are scientifically wrong, so we must be prepared to pronounce that parts of it are *morally* wrong. . . . The morally offensive passages of Scripture, such as Josh. 6-11, must be questioned, critiqued and even rejected in an open, honest and forthright way.[9]

Davies is surely right to stress the need to critique those portions of the biblical text that are morally dubious. Such a posture is especially needed when dealing with passages that portray God speaking or acting in ways that do not correspond to God's true nature.

When we encounter literary portrayals that distort God's nature, we must say clearly and unequivocally, "This is not God." If we fail to do so, we unwittingly assign attributes to God that have no relation to God's true character. Taking the initiative to question, critique, and sometimes even reject certain portrayals of God is essential if we hope to deal responsibly with problematic portrayals of God in the Old Testament.

Following in Marcion's Footsteps?

My assertion that we sometimes need to reject certain portrayals of God may lead some readers to conclude that my way of handling the problem of disturbing divine behavior is not all that different from what Marcion proposed in the second century CE. That would not be an accurate assessment. While it is true that both Marcion and I find certain portrayals of God in the Old Testament problematic and unworthy of God, our method of dealing with this dilemma differs dramatically. Marcion rejected the entire "Old Testament" as Scripture.

Obviously, that is not what I am advocating. I have no desire to discard, diminish, or otherwise discredit the Old Testament. On the contrary, I believe the Old Testament is a rich resource for spiritual and theological reflection, a point I stressed in the introduction when sharing part of my own journey with Scripture. Marcion's decision to ditch the Old Testament is extreme and unnecessary, and we should not follow in his footsteps. Since its inception, the church has regarded the Old Testament as theologically viable and valuable for Christian reflection; it must always play a vital role in our Christian conversation.

For that reason, I want to draw a clear distinction between what I am doing and what Marcion did centuries earlier. Rather than rejecting the Old Testament, I have proposed an interpretive approach that can help us evaluate the appropriateness of various portrayals of God in the Old Testament. Since *some* Old Testament portrayals of God do not accurately reflect God's character, these particular portrayals should not be used to determine our beliefs about what God is really like. This is consistent with the way Jesus used various images of God in the "Old Testament." Although Old Testament texts were obviously very important to Jesus—he quoted from them and referred to them on numerous occasions—he did not embrace every portrayal of God contained in them. Instead, he endorsed some and rejected others. Like Jesus, we too can reject certain portrayals of God without consequently rejecting the Old Testament.

Just because we find some portrayals of God problematic, we should not repeat the mistake of Marcion. Marcion treated the Old Testament as though it came from one cloth, so to speak, equally bad and problematic from start to finish. In doing so, he robbed himself of many valuable and unobjectionable insights that can be derived from the pages of the Old Testament. Moreover, by failing to appreciate the rich diversity of the Old Testament, Marcion lost the opportunity to hear the Old Testament's own critique of certain problematic portrayals of God. As Rex Mason observes:

> Some of what the Old Testament has to say about God is simply unthinkable for many people today. To imagine that God really is the kind of Being who wishes to see all Canaanites, men, women and children, exterminated,

just because they happened to be Canaanites and, very understandably, fighting in defense of their own territory, is shocking. We rightly recognize now that in this the Israelites shared very much the same religious outlook as their contemporaries. The remarkable fact is that the same Old Testament records a growth in religious understanding on the part of at least some, who did not remain satisfied with such a nationalistic, limited view of God. They began to glimpse that he cared for all people and that he looked for high standards of ethical conduct from his own people as well as others. . . . There are then glaring differences of level of religious awareness and insights in the Old Testament, and the perception of this has enabled us to judge one piece of it by another, the more bloodthirsty parts of the book of Joshua, for example, by the insights of a prophet like Amos or the author of the book of Jonah.[10]

Mason is certainly correct to recognize that the Bible is not a flat book, so to speak, since there are "glaring differences of level of religious awareness and insights in the Old Testament." Some portions are certainly more revelatory and more edifying than others. To discard the entire Old Testament, as Marcion did, is to throw out the good with the bad, and to lose much of value in the process. My proposal— that we reject certain portrayals of God that distort God's character—is not a call to discard or eliminate the Old Testament in whole or in part. Instead, it is a plea to interpret the Bible responsibly when using it to reflect on the character of God.

Of course, all this still begs the question of what to do with passages containing disturbing divine behavior. Once we identify a problematic portrayal of God, one that seriously distorts the character of God, should we simply ignore that portrayal and the passage in which it resides? I think not. As I suggest below, even some of the most troubling texts still have a great deal to offer the theologically resourceful reader.

Using a Dual Hermeneutic

In her book *Battered Love: Marriage, Sex, and Violence in the Hebrew Prophets*, Renita Weems argues that a responsible reading of prophetic passages portraying sexual violence against women requires the reader to develop "a dual hermeneutic."[11] According to Weems, such a hermeneutic allows the reader to "resist" harmful aspects of a text while still being able to "appreciate" those that are helpful. As noted in the epigraph, Weems counsels us "to read the Bible with a suspicious hope, careful of the Bible's distortions and mindful of its possibilities." Thus, when reading a troubling text, the reader need not embrace it fully or reject it completely. Instead, the reader can critique its oppressive elements and affirm its positive possibilities. In this way the reader is encouraged to utilize a "both/and" rather than an "either/or" approach. This approach is quite useful since it honestly recognizes real difficulties inherent in some texts without regarding them as theologically useless.

Although Weems's study deals exclusively with passages from prophetic literature, her proposal for dealing with these applies equally to the problematic portrayals of God in Old Testament narratives. Once we recognize that many texts have both a constructive and a corrosive side, we can employ a dual hermeneutic, one that allows us to accept what we can and reject what we cannot. This allows us to use such texts positively without ignoring their more disturbing dimensions. Dismissing a text as theologically worthless just because it contains a problematic portrayal of God is extreme and amounts to throwing out the baby with the bathwater. Even when the degree of correspondence between the textual God and the actual God is low, that does not necessarily render that text unusable. Instead, by utilizing a dual hermeneutic, it is possible to reject a problematic image of God while still finding positive ways to read and interpret the text in which that image resides.

This insight requires us to reevaluate Davies's admonition to be dissenting readers. The call to be a dissenting reader—to critique and reject that which is morally objectionable—is good as far as it goes. But it is not enough to be a *dissenting* reader and then to stop there. Rather, we need to be *discerning* readers. When reading troublesome texts, we need to discern between what is unusable and what is still salvageable from such passages. Our job is to separate the wheat from the chaff, all the while being careful not to throw out one with the other. This requires looking for value in texts that might initially be so problematic that they may not seem worth the effort. Still, as discerning readers, we can critique aspects of the text that are unacceptable without abandoning the text as theologically bankrupt. All this involves a much more nuanced way of reading and applying Old Testament texts, particularly those containing disturbing divine behavior.

This hermeneutical assumption—that theologically problematic texts can also contain theologically helpful insights—is essentially the approach taken by Jacqueline Lapsley in her recent book *Whispering the Word*. Lapsley, though keenly aware of the problem of patriarchy in biblical texts, is frustrated with her colleagues who seem unable to see past the problematic dimensions of a text to its more redeeming qualities. She writes:

> The difficulties posed by these disturbing aspects of the Bible do not mean that readers of biblical narratives must reductively conclude their interpretations with the lament that "this is a patriarchal text," as though this were the end result of interpretation or the only responsible interpretation. Many texts are patriarchal in some respects, and are *still about something else as well*.[12]

Exactly! Though I am very concerned that we name disturbing divine behavior for what it is (more on this in chapter 12), these problematic texts "are still about something else as well." Even the most theologically troubling texts contain other insights, ideas, and perspectives that can, and should, be explored. Interpreters who approach the text *primarily* with a hermeneutic of suspicion, ready to critique its shortcomings, biases, and flaws, inevitably fail to appreciate this "something else." But if we approach the Bible as Scripture, convinced that God "speaks" to us through it in various ways, then we need to do more than just reject texts containing problematic portrayals of God. We need to look carefully at other aspects of these very texts as we attempt to discern how they might function as a word from God to us.

I also like the way Ellen Davis speaks of approaching difficult texts. She advocates extending "interpretive charity," which seems a helpful way to approach such passages. As Davis explains:

> Interpretive charity does not mean pity, but rather something more like generosity and patience toward the text. . . . Charitable reading requires considerable effort; it is easier to dispense with the problematic text. Those who regard a text as religiously authoritative are willing to sustain that effort because they perceive that the text comes to them, in some sense, as a gift from God.[13]

Davis encourages us to take the time to engage even the most difficult texts in the hopes of hearing a word from God. Practicing this kind of interpretive charity is necessary to use a dual hermeneutic effectively. Davis was once asked if there was any text she would reject. Her reply, after considerable reflection on this "haunting" question, was, "No, no biblical text may be safely repudiated as a potential source of edification. . . . When we think we have reached the point of zero-edification, then that perception indicates that we are not reading deeply enough; we have not probed the layers of the text with sufficient care."[14]

This predisposition to find something of value in even the most bothersome texts is nicely expressed by Thomas Long. In an article dealing with "difficult preaching texts," Long includes a sermon he preached on a notoriously difficult text discussed previously: 2 Sam. 6:1-7. Long recognizes the difficulties of preaching from this passage about Uzzah and the ark, particularly given the view of God it presents. He writes: "The first impression of God given here is out of 'synch' with the God we meet in Jesus Christ."[15] Yet Long does not encourage us to dismiss this text quickly in order to move on to greener pastures. Instead, he believes we should wrestle with the text to see what insights it might yield despite the difficulty. As Long expresses it: "It would be a serious mistake to dismiss this story with the wave of a hand as a piece of moldy barbarism. . . . Like Jacob wrestling beside the river, *we should not let this story go until it has at least the chance to bless us.*"[16]

I think this attitude is fundamentally correct, especially when it comes to dealing with passages containing problematic portrayals of God. When we encounter texts that portray God engaged in ethically problematic or morally offensive behavior, we should not assume that the entire passage is utterly unusable. Instead, after critiquing portrayals of God that do not measure up to the God revealed in Jesus, we should then determine what other lessons might be learned from the text in question. Despite the problematic portrayal of God, what else is this passage saying and how might that help us? In short, we need to be discerning readers who apply a dual hermeneutic and are able to both critique and affirm texts simultaneously.

The Theologically Resourceful Reader

To be discerning readers who are theologically resourceful, it is very important to develop a receptive attitude toward the Bible. As we approach biblical texts, even troublesome ones, we should do so with a genuine openness to learn from them and be challenged by them. We should expect them to provide fresh insights and new perspectives even as we recognize their limitations in helping us think rightly about God. Our attitude should be characterized by respect for the text, even as we struggle with it. We come to these texts expectantly, hoping to hear a genuine word from God.

In his book *The Unfolding Drama of the Bible*, Old Testament scholar Bernhard Anderson says: "The only condition for fruitful Bible study is that you come with an infinite concern about the question, 'What is the meaning of my life, and the historical crisis in which I and my community are involved?'"[17] He continues, positing a number of things we must be willing to do if our reading of the Bible is to be truly serious and engaged:

> You must be willing to let the past—this biblical past—speak to you where you are living, to make a claim upon you in the present.

> You must come with the intention of wrestling seriously and honestly with the meaning of a biblical passage—not to air your private opinions or prejudices.

> You must expect to be questioned by the Bible, even as you bring your own questions to the Bible.

This way of reading the Bible with a willingness to learn from it—and be challenged by it—is also emphasized by Ellen Davis, who believes "friendship with the Old Testament" is something which "requires of us three kinds of willingness." Davis describes these as the "willingness to risk being 'taken in,'" the "willingness to change," and the "willingness to deal with extreme difficulty of the text."[18] According to Davis, we must be open to fresh new possibilities as we read these texts. We should avoid simply casting about for texts that support preconceived theological ideas but instead must be willing to read "against ourselves" in ways that challenge us to change. If we come to these texts only to criticize, only to stand in judgment over them, we miss the rich resources they offer us on our spiritual journey.

Obviously, when we read texts containing problematic portrayals of God, we must read them critically and carefully. We should never embrace views of God that are unworthy of God and must always be mindful of the important distinction between the textual God and the actual God. This is where applying a christocentric hermeneutic can be so helpful. But our reading cannot stop there. We must also find positive and constructive ways to use these texts. One such way is to develop the kind of reading strategy Richard Hays describes as "a hermeneutics of trust."[19] He writes:

> Reading receptively and trustingly does not mean accepting everything in the text at face value. . . . Cases may arise in which we must acknowledge internal tensions within scripture that require us to choose guidance from one biblical witness and to reject another. Because the witness of scripture itself is neither simple or univocal, the hermeneutics of trust is necessarily a matter of faithful struggle to hear and discern.[20]

Being theologically resourceful readers requires us "to hear and discern" as we read various biblical texts, even those that we find highly problematic. If we are to find ways to use troubling texts beneficially, it is important that we approach the Bible with humility and openness. Otherwise, our reading of the text will be greatly impoverished. Developing a healthy attitude toward the text is a precondition to reading it responsibly *and* constructively.

Two Problematic Portrayals and Two Problematic Passages

We are now ready to demonstrate how this dual hermeneutic works by first applying it to two problematic portrayals of God and then to two specific passages. In the book of Exodus, God is portrayed as a warrior, and on one occasion God is explicitly described as a "man of war" (Exod. 15:4). God's military prowess is on display as God systematically decimates the land of Egypt and slaughters every firstborn Egyptian. The people of Israel celebrate God's military victory over the Egyptians as they praise God for throwing horse and rider into the sea (Exod. 15:1).

This portrayal is problematic for numerous reasons, not the least of which is that it stands in tension with the character of God Jesus reveals. Jesus reveals a God who loves enemies, not one who makes war on them. Moreover, in stark contrast to the portrayal of God as warrior in Exodus, the God Jesus reveals is one who chooses to absorb violence rather than perpetuate it. Applying a christocentric hermeneutic inevitably leads one to conclude that the actual God is not a "man of war" but a God of peace. When evaluated by the standard of Jesus, the image of God as warrior is seen to be a distortion of God's true character.

But rather than just critiquing this image of God and stopping there, using a dual hermeneutic requires looking for what is positive and theologically constructive as well. For example, although the image of God as warrior fundamentally distorts God's character, there are aspects of this image that are still revelatory. For example, the way this image is used in the Exodus narrative enables us to affirm that God is against oppression and for justice (the reason God ostensibly fought for Israel in the first place) and that God is more powerful than all other gods (as some of the plagues symbolically seem to indicate). Thus, despite serious problems with this portrayal of God—problems that should be clearly identified as such—the theologically resourceful reader can still find something of value in this otherwise highly problematic image of God.

To apply this dual hermeneutic to another problematic portrayal, consider the portrayal of God as an instant executioner who intentionally kills certain individuals.[21] Once again, based on our knowledge of the God Jesus reveals, we must conclude that this image misrepresents God's character. God is not in the habit of striking people dead, regardless of how wicked they may or may not be. Yet, even though we might reject this image as fundamentally flawed, we need not conclude that it is theologically worthless. On the contrary, it reminds us that God has standards of right and wrong and that wickedness is terribly displeasing to God. This cautions us against living recklessly with no regard for the consequences of our actions. Although we may reject the notion that God goes around striking people dead on account of their misdeeds, this image still reminds us that those who blatantly disregard God's ways will ultimately be held accountable for their misdeeds.

These brief examples suggest how a discerning reader might utilize a dual hermeneutic when encountering problematic portrayals of God. As we have seen, even distorted images of God may have some redeeming qualities. But even if this is not the case, even if certain images are judged to be totally unsuitable for helping us think rightly about God, we should be careful not to reject too much since the passages in which they reside may still yield valuable insights. To illustrate this, we will consider two problematic passages: Genesis 22 and 1 Samuel 15.

The Near Sacrifice of Isaac (Gen. 22:1-19)

Many readers find the story about Abraham and Isaac in Genesis 22 unsettling, to say the least. This story, which we briefly discussed in chapter 1, portrays God commanding Abraham to sacrifice his beloved son, Isaac. This portrayal of God is problematic for at least two reasons. First and foremost is the depiction of God as one who orders child sacrifice. Second, this passage suggests that God is willing to inflict serious psychological trauma on one person (Isaac) in order to "test" another (Abraham). This portrayal of God as one who engages in psychological abuse and commands the death of a child is at odds with the character of the God Jesus reveals. Applying a christocentric hermeneutic to this text allows us to conclude that this portrayal of God significantly distorts God's character. God's behavior in this passage is morally offensive, and we should not hesitate to say so. But that is not all we should say about Genesis 22. A discerning reader using a dual hermeneutic must also explore more positive aspects of this text. Despite the problematic nature of the portrayal of God in Genesis 22, this passage still contains valuable theological insights.

To illustrate how one might utilize a dual hermeneutic when discussing Genesis 22, I want to share a portion of a sermon I preached on this passage a number of years ago at my home church in Grantham, Pennsylvania. You will detect some redundancy from my earlier discussion of Genesis 22, which I have allowed to stand in order to preserve the integrity of this part of the sermon. What follows is a slightly edited version of how I began that message:

If I were to ask you, "What is the most valuable thing you possess?," how would you respond? Of everything you have, what is it that you value the most? It may not be the most expensive thing you own, but what do you cherish more than anything else? A priceless family heirloom? Your 1972 Chevy Nova with mag wheels, dual exhaust and a 307 engine under the hood? Your baseball card collection? Your house? Your high school geometry notes? Your Nintendo Game Cube? Your photo albums? Your computer? Whatever it is, how would you feel if someone asked you to give it up or give it away? What would your response be? You'd probably say, "Not on your life. This is too important to me. I can't live without it. I wouldn't trade it for the world."

It is precisely this situation in which Abraham finds himself in Genesis 22. Only in Abraham's case the stakes are even higher. What Abraham is asked to give up is not some inanimate object. It is not his most prized possession. It is his most cherished child. According to this story, God tests Abraham by asking him to give up the most important thing in his life: his son, Isaac, the miracle boy! Actually, to be more precise, God doesn't simply ask Abraham to give up Isaac; God asks Abraham to offer up Isaac as a burnt offering. In short, God asks Abraham to sacrifice his son. And from what we can tell, Abraham seems fully intent on carrying out this request.

For many readers, this is a terribly troubling passage. Before we even get past the second verse, we are faced with a nasty moral dilemma. God is portrayed as ordering human sacrifice! What are we supposed to do with that? Did we get it wrong here at Grantham this morning? Should we have been sacrificing our children up on the altar rather than merely dedicating them? Isn't there some old saying, "A church that slays together stays together?" Something tells me that wouldn't go over very well with the church board, not to mention the parents of the affected children!

Genesis 22 is a troubling passage, one that has bothered people for many years. Some of the difficulties of this text are captured in Anne Tyler's novel titled Saint Maybe. *At one point in the novel, a teenage girl named Agatha is objecting to her uncle, who insists she attend church. Her argument is based, in part, upon passages of Scripture which annoy her. She mentions the account of Jesus cursing the fig tree, the flood recorded in Genesis that reportedly annihilates almost every human being, and this story in Genesis 22. Of this story she says:*

Or Abraham and Isaac. That one really ticks me off. God asks Abraham to kill his own son. And Abraham says, "Okay." Can you believe it? And then at the very last minute God says, "Only testing. Ha-ha." Boy, I'd like to know what Isaac thought. All the rest of his life, any time his father so much as looked in his direction Isaac would think—

At this point Agatha is cut off by her uncle who interrupts her tirade in an attempt to shut down her criticism.[22] Still, Agatha has said enough to capture something of the dilemma we face when reading this text.

Agatha's sentiments are not those of fictional characters alone. They reflect what many readers feel when encountering this story and others like it. Numerous scholars have reflected on the shadow side of this text. Old Testament scholar James Crenshaw refers to this divine command as "a monstrous test" and believes "one labors in vain . . . to find the slightest hint of divine compassion in the dreadful story recorded in Gen 22:1-19."[23] Put even more bluntly, David Gunn and Danna Fewell write:

> *We are not told what God wanted or expected to find in Abraham's performance. Most readings assume that what Abraham did met with God's approval. Abraham, on account of his radical obedience, becomes an exemplary character. Such a reading, on the other hand, leaves the character of God in a rather sticky situation. At the very best one might assert that God is simply unfathomable; at the worst, God is deranged and sadistic.[24]*

This is not the way we are used to hearing people talk about God or our beloved Bible stories. Still, Terence Fretheim warns us against the dangers of glossing over the problematic dimensions of Genesis 22 and passages like it. According to Fretheim:

> *To continue to exalt such texts as the sacrifice of Isaac (Genesis 22), and not to recognize that . . . it can be read as a case of divine child abuse, is to contribute to an atmosphere that in subtle, but insidious ways justifies the abuse of children. Both such texts and their interpreters carry deep levels of accountability for the effects they have among those who hear or read what they have to say. Lives are at stake.[25]*

Whether or not you fully agree with these sentiments, they do raise an important point. This text is difficult and potentially dangerous. It needs to be handled with care.

In light of that, let me be as clear as possible here. God does not want human sacrifice. God never has and never will. If you ever think you hear a divine voice commanding you to offer your child as a burnt offering, you have not heard the voice of God. On the contrary, the God most fully revealed in the person of Jesus blesses children and uses them as examples of the kind of character one must develop to enter the kingdom of heaven. Children are of enormous worth and importance in God's economy and must never be neglected or abused. Whatever we take away from this passage, it should not be some message suggesting that kids are disposable.

Obviously, simply saying that does not resolve all the difficulties this passage raises. We are still left with a problematic portrait of God. But that issue must be left for another time and a different conversation since I want to focus on some other dimensions of the text. Even disturbing passages of Scripture can be read in constructive ways and that is what I would like to do this morning. So without denying the problems a passage like this raises, I would like to offer a positive reading of this text, one that I think has profound implications for us today.

At this point in the sermon, I discontinued my discussion of disturbing divine behavior and turned my attention to a positive reading of Abraham's actions in the narrative. I stressed the uniqueness of Isaac and the fact that Abraham's willingness to give him up indicated his total commitment to God. I suggested God wants us to come to the same place as Abraham, to the place where we are totally committed to God, willing to withhold nothing from God. This was the major focus of my message, and I devoted most of the sermon to developing this idea.

I have used this example to illustrate what using a dual hermeneutic looks like in practical terms. I believe it is entirely appropriate to preach a sermon from Genesis 22 that emphasizes Abraham's devotion to God and that calls people to put God first, *as long as* the sermon also gives some attention to the text's shadow side. While the unsettling aspects of the text need not be the focus of the sermon, they should be honestly acknowledged. If this passage is going to be the basis for a sermon encouraging unswerving loyalty to God, it is important to state the obvious: God never requires us to kill others as a test of our loyalty. Similarly, we should clearly state that God does not—and never did—desire human sacrifice. If we neglect to do so, our silence may suggest a tacit approval of God's behavior. It may also erode the congregation's confidence in God's goodness, leaving them with a distorted view of God.

The presence of disturbing divine behavior in Genesis 22 does not render this passage theologically unusable. Instead, it requires us to be discerning readers, skilled at using a dual hermeneutic. Doing so enables us to critique certain aspects of the text while embracing others. When this is done, a powerful message can be preached responsibly from this passage.[26]

The Amalekite Genocide (1 Samuel 15)

To consider very briefly another example of how a theologically resourceful reader can use a passage containing disturbing divine behavior constructively, I want to return to the story of the Amalekite genocide (1 Samuel 15) discussed previously.[27] I have argued that the portrayal of God as a genocidal general in the opening verses of this narrative does not reflect God's true nature. God never commands ethnic cleansing. Nor is it ever God's will that one group of people traumatize, terrorize, or exterminate another. Such images of God do not correspond with the character of God Jesus reveals and thus are rightly rejected.

But once again, as discerning readers, we should explore this text for its positive potential. As we move beyond the genocidal decree in the opening verses, Saul reportedly disobeys God's clear command to totally annihilate all the Amalekites and to destroy all their livestock.[28] He does so because he is more concerned about his standing in the people's eyes than in God's. He admits as much to Samuel when he says, "I have sinned, for I have transgressed the commandment of the Lord and your words, because I feared the people and obeyed their voice" (v. 24). As a result of his disobedience, Saul loses the kingdom. This story line allows us to consider several theologically significant ideas. For instance, Saul's behavior and subsequent consequences illustrate the danger of choosing political expediency over obedience to God. Saul is portrayed as being more concerned with pleasing people than with pleasing God. In this way, the passage also challenges us to think carefully about who to listen to when confronted by competing voices. When God commands us to do one thing and people want us to do another, who do we listen to? And finally, this text stresses God's preference for obedience above sacrifice (v. 22). Obedience to God must always take priority over everything else, however worthy that something else may be. Issues like these can be profitably discussed from this passage *despite* the terribly problematic portrayal of God that confronts the reader at the beginning of the chapter. The presence of disturbing divine behavior in and of itself does not render this text theologically impotent.

To regard 1 Samuel 15 as unusable just because it contains a problematic portrayal of God is unnecessary and results in a missed opportunity to engage in constructive theological reflection. On the other hand, to use this passage without acknowledging the problematic nature of its portrayal of God runs the risk of misconstruing the essential character of God. Hence the need to be discerning readers who use a dual hermeneutic.[29]

The christocentric hermeneutic developed in chapter 10 allows us to determine the extent to which Old Testament portrayals of God do or do not reflect God's character. The dual hermeneutic developed in this chapter enables us to know what to do with distorted images of God and the passages containing them. By becoming discerning readers who are theologically resourceful, it is possible to find value in texts containing problematic portrayals of God without endorsing the distorted views of God they represent. If we are truly concerned about thinking rightly about God—as I am—and if we honestly believe the Bible should play a crucial role in that process—as I do—then we should actively attempt to determine the degree of correspondence that exists between the textual God and the actual God. While we should not hesitate to critique any portrayal that does not correspond to the God Jesus reveals, we should also be willing to recognize that even problematic portrayals may reveal something true about God, at least in a general way.

Some may regard my efforts to salvage something of value from these problematic portrayals—and the passages in which they appear—as foolhardy. Why not just admit that some portrayals of God are totally useless and reject them unconditionally? My reason for not doing so is because too much is lost in process. While some portrayals reveal God's true nature in only the most limited way, many of them—even the most problematic—have something positive to offer for those who have eyes to see.

In the sample readings offered in this chapter, I have tried to model the application of a dual hermeneutic. In both Genesis 22 and 1 Samuel 15, we saw that the degree of correspondence between the textual God and the actual God is very low since the portrayal of God in both passages fundamentally distorts God's character. Still, we were able to make some very general affirmations about God in spite of the highly problematic dimensions of these portrayals. Beyond that, we were able to identify helpful points of theological reflection despite the presence of disturbing divine behavior in these passages. This cautions us against just dismissing texts containing problematic portrayals of God. Rather, we need to be discerning readers, able to recognize the limitations of a text while simultaneously exploring positive ways it can be read and applied.

CHAPTER 12

Talking about Troubling Texts
Some Practical Suggestions

Violence-of-God traditions are the heart of the Bible. . . . This is the elephant in the room of which nobody speaks.

—JACK NELSON-PALLMEYER[1]

Christopher Columbus: Hero or Villain?

Although Christopher Columbus is typically remembered as a great explorer credited with the discovery of the new world, Howard Zinn paints a rather different picture in his superb book *A People's History of the United States.*[2] Zinn describes how Columbus mistreated the Arawak Indians from the moment he landed in the Bahamas. He immediately took some of the Arawaks by force and demanded they lead him to the gold he was so eager to find. When Columbus returned to Spain, he took some Arawaks as prisoners along with him. Many did not survive the journey. When Columbus returned to the islands a second time—with many more ships and men—he increased his acts of violence and brutality. He enslaved the Arawaks, conscripted them for forced labor, and murdered those who failed to meet work quotas.

All of this was done for one simple reason: Columbus needed gold to repay those who had invested in his voyage. When enough gold could not be found,

Columbus filled his ships with five hundred Arawak slaves who could be "cashed in" upon his return. Two hundred Arawaks died en route—no great surprise given the inhuman conditions they were forced to endure during their voyage across the Atlantic. Over time, the exploitative practices initiated by Columbus and continued by those coming after him led to the utter annihilation of the entire indigenous Arawak population.[3]

After reporting these grim facts, Zinn cites the work of Harvard historian Samuel Eliot Morison, who portrays Columbus as a great discoverer and navigator and only briefly mentions his genocidal practices. Zinn writes:

> One can outright lie about the past. Or one can omit facts which lead to unacceptable conclusions. Morison does neither. He refuses to lie about Columbus. He does not omit the story of mass murder; indeed he describes it with the harshest word one can use: genocide.
>
> But he does something else—he mentions the truth quickly and goes on to other things more important to him. Outright lying or quiet omission takes the risk of discovery which, when made, might arouse the reader to rebel against the writer. To state the facts, however, and then to bury them in a mass of other information is to say to the reader with a certain infectious calm: yes, mass murder took place, but it's not that important—it should weigh very little in our final judgments; it should affect very little what we do in the world.[4]

This seems very similar to the way many people handle disturbing divine behavior in the Old Testament. Although they recognize its presence in the Old Testament and may even be somewhat troubled by it, they tend to pass over such behavior very quickly in order to move on to "other things" they regard as "more important." But this carries significant risks. Emphasizing God's goodness and grace without critiquing portrayals of God's violence and cruelty inadvertently legitimates those very acts of brutality. With regard to Columbus, Zinn writes: "To emphasize the heroism of Columbus and his successors as navigators and discoverers, and to de-emphasize their genocide . . . serves—unwittingly—to justify what was done."[5] The same is true when problematic portrayals of God are treated superficially or passed over altogether.

General Guidelines for Dealing with Disturbing Divine Behavior in the Old Testament

A primary aim of this book has been to help people think rightly about God by dealing responsibly with disturbing divine behavior in Old Testament narratives. I hope the last few chapters have been particularly useful in this regard. In what follows, I offer several general guidelines for dealing with disturbing divine behavior that grow out of the interpretive method developed in this part of book. I then provide a number of practical suggestions for discussing problematic portrayals of God in public settings. While these comments apply to all serious readers of Scripture, they are especially intended for religious professionals and other people who preach, teach, and write from these texts. Since these individuals exert considerable influence over how people view God, they need to be particularly adept at handling disturbing divine behavior.

Start Talking about the Problems These Passages Raise

If we hope to counter some of the deleterious effects that problematic portrayals of God have on readers of the Old Testament, we must begin talking about these images and the kinds of problems they raise. We should freely admit that biblical portrayals of God have the capacity to both reveal and distort God's character, recognizing that while some portrayals help us see God clearly, others do not. Old Testament portrayals that do not reflect the true character of God should be identified as such and handled carefully. When God is portrayed behaving in ways that do not correspond to the character of God Jesus reveals, we should not shrink from saying that these portrayals fundamentally misrepresent God's true nature. We must do this if we hope to use the Bible to think rightly about God. Rather than acting as if such difficulties do not exist, or are really relatively insignificant, we must start talking about these problematic portrayals. Ignoring disturbing divine behavior is not an effective way of dealing with it.

For far too long, too many people have remained silent about the problematic nature of many of the Old Testament's portrayals of God. According to Jack Nelson-Pallmeyer, the troubling "violence-of-God traditions" in "the heart of the Bible" are "the elephant in the room of which nobody speaks."[6] This hesitancy to talk about the nastier side of God's behavior in the Old Testament is particularly acute in the church. How many times have you heard a priest or minister openly acknowledge the theologically problematic portrayals of God in the Old Testament? Or how many sermons have you heard that really grappled with a text in which God appears to be behaving badly? Very few, I imagine. On the whole, the church has not done a good job of helping people know what to do with these kinds of problem passages. The same could be said of biblical scholars generally. According to R. N. Whybray's assessment:

> The dark side of God is a subject that has received astonishingly little attention from Old Testament scholars. The standard Old Testament theologies, monographs about the Old Testament doctrine of God, articles about particular passages, even commentaries are almost completely silent on the matter. . . . It is almost as though there is a scholarly consensus that any criticism of God's character in the Old Testament is inconceivable.[7]

Although Whybray somewhat overstates the case, he is certainly right to point out that, on the whole, Old Testament scholars have been reluctant to deal directly with this issue even when writing on topics directly related to it.[8] This must change, not only among biblical scholars but among church leaders as well. Otherwise, many will take our silence to imply tacit approval of God's behavior in the Old Testament.

The manner in which problematic portrayals of God are passed over in silence is exemplified in Steven Mathewson's recent book titled *The Art of Preaching Old Testament Narrative*.[9] In a book like this, which is specifically designed to help ministers preach from Old Testament narratives, you would expect at least some acknowledgment of the difficulty of preaching from the kinds of passages we have discussed in this book. But despite a promising chapter titled "The Challenge of Preaching Old Testament Narratives," no mention is made there, or elsewhere, about disturbing divine behavior. This is especially surprising since one of the sample sermons in the book is based on the story of the near sacrifice of Isaac in Genesis 22, a passage that contains a highly problematic portrayal of God as discussed in chapter 11. Yet Mathewson says nothing about how terribly troubling God's behavior in this passage is for many readers.

This is difficult to explain. Even if Mathewson is not particularly bothered by the image of an abusive God who commands human sacrifice, he surely must realize that many people will find this portrayal of God morally questionable, if not deeply disturbing. Mathewson's silence on this point is most unfortunate. By saying nothing, he leaves the impression that God's behavior is perfectly acceptable, and he misses an opportunity to help preachers reflect on ways to deal responsibly and constructively with disturbing divine behavior in the Old Testament. If we desire to think rightly about God, and to help others do the same, then we must begin talking about the problems these kinds of passages raise.

Stop Trying to Justify God's Behavior in the Old Testament

Perhaps even more distressing than books and sermons that pass over disturbing divine behavior without comment are those that attempt to justify God's behavior in some way. We discussed several examples of this in chapter 4. Those who are convinced that the Old Testament always displays God's character accurately are forced to find some way to justify behaviors that by any other standard would be regarded as unethical or immoral. Although they realize that God's behavior may appear problematic, they are convinced that when the text is properly interpreted, it will satisfactorily explain God's behavior and vindicate God from charges of misconduct. Thus, they attempt to explain why it was "right" for God to strike people dead, wreak havoc on the land of Egypt, and command genocide. But as we have seen, the interpretations offered in these and other instances often seem strained and unconvincing.

While some of the difficulties we have with God's behavior in the Old Testament may result from inaccurate interpretations, this is not always the case. The fault does not lie simply with interpreters. Sometimes, the texts themselves are to blame. As Fretheim so keenly observes:

> One might claim that the problem is due to the distorted readings of sinful interpreters and not to the texts themselves, and that is often the case, but the texts cannot be freed from complicity in these matters. The texts *themselves* fail us at times, perhaps even often. The patriarchal bias *is* pervasive, God *is* represented as abuser and a killer of children, God *is* said to command the rape of women and the wholesale destruction of cities, including children and animals. To shrink from making such statements is dishonest. To pretend that such texts are not there, or to try to rationalize our way out of them (as I have sometimes done), is to bury our heads in the sand.[10]

I appreciate Fretheim's candor. He recognizes that it is "dishonest" to deny that certain texts are problematic in and of themselves. It is not just a matter of interpretation.

Those who attempt to defend God's behavior in the Old Testament clearly disagree. They claim "the person God instantly executed deserved to die," or "the Canaanites had to be eliminated so as not to contaminate Israel," or "the near-sacrifice of Abraham's beloved son was a necessary test of his allegiance." But doing this only redefines evil as good, legitimating actions we would otherwise never condone. When the Old Testament portrays God engaging in activities that are unethical or immoral, our first instinct should not be to come running to God's defense. Instead, we should remember to differentiate between the textual God and the actual God, keeping in mind that the two cannot simply be equated.[11] Otherwise, we will end up making claims about God that are unworthy of God and that misrepresent God's character.

As discussed in chapter 10, all portrayals of God, especially those that seem problematic, should be brought into conversation with the God Jesus reveals. Those that do not correspond to the character of the God revealed in Jesus should be regarded as distortions of God's nature—distortions that need to be corrected, not defended. When characterizations of God in the Old Testament are found to be inconsistent with the character of God revealed in Jesus, we should not hesitate to say so. When we encounter such disparities, we should clearly and unequivocally say, "God is not like this." In this way, applying a christocentric hermeneutic to problematic portrayals of God in the Old Testament frees us from the burden of having to justify divine behavior that appears ungodly and "ungodlike." It provides us with a principled approach that allows us to consider the extent to which various depictions of God represent or misrepresent the character of God. Apart from such an approach, some may feel compelled to defend God's behavior simply because it is in the Bible. But doing so is dangerous. It not only inhibits our ability to think rightly about God but actively supports and perpetuates false views of God. If we wish to deal responsibly with disturbing divine behavior in the Old Testament, we must refuse to defend problematic portrayals that do not correspond to the true character of God.

★ *Acknowledge How These Texts Have Fostered Oppression and Violence*

Rather than passing over problematic portrayals of God in silence or suggesting that they are not really all that problematic, we should use them to begin conversations about how sacred texts sometimes do inspire violence, oppression, and injustice. This is precisely what many feminist biblical scholars have been doing for years. They have exposed the patriarchal bias of biblical texts because they recognize that the patriarchal ethos of much of the Bible has been used to oppress women for centuries. One need not be a biblical scholar to appreciate this point. An undergraduate student in my Old Testament Literature class wrote these words after reading the book of Hosea:

> It really makes me angry that all the people who have major roles as either prophets or patriarchs or whatever are guys. And the women are always presented as property or as evil people who cheat on their husbands. Somehow men get all the glory; no wonder there is such discrepancy in the church today over who should be pastor and what roles women should play. Argh.

This student realized that the Bible's oppressive portrayal of women contributed to the oppression of women in the church today. The two are not disconnected.

In much the same way, problematic portrayals of God in the Old Testament, especially those that depict God engaging in acts of violence or sanctioning its use, may lead some to conclude that such behavior is, at times, appropriate for us today. Tragically, the bloody history of the Christian church has repeatedly found precisely that kind of justification for its behavior in the pages of Scripture. Though it would be overly simplistic to suggest that problematic portrayals of God in the Old Testament are directly responsible for religious violence, I cannot help but wonder whether certain ugly chapters in the history of the church—such as the Crusades, the occupation of the "New World," and the Inquisition—would have looked rather different if these texts were not in the Bible. We would be naive to underestimate the enormous power these problematic portrayals of God have exercised in shaping people's thinking about God and how God calls them to act in the world. As Fretheim so aptly puts it: "It is important to remember that these images are not 'mere metaphors'; they have a great impact on our thinking, feeling, and being. Willy-nilly, they will sink deep into our selves and shape us in ways beyond our knowing."[12] What we believe about God really matters.

When we encounter disturbing divine behavior in the Old Testament, we can use it as an opportunity to reflect on how these texts have been used to legitimate all sorts of injustice and oppression (see chapter 2). We might, for example, talk about how Old Testament laws—ostensibly given by God—that favor men over women, in addition to God's mistreatment of women in certain Old Testament passages, perpetuate the notion that men are somehow more valuable than women. Or we might discuss how problematic portrayals of God have inspired people to live and act in ways that are utterly inconsistent with Jesus' call to be peacemakers and to love enemies. We can also discuss ways to neutralize some of the more toxic effects these texts can have. My hope is that such conversations will rob these texts of some of their destructive power and will open up new possibilities to work for justice, reconciliation, and peace.

Help People Use Problematic Images Responsibly and Constructively

In chapter 11, I argued that it is not enough to critique problematic portrayals of God in the Old Testament and stop there. The real challenge for us is to be discerning readers, not just dissenting readers. Our task is to be theologically responsible and resourceful when dealing with disturbing divine behavior. While we should not shrink from rejecting problematic portrayals that do not reflect God's true character, we need not automatically dismiss these images or the passages in which they reside as theologically unusable. Instead, by using a dual hermeneutic, we can reject what we must and still use what we can.

Reading the Old Testament confessionally, as Scripture, requires us to be attentive for theological insights even in passages that sometimes seem rather unpromising. We repeat the mistake of Marcion if we dismiss certain portrayals of God as theologically deficient without offering any guidance about how to use them—and the passages containing them—constructively. Many times, significant insights can be gained from problematic passages. We miss an opportunity to benefit from these texts if we quickly dismiss them as unusable. The challenge is to deal with problematic portrayals of God in a way that minimizes neither the difficulties they raise nor the possibilities they present.

Those of us who use the Bible for religious instruction, such as preaching and teaching, have a responsibility to help people understand how to approach these troubling Old Testament images of God. People need to be aware of the problems these passages raise without failing to recognize the potential they offer the theologically resourceful reader. Since we have already developed this idea and considered a few examples of how to deal with problematic portrayals of God constructively in the previous chapter, perhaps enough has been said on this point. I would simply underscore its critical importance for those who desire to read the Bible, especially its more difficult parts, as Scripture.

Keep Disturbing Divine Behavior in Perspective

While disturbing divine behavior is prevalent—one might even say prominent—in much of the Old Testament, it represents only part of the overall characterization of God found there.[13] Therefore, when addressing this issue, it should be kept in perspective. Disturbing divine behavior is not the only kind of divine behavior in the Old Testament! On the contrary, the Old Testament contains many largely or wholly unproblematic portrayals of God, portrayals that easily coincide with the character of God Jesus reveals (as demonstrated in chapter 10). God is not murdering people on every page or behaving badly in every Old Testament narrative. Instead, the Old Testament often depicts God favorably, portraying God as gracious, compassionate, and merciful. Indeed, as we noted earlier, Israel's description of God as "gracious and merciful" was part of their core confession.

As the Old Testament portrays it, God went to great lengths to stay in relationship with Israel. The people were amazed that God continued to stick with them and extend grace to them even after they repeatedly "messed up." They did not merely recite empty words when they declared that the Lord's "steadfast love endures forever."[14] They had experienced it and were grateful for it. As the psalmist expresses it:

> He does not deal with us according to our sins, nor repay us according to our iniquities. For as the heavens are high above the earth, so great is his steadfast love toward those who fear him; as far as the east is from the west, so far he removes our transgressions from us. As a father has compassion for his children, so the LORD has compassion for those who fear him. (Ps. 103:10-13)

Some of the most beautiful and moving portrayals of God are those in which God speaks words of promise and hope to people in exile. After the Babylonians thoroughly devastated Judah in 587 BCE, destroying Jerusalem, burning down the temple, and taking people into exile, the prophets describe God's continuing care and concern for the people. They declare that God has not abandoned them or forgotten them. "Can a woman forget her nursing child, or show no compassion for the child of her womb? Even these may forget, yet I will not forget you. See, I have inscribed you on the palms of my hands," says the Lord (Isa. 49:15-16a). God had not given up on Israel. Instead, God planned to restore them.

> For surely I know the plans I have for you, says the LORD, plans for your welfare and not for harm, to give you a future with hope. Then when you call upon me and come and pray to me, I will hear you. When you search for me, you will find me; if you seek me with all your heart, I will let you find me, says the LORD, and I will restore your fortunes and gather you from all the nations

and all the places where I have driven you, says the LORD, and I will bring you back to the place from which I sent you into exile. (Jer. 29:11-14)

Despite the trauma of exile and all that the people have lost, God promises to bring them home again. Better still, God promises to transform them from the inside out.

A new heart I will give you, and a new spirit I will put within you; and I will remove from your body the heart of stone and give you a heart of flesh. I will put my spirit within you, and make you follow my statutes and be careful to observe my ordinances. Then you shall live in the land that I gave to your ancestors; and you shall be my people, and I will be your God. (Ezek. 36:26-28)

These passages—and many, many more like them throughout the Old Testament—clearly portray God's deep love for, and passionate commitment to, the people of Israel.[15]

One could easily devote an entire book to the more positive and largely unproblematic portrayals of God in the Old Testament. Given the presence of portrayals like these, it is inaccurate to generically regard the "Old Testament God" as nasty and cruel and "the New Testament God" as kind and compassionate. Marcion was surely wrong on this point. The Old Testament repeatedly illustrates the faithfulness, love, and grace of God in dramatic ways. Therefore, when discussing disturbing divine behavior in the Old Testament, it is important to keep it in perspective and not to overemphasize it by neglecting the many positive portrayals included there as well.

Talking with Others about Problematic Portrayals of God

With these suggestions in mind, I want to offer a few comments on how to talk about disturbing divine behavior with others—friends, family members, religious leaders, and so forth. As you might imagine, not everyone is eager to discuss this topic. People who hold the Bible in high regard (as I do) typically are not all that fond of someone suggesting that there are certain problems with it. This is especially true when you begin to raise questions about the appropriateness of some of the Bible's portrayals of God. For some, this conversation is unwelcome because it is regarded as an attack on the inspiration and authority of Scripture.[16] For others, this discussion seems pointless because they believe all biblical portrayals of God are trustworthy. For still others, dealing with this issue is uncomfortable because it is one they have never considered before and they are unsure how to think about it. So how can one broach this topic in a way that will engage rather than alienate individuals like these? Here are a couple of guidelines I hope will help.

Be Gracious and Sensitive

Perhaps the most important thing I can say about conducting these conversations is that they should be done with grace and sensitivity. Speaking graciously means being respectful of the other person. It involves being tactful in what we say, hopeful that the person might hear us, and might be willing to consider new possibilities. Being gracious and sensitive means we take care not to push too hard and never raise this issue just to provoke people or to suggest that their view of the Bible is naive. Instead, we speak about this subject "with all humility and gentleness, with patience, bearing with one another in love, making every effort to maintain the unity of the Spirit in the bond of peace" (Eph. 4:2-3).

As you speak with others, be aware of how they are responding. When you sense people becoming defensive, do not push the issue. In the spirit of Christian charity, be sensitive to those who are unwilling or unable to discuss this topic constructively. In such moments, you should back off. You are unlikely to persuade people whose defenses are raised. Take a step back and try again later as the opportunity presents itself. People who have always believed the Bible to be historically accurate, and its portrayals of God absolutely trustworthy, are not going to change their minds overnight. They will need to have time to reflect on what you are saying. They will need to talk with other people about the issue. They may want to read more about this topic. All of this takes time. Be patient with them. For many people, coming to terms with disturbing divine behavior is the result of a long, arduous journey. It might even help for you to share some of your own journey on this issue to help them see that you too have struggled—and perhaps continue to struggle—with these difficult texts. Validate their questions and concerns, and encourage them to keep wrestling with this issue as they read and reflect on various Old Testament passages.

Be Discerning

At the beginning of this chapter, I emphasized the need to start talking about how troubling and problematic some of these images of God really are. Obviously, I hope you do this. Still, I think there is an appropriate time and place for such conversations. It is important to be discerning so that you know when to raise this issue and when not to mention it. To illustrate, allow me to suggest two hypothetical scenarios.

SCENARIO 1: VISITING A SUNDAY CLASS

You are on vacation and are visiting a church that is unfamiliar to you. The Sunday school class you have chosen to attend is studying the book of 1 Samuel, and the passage under consideration is 1 Samuel 15. It is clear that the teacher has a carefully prepared lesson and does not seem particularly interested in deviating from it. The basic message the teacher has derived from this passage is the importance of obeying God fully (recall how Saul fails to do so by refusing to kill King Agag and by sparing some of the animals). During the entire class, nothing is said about the problematic portrayal of God at the beginning of the chapter, and no one seems particularly disturbed that God commanded Saul to commit genocide. With five minutes remaining before the end of the class, the teacher asks if there are any questions or comments. Do you raise the subject of disturbing divine behavior or not?

SCENARIO 2: HEARING A SERMON AT YOUR HOME CHURCH

At your home church, which you have faithfully attended for the past fifteen years, Pastor Jones has just preached a rousing sermon on God's faithfulness based on the book of Joshua. The sermon focused on Joshua 6–11, and Pastor Jones emphasized how perfectly God fulfilled all of the promises made to the people of Israel. Your pastor praises God for fighting on Israel's behalf in order to give them the land that was promised. Yet nothing is said about any morally problematic aspects of the text. There is no mention that "giving" Israel this land necessitated the brutal slaughter of thousands of Canaanites. Nor is there any indication that Christians might be troubled by this portrayal of a God who sides with one group of people while mercilessly annihilating another. Should you talk with your pastor about this, or should you keep quiet?

Ultimately, I cannot tell you how you should or should not act in situations like these. That is for you to decide. I can, however, suggest what *I* would probably do and why. If I found myself in scenario 1, the Sunday school class away from home, I would probably not raise the issue of disturbing divine behavior, despite how passionately I feel about it. I would make this choice for two reasons: (1) it is not the kind of issue that can be adequately explored in five minutes, and (2) as a guest in this church, I am unknown and therefore have not earned the people's trust, something that is crucial for addressing a sensitive topic like this. Additionally, I would be hesitant to raise the subject since the teacher exhibited no real openness to deal with the passage in this way. If the teacher had made some reference to the fact that some people find God's behavior troubling in this passage, I would have felt more comfortable expressing my thoughts on the matter. If I did feel compelled to say something, I would try to do so tactfully and graciously, which I hope would provide a space for discussing this issue without running the risk of immediately alienating people. Still, given the hypothetical situation as described, chances are I would not raise the issue at all.

My response would be different, however, in the second scenario, the sermon preached by my pastor at my home church. Obviously, I would not stand up in the sanctuary prior to the closing hymn and publically accuse my pastor of failing to deal responsibly with this troubling text. That would be neither gracious nor prudent. But I might talk with the pastor after the service. Better yet, I might set up an appointment to talk with the pastor at a time when it is convenient for both of us. Since many pastors feel especially vulnerable immediately after preaching a sermon, my concerns might be better received at a later time. During the course of such a conversation, I would certainly want to affirm how much I appreciated the emphasis on God's faithfulness and might even share some of the ways I have found God to be faithful in my own life. Then, I would gently ask whether he or she had considered some of the more troubling aspects of God's behavior in Joshua 6–11. I might share my own struggle with these texts and my concern about how problematic these images of God can be. I would be curious to find out how my pastor reconciles God's behavior in texts like these with other passages in the Bible that portray God in different ways. I would feel free to ask questions like these because of the longstanding relationship we have. Moreover, my intention in raising this issue would not be to embarrass or condemn the pastor but to encourage him or her to consider effective ways to deal with disturbing divine behavior from the pulpit in the future.

While these are only two hypothetical scenarios, I hope they are sufficient to demonstrate the need to be discerning when raising this issue, especially in public settings. There are times when it is entirely appropriate, even necessary, to address this issue. There are other times when it is better left alone. We need wisdom to distinguish one from the other. When we do decide to discuss disturbing divine behavior with others, being respectful, gracious, and sensitive goes a long way toward having a constructive conversation about this complicated and controversial issue.

Dealing with Disturbing Divine Behavior in the Church and the Academy

Pastors and professors often find it especially challenging to know how to broach the topic of disturbing divine behavior with congregants and students. I myself struggle with how to introduce this issue to the students I have the privilege of teaching at Messiah College. If I am teaching portions of the Old Testament that contain disturbing divine behavior and say nothing about the problematic nature of these portrayals, I worry that my students may think God really behaves the way the text suggests. On the other hand, if I critique these portrayals and claim, for example, that God did not actually murder every firstborn in Egypt or command the Israelites to slaughter all the Canaanites despite what the text says, I run the risk of alienating some students. In this way, I feel caught between a rock and hard place. Nevertheless, despite the inherent dangers of discussing this topic, I believe it is incumbent upon those of us who use the Bible for preaching and teaching to do just that. We need to find appropriate ways to talk about problematic portrayals of God if we hope to help people use the Bible to think rightly about God. To that end, I would like to offer a few additional suggestions to supplement those already discussed in this chapter. These are more specifically directed toward religious professionals.

First, pastors and professors need to help their respective audiences approach the Bible with realistic expectations. To recall the words of John Barton: "Most Christians probably read the Old Testament to learn about God. They *expect* it to tell them what God is like, what he has done and what he requires of them. But those who approach the Old Testament in this way are soon disappointed."[17] Part of our job as religious professionals is to help people realize that despite all the wonderful things the Bible reveals about God, it does not always help us think rightly about God. Some portrayals do not accurately reflect the character of God. Therefore, we have an obligation to help people be more realistic about what they can expect from the Bible, particularly from its many and varied portrayals of God.

I have sometimes wished that upon opening the Bible people would read a bold disclaimer saying, "Reader beware: the God you are about to meet in these pages does *not* always accurately reflect the true nature of God." But alas, no such warning appears. Readers are left to figure this out on their own. As religious educators, we can assist people in this regard. We can help them see the need to draw a distinction between the textual God and the actual God as they encounter various portrayals of God in the Bible. This will help them develop more realistic expectations of how to use the Bible to think about God. Specifically, it will help them realize that there is not always a direct correlation between the characterization of the textual God in the Bible and the character of the actual God in real life.

We must be very careful about what we claim the Bible will do for those who read it. If we give the impression that the Bible's portrayals of God are wholly unproblematic, we set people up for confusion, frustration, and disappointment. People are often encouraged to "dig into the Word" in order to learn more about God, and at one level such advice seems unassailable. Who would argue against reading the Bible or learning more about God? The problem comes when people actually heed this advice, "dig into the Word," and encounter portrayals of God they find problematic. What should they do then? If all they have been told is that reading the Bible will help them grow closer to God, what happens when it does not? What happens when they encounter disturbing divine behavior that does not correspond to some of their most basic beliefs about the nature and character of God? If they do not realize that some of these portrayals misrepresent God's character, they are likely to assume God is just as the Bible describes, regardless of whether or not that matches up with their previous beliefs about God. On the other hand, they might be so bothered by these images that they begin to question whether the Bible is of much use for theological reflection. Obviously, neither response is desirable. As religious educators, we have a responsibility to help people develop realistic expectations about the Bible lest they think wrongly about God or become disillusioned with the Bible when it does not function in the way they were led to believe it would.

Second, religious educators need to help people think carefully about the Bible's origins, particularly about the role humans played in its formation. Given the claims often made of the Bible—that it is authoritative in all matters of faith and practice, that it is divinely inspired by God, that it is true in all that it intends to teach—it is amazing how little most people actually know about how it came to be. People may have vague notions of people receiving words and ideas from God and writing them down, but sometimes it does not go very far beyond that. This creates a mysterious aura around the Bible that tends to discourage critical engagement with it. While such a view of the Bible is understandable among people whose access to education is limited or restricted, or among young children who cannot understand the intricacies of the Bible's development, it is more difficult to comprehend among people who are well educated, formally or otherwise. Sadly, many Christians who are extremely intelligent have never advanced beyond an elementary understanding of the Bible's origins.

When I teach the introductory Bible course at Messiah College, I devote the first unit of the course to a discussion of how the Bible came to be. Over the space of several weeks, we deal with topics like textual transmission, scribal errors, canonization, and theories of divine inspiration. For many students, this is their first encounter with many of these ideas, even though some have attended church all their lives. Many come to class with the view that the Bible is perfect, or inerrant. Yet once they begin to examine the evidence for themselves, they quickly realize the inadequacy of this view. They recognize that the Bible *does* contain certain kinds of errors and discrepancies. And while these do not necessarily shake their confidence in the authority of Scripture, it is not uncommon for them to experience a sense of betrayal. They wonder why hasn't anyone ever told us about this before? It is a very good question. Many of these students find it quite disconcerting to discover that they have been misled—or at least uninformed—about these matters by the very people they looked up to as spiritual leaders.

If we hope to help people deal responsibly with disturbing divine behavior, it is imperative to help them appreciate the human dimension of the Bible's origins. Doing this in no way denies God's involvement in the formation of Scripture, though it does help us put that involvement in proper perspective.[18] People need to understand that the biblical writers were human beings just like us. While these individuals had the capacity to communicate great truths about the character of God, they also had the ability to misrepresent God. Their worldview assumptions and presuppositions informed their writing, just as it does ours, and this inevitably colored the way they talked about God and God's role in human affairs. That is why we must be discerning readers, determining what does and does not accurately reflect the character of God. Our ability to be discerning readers who can make these kinds of distinctions rests, to a large degree, on our view of Scripture. If we believe the Bible was divinely dictated by God, we are not likely to critique anything the Bible says about God. On the other hand, if we recognize the human element in the formation of the Bible—without denying God's role in the process—we have taken a significant step forward in being able to appreciate the Bible's ability to both reveal and distort the character of God. Thus, the way we talk about the Bible and its formation can go a long way toward helping people deal responsibly with problematic portrayals of God.

Third, religious educators should encourage people to ask all kinds of questions about the Bible. Sometimes, churches or religious institutions restrict the kinds of questions that are "appropriate" or acceptable. For example, while people are encouraged to ask questions of "fact" about this or that biblical datum, questions of "factuality" about the appropriateness of certain representations of God or about whether God actually did what the Bible says God did are strictly forbidden. No pastor I know would get upset with a parishioner who asks "factual" questions such as: Where was Ur of the Chaldees? When did King Hezekiah reign? What is meant by casting lots? Questions like these are considered perfectly acceptable. But when a person begins asking questions of "factuality," he or she sometimes meets a wall of resistance. Was it right for God to instantly execute Uzzah? Did God really slaughter Israel's enemies by throwing down hailstones from heaven? Must I actually believe God wanted Saul to commit genocide by killing all the Amalekites, as the Bible claims? Questions like these are sometimes off-limits, or at least frowned upon.

I think we make a tragic mistake by discouraging people from asking questions of this nature. Not only does it stifle a healthy God-given curiosity, but it robs people of an opportunity to make sense of some of the most difficult passages in the Bible. Although some people may think it is inappropriate to ask these kinds of questions, I think something is terribly wrong when people are *not* asking these kinds of questions. It is necessary to explore these kinds of questions to keep from adopting a view of God that is unworthy of God. Mature faith requires careful thought and reflection. Thus, we should do all we can to encourage a healthy curiosity about the Bible, particularly as people engage passages containing portrayals of God they find troubling.

Fourth, the church needs to give more serious thought to how stories containing problematic portrayals of God are taught to children. Are some of these stories unsuitable for young people? Should we wait until children are a certain age before introducing them to some of the more troubling texts in the Old Testament? How do children feel when they hear a story like the one found in Genesis 22 in which where God reportedly commands Abraham to sacrifice his son? What kind of message does that communicate to them? Or what about the Exodus story? Do we want children to believe that God frees some people by killing the children of others, a lesson so graphically displayed just prior to Israel's departure from Egypt?[19] Or should we encourage our children to celebrate with the Israelites who stand singing on the seashore as they watch the bloated bodies of divinely drowned Egyptians wash up along the coast (Exod. 14:30—15:1)? In short, are there some Old Testament narratives that should not be taught to children?

The fact that some adults find these stories problematic for childhood consumption is evident in the way they are routinely sanitized in children's storybooks. Take, for example, the story of Noah's ark. In most children's books, this cataclysmic event—which reportedly resulted in the utter destruction of virtually every living thing on the planet—has been transformed into a story about cute, cuddly animals entering the ark two by two. Or consider what is done with a story like Joshua and the battle of Jericho. The focus is on trumpets, walls crumbling, and fearless obedience to the Lord, but nary a word is spoken about the brutal slaughter that follows when the city's defenses are breached (see Josh. 6:21).

Maybe it is fine to "clean up" these stories for young children, much like one might censor inappropriate parts of a video they are watching. Still, I wonder if there are some inherent dangers in doing so. The sanitized story is not the whole story and may, in fact, seriously distort what the text is really saying. Moreover, what happens when these children grow up and eventually learn "the rest of the story"? Will they feel deceived or betrayed when they realize the biblical account is a far cry from the sanitized version they got in Sunday school or at home? And how will the uncensored version affect their view of God? How does this influence the way they think about violence? These are not easy questions to answer.

In her book *How to Teach Peace to Children*, Anne Meyer Byler urges us not to whitewash the violence common to so many biblical stories. Instead, she proposes using these stories as a springboard for talking about violence and about how God wants us to live with one another. Byler writes:

> Many fairy tales and exciting children and youth books do include a lot of violence, accepting it unquestioningly . . . [and they] feature violence in overcoming evil. But then, so do many favorite Bible stories: the Flood, the exodus, the taking of the Promised Land, and Samson. It isn't fair to the biblical record to sanitize these stories. . . . We can talk with our children about the violence in books and in the Bible. We can talk about how God wanted the Israelites to depend on him, and not on their own military might . . . . We can talk about Jesus being the closest example to how God wants people to live and how he chose to be killed rather to kill.[20]

Byler offers some helpful suggestions, though I do think there are some stories in the Bible that are better left untold, or at least untold in their entirety, until children reach certain ages. Sunday school teachers, Christian educators, parents, and others should think carefully about how problematic portrayals of God are handled in church and at home. Since children as so impressionable, we want to be especially careful to represent God as accurately as possible through the stories we tell and the way we tell them.[21]

Finally, I want to direct a few words to religious educators who teach in Christian colleges and universities. A college, especially a Christian college or university, is precisely the place where the issue of disturbing divine behavior should be raised and explored. It is here, within this "safe" academic environment, that this topic can be discussed openly and honestly. Obviously, the amount of time that can be devoted to this issue will vary depending on the nature of the course and the maturity of the students enrolled in it. Less time should be spent with this issue in lower-level introductory courses, especially those that fulfill general education requirements. Substantially more time can be devoted to this issue in upper-level Bible classes, particularly those primarily populated by biblical and religious studies majors. In either case, the college classroom is an ideal place to address this issue since it naturally provides space for asking questions and holding a real dialogue, two essential ingredients for successfully discussing this difficult topic.

Raising this issue in class requires sensitivity and skill. This is especially true if a number of students come from theological traditions that have not encouraged them to ask the kinds of questions we have explored in this book. In such a context, it is especially important to make sure the presentation is not one-sided. Instead, students need to see a variety of approaches so they can consider the strengths and weaknesses of these positions. While it can be helpful to share some of our own questions, struggles, and conclusions about this topic, it is very important to give students space to form their own opinions. At the end of the day, they are the ones who need to decide which approach makes the most sense to them. By taking these kinds of considerations into account, we can help our students wrestle with this important issue productively without unnecessarily raising defenses.

———

This chapter has stressed the need to start talking more intentionally about how to deal responsibly with problematic portrayals of God. We have been far too silent for far too long about this issue. It is time we name the elephant in the room and find ways of addressing the topic that are both honest and productive. Given the complexities of this issue, there is no easy formula for discussing it constructively, though I hope some of the specific suggestions made in this chapter will help in this regard.

Those of us who use the Bible in public settings—for preaching, teaching, or other forms of Christian education—should be especially careful about how we handle passages containing problematic portrayals of God, since our respective audiences often take their cues from us. We should model good interpretive practices as we attempt to use these texts to think about God. While everyone may not be convinced by what we say or the approach we take, it is still important to raise our concerns about these images and to start conversations about how to handle them. This will enable us to counter some of the negative effects problematic portrayals of God have on readers and will allow us to articulate more clearly what God, the actual God, is really like.

Epilogue

I would just prefer things to be as black and white as they were when I was a kid listening to the Bible stories that my parents read me.

—A WISTFUL COLLEGE STUDENT[1]

When I was a child, I spoke like a child, I thought like a child, I reasoned like a child; when I became an adult, I put an end to childish ways.

—THE APOSTLE PAUL[2]

Problematic portrayals of God in the Old Testament have troubled readers of the Bible for centuries. Over the years, these depictions of God have been a source of confusion, embarrassment, and irritation for many people, especially Christians. Although numerous attempts have been made to explain these troubling images of God, many falter because they do not allow for the possibility that some portrayals might actually distort God's character. In this book, I have not only kept that option open, but have insisted that it is sometimes the only way to deal responsibly with these images.

When using the Old Testament to think about God, it is critical to avoid simplistically equating the textual God and the actual God. When we encounter portrayals of God that do not correspond to the God Jesus reveals, we should be ready and willing to say forthrightly, "This is not God." In doing so, we must be careful not to denigrate the Old Testament or give the impression that it is theologically irrelevant. On the contrary, the Old Testament is of inestimable value and conveys all sorts of truths about God, the world, and humanity. Our challenge is to be discerning readers able to differentiate between what is trustworthy and what is not.

Throughout this book I have tried to make my case both graciously *and* persuasively. I have done so because I believe a great deal is at stake. Since the way we think about God significantly affects how we relate to God and how we live our lives, it is crucial that we think about God as accurately as possible. This is why it becomes so problematic to believe that God actually said and did everything the Bible suggests. Doing so inevitably leads one to conceive of God in ways that are inappropriate and simply untrue. As we have seen, these distorted views of God can have devastating consequences.[3] If we want to use the Old Testament to think rightly about God, we must recognize that all portrayals of God are not equal. While some portrayals reveal the character of God with unmistakable clarity, others distort God's true nature. Hence the need for discernment as we read and evaluate various Old Testament images of God.

I would be very pleased if this book encourages further conversation about these troubling texts. More needs to be done to increase awareness of the kind of problems these texts raise for many readers and to offer theologically constructive suggestions for addressing these difficulties.

I hope that after reading this book you feel better equipped to interpret Old Testament passages containing disturbing divine behavior. I especially hope this book has enhanced your ability to think rightly about God and to relate meaningfully to God. If that has happened, then my time writing, and your time reading, will have been well spent.

Appendix A:
Reexamining the Nonviolent God

The revelation of Jesus in the New Testament is no less violent than the revelation of God in the Old Testament.

—Tremper Longman III[1]

From Matthew to Revelation we find a consistent witness against violence and a calling to the community to follow the example of Jesus in accepting *suffering rather than* inflicting *it.*

—Richard B. Hays[2]

Although the focus of this book has been on disturbing divine behavior in Old Testament narratives, some people believe that the most deeply disturbing portrayals of God are those found in the New Testament, particularly in eschatological, or apocalyptic, passages. These passages deal with such issues as final judgment and eternal punishment, events thought to take place during what is commonly referred to as the "end times."[3] The magnitude of divine violence portrayed in these passages, it would seem, dwarfs some of the most notoriously problematic Old Testament examples. As one scholar colorfully explains: "The final judgment with its utter destruction of the heavens and the earth and all those at enmity with God makes the most bloody warfare narratives of the Old Testament seem like children's bedtime stories."[4] What is particularly disconcerting about these passages is that they seem to portray Jesus as an "apocalyptic avenger"[5] and seem to suggest that Jesus' view of God envisions a massive amount of divine violence at the end of the age.

The primary purpose of this appendix is to explore whether New Testament passages describing eschatological judgment require us to reassess the claim that the God Jesus reveals is nonviolent. This inquiry is important lest my proposal to use a Christocentric hermeneutic meet with the same criticism leveled against C. S. Cowles.[6] Cowles is one of four authors of the book *Show Them No Mercy: Four Views on God and Canaanite Genocide*. As the subtitle suggests, this book is devoted to exploring the thorny theological problems raised by the "divine" command to exterminate all Canaanites. Like me, Cowles believes that Old Testament portrayals of God as one who initiates, sanctions, and often participates in acts of violence do not reflect God's true nature. Cowles argues that Jesus is the standard we must use to evaluate Old Testament portrayals of God. As Cowles puts it: "As the full and final revelation of God, Jesus is 'the criterion' for evaluating Scripture, the prism through which the Hebrew Scriptures must be read."[7] For Cowles, Jesus is "our final authority . . . in determining the true nature and character of God."[8] This is, in essence, what I argued in chapter 10.

The other three authors of the book all criticize Cowles for failing to address eschatological judgment in the New Testament, particularly as it relates to Jesus. Eugene Merrill disputes Cowles's assertion that the true God is not warlike but is, like Jesus, "the Prince of Peace." According to Merrill, this "overlooks eschatological descriptions of this same Prince of Peace as one who 'judges and makes war,' who is 'dressed in a robe dipped in blood,' and from whose mouth 'comes a sharp sword with which to strike down the nations' (Rev. 19:11-15)."[9]

Daniel Gard similarly finds Cowles's argument unconvincing in light of the eschatological divine violence described in the New Testament. He believes that "the New Testament eschatological texts regarding Jesus . . . shatter Cowles's radical split between God in the Old Testament and in the New Testament."[10] Tremper Longman faults Cowles with constructing a partial and biased portrait of Jesus, one that fails to account for the fuller witness of the New Testament. He writes:

> The picture of Jesus that Cowles gives us, through which he views and judges the Old Testament, is a selective one. It seems telling to me that Cowles avoids the judgment and divine warrior passages of the book of Revelation or any of the New Testament apocalyptic passages. One is led to ask why. After all, when the topic is God and violence, the apocalyptic texts are obviously relevant.[11]

Each of these authors is convinced that the eschatological judgment portrayed in the New Testament undermines the portrait of Jesus that Cowles develops. The aspect of Cowles's proposal (and mine) that seems most vulnerable to critique is the assertion that Jesus reveals a God who is nonviolent. As Longman expresses it in the epigraph: "The revelation of Jesus in the New Testament is no less violent than the revelation of God in the Old Testament."[12] If this is true, if Jesus reveals a God just as violent as some of the portrayals of God in the Old Testament suggest, it raises serious questions about the usefulness and validity of using a christocentric hermeneutic to address the problem of disturbing divine behavior in Old Testament narratives. For that reason, it is necessary to respond to this critique at some length.

Eschatological Judgment in the Gospels

Passages that contain Jesus' teaching about eschatological judgment roughly fall into one of three categories: those associated with his return, those involving judgment on specific places, and those related to eternal punishment. What follows is a brief survey designed to illustrate some examples from each category.

A Violent Second Coming

As the Gospels portray it, the second coming of Christ will not be good news for many people. Instead, it will be a day of terrible destruction and devastation. Jesus described the nature of his return by referring to two well-known Old Testament stories: the flood narrative and the destruction of Sodom and Gomorrah:

> Just as it was in the days of Noah, so too it will be in the days of the Son of Man. They were eating and drinking, and marrying and being given in marriage, until the day Noah entered the ark, and the flood came and destroyed all of them. Likewise, just as it was in the days of Lot: they were eating and drinking, buying and selling, planting and building, but on the day that Lot left Sodom, it rained fire and sulfur from heaven and destroyed all of them—it will be like that on the day that the Son of Man is revealed. (Luke 17:26-29; par. Matt. 24:37-39)

Both narratives are found in the book of Genesis. Each is a story of near total destruction, and each contains a problematic portrayal (or portrayals) of God. In the flood narrative, God is said to have "blotted out every living thing that was on the face of the ground, human beings and animals and creeping things and birds of the air; they were blotted out from the earth" (Gen. 7:23a). Only Noah and his family—his wife, three sons, and three daughters-in-law—survived. Similarly, all the inhabitants of Sodom and Gomorrah were destroyed when "the Lord rained on Sodom and Gomorrah sulfur and fire from the Lord out of heaven," with the exception of Lot, his wife (who turned into a pillar of salt while leaving the city), and his two daughters (Gen. 19:24). The level of devastation and human loss in both accounts is staggering to say the least. Yet these stories, full of divine violence and death, are the ones to which Jesus likens his return. What does this imply about the character of Jesus and the nonviolent God I have claimed he reveals?

A Judgment Worse than Sodom's

On two occasions, Jesus declared that the final judgment would be worse for some people living in his own day than for the ancient inhabitants of Sodom (and Gomorrah).[13] When Jesus sent out the disciples at one point during his ministry, he provided them with a specific set of instructions about where to go and how to behave (Matt. 10:5-10). Jesus also told them what to do about accommodations and how to respond if their message was rejected:

> Whatever town or village you enter, find out who in it is worthy, and stay there until you leave. As you enter the house, greet it. If the house is worthy, let your peace come upon it; but if it is not worthy, let your peace return to you. If anyone will not welcome you or listen to your words, shake off the dust from your feet as you leave that house or town. Truly I tell you, it will be more tolerable for the land of Sodom and Gomorrah on the day of judgment than for that town. (Matt. 10:11-15)

The town that does not welcome Jesus' disciples or heed their message will find itself in a very bad way come judgment day. It will experience even more severe judgment than did Sodom and Gomorrah. This is difficult to imagine, particularly since New Testament writers believed the destruction of these two ancient cities was "symbolic of catastrophic judgment."[14] Jesus' words surely bespeak a terrible fate.

On another occasion, when Jesus was preaching and teaching in various cities, he singled out three cities—Chorazin, Bethsaida, and Capernaum—for special condemnation. They are all faulted for their failure to repent even after experiencing tremendous miracles.

> Then he [Jesus] began to reproach the cities in which most of his deeds of power had been done, because they did not repent. "Woe to you, Chorazin! Woe to you, Bethsaida! For if the deeds of power done in you had been done in Tyre and Sidon, they would have repented long ago in sackcloth and ashes. But I tell you, on the day of judgment it will be more tolerable for Tyre and Sidon than for you. And you, Capernaum, will you be exalted to heaven? No, you will be brought down to Hades. For if the deeds of power done in you had been done in Sodom, it would have remained until this day. But I tell you that on the day of judgment it will be more tolerable for the land of Sodom than for you." (Matt. 11:20-24)

Once again, Jesus refers to the destruction of non-Israelite cities—Tyre, Sidon, Sodom—to emphasize how much worse it will be for certain inhabitants of Israel on the day of judgment.[15] It is a rhetorically powerful way of emphasizing the severity of their eschatological punishment. How can such pronouncements of utter devastation be reconciled with the portrayal of a nonviolent God?

A Fate of Eternal Consequence

Perhaps the most troubling of all Jesus' teachings are those that refer to eternal punishment. As the Gospels portray it, Jesus clearly seems to have expected eschatological judgment to have serious and irreversible consequences for those who refused the gospel. On numerous occasions, Jesus reportedly made terrifying statements about the dreadful consequences awaiting certain individuals in the hereafter. Consider this select sampling from the Gospel of Matthew:

> I tell you, many will come from east and west and will eat with Abraham and Isaac and Jacob in the kingdom of heaven, while the heirs of the kingdom will be thrown into the outer darkness, where there will be weeping and gnashing of teeth. (Matt. 8:11-12)

> Do not fear those who kill the body but cannot kill the soul; rather fear him who can destroy both soul and body in hell. (Matt. 10:28)

> The Son of Man will send his angels, and they will collect out of his kingdom all causes of sin and all evildoers, and they will throw them into the furnace of fire, where there will be weeping and gnashing of teeth. (Matt. 13:41-42)

> And if your eye causes you to stumble, tear it out and throw it away; it is better for you to enter life with one eye than to have two eyes and to be thrown into the hell of fire. (Matt. 18:9)

> Then he [the Son of Man] will say to those at his left hand, "You that are accursed, depart from me into the eternal fire prepared for the devil and his angels. . . . And these will go away into eternal punishment." (Matt. 25:41, 46a)

God's apparent willingness to inflict enormous pain and suffering upon certain people at the end of the age raises serious questions about God's character. How can a God "who can destroy both soul and body in hell" and who throws people "into the outer darkness, where there will be weeping and gnashing of teeth" legitimately be described as nonviolent?

Interpretive Options for Handling Eschatological Judgment in the Gospels

The passages we have cited raise some very difficult issues for those who contend that Jesus reveals a nonviolent God, and interpreters have responded to these challenges in various ways. In what follows, I describe three different approaches to Jesus' teaching about eschatological judgment that are all compatible with the notion that Jesus revealed a nonviolent God. While the first two completely eliminate the apparent contradiction between Jesus' teachings and the portrayal of a nonviolent God, the third significantly reduces it. I will argue that the third approach represents the best way to resolve this conundrum.

Option 1: Jesus' Teaching about Eschatological Judgment Does Not Reflect His View of God

One way to reconcile Jesus' teaching about eschatological judgment with the nonviolence of God is to argue that these teachings do not actually reflect Jesus' view of God. In other words, despite what Jesus said about God's punishment of wicked individuals at the end of time, his statements do not represent what he really thought about God's eschatological behavior. Instead, Jesus simply appropriated the language of divine judgment—language that was, after all, quite common in the first century—to emphasize the importance of living according to God's will in the present. Once readers understand that Jesus did not literally mean what he said about God in these instances, the problem of an eschatologically violent deity vanishes. According to this approach, Jesus was willing to use the language of eschatological judgment even though it carried the risk of reinforcing some mistaken notions about God's character.

The position I have described is essentially the one recently argued by New Testament scholar I. Howard Marshall in his book *Beyond the Bible*.[16] Marshall believes the teaching of Jesus was "constrained by four parameters" since it took place during a "*liminal period*."[17] He believes these parameters prevented Jesus from speaking the full truth in certain instances.For example, one parameter Marshall identifies concerns Jesus' use of "the imagery and thought forms current at the time." Since Jesus' teaching was culturally conditioned in this way, Marshall believes it does not always give a completely accurate picture of reality. He believes Jesus' use of parables containing terrifying images of divine punishment is a prime example of this. According to Marshall: "There would be universal agreement among civilized people that no human being should perpetuate horrors of the kind described in the parabolic imagery; those who do so are branded as war criminals and are guilty of crimes against humanity."[18] Therefore, Marshall does not believe that the images of God used in these parables accurately represents God's true character. He writes:

It is incredible that God should so act. . . . The imagery in the parables is imagery belonging to a time in a society that was accustomed to such things in real life and saw no incongruity in portraying divine judgement in that way. *But we can no longer think of God in that way, even if this is imagery used by Jesus.* Our basis lies in a mind nurtured by the Spirit, the mind of Christ, which has taught us that such behavior is unacceptable among human beings and that it cannot be justified in the case of God by saying that he is free to act differently from believers. True, we must leave vengeance to God (Rom. 12:19), but that does not mean that he carries out his vengeance in this kind of way. For God to be a just judge means precisely that he is not like the human tyrants portrayed in the parables. We therefore have to say that while the parables warn of the inescapable reality of divine judgment, their imagery must not be pressed too far.[19]

Marshall believes Jesus used this problematic imagery in order "to speak so that the people of his time would understand . . . [using] the standard imagery of human judgment in a way that would make it as plain as possible that God is utterly opposed to wrong behavior and will judge it perfectly."[20] Even though Jesus did not really envision God in the ways he sometimes described God, he accommodated his message to the language and culture of the time in order to make it understandable.

Marshall's proposal is certainly interesting and succeeds in relieving the tension felt between some of Jesus' teachings and the nonviolent God Jesus reveals. Still, I am not persuaded. First, it is difficult to support the claim that Jesus sometimes said one thing about God while believing something very different. Even granting this possibility, it would be even more difficult to determine when Jesus' teaching about God reflects his own beliefs and when it does not. What criteria can be used to make such determinations with any degree of confidence? It is also difficult to believe Jesus would risk perpetuating false images of God just to make a point about "the inescapable reality of divine judgment." This is especially problematic if one of the primary reasons Jesus came to earth was to reveal what God was really like! Surely there would have been other ways for Jesus to make his point without compromising the character of God in the process. Thus, while I agree with Marshall's contention that Jesus used common imagery from his day to convey his message, I am unconvinced that Jesus said one thing while believing something quite different.[21]

Option 2: "Jesus' Teachings" about Eschatological Judgment Do Not Originate with Jesus

One of the most attractive options for eliminating the tension caused by Jesus' teaching about eschatological judgment is based on contemporary research associated with the so-called "Third Quest" for the historical Jesus. Some scholars believe the historical Jesus, the one who lived in Palestine in the first century CE, never spoke of divine violence accompanying the end of the age. Despite what the Gospels claim Jesus said, these scholars believe Jesus actually rejected apocalyptic images of terrifying divine judgment at the end of the world. Accordingly, it is argued that whenever the Gospel writers attribute words of eschatological judgment to Jesus, they are putting words in his mouth and misrepresenting what he actually said. One could put it this way: while the "textual" Jesus endorses contemporary expectations about divine violence at the end of the age, the "actual" Jesus did not.

This position is taken by Walter Wink in his award-winning book *Engaging the Powers*. He writes:

> Perhaps the most frequent deviation in the New Testament itself from Jesus' standard [of God's domination-free order] is the lust for punishment of the wicked. This represents an early retrogression to mimetic rivalry, where the church seeks revenge on its persecutors. The overwhelming number of these passages appear in Matthew, and have no parallel in the other Gospels. Matthew clearly has added them out of some need the gospel had not satisfied. All the "weeping and gnashing of teeth passages" are his (8:12; 13:42, 50; 22:13; 24:51; 25:30) except one, which, however, is not set in hell (Luke 13:28). Matthew adds threats of hellfire, eternal torture, and everlasting punishment that he does not find in his sources, as their absence in the Markan and Lukan parallels attests (Matt. 5:22; 7:19; 12:36-37; 13:40, 42; 16:27; 18:34-35; 22:7; 25:41, 46). Occasionally one finds elements of this vindictiveness in Mark (9:43-48 par.; 12:1-12 par.) or Luke (12:46 [Q], 47-48a; 16:23; 19:27), but they are not made central, and in most cases do not appear to go back to Jesus either.[22]

Wink is certainly justified in emphasizing the especially problematic nature of the Gospel of Matthew in regard to the teachings of Jesus concerning eschatological judgment. What is less certain, however, is how much of this material goes back to Jesus and how much originated later with the early church.

Jack Nelson-Pallmeyer, who was one of Wink's students, believes as I do that Jesus revealed a nonviolent God. Therefore, he too must come to terms with Jesus' sayings about eschatological judgment. Nelson-Pallmeyer does this by distinguishing between what Jesus actually said and did and what the Gospel writers claim Jesus said and did. Despite what the Gospels suggest, Nelson-Pallmeyer believes Jesus never actually taught about divine eschatological judgment. He writes: "Jesus' original sayings were not apocalyptic and the apocalyptic edge, including threats of divine retribution, was added later."[23]

Nelson-Pallmeyer bases his conclusion on the work of John Dominic Crossan, a towering figure—albeit highly controversial one—in historical Jesus studies. According to Crossan, Jesus did not preach a message of God's imminent eschatological judgment. Although Crossan believes Jesus was initially persuaded by the message of divine wrath proclaimed by John the Baptist, he believes Jesus subsequently rejected that message and broke away from John.[24] "I have argued," writes Crossan, "that John the Baptist was an apocalyptic prophet preparing his followers for the imminent advent of God as the Coming One but that Jesus, after having originally accepted that vision, eventually changed his response some time after the execution of John."[25]

Crossan's assertions about a nonapocalyptic Jesus rest on his understanding of the compositional history of a hypothetical document called "Q" (from the German *Quelle*, meaning source). There is broad agreement among scholars that Q was a document that contained various sayings of Jesus found in Matthew and Luke but absent from Mark.[26] There is far less consensus, however, about the process by which this document developed. Yet this "process" is essential to Crossan's argument. Relying on the detailed compositional analysis of John Kloppenborg, Crossan argues that Q developed in at least three stages. The first two are relevant to this discussion. Crossan believes the earliest edition of Q, and the one traceable to Jesus, contained various wisdom sayings but no apocalyptic materials. Apocalyptic passages, like the ones we are considering in this chapter, are thought to have appeared only in the second edition of Q. According to Crossan, these apocalyptic passages do not reflect the actual words of the historical Jesus. Instead, he believes these words reflect common eschatological expectations and argues they were put on the lips of Jesus by early Christian writers. Even though the Gospels attribute these sayings to Jesus, Crossan believes they did not originate with Jesus since they are absent from the first edition of Q.

If Jesus never uttered a word about eschatological judgment, as Crossan claims and Nelson-Pallmeyer affirms, then the apparent tension we feel between these sayings and Jesus' revelation of a nonviolent God melts away. While this would be an easy solution, I am not convinced that Jesus never spoke about eschatological divine judgment as the Gospels suggest. It seems extremely tenuous to make such a claim on the basis of the hypothetical compositional history of a hypothetical text! Thus, while I agree that "the historical Jesus can help us decide between distortion and revelation," I am not convinced Nelson-Pallmeyer's Jesus—or Crossan's—accurately reflects the Jesus of history.[27] While I believe that some of these sayings, or at least some of these sayings in the form they now take, may be secondary, I am not convinced that every Jesus saying related to divine judgment signifies a secondary intrusion. Presumably some of these sayings did, in fact, originate with Jesus. In order to resolve the dilemma raised by Jesus' teachings about eschatological judgment, we need to consider another interpretive option.

Option 3: Jesus' Teachings about Eschatological Judgment Are Less Violent (and Less Problematic) than They Appear

Another way of trying to reconcile Jesus' teachings about eschatological judgment with his revelation of a nonviolent God is to argue that the tension between these is not as great as it appears. If this is the case, we should be careful not to overemphasize the nature of the problem. There are significant differences of opinion about how to interpret Jesus' teachings regarding eschatological judgment. This is particularly true when it comes to Jesus' teaching about "hell." While most Christians affirm the reality of hell and believe it to be the eternal fate of those who reject God, they differ significantly about the nature and duration of this dreadful reality.

Several perspectives about the nature of hell are nicely set forth in a recent book aptly titled *Four Views of Hell*. The four views under consideration are the literal view, the metaphorical view, the purgatorial view, and the conditional view. The majority of Protestants today would subscribe to either the literal or the metaphorical view.[28] Proponents of the former believe "eternal punishment is by literal fire."[29] Accordingly, sinners will experience excruciating physical pain that lasts forever. Adherents of the metaphorical view, on the other hand, contend that "hellfire and brimstone are not literal depictions of hell's furnishings, but figurative expressions warning the wicked of impending doom."[30] They believe that biblical images of hellfire should be understood figuratively as describing a state of eternal, conscious torment, not of being burned forever. As William Crockett puts it: "The most we can say is that the rebellious will be cast from the presence of God, without any hope of restoration."[31] According to this view, punishment involves mental and emotional pain rather than bodily, physical pain.

Proponents of both views—the literal and the metaphorical—imagine God inflicting a previously unprecedented amount of divine violence on recalcitrant sinners in the hereafter. With no hope of redemption, these unfortunate individuals will suffer physically or mentally (or both) for all eternity. Yet some regard this prospect as morally unacceptable. As Clark Pinnock so forcefully puts it: "Everlasting torture is intolerable from a moral point of view because it pictures God acting like a bloodthirsty monster who maintains an everlasting Auschwitz for his enemies whom he does not even allow to die."[32] That is why Pinnock and others argue that never-ending suffering is not what Jesus actually meant when he spoke of divine judgment and eternal punishment.

Conditionalists, sometimes also referred to as annihilationists, do not believe that hell represents an *unending* state of torment and despair. Instead, they believe hell is something more temporary and transitory, something that ceases to be once it has served its purpose. Hell, in their view, represents the utter and absolute destruction of an individual. They believe that people who "go to hell" are actually annihilated by God. After they are judged, they will cease to exist. Conditionalists, such as Edward Fudge, allow for the possibility of a period of conscious suffering prior to their annihilation.[33] Fudge believes the Scriptures teach that "the actual process of destruction may well involve conscious pain that differs in magnitude in each individual case.[34] Regardless of this indeterminate period of suffering, conditionalists like Fudge believe "the unrighteous will all finally die."[35] When their "judgment" has ended, God "will banish them from his presence forever. . . . They will be destroyed, both body and soul, forever."[36] In short, they will be no more. As conditionalists understand it, hell is less about duration and more about finality.

Proponents of this position believe it makes better sense of the biblical data. Both the Old and New Testaments speak of the fate of the wicked in terms of their dying, perishing, or being utterly destroyed. For example, Matt. 10:28 refers to God as one who can "destroy both soul and body in hell." This seems to imply an ultimate act of destruction that will result in permanent nonexistence. Likewise, in the parable of the weeds among the wheat, the weeds are "burned up" (Matt. 13:40). The easiest reading of such a text is that the weeds are consumed by the fire until there is nothing left of them. This represents the wicked who will be annihilated and will cease to exist. Conditionalists further contend that references to "eternal" punishment, such as the one in Matt. 25:46, do not refer to the duration of the punishment but to its finality and irreversibility. Whereas the literal and metaphorical views envision eternal *punishing* (conscious ongoing torment forever and ever), conditionalists envision eternal *punishment* (final and irreversible destruction).[37]

Conditionalists typically refrain from specifying the precise nature of the punishment they believe unrepentant sinners will experience. This is judicious since the relevant biblical texts do not demand a particular understanding of what this punishment entails and because the function of these passages is to encourage faithful living in the present, not to provide a detailed description of the judgment to come. This lack of specificity is significant since it allows for the possibility of divine punishment that is *not* violent. Since it is easy to envision various forms of punishment that are not inherently violent—consider the many kinds of noncorporal punishment parents use—one cannot simply assume that individuals who suffer eschatological divine judgment necessarily experience eschatological divine violence. We just do not know whether their punishment will—or will not—involve the use of violence.

But for the sake of argument, let us assume that the eschatological divine punishment that conditionalists envision does involve some measure of violence. What then? How would this affect the way we describe God's character? At the very least, we would need to acknowledge that God may resort to violence at the end of time. This would require us to be a bit more nuanced when speaking about God's nonviolent nature. Still, our description of God as one who does not engage in violence in *historical* time still stands. Even if we operate on the premise that eschatological judgment involves some degree of divine violence, it does not fundamentally alter our previous description or the value of using this description to evaluate disturbing divine behavior in the Old Testament since the problematic portrayals included there reportedly "took place" in historical time. Maximally then, this position suggests that God uses violence only outside the space-time continuum, only for a limited period of time, and only for the sake of final punishment. Therefore, if one accepts the conditionalists' view of eternal punishment, it is still possible to maintain that the God Jesus reveals acts nonviolently in historical time and is, therefore, fundamentally nonviolent even in the face of Jesus' teachings about eschatological judgment.

Jesus as Divine Warrior in the Book of Revelation

Most casual readers of the book of Revelation are likely to walk away from the book with the impression that God will engage in unprecedented acts of violence at the end of the age. God routinely seems to be depicted as a divine destroyer, as one who will unleash murderous waves of devastation on humankind in days to come. The ubiquitous violence in Revelation and the theological problems it raises are well expressed by Eugene Boring and are worth quoting at length. Boring writes:

> When the Lamb [Jesus] opens the sealed scroll, catastrophic violence is unleashed upon the earth and its inhabitants. The world is devastated by war, famine, plague, and death (6:1-8). People are killed because of their faithfulness to God and cry out for vengeance (6:9-11). Sun, moon, and stars are struck; mountains and islands displaced, as everyone from king to slave tries to escape the approaching wrath (6:12-17). The earth is struck with hail and fire mixed with blood (8:7) and the sea and rivers turn to blood (8:8-11; 16:3-4). Demonic locust-like creatures stream out of the abyss to torment humanity, and people cry out for death but continue to suffer (9:1-11). A twilight-zone supernatural horde of two hundred million cavalry pour across the Euphrates from the East (9:13-19). Those who worship the beast are tormented with sulphurous fire in the presence of the holy angels and the Lamb (14:10-11). Horses wade for two hundred miles in bridle-deep blood (14:20). The kings of the earth mount a final battle against God and his Messiah, and vultures are gorged with the flesh of both the lowly footsoldiers who fight the world's battles and of their high and mighty commanders (16:14-16; 19:17-18).
>
> Not only is mind and imagination overwhelmed by the quantity and unrelenting intensity of the violence perpetrated against both humans and cosmos itself, *the theological problem is compounded by the fact that the source of violence is God and the Lamb*, sometimes invoked with cries for vengeance. This whole range of imagery has posed a severe problem for interpreting Revelation as a Christian book, particularly when compared with the pictures of Jesus in the Gospels.[38]

Boring rightly observes how very problematic these images are when viewed in light of the Gospel portrayals of Jesus. The overwhelming amount of divine violence described in the book of Revelation stands in stark contrast to the nonviolent God Jesus reveals. As Walter Wink puts it: "Revelation . . . is filled with a craving, not for redemptive violence, but something even worse: punitive violence, to be carried out by God. . . . We are a long, long way from Jesus here."[39]

For the purposes of this study, it is unnecessary to reconcile the violent portrayals of God in the book of Revelation with nonviolent portrayals of God in the Gospels. As discussed previously, I am arguing that God's true nature is to be derived specifically from the God *Jesus* reveals, rather than more generally from the New Testament's various portrayals of God. Images of God in Revelation may be just as revelatory—or just as distorted—as those found elsewhere in the Bible. Each image must be evaluated by the God Jesus reveals. When this is done, Revelation's portrayal of God as a purveyor of violence on a massive scale is found wanting.

Similarly, while some portrayals of Jesus in the book of Revelation may be disturbing, they do not challenge my basic thesis. Since I have argued that the God Jesus reveals is known through Jesus' life and teachings while on earth—not descriptions of Jesus' supposed behavior at the end of time—images of Jesus in the book of Revelation that do not correspond well with descriptions of Jesus in the Gospels are ultimately unproblematic for my argument. Nevertheless, it might be helpful to comment on one particular portrayal of Jesus in the book of Revelation that many readers find especially disconcerting. In Rev. 19:11-21, Jesus is portrayed as a divine warrior, a description that would seem clearly at odds with the way Jesus is described in the Gospels.

> Then I saw heaven opened, and there was a white horse! Its rider is called Faithful and True, and in righteousness he judges and makes war. His eyes are like a flame of fire, and on his head are many diadems; and he has a name inscribed that no one knows but himself. He is clothed in a robe dipped in blood, and his name is called The Word of God. And the armies of heaven, wearing fine linen, white and pure, were following him on white horses. From his mouth comes a sharp sword with which to strike down the nations, and he will rule them with a rod of iron; he will tread the wine press of the fury of the wrath of God the Almighty. On his robe and on his thigh he has a name inscribed, "King of kings and Lord of lords." Then I saw an angel standing in the sun, and with a loud voice he called to all the birds that fly in midheaven, "Come, gather for the great supper of God, to eat the flesh of kings, the flesh of captains, the flesh of the mighty, the flesh of horses and their riders—flesh of all, both free and slave, both small and great." Then I saw the beast and the kings of the earth with their armies gathered to make war against the rider on the horse and against his army. And the beast was captured, and with it the false prophet who had performed in its presence the signs by which he deceived those who had received the mark of the beast and those who worshiped its image. These two were thrown alive into the lake of fire that burns with sulfur. And the rest were killed by the sword of the rider on the horse, the sword that

came from his mouth; and all the birds were gorged with their flesh. (Rev. 19:11-21)

Though unnamed, this rider is clearly understood to be Jesus. He is called "Faithful and True" (v. 11), his name is "the Word of God" (v. 13), and inscribed on his thigh is the name "King of kings and Lord of lords" (v. 16). Yet, in this passage, Jesus seems terribly violent. Jesus is depicted as riding a horse into battle, soundly defeating the enemy, killing the kings of the earth and their armies, and then leaving their bodies on the field of battle to be carrion for birds of prey.

Is this the right way to understand this passage? Are we intended to envision Jesus as an end-time terminator? Those who take this passage literalistically cannot help but answer in the affirmative. As Cowles observes:

> By interpreting highly symbolic language literally, the nonviolent Jesus of the Gospels is transformed into a violent warrior. . . . Thus, like Clark Kent emerging from the telephone booth as Superman, Jesus at his return will cast aside his servant garments and will disclose who he really is: a fierce, merciless, and physically violent eschatological terminator who will make the blood of his enemies flow knee-deep as in the days of Joshua.[40]

If we are correct in understanding that Jesus lived and taught nonviolence, the image of him coming back at the end of time to kill and destroy is jarring to say the least. Is it reasonable to expect Jesus, the suffering servant, to return as an extreme exterminator? As a Dr. Jekyll turned Mr. Hyde? What is going on here?

Numerous interpreters have argued that what is being described is not a literal battle but rather a symbolic victory over evil. This interpretive approach makes good sense given the genre of Revelation. Much of the book is apocalyptic literature, a genre characterized by symbols that are not meant to be interpreted literalistically. In his recent commentary on the book of Revelation, John Yeatts emphasizes the absence of physical weapons or an actual battle in Revelation 19. He observes that "in Christ's battles the only weapons are words of judgment."[41] According to Yeatts: "Christ's weapon here and throughout scripture is the Word of God, which can torment hearers by convicting them of sin and judging their deeds."[42] Similarly, J. Denny Weaver stresses "the nonviolent character of the supposed battle in the last segment of chapter 19." He explains:

> In the segment of 19:11-21, the beast and the kings and their armies are defeated not by violence and military might. They are undone—defeated—by the Word of God. This passage is another symbolic representation of the victory of the reign of God over the forces of evil that has already occurred with the death and resurrection of Jesus. It is by proclamation of the Word, not by armies and military might, that God's judgment occurs.[43]

This interpretive approach to Revelation 19 effectively eliminates the problem of Jesus physically killing people without removing the reality of divine judgment that faces those who refuse to respond positively to gospel.[44] It demonstrates that there is nothing fundamentally incompatible between this portrayal of Jesus and the portrayals we find in the Gospels.

Reconsidering the Possibility of Historical Divine Violence

Before concluding, we must consider one further objection that might be raised to the description of the God Jesus reveals described earlier in chapter 10. This objection is not related to eschatological judgment but concerns the claim that Jesus reveals a God who does not judge people through historical or natural disasters. Some biblical scholars and theologians believe Jesus taught that God was going to punish Israel by causing the destruction of Jerusalem at the hands of the Romans. Marcus Borg is among those scholars who think Jesus believed God was going to judge the inhabitants of Jerusalem in this way. Borg identifies eleven passages in which Jesus speaks about the coming destruction of Jerusalem, the temple, and/or the land.[45] Of those eleven passages, two suggest the coming destruction of Jerusalem is an act of divine judgment.

> If you, even you, had only recognized on this day the things that make for peace! But now they are hidden from your eyes. Indeed, the days will come upon you, when your enemies will set up ramparts around you and surround you, and hem you in on every side. They will crush you to the ground, you and your children within you, and they will not leave within you one stone upon another; because you did not recognize the time of your visitation from God. (Luke 19:42-44)

> Then those in Judea must flee to the mountains, and those inside the city must leave it, and those out in the country must not enter it; for these are days of vengeance, as a fulfillment of all that is written. Woe to those who are pregnant and to those who are nursing infants in those days! For there will be great distress on the earth and wrath against this people; they will fall by the edge of the sword and be taken away as captives among all nations; and Jerusalem will be trampled on by the Gentiles, until the times of the Gentiles are fulfilled. (Luke 21:21-24)

Both of these passages, found only in the Gospel of Luke, can be taken to mean God is responsible for the coming destruction of Jerusalem. According to Borg, the passage in Luke 21 contains "echoes of the Old Testament, particularly day-of-Yahweh passages, which make it clear that the fall of Jerusalem was understood as the judgment of God."[46] He believes Luke "certainly did not view it [the destruction of Jerusalem] *simply* as an event of secular history; it was divine wrath."[47]

Joel Green also believes that these passages regard the destruction of Jerusalem in 70 CE as an act of divine judgment. According to Green, Jesus' words in Luke 19:43-44 demonstrate "that divine judgment would come upon the city on account of its failure to recognize and accept the salvific visitation of God."[48] Similarly, Green believes that "the anticipated fall of Jerusalem [in Luke 21:20-24] is portrayed as divine judgment for its unfaithfulness before Yahweh."[49]

Perhaps the most influential voice to argue in favor of this position is New Testament scholar N. T. Wright. Wright also thinks Jesus believed that God's judgment would come upon Jerusalem in historical time and space.[50] Wright's argument draws on a wider array of passages than the two we have been considering. Wright believes that all of Jesus' teachings typically thought to refer to eschatological judgment are really nothing of the sort. Rather, he regards all of them as references to God's coming historical judgment. He writes:

> The great achievement of Marcus Borg, in my judgment, is to have demonstrated that the severe warnings which the gospels attribute to Jesus have little or nothing to do with either hell-fire after death or with the end of the world, in the sense of the end of the space-time universe. Instead, the warnings are to be read as typical pieces of Jewish "apocalyptic" language, as prophecies about a *this-worldly* judgment which is to be *interpreted as* the judgment of Israel's God.[51]

Wright's claim that all Jesus' supposed eschatological utterances be understood as this-worldly judgments has come under criticism and is, in my opinion, extreme.[52] While this is not the place to enter that debate, the point made by Borg, Green, Wright and others—that Jerusalem's destruction in 70 CE was an act of divine judgment—requires our consideration.

To begin, it is important to put the two Lukan passages we have been considering in perspective. First, despite what is often asserted about these passages, neither *explicitly* claims that the coming destruction of Jerusalem will be an act of divine judgment. Unlike Old Testament texts, which at times unequivocally describe historical disasters as acts of divine judgment, neither of these passages is so categorical. Second, even if one concludes that they refer to divine judgment via historical disaster, this provides only limited information about Jesus' view of God. At most, it suggests that Jesus believed that God would judge the inhabitants of Jerusalem in this particular instance through military defeat. It would not, however, imply that Jesus agreed with the perspective found in the Old Testament that historical disasters and personal tragedies should be interpreted as acts of divine judgment. For example, Jesus never affirms the idea that God might instantly annihilate a particular individual for wrongdoing, nor did Jesus ever suggest that God used war to punish other nations for their sins. At most, these passages in Luke reveal Jesus' thinking about God's actions in one particular isolated historical event.

For the sake of argument, let us assume that these Lukan passages envision the destruction of Jerusalem as an act of divine judgment. If so, the crucial question for our purposes then becomes whether these passages originated with Jesus or came later, Christian interpretations of Jerusalem's demise. Borg vigorously contends these passages do go back to Jesus and are not just Lukan creations.[53] Yet other scholars are not so sure. For example, the majority of scholars who participated in the Jesus Seminar had serious doubts about the authenticity of both Luke 19:41-44 and Luke 21:20-24.[54] Regarding the former passage, Funk and Hoover write:

> Some Fellows [of the Jesus Seminar] argued that Jesus could have uttered a prophetic oracle of this type. . . . Other Fellows took the oracle to be a prophecy that had been constructed after the fall of Jerusalem in 70 c. e. and therefore reflects events that took place long after Jesus' death. Christians regularly interpreted the fall of Jerusalem as divine retribution for the city's rejection of Jesus. The Fellows . . . also argued that the use of language from the Hebrew prophets mirrored the practice of the early church, which attributed scriptural words to Jesus.[55]

The participants of the Jesus Seminar were even less convinced that Luke 21:20-24 goes back to Jesus and clearly felt this passage was written by Luke rather than spoken by Jesus.[56] At the very least, it seems reasonably clear that this passage has been reworked by the writer of Luke. As New Testament scholar Joseph Fitzmyer puts it: "No one will contest that Luke has overlaid his form of Jesus' utterances about Jerusalem's coming desolation with various OT allusions."[57] Yet these allusions are what cause Jesus' words to have the flavor of divine judgment. Thus, given the early church's tendency to interpret the destruction of Jerusalem in 70 CE as an act of divine destruction—an interpretive move more in keeping with Old Testament perspectives on historical disasters than with the teachings of Jesus—it is not unreasonable to suggest that some of the ideas in these Lukan passages reflect the views of the early church rather than those of the historical Jesus.[58]

A similar argument could be made for the troublesome parable of the wedding banquet that occurs in Matt. 22:1-10 and Luke 14:16-24. I will focus on Matthew's version since, unlike Luke's account, it contains explicit references to divine violence.

> Once more Jesus spoke to them in parables, saying: "The kingdom of heaven may be compared to a king who gave a wedding banquet for his son. He sent his slaves to call those who had been invited to the wedding banquet, but they would not come. Again he sent other slaves, saying, "Tell those who have been invited: Look, I have prepared my dinner, my oxen and my fat calves have been slaughtered, and everything is ready; come to the wedding banquet." But they made light of it and went away, one to his farm, another to his business,

while the rest seized his slaves, mistreated them, and killed them. The king was enraged. He sent his troops, destroyed those murderers, and burned their city. Then he said to his slaves, "The wedding is ready, but those invited were not worthy. Go therefore into the main streets, and invite everyone you find to the wedding banquet." Those slaves went out into the streets and gathered all whom they found, both good and bad; so the wedding hall was filled with guests. (Matt. 22:1-10)

In this parable, the king represents God; the son, Jesus; and those initially invited, the Jews. The refusal of the initial invitees (Jews) prompts the king (God) to extend the invitation to "everyone you find" (Gentiles).[59] The parable is typically understood to reflect a new understanding of who constitutes the people of God.

The verses that are particularly curious and troubling are verses 6–7: "while the rest seized his slaves, mistreated them, and killed them. The king was enraged. He sent his troops, destroyed those murderers, and burned their city." Since these verses do not fit well in their present context, some have argued they represent a later addition to the Gospel of Matthew, going back neither to Jesus nor to the writer of Matthew. One commentator refers to them as "a post-Matthean interpolation" and claims: "The narrative makes more sense if they are omitted. How bizarre to conduct war while the roasted oxen wait to be eaten!"[60] Those who believe these verses came from the writer of the Gospel of Matthew believe that the reference to the city being burned refers to the destruction of Jerusalem by the Romans in 70 CE. As Douglas Hare puts it: "The burning of the 'rebel' city seems to be an allusion to the destruction of Jerusalem by the Romans in 70 CE, an event that Christians regarded as God's punishment upon Israel for its rejection of Jesus and the gospel."[61] Therefore, it is reasonable to conclude that these verses neither originated with Jesus nor accurately reflected his teaching. Instead, they are best understood as a Matthean (or post-Matthean) addition reflecting the early church's interpretation of the fall of Jerusalem in 70 CE.

———

In this appendix, I have reexamined the claim that Jesus reveals a nonviolent God in light of various New Testament passages about eschatological judgment. Despite certain challenges these texts raise, they do not invalidate the previous assertion that the God Jesus revealed is nonviolent. Although Jesus' eschatological teachings may allow for some measure of divine violence at the final judgment, there is no compelling evidence that Jesus envisioned God violently punishing people here and now, in time and space.[62] Allowing for the possibility that God may engage in some degree of eschatological violence does not undermine our conclusion that God's this-worldly mode of operation is that of nonviolent love.

Maximally then, Jesus' teachings about eschatological judgment suggest that at the end of the age, God will utterly destroy the wicked in an act of final and irreversible punishment. Since this is a unique, one-of-a-kind, ultimate act of judgment yet to take place, it should not cause us to redefine God as violent when all other indicators in the teachings of Jesus point in the opposite direction. Moreover, the extent to which this final judgment may be considered violent depends on how one interprets the passages in question. Some views are far less troublesome, and far less violent (if at all), than others.

Appendix B:
Inspiration and the Authority
of Scripture

Since the beginning of the Church, every Christian theology has implicitly or explicitly acknowledged the authority of Scripture. The serious question has never been whether Scripture is a primary authority for Christian faith and life but what sort of authority it is.

—Daniel L. Migliore[1]

The approach to disturbing divine behavior I have proposed in this book inevitably raises certain questions about the inspiration and authority of Scripture. If some portrayals of God distort God's character, as I have argued, then in what sense can those portrayals be said to be inspired or authoritative? Or, to put the question differently, what does the presence of disturbing divine behavior in the Old Testament suggest about God's involvement in the formation of Scripture?

A comprehensive discussion of divine inspiration and the authority of Scripture is well beyond the scope of this book. Such a discussion would require a separate book, and numerous studies have been devoted to these issues.[2] The aim of this appendix is much more modest. I hope to demonstrate that my proposal for handling problematic portrayals of God in Old Testament narratives is compatible with doctrines of divine inspiration and biblical authority. While accepting the conclusions reached in this study will undoubtedly require some readers to rethink *how* the Bible is inspired and authoritative, it will not necessitate abandoning these fundamental convictions about the nature of Scripture.

Before discussing my understanding of God's involvement in the formation of Scripture, I want to discuss some commonly held views of inspiration I regard as deficient. My quarrel with these views is that they do not satisfactorily correspond to the evidence at hand. Instead, they seem out of sync with what we know about the formation of the Bible and with the kind of things we find in the Bible itself. As we will see, these views make it difficult—if not impossible—to accept my proposal for how to handle disturbing divine behavior in Old Testament narratives. But if these views are inadequate, as I contend, then they need not be a barrier to adopting the conclusions reached in this study.

For the purposes of this discussion, I will be using the term *inspiration* to refer to God's role in the formation of Scripture, since I am interested in exploring the nature of divine involvement in the origin of the Bible. I am aware that this is not the only way of understanding what it means to speak about the inspiration of Scripture. In fact, some theological discussions of inspiration do not deal with the question of the Bible's origins at all. Instead, they refer to the way God "speaks" to people through the Bible today. But since my interest here is to look behind the Bible and to consider how it was formed, when I speak about "divine inspiration" I will be referring to God's involvement in the production of the Bible.

Plenary (Verbal) Inspiration and Conceptual Inspiration

One feature that distinguishes various views of inspiration from one another concerns how much control God is thought to have exercised over the process. Some people believe God was highly involved in the process, carefully controlling what the biblical "authors" wrote in order to insure the accuracy of the message. They believe God supplied specific ideas—if not exact words—to individuals such as Moses, David, Solomon, and Paul, who then faithfully recorded them. At the opposite end of the spectrum are those who regard the Bible as a collection of human documents and suggest that God had nothing whatsoever to do with its formation. Still others map out positions between these extremes. To begin, I want to describe two views that posit a high degree of divine control over the process: plenary inspiration and conceptual inspiration, neither of which adequately represents my understanding of God's role in the formation of Scripture.

Plenary Inspiration

The most exacting view of the inspiration of Scripture, insofar as divine control is concerned, is plenary (full or complete) inspiration, also referred to as verbal inspiration. Some advocates of this approach believe God dictated the actual words of

Scripture. God spoke, and human "stenographers" wrote down the words. Others who take this approach do not believe that God audibly spoke every word the biblical writers recorded. Instead, they allow for the possibility that some portions of the Bible contain words that God impressed upon the hearts and minds of the biblical writers. Regardles of how one understands the particular mechanism, whether God spoke audible or impressed these words upon the hearts and minds of the biblical writers, adherents of this view all agree that God's control over the specific content of the Bible is absolute.

An oft-used analogy to describe this process is that of a musician playing music on an instrument such as a flute.[3] In this analogy, the musician is God, the instrument is the human writer, and music is the biblical text that is produced as a result of this process. Obviously, a flute is not capable of producing music all by itself. It merely serves as a conduit or channel through which a musician can force air. The instrument is no more responsible for the music produced than a biblical writer is for the words written. Instead, it is God, the divine musician, who determines the specific content of the Bible. This view of inspiration emphasizes the divine origin of Scripture in the most uncompromising way possible.

Conceptual Inspiration

Like plenary inspiration, conceptual inspiration assumes that God exercised a high degree of control over the process, though in a less restrictive way.[4] According to this view, God supplied human writers with general concepts and ideas, though typically not with exact words. These human authors then had the freedom to communicate the message in various ways, using the language and literary style of their own cultural and historical settings. As Randolph Tate describes it: "God communicated a message to an individual through a dream, vision, mental impression, or some other means, and left the author free to choose the form in which the message would be conveyed."[5] Adherents of this view of conceptual inspiration believe God exercised somewhat less control over the precise content of the Bible than do adherents of plenary inspiration.

To offer an analogy of how this process is thought to have operated, consider the work of a preacher in preparing a sermon. It is not uncommon to hear preachers say that God laid a particular message on their heart. But if you were to ask them if the precise words they spoke came directly from God, most would say, "No." By saying God "laid a message" on their heart, they are claiming that God gave them certain ideas, which they themselves then crafted into a sermon. Although they believe the idea for the message—and perhaps even key parts of it—came from God, they still need to write the sermon, choose certain illustrations, and decide how it will be organized. Those who believe in conceptual inspiration feel much the same way about the formation of the Bible. They believe God gave certain individuals ideas to write but then allowed these individuals the freedom to craft the message as they saw fit. These individuals could express this God-given message in their own particular way, using a variety of literary genres, rhetorical techniques, and writing styles. It is believed that this freedom accounts for some of the diversity found in Scripture.

Proponents of the two views of inspiration just described regard God as the ultimate source of the Bible's content and believe the very reason we have a Bible is because God willed it and made it happen. While conceptual inspiration allows for more human influence in terms of how this content was communicated, both positions regard the Bible's essential message as coming from God. Both views suggest that God wanted idea "A" to be written and then prompted writer "B" to create text "C" to convey idea "A." In short, God included what God wanted in the Bible. Understandably, proponents of these views have a great deal of confidence in the trustworthiness of the Bible. If God is the source of the content of the Bible, then that content must be true and reliable. Such confidence in the divinely controlled content of the Bible leads many people to speak of the Bible as being either inerrant (without error) or infallible (true in all it intends to teach).[6]

People find these views of inspiration compelling for many reasons. Some ground their beliefs in 2 Tim. 3:16-17, which claims that "all Scripture is inspired by God." They may also embrace one of these views because it was the one favored at home, church, or a Christian school they attended. They may adopt as their own the beliefs of their parents or a trusted pastor or teacher as their own. Some resonate with this view because it coincides nicely with their view of God. People who believe that God is completely in control of world affairs are likely to carry that theological conviction into their understanding of the Bible's formation. If God is sovereign and controls all of human history, then it stands to reason that God controlled the production of the Bible.[7] Still others believe that the "unity" of the Bible reveals God's high level of involvement in the formation of Scripture. They identify certain themes and ideas that run throughout Scripture and that hold it together, in a manner of speaking. Although sometimes these individuals are not unaware of the differences that exist among various portions of the Bible, they find the unifying elements more impressive. For them, this fundamental unity in a collection of texts coming from so many different writers over such a vast span of time is clear evidence of God's control over the process. For these and other reasons, some conclude that God must have been highly involved in determining the specific content now found in the pages of Scripture.

It is not difficult to see how plenary and conceptual views of inspiration do not correspond well with some of the ideas proposed in this study. For example, if God exercised the kind of control over the content of the Bible envisioned by these approaches, it makes little sense to claim that numerous portrayals of God actually distort God's character. If God is ultimately responsible for the content of the Bible as these views claim—albeit via human agents—then it stands to reason that the Bible's portrayals of God would accurately reflect what God is really like. Surely God would not inspire these writers to depict God inaccurately! That would not make any sense. And, if all biblical portrayals of God accurately reflect God's true nature, it makes no sense to speak of differentiating between the textual God and the actual God since they are one and the same. But are these views of inspiration the best way to explain God's role in the process? Did God really exercise the high degree of control these positions imply, or have adherents of these views overemphasized God's role in the process?

Admittedly, determining the degree of God's involvement in the formation of Scripture is not an easy task. The Bible makes virtually no explicit statements about how it came to be, let alone about how God was—or was not—involved in its formation.[8] So how does one go about answering this kind of question? To begin, it helps to reflect on the nature of biblical manuscripts themselves and to consider some potential implications of the diversity we find in Scripture as we endeavor to assess God's role in the process. While this information is hardly new, and certainly not surprising to many proponents of plenary or conceptual inspiration, some of it is difficult to account for by those who wish to maintain a high degree of divine control over the process.

Issues to Consider When Assessing God's Role in the Formation of Scripture

External Factors

First, it is important to note that the English translations you and I read today are not derived from the original autographs.[9] We no longer possess any of these documents. Instead, what we have are copies of copies. It is also important to keep in mind that the Bible we read today does not come from any single ancient manuscript. In the case of the New Testament, there are more than five thousand "witnesses" (manuscripts in part or whole) to the materials that now comprise the New Testament. These witness differ from one another in various ways. Sometimes these variations are very small and relatively insignificant. Other times, the variations are much more substantial. Scholars have painstakingly analyzed these witnesses to determine which readings are thought to be the most authentic. These have been put together to form the Greek New Testament used today.[10] This text—a composite of various readings from various manuscripts—is the starting point for our modern translations. If the New Testament is actually a compilation of the best readings of various ancient manuscripts, what does this suggest about God's role in the process? How do we account for all these variations if God really exercised a high degree of control over the content of the Bible as some suggest?[11]

Similar questions exist for the Old Testament. Even though the majority of our English translation of the Old Testament comes from a single manuscript, the Leningrad Codex, there are other manuscripts that sometimes contain more authentic readings. For example, readings from the Septuagint and the Dead Sea Scrolls are sometimes closer to the original than those preserved in the Leningrad Codex. Again, the presence of various manuscripts with diverse readings raises the question of the level of divine involvement in the production of these texts. It makes little sense to speak of God tightly controlling the specific content of the Leningrad Codex, various Septuagint manuscripts, and a multitude of Dead Sea Scroll manuscripts and fragments when these sometimes differ significantly from one another. Instead, it seems that God allowed for a considerable degree of human freedom in forming and transmitting these ancient texts.

Second, and related to what has just been said, the presence of unintentional scribal errors in biblical manuscripts raises questions about the degree of divine involvement in the process of transmitting these texts. While not all variations among manuscripts resulted from unintentional scribal errors, some certainly did. Since the biblical manuscripts we now have are copies of copies, this obviously raises the question of how accurately these copies were made over the years. Thankfully, the short answer is that these texts have been transmitted reasonably accurately over time. Still, unintentional scribal errors could and did occur for a number of reasons. Sometimes the copyist's eye would skip from one word on a page to the same occurrence of that word further down the page, resulting in the omission of everything in between. Other times, copyists wrote the same thing twice. Then again, they sometimes transposed letters much like we sometimes do when we mean to type "from" and instead type "form." If the copyists were working in a scriptorium where they were listening to the text being read, there was also the danger of inaccurately writing homophones, words the sound alike but are spelled differently, such as "threw" and "through" in English.[12]

The presence of a considerable number of unintentional scribal errors in biblical manuscripts seems to suggest that God did not exercise excessive control over the process of textual transmission. If God was especially concerned with producing a "perfect" Bible, these errors could have easily been eliminated. Surely a God who can heal the blind, make the lame walk, and raise the dead could have done this. Still, the evidence at hand seems to indicate that God did not.

Third, the fact that different groups of Christians have different Bibles with different numbers of books complicates our discussion of God's role in the formation of the Bible. Christians disagree about which books should—and should not—be included in the Bible.[13] This results in Bibles of differing lengths. The Protestant Bible contains sixty-six books, the Catholic Bible contains seventy-three books, and the Greek Orthodox Bible contains seventy-six books.[14] This situation complicates any discussion of divine inspiration. Which books did God inspire? Which Bible contains those books? The Protestant one? The Catholic one? The Greek Orthodox one? None of these? How can we tell? This uncertainty about what even constitutes "the Bible" raises serious questions about the propriety of speaking of God exercising a high degree of control over the content of various books of the Bible. If God had done so, wouldn't God have also ensured that these books, and these books alone, were the ones regarded as Scripture by the Church? How then can we account for the diversity that exists?

Internal Factors

Another way to evaluate the degree of divine involvement in the formation of the Bible is to look at the internal witness of Scripture itself. Does the content of the Bible seem to indicate a high degree of divine involvement? If God exercised a high level of control over the content of the Bible, it seems reasonable to expect at least two things: (1) parallel passages—passages recounting the same story—would not contain conflicting details, and (2) God's character would be portrayed consistently.[15] Yet a close reading of the Bible does not confirm these expectations.

On numerous occasions, we find conflicting details in parallel passages. Although it is reasonable to expect different accounts to emphasize different aspects of a story, if the content of the Bible had been carefully controlled by God, we would expect the basic details to be the same. In many cases, we discover just the opposite. For example, Genesis 6 says Noah takes one pair of each kind of animal into the ark, while Genesis 7 claims he took seven pairs of all the clean animals (Gen. 6:19-20; 7:1-3).[16] First Samuel claims David killed Goliath, while 2 Samuel says Elhanan was responsible for slaying the giant (1 Sam. 17:23-51; 2 Sam. 21:19). David pays a mere fifty shekels of silver for the threshing floor of Araunah in 2 Samuel, while the Chronicler puts the price at six hundred shekels of gold (2 Sam. 24:24; 1 Chron. 21:25). The Gospel of Matthew describes Jesus cleansing the temple at the end of his ministry, while the Gospel of John portrays Jesus doing so near the beginning (Matt. 21:12-17; John 2:13-25). In Matthew's gospel, the women who arrive at the empty tomb quickly leave to tell the disciples, but Mark's account claims "they said nothing to anyone, for they were afraid" (Matt. 28:8; Mark 16:8). These are just a handful of example that could be multiplied many times over.[17] While there are reasonable explanations for these kinds of discrepancies, they are problematic for those arguing for high divine involvement in the formation of Scripture.[18] How can one talk meaningfully about God giving the specific content of the Bible to writers, even in conceptual form, when parallel passages sometimes contain conflicting accounts of what happened?

What is even more problematic for those wishing to maintain a view of inspiration that posits a high degree of divine control over the specific content of the Bible is the presence of contradictory portrayals of God. If God had been heavily invested in controlling the specific content of the Bible, it is reasonable to believe God would have taken special care to ensure that divine portrayals were consistent and congruent. It would seem that this would have been one of God's top priorities, especially if God intended those portrayals to function as a means of divine self-revelation. But as we have seen, the Bible does not speak with one voice when describing the character of God. We noted some of these inconsistencies in chapter 9: some portrayals suggest God's mind can change while others clearly state it cannot, some passages claim that God is slow to anger while others display God's anger kindling quickly, and some passages speak of God being "gracious and merciful" while others portray God ordering Israel to annihilate people without mercy. These are just a few of the many conflicted portrayals of God found in the Old Testament.[19]

The presence of contradictory portrayals of God in the Old Testament—not to mention the problems that emerge when certain Old Testament portrayals of God are compared with certain New Testament portrayals of God—raises serious questions about the degree of control God exercised over the formation of Scripture. If God exercised the kind of control over the content of Scripture that adherents of both plenary inspiration and conceptual inspiration assert, it is difficult to explain why God chose to represent God's own character in such radically different—and sometimes incongruent—ways. The evidence seems to suggest far less divine involvement in the process than such views of inspiration lead us to believe.

Inspiration by Accommodation

A more nuanced understanding of inspiration than those discussed thus far, and one that finds the presence of errors and theological diversity unremarkable, is a view that appeals to the notion of accommodation. This approach, "which has enjoyed a long and venerable history in the theology and hermeneutics of the church," has recently been promoted by Kenton Sparks in his book *God's Word in Human Words*.[20] As Sparks describes it: "Accommodation is God's adoption in inscripturation of the human audience's finite and fallen perspective. Its underlying conceptual assumption is that in many cases God does not correct our mistaken human viewpoints but merely assumes them in order to communicate with us."[21]

This view of inspiration takes both divine and human involvement in the process very seriously. Accommodationists are more willing than adherents of plenary or conceptual inspiration to recognize the limitations of human authors and to account for errors in the text. Given "the human audience's finite and fallen perspective," this view suggests that God had to speak to Israel in ways they could understand. This meant God sometimes permitted Israel to engage in practices that did always represent God's highest ideals. Still, they believe that God was fully engaged in this process. Despite certain imperfections, they contend that God has communicated—and continues to communicate—through Scripture.

An analogy often used to describe this view is that of a teacher or parent who must explain a complex concept in simplified terms to a pupil or child not fully able to understand all the complexities of the subject at hand. Sparks provides the following illustration:

> When small children ask what clouds are, the answer that we will give—if we know anything at all about relative humidity and dew point—will inevitably fall far short of the meteorological details in our head. We shall hopefully advance their knowledge of clouds, but we will privately recognize the subtle misinformation that our simplified explanation entails. This misinformation will have to stand until their minds mature and become capable of understanding a fuller, more detailed answer.[22]

In much the same way, accomodations argue, when God spoke to Israel the revelation was sometimes only partial and incomplete. Allowance of the practice of slavery would be a case in point. Although God did not forbid slavery in Israel, people of faith today would claim that such a practice does not represent God's perfect will for human relationships.

Certain aspects of inspiration by accommodation do seem an improvement over either of the views described thus far. This approach recognizes that a more complicated relationship exists between divine and human involvement in the formation of Scripture than either plenary or conceptual inspiration tends to acknowledge. It explains the nature of this divine-human partnership in a way that accounts for the presence of errors and theological diversity in the text without blaming God for the text's shortcomings.[23] This view of inspiration also seems potentially more compatible with the approach to disturbing divine behavior taken in this book. Sparks believes that "accommodated revelation provides greater access to the divine truth by depicting some things as other than they are."[24] If so, then it seems at least possible that proponents of this view could acknowledge that some portrayals of God depict God other than God really is, a point that has been key to the argument advanced in this book.[25]

Despite these advantages, inspiration by accommodation has some significant deficiencies. Although accommodationists do not maintain that God exercised the kind of control over the particular content of the Bible envisioned by proponents of plenary or conceptual inspiration, they still wish to speak of God's involvement in the process in ways that sometimes seem rather forced. To illustrate, consider the issue of Canaanite genocide. Sparks claims that "the tensions between New Testament love and Old Testament genocide may be explained by the divine genre of Scripture, by the fact that God accommodated ancient Israelite notions of ethnicity and warfare when he spoke to Israel in the Old Testament."[26] Such a claim seems to write God *into* the process based on a prior theological commitment that has decided in advance how God must have been at work in the formation of Scripture. Rather than saying,

"God accommodated ancient Israelite notions," why not simply say, in this instance and others, that Israel adopted ancient Near Eastern notions about divine involvement in warfare? After all, this essentially seems to be what Sparks claims elsewhere when he writes: "Is it only in Israel's case that divine sanction legitimizes the extermination of pagans? Or is it more likely that the biblical text has simply assumed standard but erroneous Near Eastern ideas about the relationship between ethnicity, religion, and war? Theologically speaking, the latter possibility seems more likely to me than the former."[27] If the conquest narrative in Joshua 6–11 is based on these kinds of assumptions, why refer to it as divine accommodation at all?

There are other difficulties as well. Assuming for the sake of argument that it is appropriate to speak of Canaanite genocide as an act of divine accommodation, one is hard-pressed to understand what God was trying to communicate by accommodating in that way. God would seem a rather poor teacher if the only way to communicate to Israel in this instance was through the butchery of men, women, children, and infants. Moreover, despite the obvious logic behind the accommodationist argument that God needed to communicate with Israel in understandable ways, the way God is thought to have done so is problematic. It is one thing for God to communicate complex truths to people in a simplified and less than complete manner; it is quite another to suggest that God encouraged and engaged in immoral activities like genocide in the process of that divine communiqué.

Another shortcoming of inspiration by accommodation is that it assumes God said and did certain things that there are good reasons to believe God never said or did. At one point, Sparks writes: "God has said, 'Kill the gentiles in Canaan,' but he says it no longer."[28] While I appreciate the hermeneutical sensibility that prompts Sparks (and others) to claim that genocide is not God's will for people today, assuming that genocide was commanded by God in the past is deeply troubling. It is better to be clear and unambiguous on this point. Portrayals of God commanding Israelites to kill Canaanites distort God's true character and do not reflect what God, the actual God, ever said or desired. Thus, despite certain advances that accommodation makes over other views of inspiration, it possesses significant weaknesses that render it less than satisfactory.

The Bible without Inspiration

Before stating my own views of divine inspiration, it would help to note briefly one additional approach some have taken when considering the origins of the Bible. Some have argued that God played no role in the formation of the Bible. Such is the view of Marcus Borg. In his book *Reading the Bible Again for the First Time*, Borg argues that it is inappropriate to speak of the Bible as having both human and divine origins. As he sees it, the Bible is exclusively a "human product." He believes the Bible tells us how human beings "saw things, not . . . how God sees things."[29] Borg thus denies God any involvement in the formation of Scripture. According to Borg, what makes the Bible special is not its supposed divine origins but the way God communicates through it. Thus, Borg distinguishes between the Bible's "origin" and "status." This allows him to say that even though the Bible is a human product, it functions as "sacred Scripture." He believes "the Spirit of God speaks through the human words of these ancient documents."[30] For those following Borg's lead, it makes little sense to speak of the Bible as inspired, at least not in the sense that we have been using that term here.

Borg's "human product" model is certainly one way to resolve some of the vexing issues we have raised regarding disturbing divine behavior. If the Bible is merely a human product, written over hundreds of years by many different people apart from divine prompting or input, then its contradictory passages and morally offensive divine portrayals are exactly what we might expect. Be that as it may, excluding God from the process is excessive and unwarranted. While those who advocate plenary or conceptual inspiration overemphasize God's role in the process, excluding God from the process altogether swings the pendulum too far in the other direction. Suggesting that God took a "hands-off" approach—that God was utterly uninvolved in the formation, transmission, and translation of the Bible—results in a diminished, almost deistic view of God. If we believe God to be the kind of being who is actively involved in human affairs, it seems odd to suggest that God had no influence over the formation of the Bible.

So then, if God was involved in the formation of Scripture, but not in the way envisioned by proponents of plenary or conceptual inspiration, or by those who advocate inspiration by accommodation, then what was God's role in the formation of the Bible? The view of inspiration I would like to propose is one that recognizes God's involvement in the process without minimizing the considerable freedom God gave those who wrote these texts.

Toward a More Appropriate View of Divine Involvement: General Inspiration

Rather than assuming that God was fastidiously involved in determining what went into the Bible, (an assumption that does not seem to be corroborated by the evidence), or assuming that God had nothing whatsoever to do with the formation of the Bible, (an assumption that seems illogical), I would propose an alternate way of viewing inspiration. This view, which I will call "general inspiration," acknowledges God's involvement in the process (unlike Borg's human product model) but does not conclude that God was responsible for everything in the Bible (like plenary and, to a lesser degree, conceptual inspiration). Nor does it suggest that all morally problematic passages or portrayals of God can be explained as instances of divine accommodation. Instead, the view I am proposing suggests that God exercised general divine oversight in the formation of Scripture in a way that permitted the human element to assert itself more forcefully and independently than certain other views tend to allow.

A significant difference between general inspiration and other views of inspiration is that general inspiration understands God's influence on the production of biblical texts to be more *indirect*. As people were drawn into relationship with God, their experiences of God profoundly shaped their views and their values. These perspectives inevitably influenced the texts they produced. While this view does not deny the possibility that God may have directly supplied specific words and ideas *on occasion*, it does not regard such unilateral divine activity as normative. It certainly does not envision it happening with anything approaching the frequency assumed by advocates of plenary or conceptual inspiration. Similarly, while this view does not deny the possibility that God may have accommodated to human viewpoints, it does not believe that this practice can be used as a general framework for understanding God's role in the formation of Scripture. In contrast to these views of inspiration that emphasize a top-down model in which God determines the essential content of the Bible in one way or another, general inspiration acknowledges divine involvement while maintaining that human beings are accountable for much of the content we find there.

An analogy may be useful to illustrate the nature of God's activity according to this view of inspiration. God's role in the formation of Scripture could be likened to that of a foreman. At various points, God provided input and guidance as biblical texts were produced, preserved, transmitted, and translated. Just as a foreman oversees the completion of a project without micromanaging it, God oversaw the formation of Scripture without controlling every aspect of the process. God oversaw the work of various authors and editors without overriding their humanness or preventing them from making mistakes. That God should behave this way comes as no great surprise. Just as God is pleased to work through imperfect and fallible people today, so too God worked through imperfect and fallible human beings in the production of Scripture. Recognizing the human element in the formation of the Bible helps us realize that not everything we read in the Bible reflects God's "absolute truth." While there is much that can be affirmed and embraced, there is also some that must be resisted and rejected.

In addition to affirming God's involvement in the writing stage of the Bible, this view also envisions God at work at various points along the way. One may assume that God was working behind the scenes to ensure that certain manuscripts were preserved, not because they were theologically perfect or portrayed God in unmistakably accurate ways but because they were beneficial to people of faith for various reasons. Similarly, it is not difficult to envision the spirit of God helping the community of faith recognize what texts were worth preserving and ultimately canonizing. As authoritative collections of books began to emerge and as authoritative lists were developed, lists that included certain books and excluded others, it is reasonable to assume that God was active in that process.

This understanding of general divine oversight, which allows for considerable human freedom in the process, makes it possible to affirm that Scripture is ultimately a gift from God despite its shortcomings and limitations. This means, among other things, that God did not always correct ancient writers when they depicted God in less than accurate ways. Presumably, when biblical texts were being written, God allowed the human element to be real and largely "unedited," so to speak. When people portrayed God in culturally appropriate—yet culturally conditioned—ways, God did not rush down with divine quill in hand to make the necessary corrections. Instead, God allowed these misconstruals of God's nature to coexist right alongside other portrayals that much more faithfully represent the true character of God. While we might *wish* God had exercised more divine control in the formation of Scripture by filtering out distortions, that is not what God chose to do. Apparently, creating a perfect Bible was not God's agenda.

Views of inspiration that overemphasize God's role in the formation of Scripture unnecessarily limit one's interpretive options for dealing with disturbing divine behavior in the Old Testament. Such views essentially require readers to accept all biblical portrayals of God as revelatory and thus reduce their capacity to grapple effectively with these problematic portrayals. Adhering to an improper view of divine inspiration is perhaps the greatest single obstacle to finding a responsible way of dealing with disturbing divine behavior in the Old Testament.

What is particularly troubling about an overemphasis on God's involvement in the formation of Scripture is that it sets up false expectations about what the Bible was intended to "be and do." Among other things, it conditions people to believe that the Bible *always* describes God accurately. But that puts people in a real quandary when they encounter images of God that are morally problematic. They are either forced to conclude that God sometimes behaves immorally—a conclusion few would accept—or they must try to justify God's behavior, an endeavor that requires hermeneutical gymnastics that inevitably end up clouding their vision of God's true character.

The view of general inspiration I have described avoids this dilemma. It nicely accounts for the humanness of the text without writing God out of the picture. It recognizes God's general divine oversight of the process of producing, preserving, and transmitting biblical texts while at the same time allowing for a significant degree of human freedom and creativity. This view of divine inspiration is consistent with our knowledge of human involvement in the formation of the Bible and is compatible with the approach to disturbing divine behavior advocated in this book.

The Authority of Scripture

In chapters 9–10, I suggested that we should make distinctions between the textual God and the actual God and should be ready to reject portrayals of God that do not conform to the God Jesus reveals. But what happens when we make these kinds of interpretive moves? Does it diminish the Bible's authority? If we stand in judgment over Scripture by regarding certain elements as harmful rather than helpful for understanding God's character, in what sense does Scripture have authority over us? Before we can answers these questions, it is necessary to look more specifically at what people mean when they refer to the Bible as authoritative. What do people think makes the Bible authoritative, and how does the Bible function authoritatively in people's lives?

What Makes the Bible Authoritative?

For most Christians, affirming the authority of Scripture is a given, a deeply held core conviction. But what do people mean when they speak of the authority of Scripture? Obviously, Christians who affirm the authority of Scripture are saying something very positive about the nature of the Bible. At the very least, they are saying that Scripture is of value, worth, and importance. But typically they are claiming much more than that. They are saying that the Bible is true and that its precepts are trustworthy and reliable. As such, they claim that it governs (or should govern) their theological beliefs and that it guides (or should guide) their day-to-day behavior.

Some people regard the Bible as authoritative because they believe it is divinely inspired in the "God exercised a high degree of control over the content" fashion. For these individuals, the Bible's divine origins make it intrinsically authoritative. They would argue that since God, the supreme authority of the universe, gave us the Bible, the Bible is authoritative. While there is a certain logic to this argument, I do not find it compelling because it overemphasizes God's role in the process while underestimating the human element. As discussed above, although God was active at many levels in the formation of Scripture, God is not the sole source of the Bible or its contents. Instead, God shared that process with human beings, apparently giving them a great deal of freedom in the process. This greatly complicates our efforts to describe what makes the Bible authoritative. Therefore, while basing biblical authority on Scripture's divine origins may seem pious, it fails to meaningfully account for the human element so prevalent and prominent throughout the Bible. So what makes the Bible authoritative?

First, the source of the Bible's authority is related to its *content* rather than its *origins*. To put it another way, it is authoritative because of what it says rather than because of how it originated. This is a crucial distinction. The Bible is authoritative because it contains various truths about God, the world, and humanity. From the Old Testament, we learn of God's tenacious commitment to people even after they mess up time and time again. We learn about God's passion for justice, particularly for those who are most vulnerable. We learn of God's good intentions for creation, the importance of community, and the right way to relate to God and others. In the

New Testament, Jesus teaches that the greatest commandment is to love God with all of one's heart, soul, and mind and that the second commandment is to love one's neighbor as oneself (Matt. 22:37-39). Jesus also teaches his disciples to love enemies and pray for persecutors (Matt. 5:44). Such teachings—and many others—are normative and nonnegotiable for Christians today.

The New Testament also witnesses to the fact that being in a right relationship with God involves repentance, turning from sin toward God. This involves faith on the part of the believer and grace on the part of God. As the writer of Ephesians puts it: "You have been saved by grace through faith" (2:8). Once again, Christians regard these "teachings" as authoritative. While these are just a few examples from the Old and New Testaments, they illustrate the kind of biblical *content* that enables Christians to speak *generally* of the Bible as being authoritative.

Obviously, Christians need to be discerning when reading the Bible since not everything found there is authoritative. Some portions of Scripture do not represent Christian beliefs or behaviors and should be critiqued as deficient. Still, there is much that can be wholeheartedly affirmed and embraced as being theologically true.

A second reason Christians regard the Bible as authoritative is because the church recognizes it as such. The church regards the Bible as a unique and unparalleled source for Christian edification and instruction. In the first few hundred years of its existence, the church acknowledged the distinctive nature of these texts and ultimately decided which books should and should not be included in an authoritative collection. Interestingly, one of the main determinants in this process was the degree to which the church found particular books useful.[31] Those books that faithfully reflected their understanding of Jesus, encouraged the kind of behavior they felt was representative of Christian discipleship, and were helpful for the ongoing life and worship of the church became part of the collection of texts that the church held in special regard, a collection we now call the Bible. Christians today accept the church's judgment on this matter and regard the Bible as authoritative because the church declares it to be so.

How Does the Bible Function Authoritatively for Christians?

This leaves the question of *how* the Bible functions authoritatively for Christians. As Daniel Migliore expresses it in the epigraph to this chapter: "Since the beginning of the Church, every Christian theology has implicitly or explicitly acknowledged the authority of Scripture. The serious question has never been *whether* Scripture is a primary authority for Christian faith and life but *what sort of* authority it is."[32]

As mentioned earlier, when people say they believe in the authority of Scripture, they are often claiming that for them the Bible has the final word in matters of faith and practice. They would claim that the Bible helps them know what to believe about God, sin, salvation, and the end times, among other things. They would also claim that Scripture governs their behavior and helps them distinguish between right and wrong. In order to better understand how some Christians claim the Bible functions authoritatively in their lives, it helps to consider both of these areas—beliefs and behavior—in more detail.

For all Christians, and for Protestants especially, the Bible is extremely important in doctrinal matters. When statements of faith are crafted by denominations or Christian schools, care is taken to make sure these align with "the teachings of Scripture." At the very least, the beliefs stated in these declarations cannot be in direct conflict with the Bible. For example, you would be hard-pressed to find a Christian organization claiming that salvation comes by works. Christians agree that the Scripture "speaks" clearly on this issue, and this means they are not at liberty to suggest otherwise. On the other hand, there are issues such as the practice of baptism and the Lord's Supper on which the Bible is less specific, allowing for various interpretations to emerge. Yet even when Christians disagree about these matters, they still must consider carefully the biblical evidence and do their best to faithfully reflect what they think it is saying. Using the Bible in this way, as a guide to inform theological beliefs, is entirely appropriate and necessary.

Problems arise, however, when biblical authority is viewed so rigidly and absolutely that it requires everything the Bible says to be trustworthy and reliable. Again, while we might *wish* this were so, the evidence suggests otherwise. The Bible does not always "speak" with one voice. Some passages "teach" that all people go to Sheol when they die, while others envision different fates for people after death depending on choices made here and now. Certain passages unequivocally declare that obedience to God results in physical and material blessings, while others—like some in the book of Job—clearly suggest otherwise. When reading books like Jonah or parts of Isaiah, one gets the impression that God's grace extends to all people. Yet the last chapter of the book of Ezra calls that belief into question on account of its strict exclusivistic policy. In fact, not even something as basic as monotheism—the belief that there is only one God—is consistently taught throughout the Bible. In Exod. 15:11a, we read: "Who is like you, O Lord, among the gods?" And again in Exod. 20:2, in the first of the ten commandments, Israel is prohibited from having "other gods" before Yahweh." These passages—and others like them—clearly demonstrate that some parts of the Bible assume there is more than one God. Yet other parts of the Bible, such as Isa. 44:6, seem to "teach" otherwise: "Thus says the Lord, the King of Israel, and his Redeemer, the Lord of hosts: I am the first and I am the last; besides me there is no god."

Similarly, in terms of right behavior, not everything prescribed in the Bible is equally authoritative. For example, while most Christians tend to agree that we have a responsibility to do justice, love our neighbor, and care for the most vulnerable members of our community—all of which are commanded in the Old Testament—I suspect very few Christians feel any moral dilemma about eating lobster, wearing a shirt that is 50/50, or shaving their sideburns—all of which are forbidden in the Old Testament (Lev 11:10; 19:19, 27). Likewise, most Christians today do not greet one another with a "holy kiss," forbid women to speak in church, or avoid either wearing gold jewelry or having braided hair despite what the New Testament says (Rom 16:16; 1 Cor 14:34; 1 Tim 2:9). While helpful guidelines for living can be derived from Scripture, not all biblical injunctions should be followed by Christians today.

We routinely make judgments about which parts of the Bible are normative for Christian behavior and which are not. Part of the way we do this is by attempting to differentiate between timeless truths and culturally conditioned commands, between things that apply to all people at all times and things that are situation specific. There is nothing wrong with this though there is the danger of basing our decisions on personal preferences, choosing to obey commands we find appealing while ignoring those we find less convenient. That is why we need a *principled* means of determining which passages should function authoritatively and which should not.[33]

The diversity we find in Scripture underscores the need to make *principled* judgments about which portions of Scripture are, and are not, normative for Christians. The basis for making these judgments should be the life and teachings of Jesus since Jesus is the ultimate source of authority and the one who most fully reveals the character of God.[34] A christocentric hermeneutic is crucial for guiding our thoughts about the kinds of beliefs and behaviors Christians should, and should not, affirm.[35] Scripture should be regarded as authoritative to the extent that it agrees with the will and purpose of the God Jesus reveals. Passages that stand in opposition to this revelation should *not* be regarded as determinative for Christian faith and practice but should stand under the authority of those that do.

If we wish to use the Bible responsibly, we must be discerning readers who are able to make judgments about which parts of the Bible guide the way we think and live. The fact that we make these judgments does not suggest we are denying or subverting the authority of Scripture. On the contrary, it demonstrates the seriousness with which we take the biblical text. Since the text is authoritative we cannot just ignore it or dismiss it. Instead, we must engage it, always ready to hear and obey the word of God through texts that continue to be "useful for teaching, for reproof, for correction, and for training in righteousness" (2 Tim. 3:16b). Taking the kind of principled approach I have described enables one to affirm the authority of Scripture without implying that everything in Scripture functions authoritatively.

My proposal for dealing with disturbing divine behavior works well with this understanding of biblical authority. Making distinctions between the textual God and the actual God, applying a christocentric hermeneutic, and being discerning readers are all practices that are consistent with a principled approach to biblical authority. Thus, one can deal with problematic portrayals of God as I have suggested *and* affirm the authority of Scripture without equivocation.

I began this appendix by acknowledging that the approach to disturbing divine behavior taken in this book raises certain questions about issues of divine inspiration and the authority of Scripture. I attempted to respond to these questions by proposing a view of general inspiration that I believe best accounts for the evidence at hand. This view of inspiration nicely complements the interpretive approach developed in this book and demonstrates that there is no inherent difficulty in both embracing this approach and affirming the inspiration of Scripture. Similarly, I argued that the principled hermeneutical approach I proposed for dealing with problematic portrayals of God is fully compatible with notions of biblical authority.

Throughout this appendix, our discussion focused on how we *talk* about the Bible, particularly when using such terms as *inspiration* and *authority*. This is obviously a very important matter, and we should take care to speak as accurately as possible about the nature of Scripture. That said, I would hasten to add that what is most important is not the pronouncements we make about the Bible but our obedience to it insofar as it reflects the will of the God Jesus reveals. It is easy to become so focused on defending a certain view of the Bible that we lose sight of what is most important—namely, loving and obeying the God who stands behind and above Scripture. As Glen Stassen and David Gushee put it:

> Christians must not simply assert the authority of the Scriptures, for this is not what Jesus did. He read the Scriptures as the functional daily authority for the conduct of his life and enjoined a similar approach on his followers. The goal is not to articulate the correct view of biblical authority but to hear and do the Word of God. Our commitment to the authority of Scriptures will be revealed in the laboratory of daily life.[36]

The true measure of whether or not we really believe that the Bible is authoritative is determined by how we live in light of it, not just what we say about it. For example, it does little good to proclaim the Bible's divine origins while failing to exhibit the kind of concern for the poor and needy to which the Bible calls us. Nor does it seem particularly commendable to make an eloquent defense of the authority of Scripture while at the same time ignoring some of its most central teachings about godly living. Rather, we affirm the authority of Scripture most strongly and persuasively when we live lives of faith and obedience to the God Jesus reveals. Only then will others truly know how seriously we take the words of Scripture.

Notes

Prologue

1. All Scripture quotations are from the New Revised Standard Version unless otherwise noted.

2. This excerpt was written by a student in my Old Testament Literature class at Messiah College in fall 2001. The emphasis is his.

Introduction

1. Jack Nelson-Pallmeyer, *Jesus against Christianity: Reclaiming the Missing Jesus* (Harrisburg, Pa.: Trinity Press International, 2001), 21.

2. Richard Rice, *God's Foreknowledge and Man's Free Will* (Minneapolis: Bethany House, 1985), 10.

3. This is from an assignment written by a student in the "Issues of War, Peace and Social Justice in Biblical Texts" course I taught at Messiah College in January 2007.

4. See, for example, Phyllis Trible, *Texts of Terror: Literary-Feminist Readings of Biblical Narratives*, Overtures to Biblical Theology 13 (Philadelphia: Fortress Press, 1984); Gareth Lloyd Jones, "Sacred Violence: The Dark Side of God," *Journal of Beliefs and Values* 20 (1999): 184–99; Richard Nysse, "The Dark Side of God: Considerations for Preaching and Teaching," *Word and World* 17 (1997): 437–46; Eryl W. Davies, "The Morally Dubious Passages of the Hebrew Bible: An Examination of Some Proposed Solutions," *Currents in Biblical Research* 3 (2005): 197–228.

5. The following section is adapted from a Presidential Scholar's lecture I gave at Messiah College in fall 2002 titled "Reading the Old Testament without Losing Your Faith: Connecting Biblical Scholarship and Christian Belief."

6. A. W. Tozer, *The Knowledge of the Holy; the Attributes of God: Their Meaning in the Christian Life* (New York: Harper and Row, 1961), 7.

7. Tozer, *Knowledge of the Holy*, 8.

8. Terence E. Fretheim, *The Suffering of God: An Old Testament Perspective*, Overtures to Biblical Theology 14 (Philadelphia: Fortress Press, 1984), 1.

9. For a discussion of many "unreal gods"—the inaccurate views of God some people hold—see J. B. Phillips's classic book *Your God Is Too Small* (New York: Macmillan, 1961), 15–59.

10. Obviously, a person's view of God is not the only issue that determines whether or not that person believes it is appropriate for a Christian to participate in war. Still, its importance in the decision-making process should not be underestimated.

11. John Barton, "Old Testament Theology," in *Beginning Old Testament Study*, ed. John Rogerson et al. (St. Louis: Chalice, 1998), 94.

12. For a very brief discussion of problematic portrayals of God in the New Testament, see the beginning of chapter 10. For an extended discussion of the issue of divine eschatological violence in the New Testament, see appendix A. A concise treatment of "Troubling Images of God from the New Testament" can be found in Nelson-Pallmeyer, *Jesus against Christianity*, 54–62.

13. See, for example, Terence Fretheim, "I Was Only a Little Angry": Divine Violence in the Prophets," *Interpretation* 58 (2004): 365.

14. For a discussion of the problem of sexualized divine violence in the prophets, see Renita J. Weems, *Battered Love: Marriage, Sex, and Violence in the Hebrew Prophets* (Overtures to Biblical Theology; Minneapolis: Fortress Press, 1995), and J. Cheryl Exum, "The Ethics of Violence against Women," in *The Bible in Ethics: The Second Sheffield Colloquium* (eds. John W. Rogerson, Margaret Davies and M. Daniel Carroll R.; Journal for the Study of the Old Testament: Supplement Series 207; Sheffield, U.K.: Sheffield Academic, 1995), 248-71.

15. For discussions of divine vengeance in the Psalms, see John N. Day, *Crying for Justice: What the Psalms Teach Us about Mercy and Vengeance in an Age of Terrorism* (Grand Rapids, Mich.: Kregel, 2005), and Erich Zenger, *A God of Vengeance? Understanding the Psalms of Divine Wrath* (trans. Linda M. Maloney; Louisville, Ky.: Westminster John Knox, 1996).

16. This question—"Is the Biblical Portrayal of God Always Trustworthy?"—is the title of chapter 5 in Terence E. Fretheim and Karlfried Froehlich, *The Bible as Word of God: In a Postmodern Age* (Minneapolis: Fortress Press, 1998).

17. Jack Nelson-Pallmeyer, *Is Religion Killing Us? Violence in the Bible and the Quran* (Harrisburg, Pa.: Trinity Press International, 2003), xi–xii.

18. For an analysis of why evangelical Christians fail to think critically, see Os Guinness, *Fit Bodies, Fat Minds: Why Evangelicals Don't Think and What to Do about It* (Grand Rapids, Mich.: Baker, 1994), and Mark A. Noll, *The Scandal of the Evangelical Mind* (Grand Rapids, Mich.: Eerdmans, 1994).

19. Charles Kimball, *When Religion Becomes Evil* (San Francisco: HarperSanFrancisco, 2002), 89.

20. See also Num. 14:13-25.

21. For additional examples of those who apparently had no qualms about questioning God's behavior, see the books of Job and Habakkuk.

22. As Davies ("Morally Dubious Passages," 221) observes: "The Hebrew Bible comes to us bearing clear traces of its own critique of tradition, and thus provides the contemporary reader with a warrant to dissent from its teachings and to question (and perhaps even reject) some of its ethical injunctions." See also his comments in *The Dissenting Reader: Feminist Approaches to the Hebrew Bible* (Aldershot, U.K.: Ashgate, 2003), 95.

23. The acronym is formed from the first letter of the Hebrew word designating each section of the Hebrew Bible: the Law (Torah), the Prophets (Nebiim), and the Writings (*Ketubim*). The vowels are added to make the word pronounceable.

24. See Roger Brooks and John Joseph Collins, eds., *Hebrew Bible or Old Testament? Studying the Bible in Judaism and Christianity* (Notre Dame, Ind.: University of Notre Dame Press, 1990), and, more recently, Christopher R. Seitz, "Old Testament or Hebrew Bible? Some Theological Considerations," *Pro Ecclesia* 5 (1996): 292–303. A reply and rejoinder follow in *Pro Ecclesia* 6 (1997): 133–40.

Chapter 1: Problematic Portrayals of God

1. James L. Crenshaw, *Defending God: Biblical Responses to the Problem of Evil* (New York: Oxford University Press, 2005), 178.

2. Ronald S. Hendel, "When God Acts Immorally," in *Approaches to the Bible: The Best of Bible Review*, vol. 2, *A Multitude of Perspectives*, ed. Harvey Minkoff (Washington, D.C.: Biblical Archaeology Society, 1995; reprinted in *Bible Review* 7 [June 1991]: 17).

3. Thomas Merton, *Opening the Bible* (Collegeville, Minn.: Liturgical Press, 1986), 11.

4. This is not meant to suggest that these texts are otherwise unproblematic. On the contrary, the way women are treated and portrayed in these—and other—passages creates serious difficulties for many modern readers. In recent years, feminist scholars have confronted the patriarchal bias of the biblical text and have proposed various ways of reading the Bible in light of this problem. For sample readings of the aforementioned passages (Judges 19 and 1 Samuel 13), see Phyllis Trible, *Texts of Terror: Literary-Feminist Readings of Biblical Narratives*, Overtures to Biblical Theology 13 (Philadelphia: Fortress Press, 1984), 36–91. For a general orientation to the way feminist scholars wrestle with these kind of texts, see Phyllis A. Bird, *Missing Persons and Mistaken Identities: Women and Gender in Ancient Israel*, Overtures to Biblical Theology (Minneapolis: Fortress Press, 1997), 248–64; and Eryl W. Davies, *The Dissenting Reader: Feminist Approaches to the Hebrew Bible* (Aldershot, U.K.: Ashgate, 2003), esp. chs. 2 and 3.

5. Raymund Schwager, *Must There Be Scapegoats: Violence and Redemption in the Bible*, trans. Maria L. Assad (New York: Crossroad, 2000), 55. Schwager later notes that "aside from the approximately one thousand verses in which Yahweh himself appears as the direct executioner of violent punishments, and the many texts in which the Lord delivers the criminal to the punisher's sword, in over one hundred other passages Yahweh expressly gives the command to kill people" (p. 60).

6. The passages discussed in this chapter are organized thematically rather than canonically, which has the advantage of allowing a comparison of similar passages side by side.

7. For a similar catalog of disturbing divine behavior in the Old Testament, see Jack Nelson-Pallmeyer, *Jesus against Christianity: Reclaiming the Missing Jesus* (Harrisburg, Pa.: Trinity Press International, 2001), 24–37, and David Penchansky, *What Rough Beast?: Images of God in the Hebrew Bible* (Louisville: Westminster John Knox, 1999).

8. This count was first recorded by Maimonides, an eleventh-century Jewish exegete and philosopher. For a convenient listing of all 613 laws organized categorically, see John H. Sailhamer, The Pentateuch as Narrative (Grand Rapids, Mich.: Zondervan, 1992), 481–516.

9. For a similar example, see Lev. 24:10-23.

10. "When brothers reside together, and one of them dies and has no son, the wife of the deceased shall not be married outside the family to a stranger. Her husband's brother shall go in to her, taking her in marriage, and performing the duty of a husband's brother to her, and the firstborn whom she bears shall succeed to the name of the deceased brother, so that his name may not be blotted out of Israel" (Deut. 25:5-6).

11. This number is preserved in the one version of the Greek translation of 2 Sam. 11:24. For discussion, see P. Kyle McCarter, *II Samuel*, Anchor Bible 9 (New York: Doubleday, 1984), 283.

12. While there are serious consequences for David's misdeeds—the death of his child in 2 Sam. 12:18 and the disintegration of his family reported in the remainder of 2 Samuel—unlike Uzzah, David is given the opportunity to repent and live.

13. Exod. 34:6; Num. 14:18, and so forth.

14. For another example of God as instant executioner, consider God's deadly dealings with Nabal in 1 Sam. 25:38. One might also consider Moses's near-death experience in Exod. 4:24-26, in which "the Lord met him and tried to kill him." There are other occasions in which people die because God wills it, even though God is not the executioner. See, for example, 1 Sam. 2:25 and 2 Sam. 17:14.

15. As Nancy Lee observes ("Genocide's Lament: Moses, Pharaoh's Daughter, and the Former Yugoslavia," in *God in the Fray: A Tribute to Walter Brueggemann*, ed. Tod Linafelt and Timothy K. Beal [Minneapolis: Fortress Press, 1998], 76): "The ethic of YHWH's response in threatening to kill Pharaoh's own firstborn is obviously at radical odds with the story's concern for defending Hebrew children and showing compassion for victims. The contradiction is that God resorts to the same practice, the killing of children, that Pharaoh uses in his abuse of power."

16. The Hebrew text is unclear here and actually reads "seventy men fifty thousand men."

17. For general treatments of God as warrior and war in the Old Testament, see Peter C. Craigie, *The Problem of War in the Old Testament* (Grand Rapids, Mich.: Eerdmans, 1978); Susan Niditch, *War in the Hebrew Bible: A Study in the Ethics of Violence* (New York: Oxford University Press, 1993); Tremper Longman III and Daniel G. Reid, *God Is a Warrior* (Grand Rapids, Mich.: Zondervan, 1995); and Gerhard von Rad's classic text, *Holy War in Ancient Israel*, trans. and ed. Marva J. Dawn (Grand Rapids, Mich.: Eerdmans, 1991).

18. Walter C. Kaiser Jr., *Toward Old Testament Ethics* (Grand Rapids, Mich.: Zondervan, 1983), 176.

19. Albert Curry Winn, *Ain't Gonna Study War No More: Biblical Ambiguity and the Abolition of War* (Louisville, Ky.: Westminster/John Knox, 1993), 65, emphasis mine.

20. Patrick D. Miller Jr., "God the Warrior: A Problem in Biblical Interpretation and Apologetics," *Interpretation* 19 (1965): 40.

21. For an exploration of the problem of God's genocidal portrayal in the Exodus narrative, see Lee, "Genocide's Lament," 66–82.

22. For a much more extensive discussion of God's abusiveness, and one that focuses more generally on the relationship between God and Israel, see Jeremy Young, *The Violence of God and the War on Terror* (New York: Seabury, 2008), esp. 1–58. According to Young, "*the Bible's core testimony is to the abusiveness of God*" (p. 12, emphasis in original). He sees God as "a being who is violent above all other characteristics" (p. 34) and contends that "the Hebrew Bible depicts God as a patriarchal male who is abusive towards his wife Israel" (p. 35).

23. In the Old Testament, the angel of the Lord was used as a circumlocution for speaking about God. Since certain writers were uncomfortable with the idea that God communicated directly to individuals, the angel of the Lord represented a literary way to portray *mediated* divine communication. For our purposes, what is important is recognizing that the angel of the Lord's words are, in fact, God's words.

24. Trible, *Texts of Terror*, 16.

25. Danna Nolan Fewell and David M. Gunn, *Gender, Power, and Promise: The Subject of the Bible's First Story* (Nashville, Tenn.: Abingdon, 1993), 98.

26. James L. Crenshaw, *A Whirlpool of Torment: Israelite Traditions of God as an Oppressive Presence*, Overtures to Biblical Theology 12 (Philadelphia: Fortress Press, 1984), 12.

27. See also 1 Sam. 18:10 and 19:9; and compare Judg. 9:23.

28. Exod. 9:12; 10:20, 27; 11:10; compare 14:8.

29. A number of passages state that Pharaoh's heart was hard(ened) (Exod. 7:13, 14, 22; 8:19; 9:35) or that Pharaoh hardened his own heart (Exod. 8:15, 32; 9:7, 34). While this mitigates the problem somewhat, it by no means eliminates all the difficulties associated with the image of a God who hardens hearts.

30. Interestingly, this divine behavior was so disturbing to a later scribe that the text was changed to make Satan the instigator of the census rather than Yahweh (1 Chron. 21:1). That is no small alteration! See chapter 3 for further discussion on this point.

31. No one, when tempted, should say, "I am being tempted by God"; for God cannot be tempted by evil and he himself tempts no one.

32. The designations BCE (before the common era) and CE. (common era) will be used throughout this study. They correspond to BC and AD, respectively.

33. The Hebrew word *hasatan* means "the adversary." It is not a proper name and should not be equated with New Testament depictions of "Satan." There is, in fact, no developed concept of a personal devil in the Old Testament. In the book of Job, the adversary is portrayed as working for God, functioning in the role of a prosecuting attorney. For a discussion of how "the concept of 'Satan'" develops in the Old Testament, see Rivkah Schärf Kluger, *Satan in the Old Testament*, trans. Hildegard Nagel (Evanston, Ill.: Northwestern University Press, 1967), 25–53; and Elaine Pagels, *The Origin of Satan* (New York: Random House, 1995).

34. Job regards his afflictions as coming directly from the hand of God (see, for example, Job 6:4; 16:11-17) and, according the epilogue, Job's viewpoint is to be trusted (42:7).

35. For two prophetic texts that similarly reflect the belief that God sometimes uses deception, see Jer. 4:10 and Ezek. 14:9.

36. For a discussion of Yahweh's "unreliability" and a look at Yahweh's inconsistent treatment as it relates to David and Saul, see Walter Brueggemann, *Theology of the Old Testament: Testimony, Dispute, Advocacy* (Minneapolis: Fortress Press, 1997), 367–72.

37. For example, Dwight Van Winkle ("Canaanite Genocide and Amalekite Genocide and the God of Love" [The 1989 Winifred E. Weter Faculty Award Lecture; Seattle Pacific University, Seattle, Washington, April 6, 1989, 1–45]) has argued that there are certain conditions under which God legitimately could have commanded the Canaanite and Amalekite genocides—a point to which I would take exception—but concludes that those conditions are not met in either of these cases (see esp. pp. 39–40).

Chapter 2: Problematic for Whom?

1. Robert P. Carroll, *The Bible as a Problem for Christianity* (Philadelphia: Trinity Press International, 1991), 2, emphasis in original.

2. William L. Holladay, *Long Ago God Spoke: How Christians May Hear the Old Testament Today* (Minneapolis: Fortress Press, 1995), 117. For a similar experience, see Regina M. Schwartz, *The Curse of Cain: The Violent Legacy of Monotheism* (Chicago: University of Chicago Press, 1997), ix–x. Once, when promoting a liberationist reading of the Exodus

account in an undergraduate class Schwartz was teaching, a student asked, "What about the Canaanites?" That simple question, Schwartz claims, compelled her to write the book!

3. While this discomfort can be traced back even further, the first time it is most notably an issue for the church is during the second century CE.

4. For a discussion of various expressions of pacifism, see John Howard Yoder, *Nevertheless: The Varieties and Shortcomings of Religious Pacifism*, rev. and exp. ed.(Scottdale, Pa.: Herald, 1992).

5. Martin H. Schrag and John K. Stoner, *The Ministry of Reconciliation* (Nappanee, Ind.: Evangel, 1973), 34. Christian pacifists have proposed various solutions to this dilemma. In addition to Schrag and Stoner, *Ministry of Reconciliation*, 33–51, see Dale W. Brown, *Biblical Pacifism*, 2nd ed. (Nappanee, Ind.: Evangel, 2003), 79–95; Guy Franklin Hershberger, *War, Peace, and Nonresistance*, 3rd ed. (Scottdale, Pa.: Herald, 1981), 15–42; and John Howard Yoder, *The Politics of Jesus: Vicit Agnus Noster* (Grand Rapids, Mich.: Eerdmans, 1972), 78–89.

6. Some believe the issue of divine violence is irrelevant to ethical discussions of whether or not Christians can use violence, contending that Christian ethics are not solely predicated on God's actions. For example, Miroslav Wolf (*Exclusion and Embrace: A Theological Exploration of Identity, Otherness, and Reconciliation* [Nashville, Tenn.: Abingdon, 1996], 301) argues against the notion that there is "a straightforward correspondence between divine action and human behavior." Instead, he believes "the biblical tradition insists that there are things which only God may do. One of them is to use violence."

7. Steve Johnson, the *Swinging Bridge*, October 25, 2002, 9.

8. Quoted in Terry L. Brensinger, "War in the Old Testament: A Journey toward Nonparticipation," in *A Peace Reader*, ed. E. Morris Sider and Luke Keefer Jr. (Nappanee, Ind.: Evangel, 2002), 23.

9. Jack Nelson-Pallmeyer, *Is Religion Killing Us? Violence in the Bible and the Quran* (Harrisburg, Pa.: Trinity Press International, 2003), xii.

10. Nelson-Pallmeyer, *Is Religion Killing Us?*, xv.

11. Elizabeth Achtemeier, *Preaching Hard Texts of the Old Testament* (Peabody, Mass.: Hendrickson, 1998), xii.

12. Barbara Brown Taylor, "Preaching the Terrors," *Journal for Preachers* 15, no. 2 (1992): 3.

13. In an article tellingly titled "The Problematic God of Samuel (in *Shall Not the Judge of all the Earth Do What Is Right? Studies on the Nature of God in Tribute to James L. Crenshaw*, ed. David Penchansky and Paul L. Redditt [Winona Lake, Ind.: Eisenbrauns, 2000], 127–61), Marti Steussy discusses the troubling characterization of God in the books of Samuel. Toward the end of her essay, she writes: "My seminary students will need to preach about this material. What, if anything, constructive can they say?" (158). Unfortunately, Steussy's response to that question (159) is extremely brief and provides only minimal assistance to those who attempt to preach from these challenging passages.

14. Carroll, *Bible as a Problem*, 51.

15. Katheryn Pfisterer Darr, "Ezekiel's Justifications of God: Teaching Troubling Texts," *Journal for the Study of the Old Testament* 55 (1992): 109. To her credit, Darr goes on to discuss several ways she attempts to help students who are wrestling with these troubling images.

16. Thomas Paine, *The Age of Reason* (New York: Carol, 1995).

17. Paine bolstered his case by pointing out various contradictions, curiosities, and other assorted difficulties with the Bible that, in his estimation, further demonstrated it was a fraud lacking any real authority.

18. Paine, *Age of Reason*, 109.

19. While this explains the motivation for some of what Paine wrote in *The Age of Reason*, his reasons for writing were much more complex than wanting to correct people's faulty views about God. They grew out of his belief that the organizing principles of Newtonian physics should be rigorously applied to the religious sphere as well. Philip Foner describes how Paine watched with dismay as the clergy sided with counterrevolutionaries while the populace stood against them (introduction to Paine, *Age of Reason*, 34–35). He feared that this antagonism between the priests and the people would ultimately lead them away from God. As Foner puts it: "At one stroke he might save the true religion, Deism, from atheism and republicanism from despotism. With this in mind he wrote his famous theological treatise" (35).

20. Paine, *Age of Reason*, 123–24, emphasis mine.

21. Paine, *Age of Reason*, 104, emphasis in original.

22. Paine, *Age of Reason*, 109.

23. Paine, *Age of Reason*, 115. See also 117–18.

24. Howard G. Baetzhold and Joseph B. McCullough, eds., *The Bible according to Mark Twain: Irreverent Writings on Eden, Heaven, and the Flood by America's Master Satirist* (New York: Simon and Schuster, 1996), 314.

25. Baetzhold and McCullough, *Bible According to Mark Twain*, 321, 317.

26. Baetzhold and McCullough, *Bible According to Mark Twain*, 319.

27. Baetzhold and McCullough, *Bible According to Mark Twain*, 319.

28. Martin Gardner, forward to *Steve Allen on the Bible, Religion, and Morality*, by Steve Allen (Buffalo: Prometheus Books, 1990), xii-xiii.

29. Steve Allen, *Steve Allen on the Bible, Religion, and Morality* (Buffalo, N.Y.: Prometheus, 1990), 309.

30. Allen, *Steve Allen on the Bible*, 257–58.

31. Allen, *Steve Allen on the Bible*, 312–13.

32. Allen (*Steve Allen on the Bible*, 182) writes: "I am, as a result of the present study, now of the firm opinion that *to the extent that the total goodness of God can be defended as a philosophical proposition, the last place to which the devout believer should turn for supporting evidence is the Bible*" (emphasis in original).

33. Miguel A. De La Torre, *Reading the Bible from the Margins* (Maryknoll, N.Y.: Orbis, 2002). His complete listing (pp. 89–90) is as follows: Exod. 21:1-11; 22:15-16; 23:14-19; Lev. 12:1-5; 15:19; 18:18; 21:1-9; 27:1-8; Num. 5:11-31; 27:8-9; 30:1-17; Deut. 15:19-23; 21:10-14; 22:13-21.

34. De La Torre, *Reading the Bible*, 90.

35. For an exploration of numerous Old Testament texts that contribute to the problem of domestic violence, see Gracia Fay Ellwood, *Batter My Heart*, Pendle Hill Pamphlet 282 (Wallingford, Pa.: Pendle Hill, 1988).

36. Phyllis Trible, *Texts of Terror: Literary-Feminist Readings of Biblical Narratives*, Overtures to Biblical Theology 13 (Philadelphia: Fortress Press, 1984), 8–35.

37. Renita J. Weems, *Battered Love: Marriage, Sex, and Violence in the Hebrew Prophets*, Overtures to Biblical Theology (Minneapolis: Fortress Press, 1995), 72.

38. Weems, *Battered Love*, 106.

39. Ellwood, *Batter My Heart*, 19.

40. Robert Allen Warrior, "Canaanites, Cowboys, and Indians: Deliverance, Conquest, and Liberation Theology Today," *Christianity and Crisis* 49 (1989): 261. The conquest narrative is the designation sometimes given to the story of Israel's entry into the land of Canaan described in Joshua 6–11.

41. For various readings of the Exodus-conquest narrative, including a reprint of the one by Warrior, see R. S. Sugirtharajah, *Voices from the Margin: Interpreting the Bible in the Third World*, 3rd ed. (Maryknoll, N.Y.: Orbis, 2006). See also Jack Nelson-Pallmeyer, *Jesus against Christianity: Reclaiming the Missing Jesus* (Harrisburg, Pa.: Trinity Press International, 2001), 38–53, for a trenchant critique of reading the Exodus story as a story of liberation.

42. By way of contrast, see the recent study by Stephen R. Haynes, *Noah's Curse: The Biblical Justification of American Slavery* (New York: Oxford, 2002), to consider how the Bible was used to support slavery in America.

43. Warrior, "Canaanites, Cowboys, and Indians," 262.

44. Warrior, "Canaanites, Cowboys, and Indians," 262.

45. Warrior, "Canaanites, Cowboys, and Indians," 262.

46. Warrior, "Canaanites, Cowboys, and Indians," 263.

47. Warrior, "Canaanites, Cowboys, and Indians," 264.

48. For an exposé of how textbooks routinely misrepresent Native Americans and the events surrounding the settlement of the New World, see James W. Lowen, *Lies My Teacher Told Me: Everything Your American History Textbook Got Wrong* (New York: Simon and Schuster, 1996), 98–136.

49. Susan Niditch, *War in the Hebrew Bible: A Study in the Ethics of Violence* (New York: Oxford University Press, 1993), 3–4, quoting Mather's sermon. For additional examples of this (mis)use of the biblical text, see Roland H. Bainton, *Christian Attitudes toward War and Peace: A Historical Survey and Critical Re-evaluation* (Nashville, Tenn.: Abingdon, 1960), 167–69.

50. Moshe Greenberg, "On the Political Use of the Bible in Modern Israel: An Engaged Critique," in *Pomegranates and Golden Bells: Studies in Biblical, Jewish, and Near Eastern Ritual, Law, and Literature in Honor of Jacob Milgrom* (Winona Lake, Ind.: Eisenbrauns, 1995), 461–71. For a controversial discussion of how biblical scholars have exacerbated this problem, see Keith W. Whitelam, *The Invention of Ancient Israel: The Silencing of Palestinian History* (New York: Routledge, 1995), 71–121.

51. Greenberg, "On the Political Use of the Bible," 469.

52. Greenberg, "On the Political Use of the Bible," 470.

53. Greenberg, "On the Political Use of the Bible," 471.

54. Interestingly, I found no evidence of this in Bertrand Russell, *Why I Am Not a Christian, and Other Essays on Religion and Related Subjects* (New York: Simon and Schuster, 1957). One reason he does cite, however, is Jesus' teaching about hell. That image of divine violence was totally unacceptable to him.

55. Bryan F. LeBeau, *The Atheist: Madalyn Murray O'Hair* (New York: New York University Press, 2003), 177.

56. LeBeau, *The Atheist*, 287.

57. LeBeau, *The Atheist*, 212.

58. C. S. Cowles, "A Response to Eugene H. Merrill," in C. S. Cowles et al., *Show Them No Mercy: Four Views on God and Canaanite Genocide* (Grand Rapids, Mich.: Zondervan, 2003), 97.

59. This was generally illustrated in the previous chapter by the kinds of questions that were raised regarding problematic portrayals of God in various Old Testament passages.

60. John Shelby Spong, *Rescuing the Bible from Fundamentalism: A Bishop Rethinks the Meaning of Scripture* (San Francisco: HarperSanFrancisco, 1991), 17–18.

61. Spong, *Rescuing the Bible*, 20.

62. This is taken from an assignment written by a student in the "Selected Old Testament Books" course I taught at Messiah College in fall 2003.

63. This is taken from an assignment written by a student in the "Introduction to Biblical Studies" course I taught at Messiah College in spring 2003.

Chapter 3: Ancient Approaches to Disturbing Divine Behavior

1. Joseph Wilson Trigg, *Origen: The Bible and Philosophy in the Third-Century Church* (Atlanta: John Knox, 1983), 50.

2. Jack Nelson-Pallmeyer, *Jesus against Christianity: Reclaiming the Missing Jesus* (Harrisburg, Pa.: Trinity Press International, 2001), 62.

3. For an alternate understanding, see Rivkah Schärf Kluger, *Satan in the Old Testament*, trans. Hildegard Nagel (Evanston, Ill.: Northwestern University Press, 1967), 151–62. Kluger regards Satan in the Old Testament as "a personified function of God, which . . . develops step by step and detaches itself from the divine personality" (152). She considers this detachment complete in 1 Chronicles 21. Since she regards Satan as an independent personification of the dark side of God, she sees a very close connection between the two.

4. This is the only Old Testament reference where the Hebrew word *satan* can appropriately be translated as a proper name.

5. See Robert P. Carroll, *The Bible as a Problem for Christianity* (Philadelphia: Trinity Press International, 1991), 47–48.

6. According to Carroll (*The Bible as a Problem*, 47–48), Satan and Mastema function as "narratological or mythological devices for resolving what some writers saw as problems in the representation of God as being implicated in particularly heinous offences against people."

7. O. S. Wintermute, "Jubilees: A New Translation and Introduction," in *The Old Testament Pseudepigrapha*, vol. 2, ed. James H. Charlesworth (New York: Doubleday, 1985), 47–48, emphasis mine.

8. There were, of course, many other violent images of God that do not seem to have troubled the Chronicler or the writer of Jubilees in the least. See, for example, 2 Chron. 13:13-20; Jub. 48:5, 14.

9. Both the Masorah (specialized notes related to the Hebrew Bible) and the Talmud mention these changes, though there is some debate over what these references signify. See Ellis R. Brotzman, *Old Testament Textual Criticism: A Practical Introduction* (Grand Rapids, Mich.: Baker, 1994), 117–18.

10. Brotzman, *Old Testament Textual Criticism*, 118.

11. The eighteen references are as follows: Gen. 18:22; Num. 11:15; 12:12; 1 Sam. 3:13; 2 Sam. 16:12; 20:1; 1 Kgs. 12:16; 2 Chron. 10:16; Job 7:20; 32:3; Ps. 106:20; Jer. 2:11; Lam. 3:20; Ezek. 8:17; Hos. 4:7; Zec. 2:8 (Heb. 2:12); Hab. 1:12; Mal. 1:13. This list is from Ernst Würthwein, *The Text of the Old Testament: An Introduction to the Biblia Hebraica*, trans. Erroll F. Rhodes (Grand Rapids, Mich.: Eerdmans, 1979), 18–19.

12. Broztman, *Old Testament Textual Criticism*, 55. See also Gen. 41:46; 1 Kgs. 1:2.

13. John H. Hayes, *An Introduction to Old Testament Study* (Nashville, Tenn.: Abingdon, 1979), 55.

14. For these biographical details, I am indebted to Adolf von Harnack, *Marcion: The Gospel of the Alien God*, trans. John E. Steely and Lyle D. Bierma (Durham, N.C.: Labyrinth, 1990), 15–24.

15. Harnack, *Marcion*, 16.

16. Unfortunately, neither of these works has survived, though much of the content of *Antitheses* can be reconstructed from other sources. Harnack, *Marcion*, 53.

17. These are Tertullian's words in *Against Marcion* 1.6.1; quoted in William C. Placher, *A History of Christian Thought: An Introduction* (Louisville, Ky.: Westminster, 1983), 51.

18. It is, of course, anachronistic to speak of Marcion reading the Old Testament since it had not reached canonical form by this time. On this point, see Lee M. McDonald, *The Formation of the Christian Biblical Canon*, rev. and exp. ed. (Peabody, Mass.: Hendrickson, 1995), 127–33. For further discussion of Marcion's views about allegory and his literal reading of the Old Testament, see John Barton, "Marcion Revisited," in *The Canon Debate: On the Origins and Formation of the Bible*, ed. Lee Martin McDonald and James A. Sanders (Peabody, Mass.: Hendrickson, 2002), 348–52.

19. Harnack, *Marcion*, 60–61.

21. Again, it is anachronistic to speak of Marcion producing a truncated New Testament since the New Testament as such did not exist at this time.

22. Roger E. Olson, *The Story of Christian Theology: Twenty Centuries of Tradition and Reform* (Downers Grove, Ill: InterVarsity, 1999), 133.

23. Adolf von Harnack, Militia Christi: *The Christian Religion and the Military in the First Three Centuries*, trans. David McInnes Gracie (Philadelphia: Fortress Press, 1981), 46.

24. For a discussion of how Marcion's ideas may have been a catalyst prompting the church to formulate the New Testament into a fixed collection of writings, see McDonald, *Formation of the Christian Biblical Canon*, 154–61, esp. 159–60. For an alternate view, which argues that Marcion's impact on the church's formation of the New Testament was minimal at best, see Barton, "Marcion Revisited," 341–54.

25. When Jesus refers to "the law of Moses, the prophets, and the psalms," he apparently is referring to the tripartite division of the Hebrew Bible: the Law, the Prophets, and the Writings (of which Psalms was the first book).

26. See William W. Klein, Craig L. Blomberg, and Robert L. Hubbard Jr., *Introduction to Biblical Interpretation* (Dallas: Word, 1993), 29. In the words of Robert Grant and David Tracy (*A Short History of the Interpretation of the Bible* [Philadelphia: Fortress Press, 1984], 37): "Christian exegetes, believing that the God of the Old Testament was the Father of Jesus who had raised him from the dead, could not fail to regard God's working as continuous and consistent. They therefore regarded the events described in the Old Testament as prefigurations of events in the life of Jesus and of his church."

27. Klein, Blomberg, and Hubbard, *Introduction to Biblical Interpretation*, 32.

28. It does, however, raise other kinds of problems. For instance, in the examples just given, this method results in a view of atonement that casts God in a violent role, as one who orchestrated the death of Jesus, albeit for the salvation of the world.

29. This prescription for genocide is later carried out in 1 Samuel 15.

30. Grant and Tracy, *Short History*, 33.

31. See Gal. 4:21-31 for Paul's allegorical interpretation of the two women who bore Abraham's sons.

32. Origen, *Homilies on Joshua* (in vol. 105 of *The Fathers of the Church*, trans. Barbara J. Bruce, ed. Cynthia White (Washington, D.C.: Catholic University of America Press, 2002), 1.3.

33. Origen, *Homilies on Joshua* 3.4-5.

34. Origin, *Homilies on Joshua* 11.4.

35. This quote is from Origen's homily on 1 Samuel 28, trans. Joseph W. Trigg, *Origen: The Bible and Philosophy* (London: Routledge, 1998), 200.

36. Klein, Blomberg, and Hubbard, *Introduction to Biblical Interpretation*, 34–35.

37. Trigg, *Origen*, 32.

38. Trigg, *Origen*, 33.

39. Trigg, *Origen*, 33.

40. This, however, was not Plato's position. While Plato conceded that an allegorical reading might render these stories acceptable, he nevertheless felt "the disgraceful literal meaning still would corrupt children" (Trigg, *Origen*, 33).

41. Joseph H. Lynch, "The First Crusade: Some Theological and Historical Context," in *Must Christianity Be Violent? Reflections on History, Practice, and Theology*, ed. Kenneth R. Chase and Alan Jacobs (Grand Rapids, Mich.: Brazos, 2003), 30.

42. Trigg, *Origen*, 8, 62 (quote from p. 62). For a similar assessment of how Origen saved the Old Testament, see Joseph T. Lienhard, "Origen and the Crisis of the Old Testament in the Early Church," *Pro Ecclesia* 9 (2000): 355–66, esp. 362–65.

43. For example, Origen, *Homilies on Joshua* 12.3.

44. Trigg, *Origen*, 50.

45. For a discussion of Marcion and other "Marcionites" throughout history, see John Bright, *The Authority of the Old Testament* (Nashville, Tenn.: Abingdon, 1967; reprint, Grand Rapids, Mich.: Baker, 1975), 58–79.

46. Quoted in Herbert B. Huffmon, "*Babel und Bibel*: The Encounter between Babylon and the Bible," in *Backgrounds for the Bible*, ed. Michael Patrick O'Connor and David Noel Freedman (Winona Lake, Ind.: Eisenbrauns, 1987), 130.

47. Huffmon, "*Babel und Bibel*," 134–35.

48. Harnack, Militia Christi, 47.

49. Harnack, *Marcion*, 134. In the second edition of this work, Harnack expresses his disapproval of being associated with Delitzsch (p. 177, n. 6).

50. Bright, *Authority of the Old Testament*, 17. Bright was not advocating the removal of the Old Testament but simply making a point about why it occasions such problems for Christian readers.

51. Hector Avalos, "The Letter Killeth: A Plea for Decanonizing Violent Biblical Texts," *Journal of Religion, Conflict, and Peace* 1 (2007): 16.

52. Avalos, "The Letter Killeth," under the heading "Conclusion," http://www.plowsharesproject.org/journal/php/archive/archive.php?issu_list_id=8.

53. Avalos, "The Letter Killeth," under the first section of the article, which has no heading.

54. Avalos, "The Letter Killeth," under the first section of the article, which has no heading. These quotes represent two of the five reasons Avalos gives for his call to decanonize violent texts.

55. For a sample listing of additional texts Avalos would delete, see Avalos, "The Letter Killeth," under the heading "Which Texts Should Be Decanonized?" While Avalos typically advocates removing a verse or passage, he also suggests removing the entire book of Revelation, which he regards as "a Christian revenge novel."

56. Consider the assessment of Bill Arnold and David Weisberg ("A Centennial Review of Friedrich Delitzsch's 'Babel und Bibel' Lectures," *Journal of Biblical Literature* 121 [2002]: 455), who write: "Regardless of the definition or explanation of Christianity's relationship to the Hebrew Scriptures, Christianity has continued to insist that a relationship still exists, indeed *must* exist" (emphasis in original).

57. For a helpful discussion of ten reasons why the Old Testament has often been neglected by the church, see William L. Holladay, *Long Ago God Spoke: How Christians May Hear the Old Testament Today* (Minneapolis: Fortress Press, 1995), 10–16.

58. This point is not missed by Avalos ("The Letter Killeth," under the heading "De Facto Decanonization"), who observes that "many Christians already have effectively decanonized much of the Bible because they do not find most of it relevant to their lives."

59. Ellen F. Davis, "Losing a Friend: The Loss of the Old Testament to the Church," in *Jews, Christians, and the Theology of the Hebrew Scriptures*, ed. Alice Ogden Bellis and Joel S. Kaminsky, Society of Biblical Literature Symposium Series 8 (Atlanta: Society of Biblical Literature, 2000), 83.

60. There is no question that Marcion had some very unorthodox ideas. He believed, for example, that Jesus was not really human but just appeared to be flesh and blood. He also believed that Christians should not have sex! To understand Marcion's ideas, one should view his thoughts in the broader context of Gnosticism.

Chapter 4: Defending God's Behavior in the Old Testament

1. J. C. L. Gibson, *Language and Imagery in the Old Testament* (Peabody, Mass.: Hendrickson, 1998), 24.

2. David R. Blumenthal, *Facing the Abusing God: A Theology of Protest* (Louisville, Ky.: Westminster John Knox, 1993), 249.

3. The passages are as follows: Lev. 26:27, 29; Deut. 28:63, 67; 32:39; Isa. 3:16-17; 42:24—43:4; 51:17-23; Jer. 13:25-26; Ezek. 16:6-8, 36-42; Hos. 2:12, 21-22.

4. Blumenthal, *Facing the Abusing God*, 247, emphasis in original.

5. Blumenthal, *Facing the Abusing God*, 248.

6. Blumenthal, *Facing the Abusing God*, 248.

7. As noted in the introduction, numerous examples of this kind of protest are found in the Old Testament. In addition to the biblical texts cited there, one might also note some of the speeches of Job (for example, Job 9–10) and Hab. 1:1-4, 12-17.

8. David Penchansky (*What Rough Beast? Images of God in the Hebrew Bible* [Louisville, Ky.: Westminster John Knox, 1999], 3–4) also flirts with this idea when he writes: "In the face of the experience of war and atrocity in the twentieth century . . . perhaps we need to revisit the notion of a dangerous God, perhaps even an evil God."

9. For another survey of various approaches to handling problematic portrayals of God in the Old Testament and some critiques of these approaches, see Paul N. Anderson, "Genocide or Jesus: A God of Conquest or Pacifism?," in *Contemporary Views on Spirituality and Violence*, vol. 4 of *The Destructive Power of Religion: Violence in Judaism, Christianity, and Islam*, ed. J. Harold Ellens (Westport, Conn.: Praeger, 2004), 31–52, esp. 32–35. See also Eryl W. Davies, "The Morally Dubious Passages of the Hebrew Bible: An Examination of Some Proposed Solutions," *Currents in Biblical Research* 3, no. 2 (2005): 197–228.

10. Eugene H. Merrill, "The Case for Moderate Discontinuity," in C. S. Cowles et al., *Show Them No Mercy: Four Views on God and Canaanite Genocide* (Grand Rapids, Mich.: Zondervan, 2003), 94. Similarly, he writes: "Biblical genocide was part of a Yahweh-war policy enacted for a unique situation, directed against a certain people, and in line with the character of God himself, a policy whose design is beyond human comprehension but one that is not, for that reason, unjust or immoral" (p. 93).

11. Daniel L. Gard, "A Response to C. S. Cowles," in C. S. Cowles et al., *Show Them No Mercy: Four Views on God and Canaanite Genocide* (Grand Rapids, Mich.: Zondervan, 2003), 55.

12. A. van de Beek, *Why? On Suffering, Guilt, and God*, trans. John Vriend (Grand Rapids, Mich.: Eerdmans, 1990), 263. I am indebted to C. S. Cowles ("The Case for Radical

Discontinuity," in C. S. Cowles et al., *Show Them No Mercy: Four Views on God and Canaanite Genocide* [Grand Rapids, Mich.: Zondervan, 2003], 31–32), for alerting me to A. van de Beek's position.

13. Beek, *Why?*, 263.

14. Joseph Wilson Trigg, *Origen: The Bible and Philosophy in the Third-Century Church* (Atlanta: John Knox, 1983), 50–51.

15. See, for example, Job 28, 38–41.

16. Gerd Lüdemann, *The Unholy in Holy Scripture: The Dark Side of the Bible*, trans. John Bowden (Louisville, Ky.: Westminster John Knox, 1997), 48.

17. C. S. Cowles, "A Response to Eugene H. Merrill," in C. S. Cowles et al., *Show Them No Mercy: Four Views on God and Canaanite Genocide* (Grand Rapids, Mich.: Zondervan, 2003), 100.

18. Just a few verses earlier, we were informed that "the wickedness of humankind was great in the earth . . . every inclination of the thoughts of their hearts was only evil continually" (Gen. 6:5).

19. For an account of Manasseh's repentance and subsequent restoration, see 2 Chron. 33:10-13.

20. See Walter C. Kaiser Jr., *Hard Sayings of the Old Testament* (Downers Grove, Ill.: InterVarsity, 1988), 116–18, for his treatment of 2 Sam. 6:6-7.

21. Kaiser, *Hard Sayings*, 118.

22. For a different rendition of the just cause approach, see Charles R. Swindoll, *David: A Man of Passion and Destiny* (Dallas: Word, 1997), 148–49. He places the blame on David rather than Uzzah, suggesting that God killed Uzzah because David did not pay attention to the way the ark was supposed to be transported, namely, with people carrying the ark on poles rather than allowing it to ride on a cart. This is even less appealing than Kaiser's suggestion since it implies that God killed an innocent man for David's carelessness.

23. Manasseh reigns for a very lengthy fifty-five years.

24. J. Weingreen, "The Case of the Woodgatherer (Numbers XV 32-36)," *Vetus Testamentum* 16 (1966): 363.

25. Avi Sagi, "The Punishment of Amalek in Jewish Tradition: Coping with the Moral Problem," *Harvard Theological Review* 87 (1994): 323–46.

26. Sagi, "The Punishment of Amalek," 325.

27. Sagi, "The Punishment of Amalek," 326 n. 10.

28. Sagi, "The Punishment of Amalek," 327.

29. Though one might infer this from Deut. 25:17-18.

30. Gleason L. Archer, *New International Encyclopedia of Bible Difficulties* (Grand Rapids, Mich.: Zondervan, 1982), 158.

31. Cowles, "Response to Eugene H. Merrill," 98.

32. Cowles, "Response to Eugene H. Merrill," 98.

33. Terence E. Fretheim, "God and Violence in the Old Testament," *Word and World* 24 (2004): 24–25.

34. Fretheim, "God and Violence," 25.

35. Fretheim, "God and Violence," 28, emphasis mine. In the article, these quotes appear in reverse order.

36. Tremper Longman disagrees. In "The Case for Spiritual Continuity," in C. S. Cowles et al., *Show Them No Mercy: Four Views on God and Canaanite Genocide* (Grand Rapids, Mich.: Zondervan, 2003), 173–74, he writes: "The Bible does not understand the destruction of the men, women, and children of these cities as a slaughter of innocents. *Not*

even the children are considered innocent. They are all part of an inherently wicked culture that, if allowed to live, would morally and theologically pollute the people of Israel" (emphasis mine). For an interesting discussion of Christian perspectives on the eternal fate of children and infants who die, see John Sanders, *No Other Name: An Investigation into the Destiny of the Unevangelized* (Grand Rapids, Mich.: Eerdmans, 1992), 287–305.

37. For a general discussion of the concept of accommodation as it relates to Scripture, see Kenton L. Sparks, *God's Word in Human Words: An Evangelical Appropriation of Critical Biblical Scholarship* (Grand Rapids, Mich.: Baker, 2008), 229–59.

38. Dennis P. Hollinger, *Choosing the Good: Christian Ethics in a Complex World* (Grand Rapids, Mich.: Baker, 2002), 158.

39. See Peter C. Craigie, *The Problem of War in the Old Testament* (Grand Rapids, Mich.: Eerdmans, 1978), 37. As Craigie understands it, progressive revelation represents the idea "that God's self-revelation may increase and that . . . more may be known of him over the passage of time, but the progression in revelation does not contradict or cancel out the earlier substance of revelation." Craigie draws a helpful distinction between progressive revelation and "a developmental (or evolutionary) theory of religion." Adherents of a developmental theory of religion suggest that Israel began with very primitive ideas about God and religion, which they subsequently outgrew. They believe that even though "Israel once thought this or that way about God, now they know better." Earlier and "lower" ways of thinking about God are believed to be surpassed by later and "higher" ways of understanding God's character. For an extensive application of this approach, see Harry Emerson Fosdick, *A Guide to Understanding the Bible: The Development of Ideas within the Old and New Testaments*, 12th ed. (New York: Harper and Brothers, 1938), 1–54, which describes how Fosdick believes views of God changed over time (see esp. 53–54).

40. 1 Cor. 3:2; Heb. 5:12-14.

41. Tremper Longman III, *Making Sense of the Old Testament: 3 Crucial Questions* (Grand Rapids, Mich.: Baker, 1998), 79. The five phases are as follows: (1) God's fight against the flesh-and-blood enemies of Israel, (2) God's fight against Israel, (3) postexilic anticipation of the divine warrior, (4) Jesus Christ's fight against Satan, and (5) the final battle. These are more fully developed in Tremper Longman III and Daniel G. Reid, *God Is a Warrior* (Grand Rapids, Mich.: Zondervan, 1995).

42. Longman, *Making Sense of the Old Testament*, 86.

43. Longman, *Making Sense of the Old Testament*, 71. While Longman is quick to emphasize that there is both continuity and discontinuity between the testaments, he clearly believes that God does not authorize Christians to kill or engage in acts of genocide in the name of Christ (see Longman, "Case for Spiritual Continuity, 181 n. 17, 187).

44. For a more nuanced understanding of progressive revelation that does not depend on this strictly chronological approach, see Sparks, *God's Word in Human Words*, 246–47.

45. Davies, "Morally Dubious Passages," 204.

46. Craigie, *Problem of War*, 74.

47. For an alternate view, see Guy Franklin Hershberger, *War, Peace, and Nonresistance*, 3rd ed. (Scottdale, Pa.: Herald, 1981), 36. He writes: "If all of the Israelites had been wholly obedient to the Lord it would have been possible for the Old Testament theocracy to perform all its necessary functions without the use of either the military or the civil police force."

48. Daniel L. Gard, "The Case for Eschatological Continuity," in C. S. Cowles et al., *Show Them No Mercy: Four Views on God and Canaanite Genocide* (Grand Rapids, Mich.: Zondervan, 2003), 138.

49. Tremper Longman III, *Reading the Bible with Heart and Mind* (Colorado Springs, Colo.: NavPress, 1997), 107, emphasis in original.

50. I am unconvinced by Craigie's attempt (*Problem of War*, 42) to separate God's "moral *being*" from "his will and *activity*." How do we know God's moral being except through God's words and deeds?

51. Each of these proposals represents a form of supersessionism, the idea that the New Testament and the Church supersedes the Old Testament and the people of Israel.

52. Hershberger, *War, Peace, and Nonresistance*, 25–27.

53. Hershberger, *War, Peace, and Nonresistance*, 34, emphasis mine.

54. Hershberger, *War, Peace, and Nonresistance*, 31. This grows out of his understanding of selected verses from Exod. 23:20-33.

55. Walter C. Kaiser Jr., *More Hard Sayings of the Old Testament* (Downers Grove, Ill.: InterVarsity, 1992), 153.

56. This idea is developed further in chapter 8.

57. Walter Brueggemann, *First and Second Samuel* (Louisville, Ky.: John Knox, 1990), 125.

58. See Sanders, *No Other Name*, 31–32.

59. Sanders, *No Other Name*, 31.

60. This illustration is adapted from Sanders, *No Other Name*, 31–32.

61. Scholars are sharply divided over where Columbus intended to go on his first voyage. Some believe he was heading for the Indies, while others think his plan was to go elsewhere. See Kirkpatrick Sale, *The Conquest of Paradise: Christopher Columbus and the Columbian Legacy* (New York: Knopf, 1990), 23–26.

62. Sale, *Conquest of Paradise*, 108–10.

63. See Nicholas Wolterstorff, *Reason within the Bounds of Religion*, 2nd ed. (Grand Rapids, Mich.: Eerdmans, 1984), 15–20, for the chapter titled "Some Historical Examples of Control Beliefs."

64. Sanders, *No Other Name*, 31–32.

65. Obviously, not every individual who uses one of the approaches described in this chapter thinks the same way about the historical accuracy of the Old Testament narratives. Nor do they all necessarily agree that every Old Testament portrayal of God accurately represents God's true nature. There would be some difference of opinion on these matters. My intention here is to identify a common assumption typically shared by many adherents of these approaches.

66. See esp., chapter 10.

Chapter 5: Asking the Historical Question: Did It Really Happen?

1. Tremper Longman III, *Reading the Bible with Heart and Mind* (Colorado Springs, Colo.: NavPress, 1997), 101, emphasis in original.

2. Quoted in Ronald S. Hendel, "It Ain't Necessarily So," *Bible Review* 18 (June 2002): 10. This song lyric comes from "It Ain't Necessarily So" in the opera *Porgy and Bess*.

3. For two recent representative examples, see K. A. Kitchen, *On the Reliability of the Old Testament* (Grand Rapids, Mich.: Eerdmans, 2003); and Iain Provan, V. Philips Long, and Tremper Longman III, *A Biblical History of Israel* (Louisville, Ky.: Westminster John Knox, 2003). Both attempt to defend the historicity of the Old Testament narrative, and both are fiercely critical of the minimalists' position.

4. See, for example, Philip R. Davies, *In Search of "Ancient Israel,"* Journal for the Study of the Old Testament: Supplement Series 148 (Sheffield, U.K.: Sheffield Academic, 1992); Niels Peter Lemche, *Prelude to Israel's Past: Background and Beginnings of Israelite History and Identity* (Peabody, Mass.: Hendrickson, 1998); and Thomas L. Thompson, *The Mythic Past: Biblical Archaeology and the Myth of Israel* (New York: MJF Books, 1999).

5. For some orientation to this debate, see Baruch Halpern, "Erasing History: The Minimalist Assault on Ancient Israel," *Bible Review* 11 (December 1995): 26–35, 47; and William G. Dever, *What Did the Biblical Writers Know and When Did They Know It? What Archaeology Can Tell Us about the Reality of Ancient Israel* (Grand Rapids, Mich.: Eerdmans, 2001). See, especially, chapter 2, "The Current School of Revisionists and Their Nonhistories of Ancient Israel," 23–52, for a blistering attack on revisionists.

6. As we will discuss later, these same expectations would not have been shared by our premodern counterparts. They had quite different expectations when reading and writing texts that utilized the past.

7. For a discussion of inspiration and the authority of Scripture, see appendix B.

8. John Barton, *How the Bible Came to Be* (Louisville, Ky.: Westminster John Knox, 1997), 32.

9. There are no Hebrew words in the Old Testament referring to specific species of fish. In the book of Jonah, this creature is generically referred to as "a great fish." For the sake of simplicity, I will refer to this creature as a whale since that is what is commonly envisioned by most readers of this story.

10. The story is conveniently located in Edward B. Davis, "A Whale of a Tale: Fundamentalist Fish Stories," *Perspectives on Science and Christian Faith* 43 (1991): 225–26.

11. Davis, "A Whale of a Tale," 224–37. Some evidence that betrays the inauthenticity of this account includes the following: (1) the absence of James Bartley on the voyage in question (p. 233); (2) the fact that the *Star of the East* was not a whaling ship and the fact that British whalers did not fish off the Falklands in 1891 (p. 233); and (3) the personal testimony of the captain's widow, who said, "There is not one word of truth in the whale story. I was with my husband all the years he was in the Star of the East. There was never a man lost overboard while my husband was in her" (p. 232).

12. For the details about the size of Nineveh discussed in this paragraph, see Leslie C. Allen, *The Books of Joel, Obadiah, Jonah, and Micah,* New International Commentary on the Old Testament (Grand Rapids, Mich.: Eerdmans, 1976), 221.

13. Argued, for example, by T. Desmond Alexander, "Jonah: An Introduction and Commentary," in *Obadiah, Jonah, Micah: An Introduction and Commentary* (T. Desmond Alexander, David W. Baker, and Bruce K. Waltke; Leicester, U.K.: Inter-Varsity, 1988), 57–58.

14. Allen, *The Books of Joel, Obadiah, Jonah, and Micah,* 176, emphasis mine.

15. Phyllis Trible, *Rhetorical Criticism: Context, Method, and the Book of Jonah* (Minneapolis: Fortress Press, 1994), 224.

16. For attempts to defend the historicity of Jonah, see, for example, Alexander, *Jonah,* 69–77; and Douglas Stuart, *Hosea-Jonah,* Word Biblical Commentary 31 (Waco, Tex: Word, 1987), 440–42. For a discussion of Jonah as something other than historical narrative, see Allen, *The Books of Joel, Obadiah, Jonah, and Micah,* 175–81; and Jack M. Sasson, *Jonah: A New Translation with Introduction, Commentary, and Interpretations,* Anchor Bible 24B (New York: Doubleday, 1990), 327–40.

17. Of the many recent studies, see especially William G. Dever, *Who Were the Early Israelites and Where Did They Come From?* (Grand Rapids, Mich.: Eerdmans, 2003); and

Israel Finkelstein and Neil Asher Silberman, *The Bible Unearthed: Archaeology's New Vision of Ancient Israel and the Origin of Its Sacred Texts* (New York: Free Press, 2001), 72–122.

18. Though no specific time frame is given in Joshua 6–11, based on Joshua's speech in chapter 14, it could not have taken more than five years (see Josh. 14:7, 10).

19. For a very readable account—and critique—of the effort to use archaeology to verify the historical accuracy of the Bible, see William G. Dever, *Recent Archaeological Discoveries and Biblical Research* (Seattle: University of Washington Press, 1990), 12–31.

20. The other possible date that is sometimes suggested for Israel's entry into Canaan is the fifteenth century BCE, approximately two hundred years earlier. This "early" date, which is suggested by the biblical data and was previously defended by some scholars, has largely been abandoned. The best argument for the early date is that of John J. Bimson, *Redating the Exodus and Conquest*, 2nd ed., Journal for the Study of the Old Testament: Supplement Series 5 (Sheffield, U.K.: Almond, 1981). For an extensive discussion of the issues involved in dating the exodus/settlement, see William H. Stiebing Jr., *Out of the Desert? Archaeology and the Exodus/Conquest Narratives* (Amherst, N.Y.: Prometheus, 1989), 37–63 *et passim*.

21. Finkelstein and Silberman, *Bible Unearthed*, 82–83.

22. See Bryant G. Wood, "Did the Israelites Conquer Jericho?: A New Look at the Archaeological Evidence," *Biblical Archaeology Review* 16 (April 1990): 44–58. Wood argues that the destruction of Jericho matches the archaeological record if one assumes an early date for the conquest. Wood's arguments have not found wide acceptance among scholars.

23. Dever, *Recent Archaeological Discoveries*, 47.

24. For attempts to mitigate the archaeological problems raised by Jericho and Ai, see Kitchen, *Reliability of the Old Testament*, 187–89; and Provan, Long, and Longman, *Biblical History of Israel*, 174–78.

25. For a series of convenient charts noting both points of correlation and divergence between the biblical account and the archaeological record as it relates to various cities, see Dever, *Recent Archaeological Discoveries*, 57–60.

26. Amihai Mazar, *Archaeology of the Land of the Bible: 10,000–586 B. C. E.* (New York: Doubleday, 1990), 354.

27. William G. Dever, "How to Tell a Canaanite from an Israelite," in *The Rise of Ancient Israel*, ed. Hershel Shanks et al. (Washington, D.C.: Biblical Archaeology Society, 1992), 40. For a fuller discussion, see Dever's "Ceramics, Ethnicity, and the Question of Israel's Origins," *Biblical Archaeologist* 58 (1995): 200–213.

28. Joseph A. Callaway, "The Settlement in Canaan: The Period of the Judges," in *Ancient Israel: From Abraham to the Roman Destruction of the Temple*, rev. and exp. ed., ed. Hershel Shanks (Washington, D.C.: Biblical Archaeology Society, 1999), 82.

29. Of course, one might assert that all these victories were miracles and that no rational explanation is necessary. For a different approach that attempts to explain Israel's unlikely victories as a result of their clever military strategies, see Abraham Malamat, "How Inferior Israelites Forces Conquered Fortified Canaanite Cities," *Biblical Archaeology Review* 8 (April 1982): 24–35.

30. See Finkelstein and Silberman, *Bible Unearthed*, 78–79.

31. "It is inconceivable that the destruction of so many loyal vassal [Canaanite] cities by the [Israelite] invaders would have left absolutely no trace in the extensive records of the Egyptian empire" (Finkelstein and Silberman, *Bible Unearthed*, 79).

32. See, for example, Jeffrey J. Niehaus, "Joshua and Ancient Near Eastern Warfare," *Journal of the Evangelical Theological Society* 31 (1988): 37–50; and K. Lawson Younger Jr., *Ancient Conquest Accounts: A Study in Ancient Near Eastern and Biblical History Writing*,

Journal for the Study of the Old Testament: Supplement Series 98 (Sheffield, U.K.: JSOT Press, 1990).

33. Branson L. Woodard Jr. and Michael E. Travers, "Literary Forms and Interpretation," in *Cracking Old Testament Codes: A Guide to Interpreting Literary Genres of the Old Testament*, ed. D. Brent Sandy and Ronald L. Giese Jr. (Nashville, Tenn.: Broadman and Holman, 1995), 29.

34. Hermann Gunkel, "The Prophets as Writers and Poets," in *Prophecy in Israel: Search for an Identity*, ed. David L. Petersen, Issues in Religion and Theology 10 (Philadelphia: Fortress Press, 1987), 23.

35. For some general orientation to ancient Israelite historiography, see the helpful collection of essays in V. Philips Long, ed., *Israel's Past in Present Research: Essays on Ancient Israelite Historiography* (Winona Lake, Ind.: Eisenbrauns, 1999).

36. One might, however, learn a considerable amount about important values and beliefs in the author's time. Since modern histories, like ancient ones, are written from a particular angle of vision, choices made about which stories are told, whose stories are told, and from what perspective those stories are told reveal a lot about the values of the author. This is particularly obvious in modern history books that go to great lengths to portray the country of the intended audience in the most favorable light possible.

37. The chronological gap between the author's time frame and the story's varies considerably depending on the narrative under consideration. Sometimes it is far greater than six hundred years, and sometimes it is far shorter.

38. Richard D. Nelson, *The Historical Books* (Nashville, Tenn.: Abingdon, 1998), 89. For a fuller treatment of this idea, see Richard D. Nelson, "Josiah in the Book of Joshua," *Journal of Biblical Literature* 100 (1981): 531–40.

39. Gary A. Rendsburg, "Biblical Literature as Politics: The Case of Genesis," in *Religion and Politics in the Ancient Near East* (ed. Adele Berlin; Bethesda, Md.: University Press of Maryland, 1996), 69. See also his article, "Reading David in Genesis," *Bible Review* 17 (February 2001): 20-33, 46.

40. See the examples given in Joel Rosenberg, *King and Kin: Political Allegory in the Hebrew Bible* (Bloomington: Indiana University Press, 1986); and David S. Sperling, *The Original Torah: The Political Intent of the Bible's Writers* (New York: New York University Press, 1998). It is possible that some of the Exodus traditions were shaped by the harsh policies of Solomon, who also used forced labor and appointed taskmasters. On this point, see Rainer Albertz, *A History of Israelite Religion in the Old Testament Period*, vol. 1, *From the Beginnings to the End of the Monarchy*, trans. John Bowden (Louisville, Ky.: Westminster John Knox, 1994), 142.

41. Rendsburg, "Reading David," 27.

42. Rendsburg, "Reading David," 27.

43. For a discussion of the function of direct speech in Old Testament narratives, see Robert Alter, *The Art of Biblical Narrative* (New York: Basic, 1981), 63–87.

44. Martin Noth, *The Deuteronomistic History*, 2nd ed., Journal for the Study of the Old Testament: Supplement Series 15 (Sheffield, U.K.: JSOT Press, 1991); translation of *Überlieferungsgeschichtliche Studien*, 2nd ed. (Tübingen: Max Niemeyer, 1957).

45. See Nelson, *Historical Books*, 72–73, for a fuller list and some discussion.

46. "The phrase "theologized history" is from Michael R. Cosby, *Interpreting Biblical Literature: An Introduction to Biblical Studies* (Grantham, Pa.: Stony Run Publishing, 2009), ch. 12.

47. Longman, *Reading the Bible*, 101, emphasis in original.

48. No historian today would approach an ancient document in such a credulous fashion. In fairness to Longman, I should point out that in his recent work on the history of Israel, he does pay attention to a variety of different sources in attempting to discuss what actually happened. See Proven, Long, and Longman, *Biblical History of Israel*.

49. We will say more about this in chapter 7.

50. For a moderate assessment of the historical reliability of the Bible, see Jeffrey L. Sheler, *Is the Bible True? How Modern Debates and Discoveries Affirm the Essence of Scripture* (San Francisco: HarperSanFrancisco, 1999).

51. For a brief though helpful discussion of the kind of issues to take into account when doing this, see Terence E. Fretheim, *Deuteronomic History* (Nashville, Tenn.: Abingdon, 1983), 27–35.

Chapter 6: Concerns about Raising the Historical Question

1. Quoted in Marcus J. Borg, *Reading the Bible Again for the First Time: Taking the Bible Seriously but Not Literally* (San Francisco: HarperSanFrancisco, 2001), 50.

2. See the discussion in chapter 5 under the heading, "What Is an Old Testament Narrative?"

3. For a chart displaying numerous references to Israelite kings in nonbiblical texts and inscriptions, see Baruch Halpern, "Erasing History: The Minimalist Assault on Ancient Israel," *Bible Review* 11, no. 6 (1995): 30.

4. Tremper Longman III, *Reading the Bible with Heart and Mind* (Colorado Springs, Colo.: NavPress, 1997), 104.

5. Jeffrey L. Sheler, *Is the Bible True? How Modern Debates and Discoveries Affirm the Essence of Scripture* (San Francisco: HarperSanFrancisco, 1999), 2.

6. Dr. Seuss, *The Butter Battle Book*, video, directed by Ralph Bakshi (1989; Atlanta: Turner Pictures, 1995). I am indebted to Dr. Terry L. Brensinger for introducing me to this delightful pedagogical tool, which he used similarly in some of his classes.

7. Douglas Stuart, *Hosea-Jonah*, Word Biblical Commentary 31 (Waco, Tex: Word, 1987), 440.

8. Ronald S. Hendel, "The Search for Noah's Flood," *Bible Review* 19, no. 3 (2003): 8.

9. John Goldingay, *Models for Scripture* (Grand Rapids, Mich.: Eerdmans, 1994), 74.

10. In many cases, given the lack of archives and the like, they would not have even had the means to do so!

11. For a Pulitzer Prize–winning treatment of this event, see Edward J. Larson, *Summer for the Gods: The Scopes Trial and America's Continuing Debate over Science and Religion* (Cambridge, Mass.: Harvard University Press, 1998).

12. George M. Marsden, *Fundamentalism and American Culture: The Shaping of Twentieth-Century Evangelicalism: 1870–1925* (Oxford: Oxford University Press, 1980), 186, emphasis mine.

13. William C. Placher, "Struggling with Scripture," in *Struggling with Scripture*, ed. Walter Brueggemann, William C. Placher, and Brian K. Blount (Louisville, Ky.: Westminster John Knox, 2002), 34.

14. Insisting that all the miracles in the Bible actually happened fails to appreciate the function of miracles in ancient historiography and represents a fundamental misunderstanding of a literary genre like Old Testament narrative. For a discussion of miraculous elements in the Old Testament, see John Rogerson, *The Supernatural in the Old Testament* (Guildford, U.K.: Lutterworth, 1976).

15. Mark Buchanan, "Running with Jonah: Do We Really Want to Be Closer to God?", *Christianity Today* 43 (November 15, 1999): 88. Admittedly, it is difficult to tell for certain whether Buchanan really believes the story actually happened. He does, however, operate on the assumption that what it teaches about God is reliable. In any case, Buchanan's reading is precisely the kind of conclusion that could be drawn by someone who thinks the story of Jonah is historical.

16. See chapter 1.

Chapter 7: The Functions of Old Testament Narrative

1. L. P. Hartley, *The Go-Between* (New York: Knopf, 1953), 3. For this quote, I am indebted to Ben Witherington III, *The Jesus Quest: The Third Search for the Jew of Nazareth* (Downers Grove, Ill.: InterVarsity, 1995), 15.

2. There are exceptions, as Luke 1:1-4 demonstrates. See also John 20:30-31.

3. Scholars differ over the degree to which one can ascertain authorial intent when reading biblical texts. For a brief discussion of textual indeterminacy and related issues, see my *Subversive Scribes and the Solomonic Narrative: A Rereading of 1 Kings 1–11*, Library of Hebrew Bible/Old Testament Studies 436 (New York: Clark, 2006), 77–86, and the references given there.

4. While the term *Canaanite* is sometimes used to designate one of many groups of people living in Canaan prior to Israel's occupation of the land, other times it is used more generically to refer to the entire indigenous population of Canaan. This latter sense is how I am using it here and elsewhere in this chapter.

5. For an attempt to reconcile these "seemingly contradictory reasons," see Dennis T. Olsen, *The Book of Judges: Introduction, Commentary, and Reflections*, vol. 2 of *The New Interpreter's Bible: A Commentary in Twelve Volumes* (Nashville, Tenn.: Abingdon, 1998), 759.

6. An additional explanation for the continuing presence of Canaanites in the land is that God intended to drive out the inhabitants of the land in stages lest wild animals overrun the place before Israel could take up full residence there (Exod. 23:29-30; Deut. 7:22-23).

7. As John Gray, in *Joshua, Judges, Ruth*, New Century Bible Commentary (Grand Rapids, Mich.: Eerdmans, 1986), 246, observes: "The various answers reflect the measure of theological embarrassment."

8. John Horgan and Frank Geer, *Where Was God on September 11?* (San Francisco: BrownTrout, 2002); Donald B. Kraybill and Linda Gehman Peachey, *Where Was God on Sept. 11? Seeds of Faith and Hope* (Scottdale, Pa.: Herald, 2002).

9. The classic exposition of this is found in Martin Noth, *The Deuteronomistic History*, 2nd ed., Journal for the Study of the Old Testament: Supplement Series 15 (Sheffield, U.K.: JSOT Press, 1991); translation of *Überlieferungsgeschichtliche Studien*, 2nd ed. (Tübingen: Max Niemeyer, 1957).

10. See, for example, 2 Kgs. 24:1-4; 2 Chron. 36:11-21.

11. For a definition of propaganda and a discussion of the appropriateness of this classification for certain portions of the Old Testament, see my *Subversive Scribes and the Solomonic Narrative: A Rereading of 1 Kings 1-11* (Library of Hebrew Bible/Old Testament Studies 436; New York: T & T Clark, 2006), 6-14.

12. For translation, see Benjamin R. Foster, *From Distant Days: Myths, Tales, and Poetry of Ancient Mesopotamia* (Bethesda, Md.: CDL Press, 1995), 178–96. The best discussion of the political and propagandistic features of this text is Peter Machinist, "Literature as Politics: The Tulkulti-Ninurta Epic and the Bible," *Catholic Biblical Quarterly* 38 (1976): 455–82.

See also John Van Seters, *In Search of History: Historiography in the Ancient World and the Origins of Biblical History* (New Haven, Conn.: Yale University Press, 1983; repr., Winona Lake, Ind.: Eisenbrauns, 1997), 93–95.

13. Machinist, "Literature as Politics," 464.

14. Machinist, "Literature as Politics," 458.

15. See, for example, 2 Sam. 3:1; 16:5-8; 20:1-22.

16. P. Kyle McCarter Jr., "The Apology of David," *Journal of Biblical Literature* 99 (1980): 499–502. For other studies, see Neils Peter Lemche, "David's Rise," *Journal for the Study of the Old Testament* 10 (1978): 2–25; Keith W. Whitelam, "The Defense of David," *Journal for the Study of the Old Testament* 29 (1984): 61–87; Marc Zvi Brettler, *The Creation of History in Ancient Israel* (London: Routledge, 1995), 91–111, and in an abbreviated form, "Biblical Literature as Politics: The Case of Samuel," in *Religion and Politics in the Ancient Near East*, ed. Adele Berlin (Bethesda, Md.: University Press of Maryland, 1996), 71–96; and Steven L. McKenzie, *King David: A Biography* (New York: Oxford University 2000), esp. 30-36. See also Tryggve N. D. Mettinger, *King and Messiah: The Civil and Sacral Legitimation of the Israelite Kings*, Coniectanea biblica: Old Testament Series 8 (Lund: CWK Gleerup, 1976), 38–41.

17. McCarter, "Apology of David," 502.

18. Douglas Stuart, *Hosea-Jonah*, Word Biblical Commentary 31 (Waco, Tex: Word, 1987), 434–35.

19. Stuart, *Hosea-Jonah*, 506.

20. Leslie C. Allen, *The Books of Joel, Obadiah, Jonah, and Micah*, New International Commentary on the Old Testament (Grand Rapids, Mich.: Eerdmans, 1976), 190.

21. See, for example, William L. Holladay, *Long Ago God Spoke: How Christians May Hear the Old Testament Today* (Minneapolis: Fortress Press, 1995), 99–100. Holladay emphasizes three functions of Old Testament narratives: celebration, instruction, and warning.

22. See, for example, Marc Brettler's discussion of the Ehud narrative (*Creation of History*, 79–90), and Ze'ev Weisman, *Political Satire in the Bible* (Atlanta: Scholars, 1998).

23. Richard D. Nelson, *The Historical Books* (Nashville, Tenn.: Abingdon, 1998), 85–88.

24. As Nelson uses the following chronological designations, the monarchical period spans from the tenth century to a little bit past the seventh, the DtrH refers to an author/editor who wrote during the late seventh century, and the exilic period commences with the fall of Jerusalem in 587 BCE.

25. See, for example, Josh. 1:2-4, 6, 11.

26. As noted earlier, Joshua can be understood as symbolically representing Josiah.

27. Richard D. Nelson, *Joshua: A Commentary*, Old Testament Library (Louisville, Ky.: Westminster John Knox, 1997), 15.

28. Nelson, *Joshua*, 18. See also Nelson, *Historical Books*, 82.

29. John Barton, "Old Testament Theology," in *Beginning Old Testament Study*, ed. John Rogerson et al. (St. Louis: Chalice, 1998), 107.

30. Barton, "Old Testament Theology," 108, emphasis mine.

Chapter 8: Israel's Theological Worldview

1. T. R. Hobbs, *A Time for War: A Study of Warfare in the Old Testament* (Wilmington, Del.: Michael Glazier, 1989), 9–10.

2. K. L. Noll, "Is There a Text in This Tradition? Readers' Response and the Taming of Samuel's God," *Journal for the Study of the Old Testament* 83 (1999): 36.

3. Gen. 6:5—7:24; Josh. 10:11; 2 Chron. 14:9-13.

4. Noll, "Is There a Text?," 33 n. 7. Noll's description of God here is based on 1 Samuel 1–15. On the problematic portrayal of God in the books of Samuel, see also Marti J. Steussy, "The Problematic God of Samuel," in *Shall Not the Judge of All the Earth Do What Is Right? Studies on the Nature of God in Tribute to James L. Crenshaw*, ed. David Penchansky and Paul L. Redditt (Winona Lake, Ind.: Eisenbrauns, 2000), 127–61.

5. Noll, "Is There a Text?," 36.

6. Noll, "Is There a Text?," 38–39.

7. Noll, "Is There a Text?," 33–34.

8. Noll, "Is There a Text?," 38.

9. Noll, "Is There a Text?," 39 n. 26.

10. Michael Carasik, "The Limits of Omniscience," *Journal of Biblical Literature* 119 (2000): 221–32. See also his more popular and abbreviated version, "Can God Read Minds?" *Bible Review* 18 (June 2002): 32–36, 44–45.

11. Carasik, "Can God Read Minds?," 36, emphasis mine.

12. Carasik, "Can God Read Minds?," 44.

13. James W. Sire, *The Universe Next Door*, 3rd ed. (Downers Grove, Ill: InterVarsity, 1997), 16. If there is fault to be found with this definition, it resides in the absence of any *active* component. Whether realized or not, the ideological assumptions undergirding our worldview constitute more than just a cognitive framework that travels around with us. Instead, our worldview is an active agent that, to a greater or lesser degree, motivates our behavior.

14. J. C. L. Gibson, *Language and Imagery in the Old Testament* (Peabody, Mass.: Hendrickson, 1998), 26. For an extended treatment of the characterization of God in the Old Testament, see Dale Patrick, *The Rendering of God in the Old Testament*, Overtures to Biblical Theology 10 (Philadelphia: Fortress Press, 1981).

15. For two relatively recent examples, see Walter Brueggemann, *Theology of the Old Testament: Testimony, Dispute, Advocacy* (Minneapolis: Fortress Press, 1997); and Bernhard W. Anderson, *Contours of Old Testament Theology* (Minneapolis: Fortress Press, 1999).

16. Interestingly, there is no other biblical reference to Saul's Gibeonite slaughter. This has led some to surmise that it was fabricated as a pretext to justify David's slaughter of the remaining royal house of Saul. In any case, the narrative accurately reflects the widely held belief that a natural disaster, such as a famine, resulted from divine displeasure.

17. See Matt. 5:45.

18. As Carole Fontaine has pointed out ("The Abusive Bible: On the Use of Feminist Method in Pastoral Contexts," in *A Feminist Companion to Reading the Bible: Approaches, Methods and Strategies*, ed. Athalya Brenner and Carole Fontaine [Sheffield, U.K.: Sheffield Academic, 1997], 105), this "role reversal" is yet another example of the patriarchal bias of the text. She writes: "Powers that have to do with women's 'biological creativity' are transferred wholesale to the father-god, who is now considered to be the one who opens and closes wombs." She goes on to note that this is most strikingly demonstrated in Gen. 2:21-22, a passage that records the only time a man ever "gave birth"!

19. See 1 Sam. 1:4-6.

20. Individuals whose disease is regarded as coming from God in response to sinful behavior include Miriam (Num. 12:10), Gehazi (2 Kgs. 5:27), Azariah (2 Kgs. 15:5), and Uzziah (2 Chron. 26:19-20). All of these individuals get "leprosy," while Jehoram is stricken with diseased bowels (2 Chron. 21:15-19). See also Ps. 106:15.

21. Benjamin R. Foster, *From Distant Days: Myths, Tales, and Poetry of Ancient Mesopotamia* (Bethesda, Md.: CDL Press, 1995), 276–77, with some slight changes in punctuation.

22. Even within the Old Testament itself there are countervoices to this theological perspective. Not everyone in ancient Israel believed God operated in this quid pro quo fashion. See, for example, the book of Job and Eccl. 7:15.

23. See, for example, Patrick D. Miller Jr., *The Divine Warrior in Early Israel* (Cambridge, Mass.: Harvard University Press, 1973); and Sa-Moon Kang, *Divine War in the Old Testament and in the Ancient Near East*, Beihefte zur Zeitschrift für die alttestamentliche Wissenschaft 177 (Berlin: de Gruyter, 1989).

24. Quoted in Kang, *Divine War in the Old Testament*, 68.

25. For a convenient survey of the Moabites, see Gerald L. Mattingly, "Moabites," in *Peoples of the Old Testament World*, ed. Alfred J. Hoerth, Gerald L. Mattingly, and Edwin M. Yamauchi (Grand Rapids, Mich.: Baker, 1994), 317–33. On the Mesha inscription, see also Gerald L. Mattingly, "Moabite Religion and the Mesha' Inscription," in *Studies in the Mesha Inscription and Moab*, ed. J. Andrew Dearman (Atlanta: Scholars, 1989), 211–38.

26. See 2 Kgs. 3:4-8.

27. Interestingly, the Old Testament makes no reference to Omri's notable victory over King Mesha. The formal account of Omri's kingship receives scant attention—only 1 Kgs. 16:21-28—because this apostate king was a theological failure from the historian's perspective. "Omri did what was evil in the sight of the Lord; he did more evil than all who were before him. For he walked in all the way of Jeroboam son of Nebat, and in the sins that he caused Israel to commit, provoking the Lord, the God of Israel, to anger by their idols" (1 Kgs. 16:25-26). Had the historian recorded Omri's victory over Mesha, it would have suggested Yahweh's divine blessing and favor upon this king. Since this was not the desired impression, one could reasonably assume that this is the reason this significant event is passed over in silence.

28. All quotations from this inscription are from "The Moabite Stone," trans. W. F. Albright, in *Ancient Near Eastern Texts Relating to the Old Testament*, 3rd ed., ed. J. B. Pritchard (Princeton, N.J.: Princeton University Press, 1969), 320–21.

29. See Judg. 3:8; 10:7.

30. As noted earlier, this position softens over time to allow for secondary causes. See chapter 3.

31. It is interesting to note that this emphasis on divine causality never excuses the biblical characters from responsibility for their own actions. The tension between divine sovereignty and human freedom is allowed to coexist within the pages of the Old Testament, with neither one finally cancelling out the other.

32. Robert P. Carroll, *The Bible as a Problem for Christianity* (Philadelphia: Trinity Press International, 1991), 46.

33. Carroll, *The Bible as a Problem*, 48.

34. Thomas W. Mann, *The Book of the Torah: The Narrative Integrity of the Pentateuch* (Atlanta: John Knox, 1988), 94.

35. Gibson, *Language and Imagery*, 23. In addition to the heart-hardening passage in Exod. 7:1-4, the other two passages are Gen. 2:17; 3:22, which Gibson regards as an act of divine deception, and Job 1–2, in which he regards God as wanting "to score a petulant point off Satan" (Gibson, *Language and Imagery*, 23–24).

36. Gibson, *Language and Imagery*, 25.

37. For a discussion of cosmology in Israel and the ancient Near East, see John H. Walton, *Ancient Near Eastern Thought and the Old Testament: Introducing the Conceptual World of the Hebrew Bible* (Grand Rapids, Mich.: Baker, 2006), 165–99.

38. 1 Sam. 2:8b. See also Job 9:6; Ps. 75:3.

39. See, for example, Gen. 37:35; Num. 16:30; 1 Sam. 2:6; 1 Kgs. 2:9; Job 7:9-10; Ps. 9:17; 89:48.

40. Gibson, *Language and Imagery*, 25.

Chapter 9: Distinguishing between the Textual God and the Actual God

1. John H. Walton and Andrew E. Hill, *Old Testament Today: A Journey from Original Meaning to Contemporary Significance* (Grand Rapids, Mich.: Zondervan, 2004), 3, emphasis mine.

2. Danna Nolan Fewell and David M. Gunn, *Gender, Power, and Promise: The Subject of the Bible's First Story* (Nashville, Tenn.: Abingdon, 1993), 18.

3. See the first epigraph at the beginning of the chapter.

4. This language of revealing and distorting God's character occurs repeatedly throughout Jack Nelson-Pallmeyer, *Jesus against Christianity: Reclaiming the Missing Jesus* (Harrisburg, Pa.: Trinity Press International, 2001). See, for example, pp. 16, 65, 88, and 137.

5. Terence E. Fretheim and Karlfried Froehlich, *The Bible as Word of God: In a Postmodern Age* (Minneapolis: Fortress Press, 1998), 116–17.

6. Fretheim and Froehlich, *Bible as Word of God*, 116.

7. The phrase "the textual God" is not entirely satisfactory since it might give the misleading impression that the Old Testament presents an entirely unified portrait of God, something that is certainly not the case.

8. For a discussion of the inspiration of Scripture, see appendix B.

9. For a range of options Jewish interpreters have offered to the troubling moral implications of the Amalekite traditions in the biblical text, see Avi Sagi, "The Punishment of Amalek in Jewish Tradition: Coping with the Moral Problem," *Harvard Theological Review* 87 (1994): 323–46.

10. Later in this passage, Saul invites the Kenites to separate themselves from the Amalekites (see Judg. 1:16) since they "showed kindness to all the people of Israel when they came up out of Egypt" (1 Sam. 15:6). Although there is no prior record of this act of kindness, the Hebrew Bible indicates that the Israelites and the Kenites enjoyed close and friendly relations (see, for example, Judg. 4:11-22; 5:24). The implicit contrast to Amalek's behavior at the very same moment in Israel's experience reinforces the negative characterization of the Amalekites, though it fails to provide any additional insight into the nature of their misconduct.

11. For a brief collection of early Christian typological understandings of Exod. 17:8-13, see James L. Kugel, *The Bible as It Was* (Cambridge, Mass.: Harvard University Press, 1997), 366–67.

12. In addition to the references already noted in the discussion about David and political propaganda in chapter 7, see P. Kyle McCarter Jr., "Plots, True or False: The Succession Narrative as Court Apologetic," *Interpretation* 35 (1981): 355–67; and Keith W. Whitelam, "Israelite Kingship: The Royal Ideology and Its Opponents," in *The World of Ancient Israel: Sociological, Anthropological and Political Perspectives*, ed. R. E. Clements (Cambridge: Cambridge University Press, 1989), 119–39. For an alternate understanding of the purpose of the first half of 1 Samuel, see Marsha White, "'The History of Saul's Rise': Saulide State Propaganda in 1 Samuel 1–14," *"A Wise and Discerning Mind": Essays in Honor of Burke O. Long*, ed. Saul M. Olyan and Robert C. Culley, 271–92 (Providence, R.I.: Brown University Press, 2000).

13. Particularly noteworthy in this regard are Saul's self-incriminatory speeches. For discussion, see Amos Frisch, "'For I Feared the People, and I Yielded to Them' (I Sam 15, 24): Is Saul's Guilt Attenuated or Intensified?" *Zeitschrift für die alttestamentliche Wissenschaft*

108 (1996): 98–104; and V. Philips Long, "Interpolation or Characterization: How Are We to Understand Saul's Two Confessions?" *Presbyterion* 19 (Spring 1993): 49–53.

14. See 1 Sam. 28:18. See Galen Marquis, "Samuel's Cloak: Aspects of Intertextuality and Allusiveness in Biblical Historiography," in *Proceedings of the 10th World Congress of Jewish Studies, Division A: The Bible and Its World*, ed. David Assaf (Jerusalem: Magnes, 1990), 99–106, for a discussion of connections between 1 Samuel 15 and 28.

15. 1 Sam. 15:3. See also Josh. 6:21; 1 Sam. 22:19.

16. Walter Brueggemann, *First and Second Samuel*, Interpretation: A Bible Commentary for Teaching and Preaching (Louisville, Ky.: John Knox, 1990), 108, writes: "A careful reading . . . suggests that the conflict with the Amalekites is simply used as an occasion for a formal, authoritative theological statement in the mouth of Samuel. . . . The stringent and uncompromising requirements of this theology make it inevitable and inescapable that Saul will be judged a failure."

17. See the quotation from Michal Carasik in chapter 8, p. ___.

18. For a rather different approach that arrives at the same conclusion, see Dwight Van Winkle, "Canaanite Genocide and Amalekite Genocide and the God of Love" (1989 Winifred E. Weter Faculty Award Lecture; Seattle Pacific University, Washington, April 6, 1989), 1–45. Van Winkle explores the conditions under which he believes God could have legitimately ordered genocide and concludes that these conditions are unmet in both cases.

19. As Walter Brueggemann (*Theology of the Old Testament: Testimony, Dispute, Advocacy* [Minneapolis: Fortress Press, 1997], 367–68 n. 15) expresses it: "It is never without problem to take what is a literary and artistic rendering, as we have it in the Saul-David narrative, and to treat it as theological substance. The artistic and theological are not necessarily distinct from each other, but they are acts with very different perspectives."

20. The most compelling reason to regard this portrayal of God as a literary creation rather than a historical reality is because it does not correspond to the God Jesus reveals. The idea of using a christocentric hermeneutic to evaluate the reliability of biblical portrayals of God is developed at length in chapter 10.

21. Walter C. Kaiser, Jr., *Hard Sayings of the Old Testament* (Downers Grove, Ill.: Inter-Varsity, 1988), 106–9.

22. For more imaginative efforts to emphasize—and intensify—Amalek's evilness, see certain Jewish interpretations cited in Sagi, "Punishment of Amalek," 325–327; and Louis H. Feldman, "Josephus's View of the Amalekites," *Bulletin for Biblical Research* 12 (2002): 164–68.

23. See Esth. 3:5-15. Kaiser, *Hard Sayings*, 108–9, quotes at 109, emphasis mine.

24. Kaiser, *Hard Sayings*, 107.

25. Kaiser, *Hard Sayings*, 107.

26. It is best to classify this passage in the general category of *vaticinia ex eventu*—that is, as a prophecy that takes place after the event it ostensibly predicts. For a discussion of this concept, see Rex Mason, *Propaganda and Subversion in the Old Testament* (London: SPCK, 1997), 2–3, 14–15.

27. See Num. 13:29.

28. Kaiser, *Hard Sayings*, 107, emphasis mine.

29. I am basing this figure on the internal chronology of the Bible suggested by 1 Kgs. 6:1.

30. David J. A. Clines, *Interested Parties: The Ideology of Writers and Readers of the Hebrew Bible*, Journal for the Study of the Old Testament: Supplement Series 205 (Sheffield, U.K.: Sheffield Academic Press, 1995), 190–91.

31. Robert P. Carroll, *The Bible as a Problem for Christianity* (Philadelphia: Trinity Press International, 1992), 42.

32. For a discussion of how to use these troubling texts in theologically responsible and resourceful ways, see chapter 12.

Chapter 10: Evaluating Disturbing Divine Behavior by the God Jesus Reveals

1. Gareth Lloyd Jones, "Sacred Violence: The Dark Side of God," *Journal of Beliefs and Values* 20 (1999): 198.

2. See also the story of Ananias and Sapphira in Acts 5:1-11. Both individuals die because they lie about the selling price of a piece of land. Although the text does not directly suggest that God is responsible for their deaths, many interpreters believe this is implied.

3. Tim LaHaye and Jerry B. Jenkins, *Are We Living in the End Times?* (Wheaton, Ill.: Tyndale House, 1999), 250.

4. Tremper Longman III, "The Case for Spiritual Continuity," in C. S. Cowles et al., *Show Them No Mercy: Four Views on God and Canaanite Genocide* (Grand Rapids, Mich.: Zondervan, 2003), 174.

5. Longman, "Case for Spiritual Continuity," 185.

6. For examples of other interpreters using a christocentric hermeneutic to deal with problematic portrayals of God, see especially Jack Nelson-Pallmeyer, *Jesus against Christianity: Reclaiming the Missing Jesus* (Harrisburg, Pa.: Trinity Press International, 2001); and C. S. Cowles, "The Case for Radical Discontinuity," in C. S. Cowles et al., *Show Them No Mercy: Four Views on God and Canaanite Genocide* (Grand Rapids, Mich.: Zondervan, 2003), 13–44. For a shorter treatment, see David Janzen, "The God of the Bible and the Nonviolence of Jesus," in *Teaching Peace: Nonviolence and the Liberal Arts*, ed. J. Denny Weaver and Gerald Biesecker-Mast (Lanham, Md.: Rowman and Littlefield, 2003), 53–63.

7. This approach is particularly beneficial when using Scripture as a basis for Christian ethics. See, for example, Glen H. Stassen and David P. Gushee, *Kingdom Ethics: Following Jesus in Contemporary Context* (Downers Grove, Ill.: InterVarsity Press, 2003), esp. 81–98.

8. See, for example, Phil. 2:5-8.

9. Here I follow Cowles ("Case for Radical Discontinuity," 22, 36) in appealing to Col. 1:15 and John 14:8-9 (discussed later in this chapter).

10. Cowles, "Case for Radical Discontinuity," 22.

11. Cowles, "Case for Radical Discontinuity," 42.

12. Quoted in Bruce A. Stevens, "Jesus as the Divine Warrior," *Expository Times* 94 (1983): 325.

13. Janzen, "God of the Bible," 57.

14. Janzen, "God of the Bible," 59.

15. Janzen, "God of the Bible," 61.

16. Jones, "Sacred Violence," 198.

17. For a brief survey of these quests, see N. T. Wright, *Who Was Jesus?* (Grand Rapids, Mich.: Eerdmans, 1993), 1–18. For an introduction to more recent attempts to identify the historical Jesus, see Ben Witherington III, *The Jesus Quest: The Third Search for the Jew of Nazareth* (Downers Grove, Ill.: InterVarsity, 1995).

18. This is most clearly evident in the Gospel of Luke, which begins with these words: "Since many have undertaken to set down an orderly account of the events that have been fulfilled among us, just as they were handed on to us by those who from the beginning were

eyewitnesses and servants of the word, I too decided, after investigating everything carefully from the very first, to write an orderly account for you, most excellent Theophilus, so that you may know the truth concerning the things about which you have been instructed" (Luke 1:1-4).

19. It is anachronistic to speak of Jesus using the Old Testament since the Old Testament was not recognized as such until some time after Jesus.

20. Joel B. Green, *The Gospel of Luke*, New International Commentary on the New Testament (Grand Rapids, Mich.: Eerdmans, 1997), 218.

21. See appendix A.

22. Donald A. Hagner, *Matthew 1–13*, Word Biblical Commentary 33a (Dallas: Word, 1993), 134.

23. Obviously, there are numerous passages in the Old Testament that contain depictions of God's extravagant mercy and grace. See chapter 12 of this book for a brief discussion.

24. Gerd Lüdemann, *The Unholy in Holy Scripture: The Dark Side of the Bible*, trans. John Bowden (Louisville, Ky.: Westminster John Knox, 1997), 128.

25. It would be more accurate to speak of this as the story of the woman *and man* caught in the act of adultery; however, given the patriarchal culture, the man unsurprisingly is not called to account.

26. Since the earliest and best manuscripts of the Gospel of John do not include this passage, many scholars believe it was not originally part of the Gospel of John. This does not imply that the story is inauthentic but indicates that when the Gospel of John was first written, this particular story was not located where it now resides. As Leon Morris (*The Gospel of John*, rev. ed., New International Commentary on the New Testament [Grand Rapids, Mich.: Eerdmans, 1995], 779) observes: "Throughout the history of the church it has been held that, whoever wrote it, this little story is authentic."

27. Ben Witherington III, *The Christology of Jesus* (Minneapolis: Fortress Press, 1990), 73.

28. Witherington, *Christology of Jesus*, 77.

29. John Dear, *Our God Is Nonviolent: Witnesses in the Struggle for Peace and Justice* (New York: Pilgrim, 1990), 2.

30. Tremper Longman III and Daniel G. Reid, "When God Declares War," *Christianity Today* 40 (October 28, 1996): 14.

31. For a collection of essays on the topic, see Stephen Jones, ed., "Is God Nonviolent? A Mennonite Symposium," *Conrad Grebel Review* 21 (2003): 3–55.

32. Cowles, "Case for Radical Discontinuity," 24.

33. Cowles, "Case for Radical Discontinuity," 24. For a critique of Cowles's explanation, see Eugene H. Merrill, "A Response to C. S. Cowles," in C. S. Cowles et al., *Show Them No Mercy: Four Views on God and Canaanite Genocide* (Grand Rapids, Mich.: Zondervan, 2003), 50.

34. Witherington, *Christology of Jesus*, 273.

35. This is clearly an allusion to Elijah in 2 Kgs. 1:1-16. Contra Cowles ("Case for Radical Discontinuity," 25), who believes it refers to the destruction of Sodom and Gomorrah.

36. For a list of the manuscripts and a brief discussion of evidence for and against the authenticity of this saying, see I. Howard Marshall, *The Gospel of Luke*, New International Greek Testament Commentary (Grand Rapids, Mich.: Eerdmans, 1978), 407–408.

37. Cowles, "Case for Radical Discontinuity," 25–26.

38. For an alternate understanding, see Stephen Charles Mott, *Biblical Ethics and Social Change* (New York: Oxford University Press, 1982), 178–83.

39. For a concerted effort to confront this trend, see J. Denny Weaver, *The Nonviolent Atonement* (Grand Rapids, Mich.: Eerdmans, 2001). For a variety of perspectives on the atonement as it relates to issues of violence and nonviolence, see John Sanders, ed., *Atonement and Violence: A Theological Conversation* (Nashville, Tenn.: Abingdon, 2006).

40. For a more comprehensive critique of penal substitutionary atonement, see Joel B. Green and Mark D. Baker, *Recovering the Scandal of the Cross: Atonement in New Testament and Contemporary Contexts* (Downers Grove, Ill.: InterVarsity, 2000), 11–34.

41. For a recent collection of essays rethinking traditional understandings of the atonement, see Brad Jersak and Michael Hardin, eds., *Stricken by God?: Nonviolent Identification and the Victory of Christ* (Grand Rapids, Mich.: Eerdmans, 2007).

42. J. Denny Weaver, "Narrative Christus Victor: The Answer to Anselmian Atonement Violence," in *Atonement and Violence: A Theological Conversation*, ed. John Sanders (Nashville, Tenn.: Abingdon, 2006), 25.

43. Dear, *Our God Is Nonviolent*, 49.

44. See George Aichele, "Jesus' Violence," in *Violence, Utopia and the Kingdom of God: Fantasy and Ideology in the Bible*, ed. George Aichele and Tina Pippin (London: Routledge, 1998), 72–91; and Michel Desjardins, *Peace, Violence and the New Testament* (Sheffield, U.K.: Sheffield Academic, 1997), 62–110, esp. 72–78.

45. See Richard B. Hays, *The Moral Vision of the New Testament: Community, Cross, New Creation: A Contemporary Introduction to New Testament Ethics* (San Francisco: HarperSanFrancisco, 1996), 332–36; and Willard M. Swartley, *Slavery, Sabbath, War, and Women* (Scottdale, Pa.: Herald, 1983), 250–55. Swartley has a chart that indicates the page references of where eight writers respond to twenty-four passages sometimes regarded as being problematic for pacifists.

46. See, for example, Matt. 25:31-46.

47. For a discussion of creation traditions in the Old Testament that suggest the use of violence in the creative process, see John Day, *God's Conflict with the Dragon and the Sea: Echoes of a Canaanite Myth in the Old Testament* (Cambridge: Cambridge University Press, 1985); and Jon D. Levenson, *Creation and the Persistence of Evil: The Jewish Drama of Divine Omnipotence* (San Francisco: Harper and Row, 1988).

48. J. Richard Middleton, "Created in the Image of a Violent God? The Ethical Problem of the Conquest of Chaos in Biblical Creation Texts," *Interpretation* 58 (2004): 355.

49. For examples, see chapter 8, note 20.

50. Charles H. Talbert, *Reading Luke: A Literary and Theological Commentary on the Third Gospel* (New York: Crossroad, 1982), 145.

51. Marshall, *Gospel of Luke*, 554. Marshall does, however, allow for the possibility of this being a reference "to the destruction of Jerusalem."

52. Cowles, "Case for Radical Discontinuity," 27.

53. For further discussion of this point, see appendix A.

54. Gen. 18:25b.

55. Cowles, "Case for Radical Discontinuity," 30.

56. Katheryn Pfisterer Darr, "Ezekiel's Justifications of God: Teaching Troubling Texts," *Journal for the Study of the Old Testament* 55 (1992): 114.

Chapter 11: Using Problematic Passages Responsibly

1. Renita J. Weems, *Battered Love: Marriage, Sex, and Violence in the Hebrew Prophets*, Overtures to Biblical Theology (Minneapolis: Fortress Press, 1995), 123 n. 7.

2. According Pamela Milne ("No Promised Land: Rejecting the Authority of the Bible," in *Feminist Approaches to the Bible*, ed. Hershel Shanks [Washington, D.C.: Biblical Archaeology Society, 1995], 47–48): "Feminists generally use the term 'patriarchy' to refer to the manifestation and institutionalization of male dominance over women and children."

3. For a general orientation to this approach, see Edgar V. McKnight, "Reader-Response Criticism," in *To Each Its Own Meaning: An Introduction to Biblical Criticisms and Their Application*, ed. Steven L. McKenzie and Stephen R. Haynes, rev. and exp. ed. (Louisville, Ky.: Westminster John Knox, 1999), 230–52.

4. Eryl W. Davies, *The Dissenting Reader: Feminist Approaches to the Hebrew Bible* (Aldershot, U. K.: Ashgate, 2003), 47.

5. Davies, *Dissenting Reader*, 46.

6. Davies (*Dissenting Reader*, viii, 94–99) is keenly aware that taking such an approach raises questions about biblical authority. If people can stand in judgment over the text, critique it, and ultimately reject aspects they find morally problematic, in what sense is the text functioning authoritatively? Although some might argue that such an approach undermines biblical authority, Davies disagrees. Instead, he argues that there is an inner-biblical warrant for engaging in this kind of honest questioning. This inner-biblical warrant is found in two kinds of Old Testament passages: (1) those that portray individuals questioning God's justice and which demonstrate a critique and reworking of earlier traditions, and (2) those that betray an "anti-patriarchal perspective." In both cases, Davies emphasizes that a critique of the Old Testament's "own values, principles and assumptions" is *already* part of the biblical witness (p. 95). Therefore, Davies believes that feminists who choose to critique patriarchy in the Old Testament simply follow in that same venerable tradition.

7. Davies, *Dissenting Reader*, 109.

8. Eryl W. Davies, "The Morally Dubious Passages of the Hebrew Bible: An Examination of Some Proposed Solutions," *Currents in Biblical Research* 3 (2005): 197–228.

9. Davies, "Morally Dubious Passages," 221–22, emphasis in original.

10. Rex Mason, *Propaganda and Subversion in the Old Testament* (London: SPCK, 1997), 6–7.

11. Weems, *Battered Love*, 100.

12. Jacqueline E. Lapsley, *Whispering the Word: Hearing Women's Stories in the Old Testament* (Louisville, Ky.: Westminster John Knox, 2005), 7, emphasis in original.

13. Ellen F. Davis, "Critical Traditioning: Seeking an Inner Biblical Hermeneutic," *Anglican Theological Review* 82 (2000): 749.

14. Davis, "Critical Traditioning," 734.

15. Thomas G. Long, "The Fall of the House of Uzzah . . . and Other Difficult Preaching Texts," *Journal for Preachers* 7 (Advent 1983): 17.

16. Long, "Fall of the House of Uzzah," emphasis mine.

17. Bernhard W. Anderson, *The Unfolding Drama of the Bible*, 3rd ed. (Philadelphia: Fortress Press, 1988), 13.

18. Ellen F. Davis, "Losing a Friend: The Loss of the Old Testament to the Church," in *Jews, Christians, and the Theology of the Hebrew Scriptures*, ed. Alice Ogden Bellis and Joel S. Kaminsky, Society of Biblical Literature Symposium Series 8 (Atlanta: Society of Biblical Literature, 2000), 85.

19. Richard B. Hays, "Salvation by Trust? Reading the Bible Faithfully," *Christian Century* 114 (1997): 218–23. Similarly, Lapsley (*Whispering the Word*, 19) speaks of "a hermeneutic of informed trust," which "frees us to encounter God in Scripture . . . to expect that God

is telling us something significant, even revelatory about ourselves, about who God is, and about our life together."

20. Hays, "Salvation by Trust?," 221–22.

21. Gen. 38:7-10; Lev. 10:1-2; 2 Sam. 6:6-11.

22. Quoted in William L. Holladay, *Long Ago God Spoke: How Christians May Hear the Old Testament Today* (Minneapolis: Fortress Press, 1995), 114.

23. James L. Crenshaw, *A Whirlpool of Torment: Israelite Traditions of God as an Oppressive Presence*, Overtures to Biblical Theology 12 (Philadelphia: Fortress Press, 1984), 12.

24. David M. Gunn and Danna Nolan Fewell, *Narrative in the Hebrew Bible* (Oxford: Oxford University Press, 1993), 98.

25. Terence E. Fretheim and Karlfried Froehlich, *The Bible as Word of God: In a Postmodern Age* (Minneapolis: Fortress Press, 1998), 100.

26. For an essay that recognizes both the difficulties and possibilities of Genesis 22, see R. W. L. Moberly, "Living Dangerously: Genesis 22 and the Quest for Good Biblical Interpretation," in *The Art of Reading Scripture*, ed. Ellen F. Davis and Richard B. Hays (Grand Rapids, Mich.: Eerdmans, 2003), 181–97.

27. See chapter 9.

28. For a more positive reading of Saul, see David M. Gunn, *The Fate of King Saul: An Interpretation of a Biblical Story*, Journal for the Study of the Old Testament: Supplement Series 14. (Sheffield, U.K.: JSOT Press, 1980).

29. For an attempt to approach the troublesome passages concerning Canaanite genocide in a theologically constructive manner similar to the one I have presented here, consider these remarks from Kenton Sparks (*God's Word in Human Words: An Evangelical Appropriation of Critical Biblical Scholarship* [Grand Rapids, Mich.: Baker, 2008], 325–26): "While modern exegetes will not wish to use the Old Testament's Canaanite genocide as a behavior for Christians to imitate, we can still discern—if we are willing to look carefully—a significant connection between God's command to destroy the Canaanites and the Bible's other theological priorities, which include a determined effort to eradicate sin and sinful influences from the life of the church. So there is something of genuine theological value in the Old Testament conquest account, even if we embrace not the whole but only aspects of it."

Chapter 12: Talking about Troubling Texts

1. Jack Nelson-Pallmeyer, *Is Religion Killing Us? Violence in the Bible and the Quran* (Harrisburg, Pa.: Trinity Press International, 2003), xiv.

2. Howard Zinn, *A People's History of the United States: 1492–Present* (New York: Perennial, 2003).

3. Zinn, *A People's History*, 7.

4. Zinn, *A People's History*, 8.

5. Zinn, *A People's History*, 9.

6. Nelson-Pallmeyer, *Is Religion Killing Us?*, xiv.

7. R. N. Whybray, "'Shall Not the Judge of All the Earth Do What Is Just?' God's Oppression of the Innocent in the Old Testament," in *Shall Not the Judge of All the Earth Do What Is Right? Studies on the Nature of God in Tribute to James L. Crenshaw*, ed. David Penchansky and Paul L. Redditt (Winona Lake, Ind.: Eisenbrauns, 2000), 2.

8. For example, one might reasonably expect books devoted to Old Testament images of God to include some discussion about the problem of disturbing divine behavior. Yet neither

Claus Westermann, *What Does the Old Testament Say about God?* ed. Friedemann W. Golka (Atlanta: John Knox, 1979), nor Rex Mason, *Old Testament Pictures of God* (Oxford: Regent's Park College, 1993), nor Mary Mills, *Images of God in the Old Testament* (Collegeville, Minn.: Liturgical Press, 1998), contains any discussion about this crucial issue.

9. Steven D. Mathewson, *The Art of Preaching Old Testament Narrative* (Grand Rapids, Mich.: Baker, 2002.

10. Terence E. Fretheim and Karlfried Froehlich, *The Bible as Word of God: In a Postmodern Age* (Minneapolis: Fortress Press, 1998), 100, emphasis in original.

11. See chapter 9 for differentiating between the textual God and the actual God.

12. Terence E. Fretheim, "The Character of God in Jeremiah," in *Character and Scripture: Moral Formation, Community, and Biblical Interpretation*, ed. William P. Brown (Grand Rapids, Mich.: Eerdmans, 2002), 229.

13. For studies exploring a broad array of Old Testament portrayals of God, see the sources in note 8 above.

14. See, for example, Psalm 136.

15. For a few other examples, see Exod. 3:7-8; Deut. 7:7-8; 32:7-14; Ps. 105:12-15; Isa. 40:1-2; 43:1-7; Hos. 14:4-7; and Joel 2:23-27.

16. This issue is addressed at length in appendix B.

17. Barton, "Old Testament Theology," 94, emphasis mine.

18. For a discussion of God's involvement in the formation of Scripture and the authority of Scripture, see appendix B.

19. See Exod. 12:29.

20. Anne Meyer Byler, *How to Teach Peace to Children* (Scottdale, Pa.: Herald, 2003), 45.

21. I have found very little written on this topic. It seems to be one in need of a lot more thought and attention. For a discussion of whether children should be taught the New Testament, see Christopher Evans, *Is "Holy Scripture" Christian? and Other Questions* (London: SCM Press, 1971), 37–50.

Afterword

1. This is from an assignment written by a student in my "Old Testament Literature" course (Fall 2001) after reflecting on the issue of the historicity of the book of Joshua.

2. 1 Cor. 13:11.

3. See chapter 2.

Appendix A: Reexamining the Nonviolent God

1. Tremper Longman III, "A Response to C. S. Cowles," in C. S. Cowles et al., *Show Them No Mercy: Four Views on God and Canaanite Genocide* (Grand Rapids, Mich.: Zondervan, 2003), 58–59.

2. Richard B. Hays, *The Moral Vision of the New Testament: Community, Cross, New Creation: A Contemporary Introduction to New Testament Ethics* (San Francisco: HarperSanFrancisco, 1996), 332.

3. This issue has already been raised briefly at the beginning of chapter 10.

4. Daniel L. Gard, "A Response to C. S. Cowles," in C. S. Cowles et al., *Show Them No Mercy: Four Views on God and Canaanite Genocide* (Grand Rapids, Mich.: Zondervan, 2003), 56.

5. This phrase is from John Dominic Crossan, *The Historical Jesus: The Life of a Mediterranean Jewish Peasant* (San Francisco: HarperSanFrancisco, 1991), 235.

6. C. S. Cowles, "The Case for Radical Discontinuity," in C. S. Cowles et al., *Show Them No Mercy: Four Views on God and Canaanite Genocide* (Grand Rapids, Mich.: Zondervan, 2003), 13–44.

7. Cowles, "Case for Radical Discontinuity," 32.

8. Cowles, "Case for Radical Discontinuity," 42.

9. Eugene H. Merrill, "A Response to C. S. Cowles," in C. S. Cowles et al., *Show Them No Mercy: Four Views on God and Canaanite Genocide* (Grand Rapids, Mich.: Zondervan, 2003), 49.

10. Gard, "Response to C. S. Cowles," 56.

11. Longman, "Response to C. S. Cowles," 59–60.

12. Longman, "Response to C. S. Cowles," 58–59.

13. Matt. 10:11-15; 11:20-24, par. Luke 10:10-15. Luke connects these incidents, placing the pronouncement of judgment on certain cities after Jesus' instructions to the seventy who are sent out by Jesus.

14. Donald A. Hagner, *Matthew 1–13*, Word Biblical Commentary 33a (Dallas: Word, 1993), 273, citing Rom. 9:29; 2 Pet. 2:6; and Jude 7 in support.

15. For judgment oracles against the cities of Tyre and Sidon, see, for example, Isaiah 23 and Ezekiel 26–28.

16. I. Howard Marshall, *Beyond the Bible: Moving from Scripture to Theology* (Grand Rapids, Mich.: Baker, 2004). I am uncertain whether Marshall objects in principle to the idea that God sometimes uses violence. His argument is not for a nonviolent God per se but is against various violent portrayals of God in the New Testament that he finds unconscionable. Marshall's book contains three lectures he gave at Acadia Divinity College along with two responses from other scholars. Marshall is interested in finding criteria derived from the Bible that provide a method for moving beyond the Bible to develop Christian doctrine. Marshall believes such a move is warranted since the New Testament exceeds the Old in many ways and since the teachings of the early church move beyond the teaching of Jesus.

17. The four parameters that constrain Jesus' teaching, according to Marshall (*Beyond the Bible*, 63) are as follows: "1) It is given in the time of the dawn of the kingdom of God, the period prior to the death and resurrection of Jesus, which dramatically alter the situation, 2) It is elementary instruction because it is for beginners starting from scratch, 3) It is given within the conditions of life under Judaism because it is for the most part addressed to Jews, 4) It uses the imagery and thought forms current at the time."

18. Marshall, *Beyond the Bible*, 67.

19. Marshall, *Beyond the Bible*, 67, emphasis mine.

20. Marshall, *Beyond the Bible*, 67.

21. While Marshall's suggestion that we have "a mind nurtured by the Spirit, the mind of Christ, which has taught us that such behavior is unacceptable among human beings" is true enough, it seems an inadequate basis for concluding that Jesus therefore *thought* differently than he *taught*.

22. Wink, *Engaging the Powers*, 135–36.

23. Jack Nelson-Pallmeyer, *Jesus against Christianity: Reclaiming the Missing Jesus* (Harrisburg, Pa.: Trinity Press International, 2001), 227.

24. See Crossan, *Historical Jesus*, 225–64; and John Dominic Crossan, *The Birth of Christianity: Discovering What Happened in the Years Immediately after the Execution of Jesus* (San Francisco: HarperSanFrancisco, 1998), 247–56. Crossan (*Birth of Christianity*, 287)

speculates that "it may well have been the absence of an avenging God before, during, or after John the Baptist's own execution that convinced Jesus of a different type of God."

25. Crossan, *Historical Jesus*, 259.

26. For a discussion of this hypothetical document and a table listing "material usually allotted to Q," see Raymond E. Brown, *An Introduction to the New Testament* (New York: Doubleday, 1997), 116–22.

27. Nelson-Pallmeyer, *Jesus against Christianity*, 159.

28. In some discussions, the first two views are lumped together and discussed as the "traditional" view. See, for example, Edward William Fudge and Robert A. Peterson, *Two Views of Hell: A Biblical and Theological Dialogue* (Downers Grove, Ill.: InterVarsity, 2000), which sets traditionalism and conditionalism in dialogue. See also Gregory A. Boyd and Paul R. Eddy, *Across the Spectrum: Understanding Issues in Evangelical Theology* (Grand Rapids, Mich.: Baker, 2002), 254–64.

29. John F. Walvoord, "The Literal View," in *Four Views on Hell*, ed. William Crockett (Grand Rapids, Mich.: Zondervan, 1992), 28.

30. William V. Crockett, "The Metaphorical View," in *Four Views on Hell*, ed. William Crockett (Grand Rapids, Mich.: Zondervan, 1992), 44.

31. Crockett, "Metaphorical View," 61.

32. Clark H. Pinnock, "The Conditional View," in *Four Views on Hell*, ed. William Crockett (Grand Rapids, Mich.: Zondervan, 1992), 149.

33. Pinnock, "Conditional View," 154.

34. Fudge and Peterson, *Two Views of Hell*, 21.

35. Fudge and Peterson, *Two Views of Hell*, 82.

36. Fudge and Peterson, *Two Views of Hell*, 80–81.

37. My discussion in this paragraph is derived from Pinnock, "Conditional View," 143–58.

38. M. Eugene Boring, *Revelation*, Interpretation: A Bible Commentary for Teaching and Preaching. (Louisville, Ky.: John Knox, 1989), 112–13, emphasis mine. Boring offers some guidance for dealing with this imagery in a section aptly titled "Interpreting Revelation's Violent Imagery," 112–19.

39. Wink, *Engaging the Powers*, 136.

40. C. S. Cowles, "A Response to Tremper Longman III," in C. S. Cowles et al., *Show Them No Mercy: Four Views on God and Canaanite Genocide* (Grand Rapids, Mich.: Zondervan, 2003), 193.

41. John R. Yeatts, *Revelation*, Believers Church Bible Commentary. Scottdale, Pa.: Herald, 2003), 356.

42. Yeatts, *Revelation*, 362.

43. J. Denny Weaver, *The Nonviolent Atonement* (Grand Rapids, Mich.: Eerdmans, 2001), 33.

44. For other interpretations emphasizing the nonviolent nature of Jesus in the book of Revelation, see Mark Bredin, *Jesus, Revolutionary of Peace: A Nonviolent Christology in the Book of Revelation* (Carlisle, U.K.: Paternoster, 2003); and Loren L. Johns, *The Lamb Christology of the Apocalypse of John: An Investigation into Its Origins and Rhetorical Force*, *Wissenschaftliche Untersuchungen zum Neuen Testament* 2/167 (Tübingen: Mohr Siebeck, 2003).

45. Luke 13:1-5; 13:34-35 par.; 17:31-36 par.; 19:42-44; 21:20, 21b-22, 23b-24; 23:28-31; Mark 11:15-17; 13:2; 13:14-18; 14:58; 15:29; Matt. 26:52.

46. Borg, *Conflict, Holiness and Politics*, 189.

47. Borg, *Conflict, Holiness and Politics*, 189.

48. Joel B. Green, *The Gospel of Luke*, New International Commentary on the New Testament (Grand Rapids, Mich.: Eerdmans, 1997), 738.

49. Green, *Gospel of Luke*, 739.

50. In reference to Mark 13, N. T. Wright (*Jesus and the Victory of God*, vol. 2 of *Christian Origins and the Question of God* [Minneapolis: Fortress Press, 1996], 342) claims: "The event that was coming swiftly upon Jerusalem would be the divine judgment on YHWH's rebellious people, exercised through Rome's judgment on her rebellious subject." Wright clearly understands this text, and others like it, to refer to God's judgment upon Jerusalem in the first century CE.

51. N. T. Wright, *Who Was Jesus?* (Grand Rapids, Mich.: Eerdmans, 1993), 15.

52. This claim is argued at length by Wright, *Jesus and the Victory of God*, 320–68. For a critique, see Dale C. Allison Jr., "Jesus and the Victory of Apocalyptic," in *Jesus and the Restoration of Israel: A Critical Assessment of N. T. Wright's* Jesus and the Victory of God, ed. Carey C. Newman (Downers Grove, Ill.: InterVarsity, 1999), 126–41.

53. Marcus J. Borg, *Conflict, Holiness and Politics in the Teachings of Jesus* (New York: Mellen, 1984), 186–90. See also Wright, *Jesus and the Victory of God*, 348–49.

54. Robert W. Funk, Roy W. Hoover, and the Jesus Seminar, *The Five Gospels: The Search for the Authentic Words of Jesus: New Translation and Commentary* (New York: Polebridge, 1993), 34. The Jesus Seminar used various criteria to ascertain the authenticity of the sayings of Jesus recorded in the Gospels and voted on these. Their results are found in a color-coded rendition of the four canonical Gospels and the Gospel of Thomas. Starting with thirty scholars, more than two hundred specialists ultimately participated in this project. For a strong critique of the Jesus Seminar, see Ben Witherington III, *The Jesus Quest: The Third Search for the Jew of Nazareth* (Downers Grove, Ill.: InterVarsity, 1995), 42–57.

55. Funk, Hoover, and the Jesus Seminar, *Five Gospels*, 376. In their color-coded Gospels, Luke 19:42–44 is presented in gray, which indicates "Jesus did not say this, but the ideas contained in it are close to his own" (*Five Gospels*, 36).

56. Funk, Hoover, and the Jesus Seminar, *Five Gospels*, 383–84. This passage is written in black, which indicates "Jesus did not say this; it represents the perspective or content of a later or different tradition" (*Five Gospels*, 36).

57. Joseph A. Fitzmyer, *The Gospel according to Luke (X–XXIV): Introduction, Translation, and Notes*, Anchor Bible 28A (Garden City, N.Y.: Doubleday, 1985), 1344. Fitzmyer does not deny that Jesus may have said something like what we find here. Earlier, when referring to Luke 19:41-44, Fitzmyer says: "There is . . . reason to think that Jesus did actually say something similar to this prophetic pronouncement about the fate of Jerusalem or at least its Temple" (p. 1254). Still, he believes that whatever Jesus said in these instances has been reworked by the writer of Luke (pp. 1255, 1344).

58. Another way of mitigating the dilemma raised by Luke 19:41-44; 21:20-24 would be to argue that these are authentic Jesus sayings but that Jesus was wrong about God's role in the coming destruction of Jerusalem. As Marcus Borg (*Jesus in Contemporary Scholarship* [Valley Forge, Pa.: Trinity Press International, 1994], 65 n. 19) puts it: "I have no problems myself in affirming that Jesus could be mistaken about various things. I take it for granted that he believed many things that we quite properly do not believe (e.g. he probably thought the world was flat, that the universe was relatively small and not very old, that the Torah was written by Moses, etc.)."

59. On Israel's rejection of the Messiah and the kingdom of heaven, see Jack Dean Kingsbury, *Matthew*, 2nd ed., Proclamation Commentaries (Philadelphia: Fortress Press, 1986), 78–81.

60. Douglas R. A. Hare, *Matthew*, Interpretation: A Bible Commentary for Teaching and Preaching (Louisville, Ky.: John Knox, 1993), 251.

61. Hare, *Matthew*, 251.

62. Even if one follows scholars like Marcus Borg and N. T. Wright, who believe Jesus did teach that God was going to judge Israel by allowing the Romans to destroy Jerusalem, this would be the only example of such a view in all of Jesus' teachings.

Appendix B: Inspiration and the Authority of Scripture

1. Daniel L. Migliore, *Faith Seeking Understanding: An Introduction to Christian Theology*, 2nd ed. (Grand Rapids, Mich.,: Eerdmans, 2004), 40, emphasis in original.

2. To cite just a few examples, see Paul J. Achtemeier, *Inspiration and Authority: Nature and Function of Christian Scripture*, rev. and exp. ed. (Peabody, Mass.: Hendrickson, 1999); Robert Gnuse, *The Authority of the Bible: Theories of Inspiration, Revelation and the Canon of Scripture* (New York: Paulist, 1985); and N. T. Wright, *The Last Word: Beyond the Bible Wars to a New Understanding of the Authority of Scripture* (San Francisco: HarperSanFrancisco, 2005).

3. Achtemeier, *Inspiration and Authority*, 18 n. 20.

4. For a brief discussion of conceptual inspiration as well as verbal inspiration, see W. Randolph Tate, *Biblical Interpretation: An Integrated Approach*, rev. ed. (Peabody, Mass.: Hendrickson, 1997), 192–93.

5. Tate, *Biblical Interpretation*, 192.

6. For discussion and critique of these perspectives, see Gnuse, *Authority of the Bible*, 22–41.

7. On the other hand, it is quite possible to believe that God exercised a high degree of control over the formation of the Bible without subscribing to views of divine sovereignty that are deterministic. For a discussion of various views of divine sovereignty, see David Basinger and Randall Basinger, *Predestination and Free Will: Four Views of Divine Sovereignty and Human Freedom* (Downers Grove, Ill.: InterVarsity, 1986).

8. See 1 Tim. 3:16-17; 2 Pet. 1:20-21.

9. In biblical studies, the term *autograph* is used to refer to an original document rather than a copy. The actual piece of parchment on which Paul (or his scribe) wrote the letter to the Thessalonians, for example, would be considered an autograph.

10. For an introduction to textual criticism, the goal of which is to determine the most authentic reading, see Paul D. Wegner, *A Student's Guide to Textual Criticism of the Bible: Its History, Methods, and Results* (Downers Grove, Ill.: InterVarsity, 2006).

11. Some argue that God inspired the original autographs, but that argument is problematic since we no longer have any of these. It is also complicated by that fact that speaking of original autographs makes little sense for many biblical texts, particularly those in the Old Testament, which underwent multiple revisions and existed in various forms.

12. See, for example, Ps. 100:3. For a discussion of other kinds of unintentional errors, see Wegner, *Student's Guide to Textual Criticism*, 44–50.

13. See Robert P. Carroll, *The Bible as a Problem for Christianity* (Philadelphia: Trinity Press International, 1991), 14–21.

14. Depending on how they are counted, you will find differing totals for the number of books in the Catholic Bible. Similarly, there are also different totals for the number of books in the Greek Orthodox Bible, in this case because there is some question over which books should be included.

15. For an alternate perspective that would particularly take issue with the second assumption, see Peter Enns, *Inspiration and Incarnation: Evangelicals and the Problem of the Old Testament* (Grand Rapids, Mich.: Baker, 2005), 97–111.

16. Clean and unclean are classifications that refer to animals the Israelites were—or were not—allowed to eat (see Leviticus 11; Deut. 14:3-21).

17. For additional examples, see Achtemeier, *Inspiration and Authority*, 50–54.

18. For a conservative attempt to "solve" these kinds of problems, see, for example, Gleason L. Archer, *New International Encyclopedia of Bible Difficulties* (Grand Rapids, Mich.: Zondervan, 1982). For a recent critique of the way traditional scholars respond to difficulties raised by biblical criticism, see Kenton L. Sparks, *God's Word in Human Words: An Evangelical Appropriation of Critical Biblical Scholarship* (Grand Rapids, Mich.: Baker, 2008), 133–70.

19. Consider, for example, Brueggemann's discussion of "Israel's Core Testimony" and "Israel's Countertestimony" as it relates to the character of Yahweh in his *Theology of the Old Testament: Testimony, Dispute, Advocacy* (Minneapolis: Fortress, 1997), 117–403.

20. Sparks, *God's Word in Human Words*, 258.

21. Sparks, *God's Word in Human Words*, 230-31.

22. Sparks, *God's Word in Human Words*, 249.

23. As Sparks (*God's Word in Human Words*, 256) emphasizes: "Accommodation does not introduce errors into Scripture; it is instead a theological explanation for the presence of human errors in Scripture."

24. Sparks, *God's Word in Human Words*, 239.

25. This is exactly what accommodationists do in the case of anthropomorphisms. See Sparks, *God's Word in Human Words*, 231.

26. Sparks, *God's Word in Human Words*, 326.

27. Sparks, *God's Word in Human Words*, 297.

28. Sparks, *God's Word in Human Words*, 243. Sparks uses this example as a means of explaining the ideas of Nicholas Wolterstorff, with which he agrees, as far as I can tell.

29. Marcus J. Borg, *Reading the Bible Again for the First Time: Taking the Bible Seriously but Not Literally* (San Francisco: HarperSanFrancisco, 2001), 23.

30. Borg, *Reading the Bible Again*, 33.

31. See the discussion in Lee M. McDonald, *The Formation of the Christian Biblical Canon*, rev. and exp. ed. (Peabody, Mass.: Hendrickson, 1995), 246–49.

32. Migliore, *Faith Seeking Understanding*, 40, emphasis in original.

33. See Glen H. Stassen and David P. Gushee, *Kingdom Ethics: Following Jesus in Contemporary Context* (Downers Grove, Ill.: InterVarsity, 2003). For a somewhat different approach predicated on taking the whole context of Scripture into account and discerning where it seems to be heading, see the discussion of "trajectory theology" in Sparks, *God's Word in Human Words*, 279–328.

34. See Matt. 28:18.

35. See chapter 10.

36. Stassen and Gushee, *Kingdom Ethics*, 98.

Bibliography

Achtemeier, Elizabeth. *Preaching Hard Texts of the Old Testament*. Peabody, Mass.: Hendrickson, 1998.

Achtemeier, Paul J. *Inspiration and Authority: Nature and Function of Christian Scripture*. Rev. and exp. ed. Peabody, Mass.: Hendrickson, 1999.

Aichele, George. "Jesus' Violence." Pages 72–91 in *Violence, Utopia and the Kingdom of God: Fantasy and Ideology in the Bible*. Edited by George Aichele and Tina Pippin. London: Routledge, 1998.

Albertz, Rainer. *A History of Israelite Religion in the Old Testament Period*. Volume 1, *From the Beginnings to the End of the Monarchy*. Translated by John Bowden. Louisville, Ky.: Westminster/John Knox, 1994.

Alexander, T. Desmond. "Jonah: An Introduction and Commentary." Pages 45–131 in *Obadiah, Jonah, Micah: An Introduction and Commentary*. Edited by T. Desmond Alexander, David W. Baker, and Bruce K. Waltke. Leicester, U.K.: InterVarsity, 1988.

Allen, Leslie C. *The Books of Joel, Obadiah, Jonah, and Micah*. New International Commentary on the Old Testament. Grand Rapids, Mich.: Eerdmans, 1976.

Allen, Steve. *Steve Allen on the Bible, Religion, and Morality*. Buffalo, N.Y.: Prometheus, 1990.

Allison, Dale C., Jr. "Jesus and the Victory of Apocalyptic." Pages 126–41 in *Jesus and the Restoration of Israel: A Critical Assessment of N. T. Wright's* Jesus and the Victory of God. Edited by Carey C. Newman. Downers Grove, Ill: InterVarsity, 1999.

Alter, Robert. *The Art of Biblical Narrative*. New York: Basic, 1981.

Anderson, Bernhard W. *Contours of Old Testament Theology*. Minneapolis: Fortress Press, 1999.

————. *The Unfolding Drama of the Bible*. 3rd ed. Philadelphia: Fortress Press, 1988.

Anderson, Paul N. "Genocide or Jesus: A God of Conquest or Pacifism?" Pages 31–52 in *Contemporary Views on Spirituality and Violence*. Vol. 4 of *The Destructive Power of Religion: Violence in Judaism, Christianity, and Islam*. Edited by J. Harold Ellens. Westport, Conn.: Praeger, 2004.

Archer, Gleason L. *New International Encyclopedia of Bible Difficulties*. Grand Rapids, Mich.: Zondervan, 1982.

Arnold, Bill T., and David B. Weisberg. "A Centennial Review of Friedrich Delitzsch's 'Babel und Bibel' Lectures." *Journal of Biblical Literature* 121 (2002): 441–57.

Avalos, Hector. *Fighting Words: The Origins of Religious Violence*. Amherst, N.Y.: Prometheus, 2005.

————. "The Letter Killeth: A Plea for Decanonizing Violent Biblical Texts." *Journal of Religion, Conflict, and Peace* 1 (2007). http://www.plowsharesproject.org/journal/php/archive/archive.php?issu_list_id=8.

Baetzhold, Howard G., and Joseph B. McCullough, eds. *The Bible according to Mark Twain: Irreverent Writings on Eden, Heaven, and the Flood by America's Master Satirist*. New York: Simon and Schuster, 1996.

Bainton, Roland H. *Christian Attitudes toward War and Peace: A Historical Survey and Critical Re-evaluation*. Nashville, Tenn.: Abingdon Press, 1960.

Barton, John. *How the Bible Came to Be*. Louisville, Ky.: Westminster John Knox, 1997.

————. "Marcion Revisited." Pages 341–54 in *The Canon Debate: On the Origins and Formation of the Bible*. Edited by Lee Martin McDonald and James A. Sanders. Peabody, Mass.: Hendrickson, 2002.

————. "Old Testament Theology." Pages 94–113 in *Beginning Old Testament Study*. Edited by John Rogerson et al. St. Louis: Chalice, 1998.

Basinger, David, and Randall Basinger. *Predestination and Free Will: Four Views of Divine Sovereignty and Human Freedom*. Downers Grove, Ill.: InterVarsity, 1986.

Beek, A. van de. *Why? On Suffering, Guilt, and God*. Translated by John Vriend. Grand Rapids, Mich.: Eerdmans, 1990.

Bimson, John J. *Redating the Exodus and Conquest*. 2nd ed. Journal for the Study of the Old Testament: Supplement Series 5. Sheffield, U.K.: Almond, 1981.

Bird, Phyllis A. *Missing Persons and Mistaken Identities: Women and Gender in Ancient Israel*. Overtures to Biblical Theology. Minneapolis: Fortress Press, 1997.

Blumenthal, David R. *Facing the Abusing God: A Theology of Protest*. Louisville, Ky.: Westminster John Knox, 1993.

Borg, Marcus J. *Conflict, Holiness and Politics in the Teachings of Jesus*. New York: Mellen, 1984.

————. *Jesus in Contemporary Scholarship*. Valley Forge, Pa.: Trinity Press International, 1994.

————. "An Orthodoxy Reconsidered: The 'End-of-the-World Jesus.'" Pages 207–17 in *The Glory of Christ in the New Testament: Studies in Christology in Memory of George Bradford Caird*. Edited by L. D. Hurst and N. T. Wright. Oxford: Oxford University Press, 1987.

————. *Reading the Bible Again for the First Time: Taking the Bible Seriously but Not Literally*. San Francisco: HarperSanFrancisco, 2001.

Boring, M. Eugene. *Revelation*. Interpretation: A Bible Commentary for Teaching and Preaching. Louisville, Ky.: John Knox, 1989.

Boyd, Gregory A. *Is God to Blame? Beyond Pat Answers to the Problem of Suffering*. Downers Grove, Ill.: InterVarsity, 2003.

Boyd, Gregory A., and Paul R. Eddy. *Across the Spectrum: Understanding Issues in Evangelical Theology*. Grand Rapids, Mich.: Baker, 2002.

Bredin, Mark. *Jesus, Revolutionary of Peace: A Nonviolent Christology in the Book of Revelation*. Carlisle, U.K.: Paternoster, 2003.

Brensinger, Terry L. "War in the Old Testament: A Journey Toward Nonparticipation." Pages 22-31 in *A Peace Reader*. Edited by E. Morris Sider and Luke Keefer, Jr. Nappanee, Ind.: Evangel, 2002.

Brettler, Marc Zvi. "Biblical Literature as Politics: The Case of Samuel." Pages 71–92 in *Religion and Politics in the Ancient Near East*. Edited by Adele Berlin. Bethesda, Md.: University Press of Maryland, 1996.

————. *The Creation of History in Ancient Israel*. London: Routledge, 1995.

Bright, John. *The Authority of the Old Testament*. Nashville, Tenn.: Abingdon, 1967. Repr. Grand Rapids, Mich.: Baker, 1975.

Brooks, Roger, and John Joseph Collins, eds. *Hebrew Bible or Old Testament? Studying the Bible in Judaism and Christianity*. Notre Dame: University of Notre Dame Press, 1990.

Brotzman, Ellis R. *Old Testament Textual Criticism: A Practical Introduction*. Grand Rapids, Mich.: Baker, 1994.

Brown, Dale W. *Biblical Pacifism*. 2nd ed. Nappanee, Ind.: Evangel, 2003.

Brown, Raymond E. *An Introduction to the New Testament*. New York: Doubleday, 1997.

Brueggemann, Walter. *First and Second Samuel*. Interpretation: A Bible Commentary for Teaching and Preaching.. Louisville, Ky.: John Knox, 1990.

————. *Theology of the Old Testament: Testimony, Dispute, Advocacy*. Minneapolis: Fortress Press, 1997.

Buchanan, Mark. "Running with Jonah: Do We Really Want to Be Closer to God?" *Christianity Today* 43 (November 15, 1999): 87–88, 90–91.

Byler, Anne Meyer. *How to Teach Peace to Children*. Scottdale, Pa.: Herald, 2003.

Callaway, Joseph A. "The Settlement in Canaan: The Period of the Judges." Pages 55–89 in *Ancient Israel: From Abraham to the Roman Destruction of the Temple*. Revised by J. Maxwell Miller. Rev. and exp. ed. Edited by Hershel Shanks. Washington, D.C.: Biblical Archaeology Society, 1999.

Carasik, Michael. "Can God Read Minds?" *Bible Review* 18 (June 2002): 32–36, 44–45.

———. "The Limits of Omniscience." *Journal of Biblical Literature* 119 (2000): 221–32.

Carroll, Robert P. *The Bible as a Problem for Christianity*. Philadelphia: Trinity Press International, 1991.

Clines, David J. A. *Interested Parties: The Ideology of Writers and Readers of the Hebrew Bible*. Journal for the Study of the Old Testament: Supplement Series 205. Sheffield, U.K.: Sheffield Academic, 1995.

Collins, John J. "The Zeal of Phinehas: The Bible and the Legitimation of Violence." *Journal of Biblical Literature* 122 (2003): 3–21.

Cosby, Michael R. *Interpreting Biblical Literature: An Introduction to Biblical Studies*. Grantham, Pa.: Stony Run Publishing, 2009.

Cowles, C. S. "The Case for Radical Discontinuity." Pages 13–44 in C. S. Cowles et al., *Show Them No Mercy: Four Views on God and Canaanite Genocide*. Grand Rapids, Mich.: Zondervan, 2003.

———. "A Response to Eugene H. Merrill." Pages 97–101 in C. S. Cowles et al., *Show Them No Mercy: Four Views on God and Canaanite Genocide*. Grand Rapids, Mich.: Zondervan, 2003.

———. "A Response to Tremper Longman III." Pages 191–95 in C. S. Cowles et al., *Show Them No Mercy: Four Views on God and Canaanite Genocide*. Grand Rapids, Mich.: Zondervan, 2003.

Cowles, C. S., et al. *Show Them No Mercy: Four Views on God and Canaanite Genocide*. Grand Rapids, Mich.: Zondervan, 2003.

Craigie, Peter C. *The Problem of War in the Old Testament*. Grand Rapids, Mich.: Eerdmans, 1978.

Crenshaw, James L. *Defending God: Biblical Responses to the Problem of Evil*. New York: Oxford University Press, 2005.

———. *A Whirlpool of Torment: Israelite Traditions of God as an Oppressive Presence*. Overtures to Biblical Theology 12. Philadelphia: Fortress Press, 1984.

Crockett, William, ed. *Four Views on Hell*. Grand Rapids, Mich.: Zondervan, 1992.

Crockett, William V. "The Metaphorical View." Pages 43–76 in *Four Views on Hell*. Edited by William Crockett. Grand Rapids, Mich.: Zondervan, 1992.

Crossan, John Dominic. *The Birth of Christianity: Discovering What Happened in the Years Immediately after the Execution of Jesus*. San Francisco: HarperSanFrancisco, 1998.

———. *The Historical Jesus: The Life of a Mediterranean Jewish Peasant.* San Francisco: HarperSanFrancisco, 1991.

Darr, Katheryn Pfisterer. "Ezekiel's Justifications of God: Teaching Troubling Texts." *Journal for the Study of the Old Testament* 55 (1992): 97–117.

Davies, Eryl W. *The Dissenting Reader: Feminist Approaches to the Hebrew Bible.* Aldershot, U.K.: Ashgate, 2003.

———. "The Morally Dubious Passages of the Hebrew Bible: An Examination of Some Proposed Solutions." *Currents in Biblical Research* 3 (2005): 197–228.

Davies, Philip R. *In Search of "Ancient Israel."* Journal for the Study of the Old Testament: Supplement Series 148. Sheffield, U.K.: Sheffield Academic, 1992.

Davis, Edward B. "A Whale of a Tale: Fundamentalist Fish Stories." *Perspectives on Science and Christian Faith* 43 (1991): 224–37.

Davis, Ellen F. "Critical Traditioning: Seeking an Inner Biblical Hermeneutic." *Anglican Theological Review* 82 (2000): 733–51.

———. "Losing a Friend: The Loss of the Old Testament to the Church." Pages 83–94 in *Jews, Christians, and the Theology of the Hebrew Scriptures.* Edited by Alice Ogden Bellis and Joel S. Kaminsky. Society of Biblical Literature Symposium Series 8. Atlanta: Society of Biblical Literature, 2000.

Day, John. *Crying for Justice: What the Psalms Teach Us about Mercy and Vengeance in an Age of Terrorism.* Grand Rapids, Mich.: Kregel, 2005.

———. *God's Conflict with the Dragon and the Sea: Echoes of a Canaanite Myth in the Old Testament.* Cambridge: Cambridge University Press, 1985.

De La Torre, Miguel A. *Reading the Bible from the Margins.* Maryknoll, N.Y.: Orbis, 2002.

Dear, John. *Our God Is Nonviolent: Witnesses in the Struggle for Peace and Justice.* New York: Pilgrim, 1990.

Dearman, J. Andrew, ed. *Studies in the Mesha Inscription and Moab.* Atlanta: Scholars, 1989.

Desjardins, Michel. *Peace, Violence and the New Testament.* Sheffield, U.K.: Sheffield Academic, 1997.

Dever, William G. "Ceramics, Ethnicity, and the Question of Israel's Origins." *Biblical Archaeologist* 58 (1995): 200–213.

———. "How to Tell a Canaanite from an Israelite." Pages 26–56 in Hershel Shanks et al., *The Rise of Ancient Israel.* Washington, D.C.: Biblical Archaeology Society, 1992.

———. *Recent Archaeological Discoveries and Biblical Research.* Seattle: University of Washington Press, 1990.

———. *What Did the Biblical Writers Know and When Did They Know It? What Archaeology Can Tell Us about the Reality of Ancient Israel.* Grand Rapids, Mich.: Eerdmans, 2001.

————. *Who Were the Early Israelites and Where Did They Come From?* Grand Rapids, Mich.: Eerdmans, 2003.

Edelman, Diana. "Saul's Battle against Amaleq (1 Sam. 15)." *Journal for the Study of the Old Testament* 35 (1986): 71–84.

Ellwood, Gracia Fay. *Batter My Heart.* Pendle Hill Pamphlet 282. Wallingford, Pa.: Pendle Hill Publications, 1988.

Enns, Peter. *Inspiration and Incarnation: Evangelicals and the Problem of the Old Testament.* Grand Rapids, Mich.: Baker, 2005.

Evans, Christopher. *Is "Holy Scripture" Christian? and Other Questions.* London: SCM Press, 1971.

Exum, J. Cheryl. "The Ethics of Violence against Women." Pages 248–271 in *The Bible in Ethics: The Second Sheffield Colloquium.* Edited by John W. Rogerson, Margaret Davies, and M. Daniel Carroll R. Journal for the Study of the Old Testament: Supplement Series 207. Sheffield, U.K.: Sheffield Academic, 1995.

Feldman, Louis H. "Josephus's View of the Amalekites." *Bulletin for Biblical Research* 12 (2002): 161–86.

Fewell, Danna Nolan, and David M. Gunn. *Gender, Power, and Promise: The Subject of the Bible's First Story.* Nashville, Tenn.: Abingdon, 1993.

Finkelstein, Israel, and Neil Asher Silberman. *The Bible Unearthed: Archaeology's New Vision of Ancient Israel and the Origin of Its Sacred Texts.* New York: Free Press, 2001.

Fitzmyer, Joseph A. *The Gospel according to Luke (X–XXIV): Introduction, Translation, and Notes.* Anchor Bible 28A. Garden City, N.Y.: Doubleday, 1985.

Foner, Philip S. Introduction to *The Age of Reason*, by Thomas Paine. New York: Carol Publishing Group, 1995.

Fontaine, Carole E. "The Abusive Bible: On the Use of Feminist Method in Pastoral Contexts." Pages 84–113 in *A Feminist Companion to Reading the Bible: Approaches, Methods and Strategies.* Edited by Athalya Brenner and Carole Fontaine. Sheffield, U.K.: Sheffield Academic Press, 1997.

Fosdick, Harry Emerson. *A Guide to Understanding the Bible: The Development of Ideas within the Old and New Testaments.* 12th ed. New York: Harper and Brothers, 1938.

Foster, Benjamin R. *From Distant Days: Myths, Tales, and Poetry of Ancient Mesopotamia.* Bethesda, Md.: CDL Press, 1995.

Fretheim, Terence E. "The Character of God in Jeremiah." Pages 211–30 in *Character and Scripture: Moral Formation, Community, and Biblical Interpretation.* Edited by William P. Brown. Grand Rapids, Mich.: Eerdmans, 2002.

————. *Deuteronomic History.* Nashville, Tenn.: Abingdon, 1983.

————. "God and Violence in the Old Testament." *Word and World* 24 (2004): 18–28.

————. "I Was Only a Little Angry": Divine Violence in the Prophets. *Interpretation* 58 (2004): 365–75.

————. *The Suffering of God: An Old Testament Perspective*. Overtures to Biblical Theology 14. Philadelphia: Fortress Press, 1984.

Fretheim, Terence E., and Karlfried Froehlich. *The Bible as Word of God: In a Postmodern Age*. Minneapolis: Fortress Press, 1998.

Frisch, Amos. "'For I Feared the People, and I Yielded to Them' (I Sam 15, 24): Is Saul's Guilt Attenuated or Intensified?" *Zeitschrift für die alttestamentliche Wissenschaft* 108 (1996): 98–104.

Fudge, Edward William, and Robert A. Peterson. *Two Views of Hell: A Biblical and Theological Dialogue*. Downers Grove, Ill.: InterVarsity, 2000.

Funk, Robert W., Roy W. Hoover, and the Jesus Seminar. *The Five Gospels: The Search for the Authentic Words of Jesus: New Translation and Commentary*. New York: Polebridge, 1993.

Gard, Daniel L. "The Case for Eschatological Continuity." Pages 111–141 in C. S. Cowles et al., *Show Them No Mercy: Four Views on God and Canaanite Genocide*. Grand Rapids, Mich.: Zondervan, 2003.

————. "A Response to C. S. Cowles." Pages 55–56 in C. S. Cowles et al., *Show Them No Mercy: Four Views on God and Canaanite Genocide*. Grand Rapids, Mich.: Zondervan, 2003.

Gardner, Martin. Forward to *Steve Allen on the Bible, Religion, and Morality*, by Steve Allen. Buffalo: Prometheus Books, 1990.

Gibson, J. C. L. *Language and Imagery in the Old Testament*. Peabody, Mass.: Hendrickson, 1998.

Gnuse, Robert. *The Authority of the Bible: Theories of Inspiration, Revelation and the Canon of Scripture*. New York: Paulist, 1985.

Goldingay, John. *Models for Interpretation of Scripture*. Grand Rapids, Mich.: Eerdmans, 1995.

————. *Models for Scripture*. Grand Rapids, Mich.: Eerdmans, 1994.

Grant, Robert M., and David Tracy. 2nd ed. Rev. and exp. ed. *A Short History of the Interpretation of the Bible*. Philadelphia: Fortress Press, 1984.

Gray, John. *Joshua, Judges, Ruth*. New Century Bible Commentary. Grand Rapids, Mich.: Eerdmans, 1986.

Green, Joel B. *The Gospel of Luke*. New International Commentary on the New Testament. Grand Rapids, Mich.: Eerdmans, 1997.

Green, Joel B., and Mark D. Baker. *Recovering the Scandal of the Cross: Atonement in New Testament and Contemporary Contexts*. Downers Grove, Ill.: InterVarsity, 2000.

Greenberg, Moshe. "On the Political Use of the Bible in Modern Israel: An Engaged Critique." Pages 461–71 in *Pomegranates and Golden Bells: Studies in Biblical, Jewish, and Near Eastern Ritual, Law, and Literature in Honor of Jacob Milgrom*. Winona Lake, Ind.: Eisenbrauns, 1995.

Guinness, Os. *Fit Bodies, Fat Minds: Why Evangelicals Don't Think and What to Do about It*. Grand Rapids, Mich.: Baker, 1994.

Gunkel, Hermann. "The Prophets as Writers and Poets." Pages 22–73 in *Prophecy in Israel: Search for an Identity*. Edited by David L. Petersen. Issues in Religion and Theology 10. Philadelphia: Fortress Press, 1987.

Gunn, David M. *The Fate of King Saul: An Interpretation of a Biblical Story*. Journal for the Study of the Old Testament: Supplement Series 14. Sheffield, U.K.: JSOT Press, 1980.

Gunn, David M., and Danna Nolan Fewell. *Narrative in the Hebrew Bible*. Oxford: Oxford University Press, 1993.

Hagner, Donald A. *Matthew 1–13*. Word Biblical Commentary 33a. Dallas: Word, 1993.

Halpern, Baruch. "Erasing History: The Minimalist Assault on Ancient Israel." *Bible Review* 11 (December 1995): 26–35, 47.

Hare, Douglas R. A. *Matthew*. Interpretation: A Bible Commentary for Teaching and Preaching.. Louisville, Ky.: John Knox, 1993.

Harnack, Adolf von. *Marcion: The Gospel of the Alien God*. Translated by John E. Steely and Lyle D. Bierma. Durham, N.C.: Labyrinth, 1990. Translation of *Neue Studien zu Marcion*. 2nd ed. Leipzig: J. C. Hinrichs, 1924.

———. Militia Christi: *The Christian Religion and the Military in the First Three Centuries*. Translated by David McInnes Gracie. Philadelphia: Fortress Press, 1981.

Hartley, L. P. *The Go-Between*. New York: Knopf, 1953.

Hayes, John H. *An Introduction to Old Testament Study*. Nashville, Tenn.: Abingdon, 1979.

Haynes, Stephen R. *Noah's Curse: The Biblical Justification of American Slavery*. New York: Oxford, 2002.

Hays, Richard B. *The Moral Vision of the New Testament: Community, Cross, New Creation: A Contemporary Introduction to New Testament Ethics*. San Francisco: HarperSanFrancisco, 1996.

———. "Salvation by Trust? Reading the Bible Faithfully." *Christian Century* 114 (1997): 218–23.

Hendel, Ronald S. "It Ain't Necessarily So." *Bible Review* 18 (June 2002): 10.

———. "The Search for Noah's Flood." *Bible Review* 19 (June 2003): 8.

———. "When God Acts Immorally." Pages 16–25, 310–11 in *Approaches to the Bible: The Best of Bible Review*. Vol. 2: *A Multitude of Perspectives*. Edited by Harvey Minkoff. Washington, D.C.: Biblical Archaeology Society, 1995. Repr. *Bible Review* 7 (June 1991): 34, 37, 46, 48, 50.

Hershberger, Guy Franklin. *War, Peace, and Nonresistance*. 3rd ed. Scottdale, Pa.: Herald, 1981.

Hobbs, T. R. *A Time for War: A Study of Warfare in the Old Testament*. Wilmington, Del.: Michael Glazier, 1989.

Holladay, William L. *Long Ago God Spoke: How Christians May Hear the Old Testament Today*. Minneapolis: Fortress Press, 1995.

Hollinger, Dennis P. *Choosing the Good: Christian Ethics in a Complex World*. Grand Rapids, Mich.: Baker, 2002.

Horgan, John, and Frank Geer. *Where Was God on September 11?* San Francisco: BrownTrout, 2002.

Huffmon, Herbert B. "*Babel und Bibel*: The Encounter between Babylon and the Bible." Pages 125–36 in *Backgrounds for the Bible*. Edited by Michael Patrick O'Connor and David Noel Freedman. Winona Lake, Ind.: Eisenbrauns, 1987. Repr. *Michigan Quarterly Review* 22 (1983): 309–20.

Janzen, David. "The God of the Bible and the Nonviolence of Jesus." Pages 53–63 in *Teaching Peace: Nonviolence and the Liberal Arts*. Edited by J. Denny Weaver and Gerald Biesecker-Mast. Lanham, Md.: Rowman and Littlefield, 2003.

Jersak, Brad, and Michael Hardin, eds. *Stricken by God? Nonviolent Identification and the Victory of Christ*. Grand Rapids, Mich.: Eerdmans, 2007.

Johns, Loren L. *The Lamb Christology of the Apocalypse of John: An Investigation into Its Origins and Rhetorical Force*. Wissenschaftliche Untersuchungen zum Neuen Testament 2/167. Tübingen: Mohr Siebeck, 2003.

Jones, Gareth Lloyd. "Sacred Violence: The Dark Side of God." *Journal of Beliefs and Values* 20 (1999): 184–99.

Jones, Stephen, ed. "Is God Nonviolent? A Mennonite Symposium." *Conrad Grebel Review* 21 (2003).

Kaiser, Jr., Walter C. *Hard Sayings of the Old Testament*. Downers Grove, Ill.: InterVarsity, 1988.

———. *More Hard Sayings of the Old Testament*. Downers Grove, Ill.: InterVarsity, 1992.

———. *The Old Testament Documents: Are They Reliable and Relevant?* Downers Grove, Ill.: InterVarsity, 2001.

———. *Toward Old Testament Ethics*. Grand Rapids, Mich.: Zondervan, 1983.

Kang, Sa-Moon. *Divine War in the Old Testament and in the Ancient Near East*. Beihefte zur Zeitschrift für die alttestamentliche Wissenschaft 177. Berlin: de Gruyter, 1989.

Kimbell, Charles. *When Religion Becomes Evil*. San Francisco: HarperSanFrancisco, 2002.

Kingsbury, Jack Dean. *Matthew*. Proclamation Commentaries. 2nd ed. Philadelphia: Fortress Press, 1986.

Kitchen, K. A. *On the Reliability of the Old Testament*. Grand Rapids, Mich.: Eerdmans, 2003.

Klein, William W., Craig L. Blomberg, and Robert L. Hubbard Jr. *Introduction to Biblical Interpretation*. Dallas: Word, 1993.

Kluger, Rivkah Schärf. *Satan in the Old Testament*. Translated by Hildegard Nagel. Evanston, Ill.: Northwestern University Press, 1967.

Kraybill, Donald B., and Linda Gehman Peachey. *Where Was God on September 11? Seeds of Faith and Hope*. Scottdale, Pa.: Herald, 2002.

Kugel, James L. *The Bible as It Was*. Cambridge, Mass.: Harvard University Press, 1997.

LaHaye, Tim, and Jerry B. Jenkins. *Are We Living in the End Times?* Wheaton, Ill.: Tyndale House, 1999.

Lapsley, Jacqueline E. *Whispering the Word: Hearing Women's Stories in the Old Testament*. Louisville, Ky.: Westminster John Knox, 2005.

Larson, Edward J. *Summer for the Gods: The Scopes Trial and America's Continuing Debate over Science and Religion*. Cambridge, Mass.: Harvard University Press, 1998.

LeBeau, Bryan F. *The Atheist: Madalyn Murray O'Hair*. New York: New York University Press, 2003.

Lee, Nancy C. "Genocide's Lament: Moses, Pharaoh's Daughter, and the Former Yugoslavia." Pages 66–82 in *God in the Fray: A Tribute to Walter Brueggemann*. Edited by Tod Linafelt and Timothy K. Beal. Minneapolis: Fortress Press, 1998.

Lemche, Niels Peter. "David's Rise." *Journal for the Study of the Old Testament* 10 (1978): 2–25.

———. *Prelude to Israel's Past: Background and Beginnings of Israelite History and Identity*. Peabody, Mass.: Hendrickson, 1998.

Levenson, Jon D. *Creation and the Persistence of Evil: The Jewish Drama of Divine Omnipotence*. San Francisco: Harper and Row, 1988.

Lienhard, Joseph T. "Origen and the Crisis of the Old Testament in the Early Church," *Pro Ecclesia* 9 (2000): 355–66.

Long, Thomas G. "The Fall of the House of Uzzah . . . and Other Difficult Preaching Texts." *Journal for Preachers* 7 (Advent 1983): 13–19.

Long, V. Philips. *The Art of Biblical History*. Grand Rapids, Mich.: Zondervan, 1994.

———. "Interpolation or Characterization: How Are We to Understand Saul's Two Confessions?" *Presbyterion* 19 (Spring 1993): 49–53.

———, ed. *Israel's Past in Present Research: Essays on Ancient Israelite Historiography*. Winona Lake, Ind.: Eisenbrauns, 1999.

———. *The Reign and Rejection of King Saul: A Case for Literary and Theological Coherence*. Society of Biblical Literature Dissertation Series 118. Atlanta: Scholars, 1989.

Longman III, Tremper. "The Case for Spiritual Continuity." Pages 161–87 in C. S. Cowles et al., *Show Them No Mercy: Four Views on God and Canaanite Genocide*. Grand Rapids, Mich.: Zondervan, 2003.

———. *Making Sense of the Old Testament: 3 Crucial Questions*. Grand Rapids, Mich.: Baker, 1998.

———. *Reading the Bible with Heart and Mind*. Colorado Springs, Colo.: NavPress, 1997.

———. "A Response to C. S. Cowles." Pages 57–60 in C. S. Cowles et al., *Show Them No Mercy: Four Views on God and Canaanite Genocide*. Grand Rapids, Mich.: Zondervan, 2003.

Longman III, Tremper, and Daniel G. Reid. *God Is a Warrior*. Grand Rapids, Mich.: Zondervan, 1995.

———. "When God Declares War." *Christianity Today* 40 (October 28, 1996): 14–21.

Lowen, James W. *Lies My Teacher Told Me: Everything Your American History Textbook Got Wrong*. New York: Simon and Schuster, 1996.

Lüdemann, Gerd. *The Unholy in Holy Scripture: The Dark Side of the Bible*. Translated by John Bowden. Louisville, Ky.: Westminster John Knox, 1997.

Lynch, Joseph H. "The First Crusade: Some Theological and Historical Context." Pages 23–36 in *Must Christianity Be Violent? Reflections on History, Practice, and Theology*. Edited by Kenneth R. Chase and Alan Jacobs. Grand Rapids, Mich.: Brazos, 2003.

Machinist, Peter. "Literature as Politics: The Tulkulti-Ninurta Epic and the Bible." *Catholic Biblical Quarterly* 38 (1976): 455–82.

Malamat, Abraham. "How Inferior Israelites Forces Conquered Fortified Canaanite Cities." *Biblical Archaeology Review* 8 (April 1982): 24–35.

Mann, Thomas W. *The Book of the Torah: The Narrative Integrity of the Pentateuch*. Atlanta: John Knox, 1988.

Marquis, Galen. "Samuel's Cloak: Aspects of Intertextuality and Allusiveness in Biblical Historiography." Pages 99–106 in *Proceedings of the 10th World Congress of Jewish Studies, Division A: The Bible and Its World*. Edited by David Assaf. Jerusalem: Magnes, 1990.

Marsden, George M. *Fundamentalism and American Culture: The Shaping of Twentieth-Century Evangelicalism: 1870–1925*. Oxford: Oxford University Press, 1980.

Marshall, I. Howard. *Beyond the Bible: Moving from Scripture to Theology*. Grand Rapids, Mich.: Baker, 2004.

———. *The Gospel of Luke*. New International Greek Testament Commentary. Grand Rapids, Mich.: Eerdmans, 1978.

———. "New Testament Perspectives on War." *Evangelical Quarterly* 57 (1985): 115–32.

Mason, Rex. *Old Testament Pictures of God*. Oxford: Regent's Park College, 1993.

———. *Propaganda and Subversion in the Old Testament*. London: SPCK, 1997.

Mathewson, Steven D. *The Art of Preaching Old Testament Narrative*. Grand Rapids, Mich.: Baker, 2002.

Mattingly, Gerald L. "Moabites." Pages 317–33 in *Peoples of the Old Testament World*. Edited by Alfred J. Hoerth, Gerald L. Mattingly, and Edwin M. Yamauchi. Grand Rapids, Mich.: Baker, 1994.

———. "Moabite Religion and the Mesha' Inscription." Pages 211–38 in *Studies in the Mesha Inscription and Moab*. Edited by J. Andrew Dearman. Atlanta: Scholars, 1989.

Mazar, Amihai. *Archaeology of the Land of the Bible: 10,000–586 B. C. E.* New York: Doubleday, 1990.

McCarter, Jr., P. Kyle. "The Apology of David." *Journal of Biblical Literature* 99 (1980): 489–504.

———. "Plots, True or False: The Succession Narrative as Court Apologetic." *Interpretation* 35 (1981): 355–367.

———. *I Samuel: A New Translation with Introduction and Commentary*. Anchor Bible 8. New York: Doubleday, 1980.

———. *II Samuel*. Anchor Bible 9. New York: Doubleday, 1984.

McDonald, Lee M. *The Formation of the Christian Biblical Canon*. Rev. and exp. ed. Peabody, Mass.: Hendrickson, 1995.

McKenzie, Steven L. *King David: A Biography*. New York: Oxford University Press, 2000.

McKnight, Edgar V. "Reader-Response Criticism." Pages 230–52 in *To Each Its Own Meaning: An Introduction to Biblical Criticisms and Their Application*. Edited by Steven L. McKenzie and Stephen R. Haynes. Rev. and exp. ed. Louisville, Ky.: Westminster John Knox, 1999.

Merrill, Eugene H. "The Case for Moderate Discontinuity." Pages 63–94 in C. S. Cowles et al., *Show Them No Mercy: Four Views on God and Canaanite Genocide*. Grand Rapids, Mich.: Zondervan, 2003.

———. "A Response to C. S. Cowles." Pages 47–52 in C. S. Cowles et al., *Show Them No Mercy: Four Views on God and Canaanite Genocide*. Grand Rapids, Mich.: Zondervan, 2003.

Merton, Thomas. *Opening the Bible*. Collegeville, Minn.: Liturgical Press, 1986.

Mettinger, Tryggve N. D. *King and Messiah: The Civil and Sacral Legitimation of the Israelite Kings*. Coniectanea biblica: Old Testament Series 8. Lund: CWK Gleerup, 1976.

Middleton, J. Richard. "Created in the Image of a Violent God? The Ethical Problem of the Conquest of Chaos in Biblical Creation Texts." *Interpretation* 58 (2004): 341–55.

Migliore, Daniel L. *Faith Seeking Understanding: An Introduction to Christian Theology*. 2nd ed. Grand Rapids, Mich.: Eerdmans, 2004.

Miller, Patrick D., Jr. *The Divine Warrior in Early Israel*. Cambridge, Mass.: Harvard University Press, 1973.

————. "God the Warrior: A Problem in Biblical Interpretation and Apologetics." *Interpretation* 19 (1965): 39–46.

Mills, Mary E. *Images of God in the Old Testament*. Collegeville, Minn.: Liturgical Press, 1998.

Milne, Pamela J. "No Promised Land: Rejecting the Authority of the Bible." Pages 47–73 in *Feminist Approaches to the Bible*. Edited by Hershel Shanks. Washington, D.C.: Biblical Archaeology Society, 1995.

Moberly, R. W. L. "Living Dangerously: Genesis 22 and the Quest for Good Biblical Interpretation." Pages 181–97 in *The Art of Reading Scripture*. Edited by Ellen F. Davis and Richard B. Hays. Grand Rapids, Mich.: Eerdmans, 2003.

Morris, Leon. *The Gospel of John*. Rev. ed. New International Commentary on the New Testament. Grand Rapids, Mich.: Eerdmans, 1995.

Mott, Stephen Charles. *Biblical Ethics and Social Change*. New York: Oxford University Press, 1982.

Nelson, Richard D. *The Historical Books*. Nashville, Tenn.: Abingdon, 1998.

————. *Joshua: A Commentary*. Old Testament Library. Louisville, Ky.: Westminster John Knox, 1997.

————. "Josiah in the Book of Joshua." *Journal of Biblical Literature* 100 (1981): 531–40.

Nelson-Pallmeyer, Jack. *Is Religion Killing Us? Violence in the Bible and the Quran*. Harrisburg, Pa.: Trinity Press International, 2003.

————. *Jesus against Christianity: Reclaiming the Missing Jesus*. Harrisburg, Pa.: Trinity Press International, 2001.

Niditch, Susan. *War in the Hebrew Bible: A Study in the Ethics of Violence*. New York: Oxford University Press, 1993.

Niehaus, Jeffrey J. "Joshua and Ancient Near Eastern Warfare." *Journal of the Evangelical Theological Society* 31 (1988): 37–50.

Noll, K. L. "Is There a Text in This Tradition? Readers' Response and the Taming of Samuel's God." *Journal for the Study of the Old Testament* 83 (1999): 31–51.

Noll, Mark A. *Between Faith and Criticism: Evangelicals, Scholarship, and the Bible in America*. 2nd ed. Grand Rapids, Mich.: Baker, 1991.

————. *The Scandal of the Evangelical Mind*. Grand Rapids, Mich.: Eerdmans, 1994.

Noth, Martin. *The Deuteronomistic History*. 2nd ed. Journal for the Study of the Old Testament: Supplement Series 15. Sheffield, U.K.: JSOT Press, 1991. Translation of *Überlieferungsgeschichtliche Studien*. 2nd ed. Tübingen: Max Niemeyer, 1957.

Nysse, Richard. "The Dark Side of God: Considerations for Preaching and Teaching." *Word and World* 17 (1997): 437–46.

Olson, Dennis T. *The Book of Judges: Introduction, Commentary, and Reflections*. Pages 721–888 in *The New Interpreter's Bible: A Commentary in Twelve Volumes*. Vol. 2. Nashville, Tenn.: Abingdon, 1998.

Olson, Roger E. *The Story of Christian Theology: Twenty Centuries of Tradition and Reform.* Downers Grove, Ill: InterVarsity, 1999.

Origen. *Homilies on Joshua.* In vol. 105 of *The Fathers of the Church.* Translated by Barbara J. Bruce. Edited by Cynthia White. Washington, D.C.: Catholic University of America Press, 2002.

Pagels, Elaine. *The Origin of Satan.* New York: Random House, 1995.

Paine, Thomas. *The Age of Reason.* New York: Carol Publishing Group, 1995.

Patrick, Dale. *The Rendering of God in the Old Testament.* Overtures to Biblical Theology 10. Philadelphia: Fortress Press, 1981.

Penchansky, David. *What Rough Beast? Images of God in the Hebrew Bible.* Louisville, Ky.: Westminster John Knox, 1999.

Phillips, J. B. *Your God Is Too Small.* New York: Macmillan, 1961.

Pinnock, Clark H. "The Conditional View." Pages 135–66 in *Four Views on Hell.* Edited by William Crockett. Grand Rapids, Mich.: Zondervan, 1992.

Placher, William C. *A History of Christian Thought: An Introduction.* Louisville, Ky.: Westminster, 1983.

———. "Struggling with Scripture." Pages 32–50 in Walter Brueggemann, William C. Placher, and Brian K. Blount, *Struggling with Scripture.* Louisville, Ky.: Westminster John Knox, 2002.

Pritchard, James B., ed. *Ancient Near Eastern Texts Relating to the Old Testament.* 3rd ed. Princeton, N.J.: Princeton University Press, 1969.

Provan, Iain W. *1 and 2 Kings.* New International Biblical Commentary on the Old Testament. Peabody, Mass.: Hendrickson, 1995.

Provan, Iain, V. Philips Long, and Tremper Longman III. *A Biblical History of Israel.* Louisville, Ky.: Westminster John Knox, 2003.

Rad, Gerhard von. *Holy War in Ancient Israel.* Translated and edited by Marva J. Dawn. Grand Rapids, Mich.: Eerdmans, 1991.

Rendsburg, Gary A. "Biblical Literature as Politics: The Case of Genesis." Pages 47–70 in *Religion and Politics in the Ancient Near East.* Edited by Adele Berlin. Bethesda, Md.: University Press of Maryland, 1996.

———. "Reading David in Genesis." *Bible Review* 17 (February 2001): 20–33, 46.

Rice, Richard. *God's Foreknowledge and Man's Free Will.* Minneapolis: Bethany House, 1985.

Rogerson, John. *The Supernatural in the Old Testament.* Guildford, U.K.: Lutterworth, 1976.

Rosenberg, Joel. *King and Kin: Political Allegory in the Hebrew Bible.* Bloomington: Indiana University Press, 1986.

Russell, Bertrand. *Why I Am Not a Christian, and Other Essays on Religion and Related Subjects.* New York: Simon and Schuster, 1957.

Sagi, Avi. "The Punishment of Amalek in Jewish Tradition: Coping with the Moral Problem." *Harvard Theological Review* 87 (1994): 323–46.

Sailhamer, John H. *The Pentateuch as Narrative*. Grand Rapids, Mich.: Zondervan, 1992.

Sale, Kirkpatrick. *The Conquest of Paradise: Christopher Columbus and the Columbian Legacy*. New York: Knopf, 1990.

Sanders, John. *No Other Name: An Investigation into the Destiny of the Unevangelized*. Grand Rapids, Mich.: Eerdmans, 1992.

———, ed. *Atonement and Violence: A Theological Conversation*. Nashville, Tenn.: Abingdon, 2006.

Sasson, Jack M. *Jonah: A New Translation with Introduction, Commentary, and Interpretations*. Anchor Bible 24B. New York: Doubleday, 1990.

Schrag, Martin H., and John K. Stoner. *The Ministry of Reconciliation*. Nappanee, Ind.: Evangel, 1973.

Schwager, Raymund. *Must There Be Scapegoats: Violence and Redemption in the Bible*. Translated by Maria L. Assad. New York: Crossroad, 2000.

Schwartz, Regina. *The Curse of Cain: The Violent Legacy of Monotheism*. Chicago: University of Chicago Press, 1997.

Seibert, Eric A. *Subversive Scribes and the Solomonic Narrative: A Rereading of 1 Kings 1–11*. Library of Hebrew Bible/Old Testament Studies 436. New York: T & T Clark, 2006.

Seitz, Christopher R. "Old Testament or Hebrew Bible? Some Theological Considerations." *Pro Ecclesia* 5 (1996): 292–303.

Seuss, Dr. *The Butter Battle Book*. Video. Directed by Ralph Bakshi. 1989; Atlanta: Turner Pictures, 1995.

Sheler, Jeffrey L. *Is the Bible True? How Modern Debates and Discoveries Affirm the Essence of Scripture*. San Francisco: HarperSanFrancisco, 1999.

Shields, Mary E. "An Abusive God? Identity and Power/Gender and Violence in Ezekiel 23." Pages 129–51 in *Postmodern Interpretations of the Bible: A Reader*. Edited by A. K. A. Adam. St. Louis: Chalice, 2001.

Sire, James W. *The Universe Next Door*. 3rd ed. Downers Grove, Ill: InterVarsity, 1997.

Sparks, Kenton L. *God's Word in Human Words: An Evangelical Appropriation of Critical Biblical Scholarship*. Grand Rapids, Mich.: Baker, 2008.

Sperling, David S. *The Original Torah: The Political Intent of the Bible's Writers*. New York: New York University Press, 1998.

Spong, John Shelby. *Rescuing the Bible from Fundamentalism: A Bishop Rethinks the Meaning of Scripture*. San Francisco: HarperSanFrancisco, 1991.

Stassen, Glen H., and David P. Gushee. *Kingdom Ethics: Following Jesus in Contemporary Context*. Downers Grove, Ill.: InterVarsity, 2003.

Steussy, Marti J. "The Problematic God of Samuel." Pages 127–61 in *Shall Not the Judge of All the Earth Do What Is Right? Studies on the Nature of God in Tribute to*

James L. Crenshaw. Edited by David Penchansky and Paul L. Redditt. Winona Lake, Ind.: Eisenbrauns, 2000.

Stevens, Bruce A. "Jesus as the Divine Warrior." *Expository Times* 94 (1983): 326–29.

Stiebing, William H., Jr. *Out of the Desert? Archaeology and the Exodus/Conquest Narratives.* Amherst, N.Y.: Prometheus, 1989.

Stuart, Douglas. *Hosea-Jonah.* Word Biblical Commentary 31. Waco, Tex: Word, 1987.

Sugirtharajah, R. S. *Voices from the Margin: Interpreting the Bible in the Third World.* 3rd ed. Maryknoll, N.Y.: Orbis, 2006.

Swartley, Willard M. *Covenant of Peace: The Missing Peace in New Testament Theology and Ethics.* Grand Rapids, Mich.: Eerdmans, 2006.

———. *Slavery, Sabbath, War, and Women.* Scottdale, Pa.: Herald, 1983.

Swindoll, Charles R. *David: A Man of Passion and Destiny.* Dallas: Word, 1997.

Talbert, Charles H. *Reading Luke: A Literary and Theological Commentary on the Third Gospel.* New York: Crossroad, 1982.

Tate, W. Randolph. *Biblical Interpretation: An Integrated Approach.* Rev. ed. Peabody, Mass.: Hendrickson, 1997.

Taylor, Barbara Brown. "Preaching the Terrors." *Journal for Preachers* 15 (Spring 1992): 3–7.

Thompson, Thomas L. *The Mythic Past: Biblical Archaeology and the Myth of Israel.* New York: MJF Books, 1999.

Tozer, A. W. *The Knowledge of the Holy: The Attributes of God: Their Meaning in the Christian Life.* New York: Harper and Row, 1961.

Trible, Phyllis. *Rhetorical Criticism: Context, Method, and the Book of Jonah.* Minneapolis: Fortress Press, 1994.

———. *Texts of Terror: Literary-Feminist Readings of Biblical Narratives.* Overtures to Biblical Theology 13. Philadelphia: Fortress Press, 1984.

Trigg, Joseph Wilson. *Origen.* London: Routledge, 1998.

———. *Origen: The Bible and Philosophy in the Third-Century Church.* Atlanta: John Knox, 1983.

Tyler, Anne. *Saint Maybe.* New York: Knopf, 1991.

Van Seters, John. *In Search of History: Historiography in the Ancient World and the Origins of Biblical History.* New Haven, Conn.: Yale University Press, 1983. Repr., Winona Lake, Ind.: Eisenbrauns, 1997.

Van Winkle, Dwight. "Canaanite Genocide and Amalekite Genocide and the God of Love." The 1989 Winifred E. Weter Faculty Award Lecture. Seattle Pacific University, Washington, April 6, 1989, 1–45.

Walton, John H. *Ancient Near Eastern Thought and the Old Testament: Introducing the Conceptual World of the Hebrew Bible.* Grand Rapids, Mich.: Baker, 2006.

Walton, John H., and Andrew E. Hill. *Old Testament Today: A Journey from Original Meaning to Contemporary Significance.* Grand Rapids, Mich.: Zondervan, 2004.

Walvoord, John F. "The Literal View." Pages 11–28 in *Four Views on Hell*. Edited by William Crockett. Grand Rapids, Mich.: Zondervan, 1992.

Warrior, Robert Allen. "Canaanites, Cowboys, and Indians: Deliverance, Conquest, and Liberation Theology Today." *Christianity and Crisis* 49 (1989): 261–65.

Weaver, J. Denny. "Narrative Christus Victor: The Answer to Anselmian Atonement Violence." Pages 1–46 in *Atonement and Violence: A Theological Conversation*. Edited by John Sanders. Nashville, Tenn.: Abingdon, 2006.

———. *The Nonviolent Atonement*. Grand Rapids, Mich.: Eerdmans, 2001.

Weems, Renita J. *Battered Love: Marriage, Sex, and Violence in the Hebrew Prophets*. Overtures to Biblical Theology. Minneapolis: Fortress Press, 1995.

Wegner, Paul D. *A Student's Guide to Textual Criticism of the Bible: Its History, Methods, and Results*. Downers Grove, Ill.: InterVarsity, 2006.

Weingreen, J. "The Case of the Woodgatherer (Numbers XV 32-36)." *Vetus Testamentum* 16 (1966): 361–64.

Weisman, Ze'ev. *Political Satire in the Bible*. Atlanta: Scholars, 1998.

Westermann, Claus. *What Does the Old Testament Say about God?* Edited by Friedemann W. Golka. Atlanta: John Knox, 1979.

White, Marsha. "'The History of Saul's Rise': Saulide State Propaganda in 1 Samuel 1–14." Pages 271–92 in *"A Wise and Discerning Mind": Essays in Honor of Burke O. Long*. Edited by Saul M. Olyan and Robert C. Culley. Providence, R.I.: Brown University, 2000.

Whitelam, Keith W. "The Defense of David." *Journal for the Study of the Old Testament* 29 (1984): 61–87.

———. *The Invention of Ancient Israel: The Silencing of Palestinian History*. New York: Routledge, 1995.

———. "Israelite Kingship: The Royal Ideology and Its Opponents." Pages 119–39 in *The World of Ancient Israel: Sociological, Anthropological and Political Perspectives*. Edited by R. E. Clements. Cambridge: Cambridge University Press, 1989.

Whybray, R. N. "The Immorality of God: Reflections on Some Passages in Genesis, Job, Exodus and Numbers." *Journal for the Study of the Old Testament* 72 (1996): 89–120.

———. "'Shall Not the Judge of All the Earth Do What Is Just?' God's Oppression of the Innocent in the Old Testament." Pages 1–19 in *Shall Not the Judge of All the Earth Do What Is Right? Studies on the Nature of God in Tribute to James L. Crenshaw*. Edited by David Penchansky and Paul L. Redditt. Winona Lake, Ind.: Eisenbrauns, 2000.

Wink, Walter. *Engaging the Powers: Discernment and Resistance in a World of Domination*. Minneapolis: Fortress Press, 1992.

Winn, Albert Curry. *Ain't Gonna Study War No More: Biblical Ambiguity and the Abolition of War*. Louisville, Ky.: Westminster John Knox, 1993.

Wintermute, O. S. "Jubilees: A New Translation and Introduction." Pages 35–142 in *The Old Testament Pseudepigrapha*. Vol. 2. Edited by James H. Charlesworth. New York: Doubleday, 1985.

Witherington III, Ben. *The Christology of Jesus*. Minneapolis: Fortress Press, 1990.

———. *The Jesus Quest: The Third Search for the Jew of Nazareth*. Downers Grove, Ill.: InterVarsity, 1995.

Wolf, Miroslav. *Exclusion and Embrace: A Theological Exploration of Identity, Otherness, and Reconciliation*. Nashville, Tenn.: Abingdon, 1996.

Wolterstorff, Nicholas. *Reason within the Bounds of Religion*. 2nd ed. Grand Rapids, Mich.: Eerdmans, 1984.

Wood, Bryant G. "Did the Israelites Conquer Jericho?: A New Look at the Archaeological Evidence." *Biblical Archaeology Review* 16 (April 1990): 44–58.

Woodard, Branson L., Jr., and Michael E. Travers. "Literary Forms and Interpretation." Pages 29–43 in *Cracking Old Testament Codes: A Guide to Interpreting the Literary Genres of the Old Testament*. Edited by D. Brent Sandy and Ronald L. Giese Jr. Nashville, Tenn.: Broadman and Holman, 1995.

Wright, N. T. *Jesus and the Victory of God*. Vol. 2 of *Christian Origins and the Question of God*. Minneapolis: Fortress Press, 1996.

———. *The Last Word: Beyond the Bible Wars to a New Understanding of the Authority of Scripture*. San Francisco: HarperSanFrancisco, 2005.

———. *Who Was Jesus?* Grand Rapids, Mich.: Eerdmans, 1993.

Würthwein, Ernst. *The Text of the Old Testament: An Introduction to the* Biblia Hebraica. Translated by Erroll F. Rhodes. Grand Rapids, Mich.: Eerdmans, 1979.

Yeatts, John R. *Revelation*. Believers Church Bible Commentary. Scottdale, Pa.: Herald, 2003.

Yoder, John Howard. *Nevertheless: The Varieties and Shortcomings of Religious Pacifism*. Rev. and exp. ed. Scottdale, Pa.: Herald, 1992.

———. *The Politics of Jesus: Vicit Agnus Noster*. Grand Rapids, Mich.: Eerdmans, 1972.

Young, Jeremy. *The Violence of God and the War on Terror*. New York: Seabury, 2008.

Younger, K. Lawson, Jr. *Ancient Conquest Accounts: A Study in Ancient Near Eastern and Biblical History Writing*. Journal for the Study of the Old Testament: Supplement Series 98. Sheffield, U.K.: JSOT Press, 1990.

Zenger, Erich. *A God of Vengeance? Understanding the Psalms of Divine Wrath*. Translated by Linda M. Maloney. Louisville, Ky.: Westminster John Knox, 1996.

Zinn, Howard. *A People's History of the United States: 1492–Present*. New York: Perennial, 2003.

Index of Biblical References

Romans

5:8	192
9:29	312
12:19	249
16:16	279

1 Corinthians

3:2	294
13:11	311
14:34	279
15:14	120

Galatians

4:21-31	290

Ephesians

2:4-5a	203
2:8	277
4:2-3	232
6:10-20	83

Philippians

2:5-8	306

Colossians

1:15	186, 306
1:19	186

1 Timothy

2:9	279
3:16-17	315

2 Timothy

3:16-17	266
3:16b	279

Hebrews

1:3a	186
2:12	289
5:12-14	294

James

1:13	29

2 Peter

1:20-21	315
2:6	312

1 John

4:8b	203
4:19	203

Jude

7	312

Revelation

6:1-8	254
6:9-11	254
6:12-17	254
8:7	254
8:8-11	254
9:1-11	254
9:13-19	254
14:10-11	254
14:20	254
16:3-4	254
16:14-16	254
19	256, 257
19:11	256
19:11-15	244
19:11-21	255–56
19:13	256
19:16	256
19:17-18	254
20:11-15	184

Index of Modern Authors

Weisberg, David B., 66–67, 291
Weisman, Ze'ev, 301
Westermann, Claus, 310–11
White, Marsha, 304
Whitelam, Keith W., 288, 301, 304
Whybray, R. N., 225–26, 310
Wink, Walter, 250, 254–55, 312, 313
Winn, Albert Curry, 24, 284
Wintermute, O. S., 55–56, 289
Witherington, Ben, III, 194, 195, 300, 306, 307, 314
Wolf, Miroslav, 286
Wolterstorff, Nicholas, 295, 316
Wood, Bryant G., 297

Woodard, Branson L., Jr., 298
Wright, N. T., 258, 306, 314, 315
Würthwein, Ernst, 289

Y
Yeatts, John R., 256, 313
Yoder, John Howard, 286
Young, Jeremy, 284
Younger, K. Lawson, Jr., 297–98

Z
Zenger, Erich, 282
Zinn, Howard, 223–24, 310